LAST CHANCE ALASKA 2
Grayscale Edition

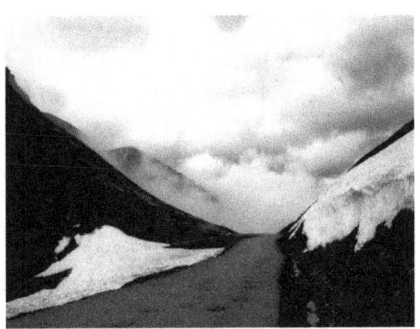

Hatcher Pass, Alaska. 2001   JDH

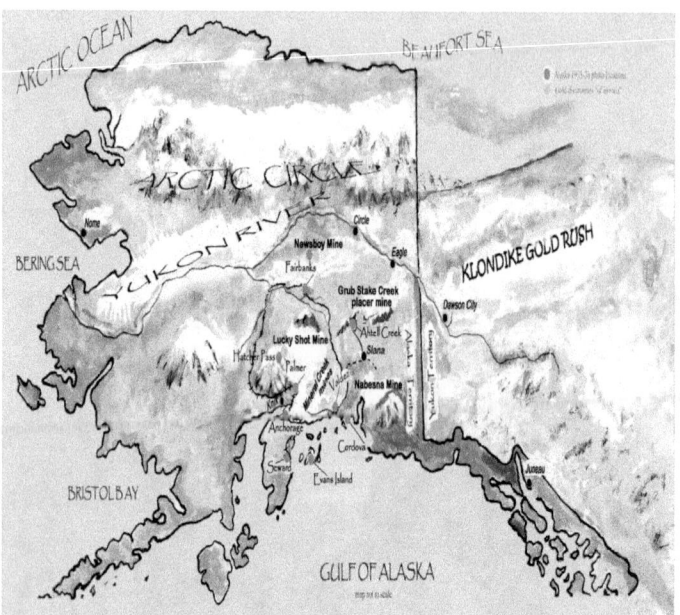

Map 1. Alaska 1935-36   photo locations and repeat photography

LAST CHANCE

ALASKA 2

Grayscale Edition

Chapter VIII
DIRECTOR'S CUT

JILL DOUGLAS HOPPER

FOREWORD BY
ALISON M. VAN ARSDEL

LAST CHANCE ALASKA 2
Grayscale Edition

ISBN 10   1519620535
ISBN 13   9781519620538
Library of Congress Control Number: 201790767
CreateSpace Independent Publishing Platform
North Charleston, SC

Cover design by Jim Breckenridge
Pip Printing, Palm Bay, FL.

Cover jacket Photos by
Randolph Angus Douglas and Jill Douglas Hopper

LAST CHANCE ALASKA

Copyright © March 3, 2009 VAu 1-010-931
by Jill Douglas Hopper
ISBN 1439229090
Library of Congress Control Number: 2010902303

CreateSpace Independent Publishing Platform
North Charleston, SC
Cover design by Leslie Wiggins
Pip Printing, Palm Bay, FL.

Cover jacket Photos by
Randolph Angus Douglas

Printed in the USA

www.createspace.com
www.amazon.com
www.lastchancealaska.com

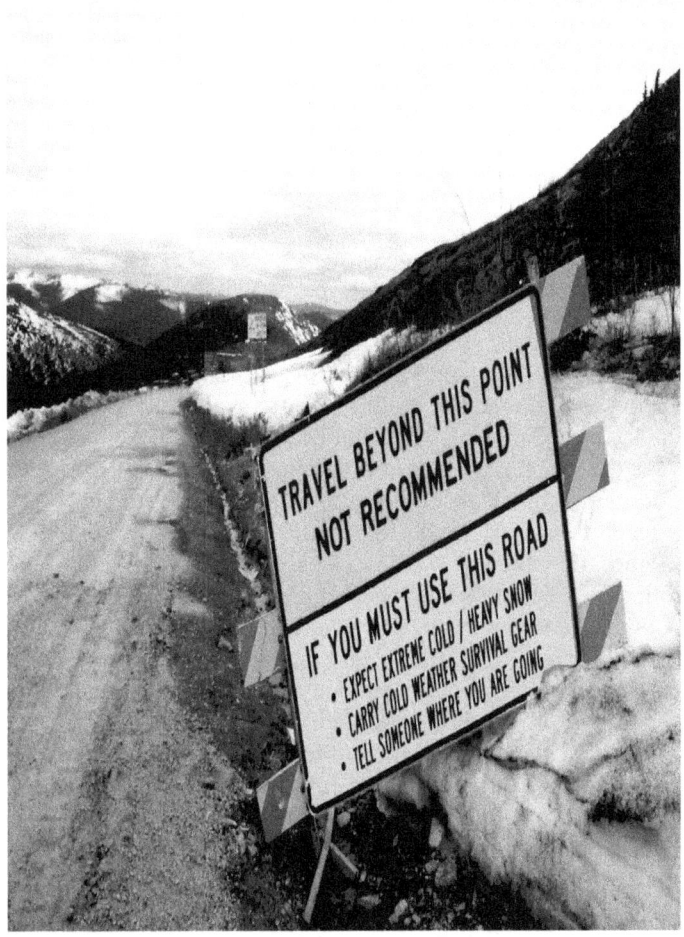

Top of the World Highway (looking w), Alaska-Yukon Border. 2001   JDH

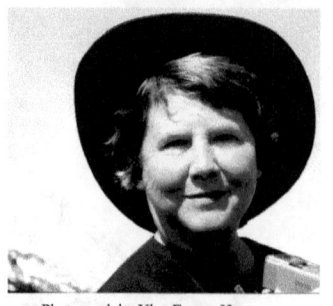

Thompson Pass, Alaska. 2001

   LAST CHANCE ALASKA was inspired as a result of a
mid-thirties journey to look for gold in the Alaska Territory
by the Author's father, Randolph Angus Douglas. All
through childhood she and her siblings heard stories of
a land very far away. A land of bears and gold.
   As the twentieth century was coming to a close, a second
journey began. Hopper followed Douglas's footsteps to the
rugged frontier of Alaska to capture his 1935-36 photographs
in repeat photography. She was guided only by the scribbling on the backs of old photographs, the transcription of
Douglas's original diary and a copy of a 1935 hand drawn
map to an old Ahtell Creek gold mining cabin. Locating
each photo area became a passion and an extraordinary five
year quest. Each photo was a story all its own.
   Enjoy this unique collection of repeat photography that only
the advantage of a still camera can bring. The photographs
encompass over half a century of post gold rush Alaska. The
transcontinental highway was just reaching completion in the
lower forty-eight and Alaska did not reach statehood until
1959.
   Glimpses of a 1935 lower forty-eight auto crossing from
New Jersey to Seattle, WA. are included in the opening
chapter where the Steamer Yukon was waiting to sail
Douglas and his dog, Spot, to Valdez, Alaska.
   Jill was born in upstate New York just before Pearl Harbor
in 1941 She attended Fairleigh Dickinson University, major-
ing in English and also attended evening classes at Montclair
State University before pursuing a short career in ballet at
Radio City Music Hall in NYC. Her four children consider
her an animal advocate—motivated throughout her life by
writers such as Jack London, author of *CALL OF THE
WILD,* who saw cruelty first hand in the wilds of northern
Canada and Cleveland Amory who wrote and founded the
Black Beauty Ranch in Texas.

vi

To order copies of

LAST CHANCE ALASKA
Color Interior Edition

LAST CHANCE ALASKA 2
Grayscale Edition
or

NELLIE'S HILL

please contact
www.createspace.com
or www.amazon.com

www.lastchancealaska.com

CONTENTS

INTRODUCTION by Author

*1935*_____The Great Depression began in late 1929. It left many men jobless and without a sense of purpose. A young man from the northeast named Randolph Angus Douglas was also struggling through the depression — a melancholy that lasted over a decade. In 1934, a family member proposed a two year trip to the Alaska Territory to search for gold. Douglas's immediate response was, "yes."

Looking back, one could draw the conclusion that it was terribly naive to expect to locate a gold strike in the narrow confines of a couple of Alaska summers. Mountain passes did not open up in those days until mid or late June. Snowflakes were recorded as early as August 3rd in Douglas's 1935 diary. Roads to the Alaska interior were no more than enlarged gold rush trails. Trucks ran the roads every day or two, making deliveries to remote towns and mining areas. Poorly constructed bridges would frequently wash out, or buckle under the harsh weather conditions. This left men and vehicles stranded for days waiting for the repairs to be completed. Many times the men themselves would lend a hand to hasten the reopening. Nevertheless, there was gold to be found. The lure of this precious metal had Douglas preparing for a journey of 5,500 miles. How would he have prepared for such a journey? The assets Douglas had were a camera, an old Ford auto and a relative's investment in his gold finding abilities (which included a life insurance policy).

*2000*_____The arrival of the Millennium in the year 2000 brought out different responses from different people. Some thought the world was coming to an end, others thought terrorists might strike, and still others were concerned with computers shutting down causing chaos in a high tech world. In other words, jitters had taken over the planet. Never fearing the uncertainty of tomorrow, I remained focused on my goal of retracing the old Alaska photo sites of 1935-36. We continued preparing for a risky, but adventurous trip by foot into the Alaska back-country to locate an old cabin lived in by Douglas while prospecting for gold in the Ahtell Creek Valley.

After driving to Seattle, Washington, from Florida, we were joined by three of Douglas's grandchildren from the east coast. Upon arriving in Anchorage, we were met by a forth "grand." Our backup was now in place. After a few days of enticement, we rendezvoused at the Caribou Café in Glennallen to strategize for the ultimate goal of backpacking the Ahtell Creek Trail to search for the old gold mining cabin. With the assistance of the Glennallen Bureau of Land Management (BLM), I felt confident our trek into the wilderness would yield some very unique photography, as can be seen in Chapter III.

*2001___*The book was now taking on a life of its own. We felt compelled to return to Alaska for the 2001 summer window to complete some unfinished repeat photography. That summer we lived among the Alaska residents, revisited old photo sites, and listened to tapes made available by old-timers who had the foresight to record history before it became tangled with tomorrow. Those voices from the past accurately enriched the quest to find out what life was like in Alaska in the early 1900's. Together we visited town archives, libraries, museums and asked many, many questions. In Valdez, I conducted several phone interviews with some old-time Valdezeans and enjoyed some memorable lunches with those who had touched Douglas's life in 1935-36 during his tenure in the Alaska territory.

While a mother bear and her cubs were walking the ridges on the north side of town in Valdez, we climbed the nearby mountains and hiked washed out, sometimes very dangerous trails for that perfect photo. After several attempts, we located the terminal moraine of the much retreated Valdez Glacier. Searching out old gold mines was also high on the list—many unreachable.

Soon it would be time to pack up our camper and head for the Canadian border. Maybe we could take that trip to the Arctic Ocean region after all. An area not accessible to us on our way up due to weather. Several last minute salmon fishing trips were made before we left Eagle's Rest.

*2002___*A road trip was made from Florida to Pennsylvania to acquire the last two pictures of repeat photography to complete this book. Unexpectedly, these were Douglas's first two 1935 photos beginning his cross-country trip from New Jersey to Washington. All of the 2000-01 photographs in this book were taken before the event of September 11, 2001 with the exception of the two 2002 Pennsylvania bridge pictures. In the summer of 2002 it was more important to frame the flag than to frame the two bridges.

FOREWORD

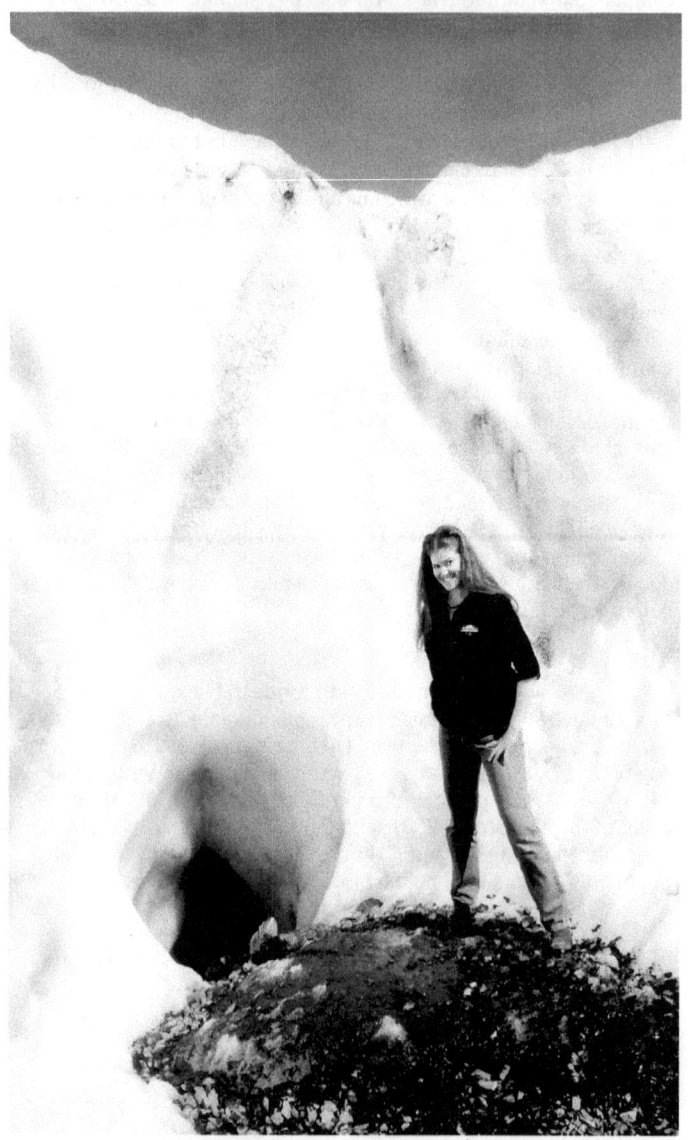

Alison M. Van Arsdel on the Matanuska Glacier, Alaska. 2000   JDH

FOREWORD by Alison M. Van Arsdel

My mom is traveling across the country in an RV."
That is what each of her children said at one point or
another over these years of her dedicating herself to this
adventure. It was our little source of bragging, that our
mom is "cool" and active in her retirement years. The
prospector in the following pages was my grandpa. I knew
him for sixteen years before he passed away. Jill wanted to
feel that excitement of travel with a purpose. By following
in her father's footsteps, she relived the moments of the
earlier part of the 1900's through her camera. She will do
anything for a good photograph. When her eyes become
the camera she is suddenly capable of a marathon run, a
rock climb, strange balancing acts and becoming a thief
in the night to snatch that final photo.

No journey, whether successful or not, is a wasted one. It
is in the hunt for gold that gold is found. We profit most
by allowing ourselves to live and do even that which might
at first seem frightening or even impossible. We benefit
by taking chances, working hard and knowing when to
change directions. Perhaps my grandpa found exactly
what he was looking for.

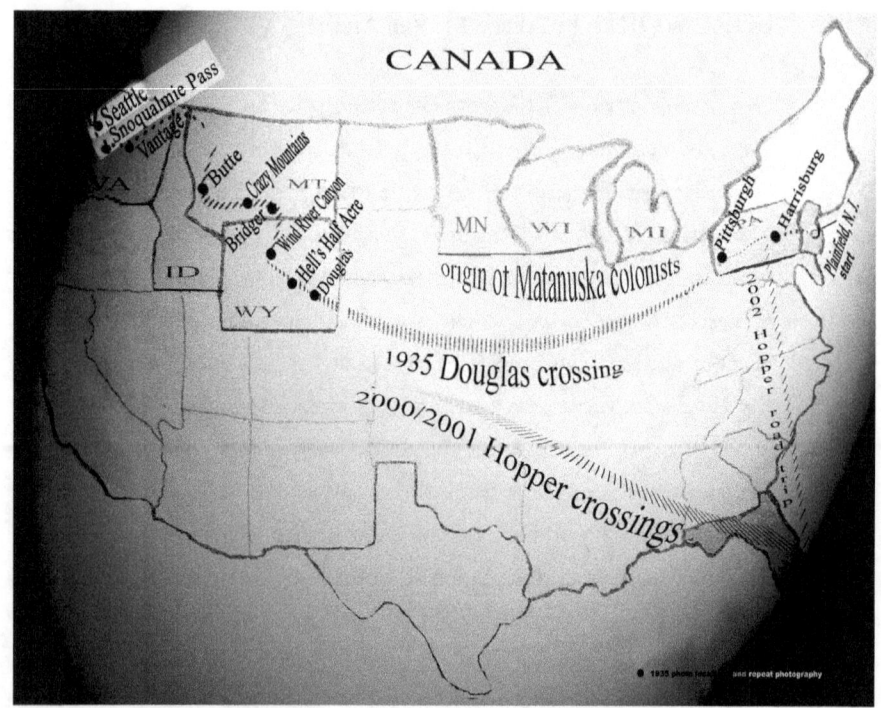

Map 2. Lower forty-eight and 1935 photo locations

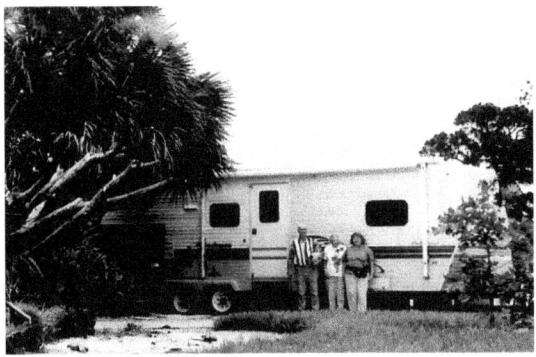

Titusville, Florida. 2000

Our repeat photography adventure began in Florida in the early morning hours of July 1, 2000. My husband, Emory, my mother, Nellie (the late prospector's wife of forty-five years) and our family pet, Little Jon, were traveling companions on this remarkable journey. We all rode through the Gateway Arch in St. Louis, Missouri, on July forth during an incredible heat wave. We traveled and camped along the way in a "new"30 foot travel trailer. Douglas's routes were traced and photographed through Wyoming, Montana, Idaho and Washington.

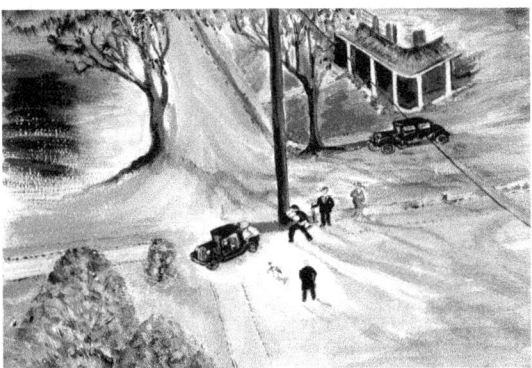

Illustration I. Hard Going Ahead

On the morning of May 8, 1935, Randolph Angus Douglas waved farewell to his comfortable home in Plainfield, New Jersey, and began his journey of over 5,500 miles to the rugged outposts of the Alaska Territory — *"the unknown,"* as he put it. Douglas was armed with only a 30.30 high-powered rifle, a camera, an old auto packed with warm clothes, camping gear, some "high tech" mining equipment for that period of time and his dog, Spot. That evening he wrote in his diary, *"Spot has a lot of hard going before him."*

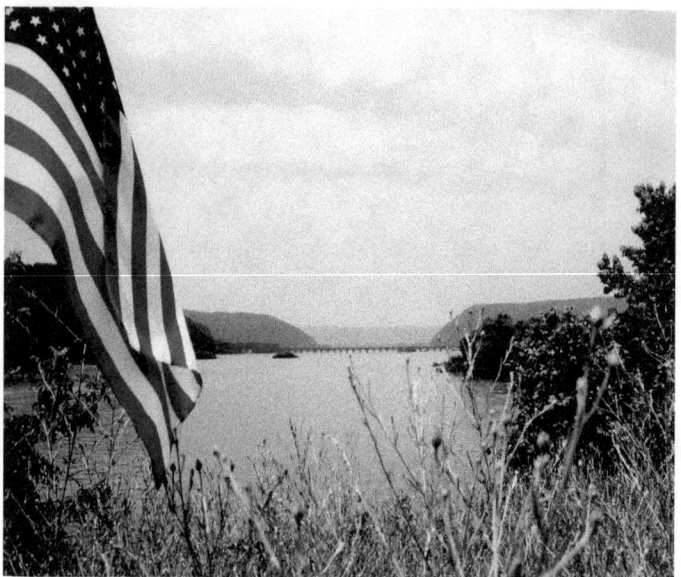

Rockville Bridge, Harrisburg, Pennsylvania. 2002   JDH

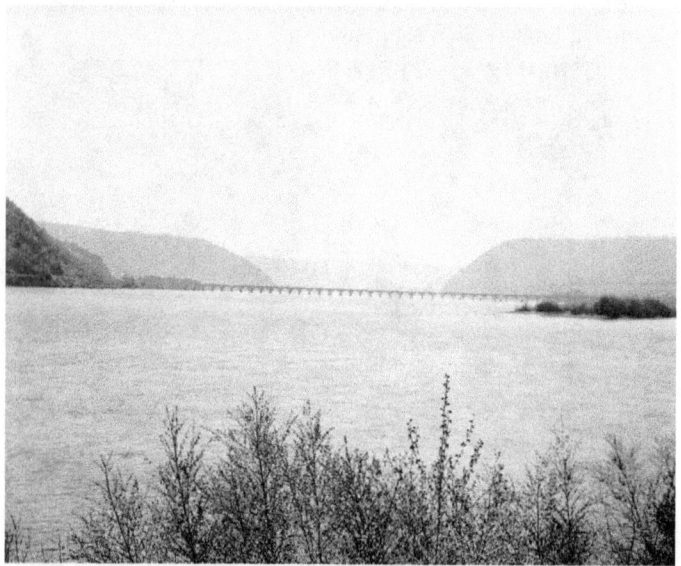

"Susquehanna Rv. near Harrisburg, Pennsylvania (L north) 1935" RAD

   This was the first photograph of Douglas's one–man
expedition. The Rockville Bridge is the longest stone arch
bridge in the world, with a length of 3,810 feet.

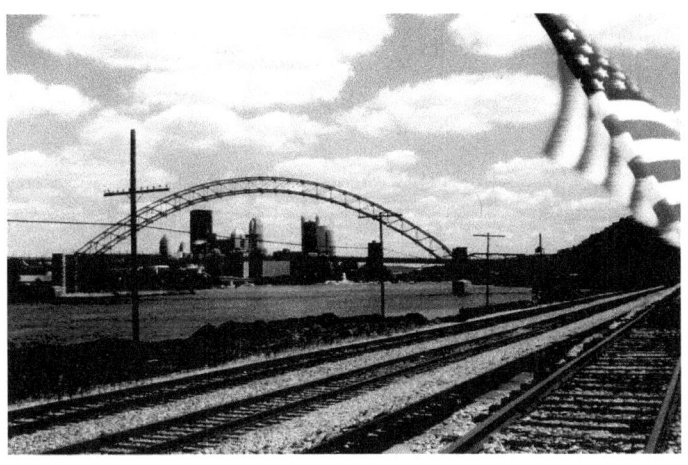

Westend Bridge, Pittsburgh, Pennsylvania. 2002   JDH

For one glorious moment, we were Pittsburgh Steeler fans walking across a bridge with an excited group of revelers to the Heinz Stadium (left). In a city where three rivers converge — the Allegheny (out of photo left), the Monongahela (out of photo right) and the Ohio (center) — there were numerous bridges to search out. The old Westend Bridge spans the Ohio River in a city now known as the Golden Triangle.

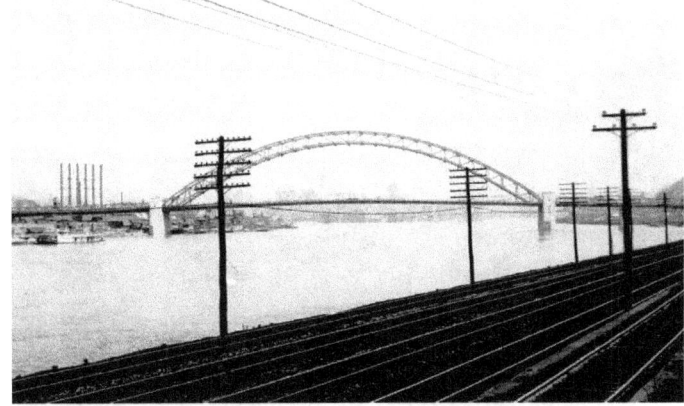

"Pittsburgh, Pennsylvania...Ohio River (L east)...May, 1935"   RAD

The original Lincoln Highway 2 — first named and most direct route from New York to San Francisco — was Douglas's likely road of choice out of Pittsburgh. He arrived in Douglas, Wyoming three days later. Thirty-one thousand miles of concrete road stretched around the United States by 1925. The transcontinental highway closed its gap in Nebraska in 1935.

3

NEW CHAPTER

CONTENTS   182

Book covers
Illustrations
Maps
Alaska train depots
Behind the Scenes **2000 / 2001**

Including: Eight (not to scale) maps by Author
inserted on pgs. 232, 249, 262, 287, 296, 307, 311 & 330

LAST CHANCE ALASKA
ILLUSTRATIONS by Author

MAPS (not to scale) by Author

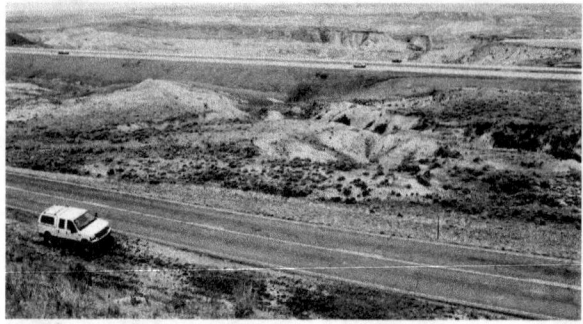

East of Douglas, Wyoming. 2001   JDH

It was amazing that this photo area was located. Drivers now travel on Interstate 25 which can be seen near the top of the above photo. We too, climbed up a hill to acquire a photograph — this time not of the Wyoming badlands east of Douglas, but to contrast yesterday's and today's highways. In 1860-61 the Pony Express was running this stretch of land by horseback on a dusty trail. Wyoming became a territory in 1868 and achieved statehood twenty-two years later in 1890. It was our 44th state. It is also home of the Wyoming Pioneer Memorial Museum in Douglas, Wyoming.

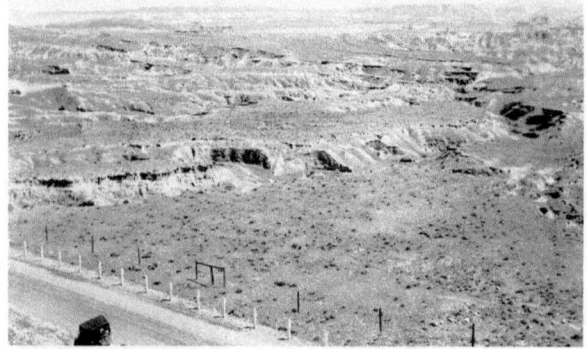

"The badlands of Wyoming...May 12, 1935"   RAD

Traveling the early roads of the twentieth century, an old 1920's auto inched its way on a journey towards a pier in Seattle, Washington. A man with high hopes pulled off, got out of the vehicle, and climbed up a hill to photograph this strange barren land stretching as far as the eye could see. This was his first cross-country trip. It is here east of Douglas, Wyoming, that he developed an immediate fascination for the badlands as reflected in the number of photos taken in this state.

4

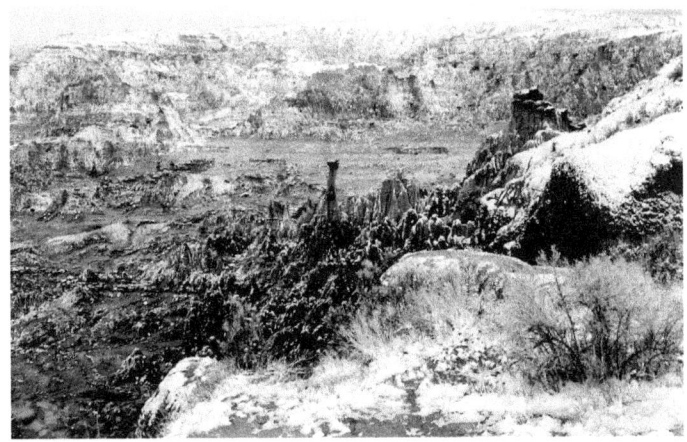

Hell's Half Acre, Wyoming. 2001   JDH

Our first view of this area of land was in the middle of the 2000 summer. We traveled on a clockwise road trip from Buffalo, Wyoming. It was as hot as the name implies. The next time through in April of 2001, we were pleased to notice the snow. Emory promptly renamed it "hell frozen over." We received permission from the owner to photograph from a small area of land extending out into the canyon behind their restaurant and motel. Hell's Half Acre is a unique place to visit.

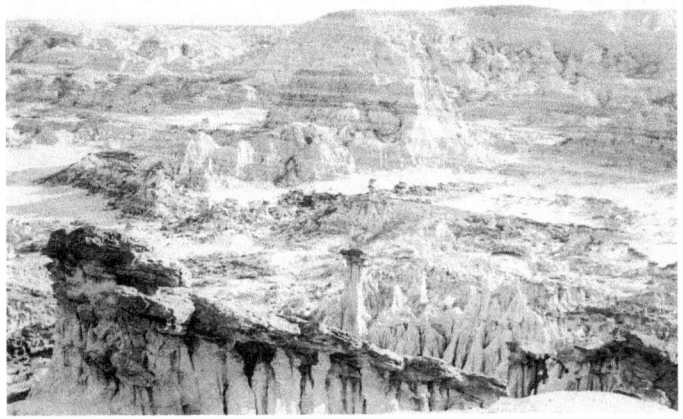

"Hell's Half Acre, Wyoming...looking southeast...May 12, 1935"   RAD

Unsurpassed only by the badlands of South Dakota, which Douglas had not seen, Hell's Half Acre presented itself to him as a land of limitless extremes. Five more photographs were taken. He continued west on the present highway 20/26, making a sharp turn to the right at Shoshoni where he began entertaining thoughts of viewing Yellowstone N. P.

5

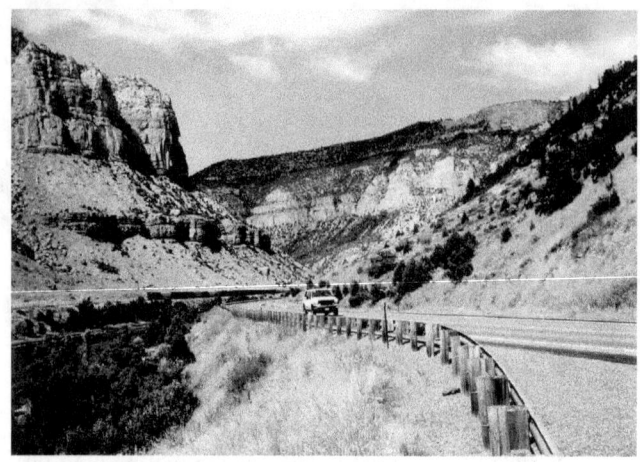

Wind River Canyon, Wyoming. 2000   JDH

Crossing the United States in 2000, Nellie could not understand what all the fuss was about at finding this hot, isolated curve in the road just north of Boysen State Park in Wyoming. After a u-turn, Emory drove Nellie around the bend and straight for Jill, who was standing on top of a guard post with the camera poised. Had her daughter lost her mind?

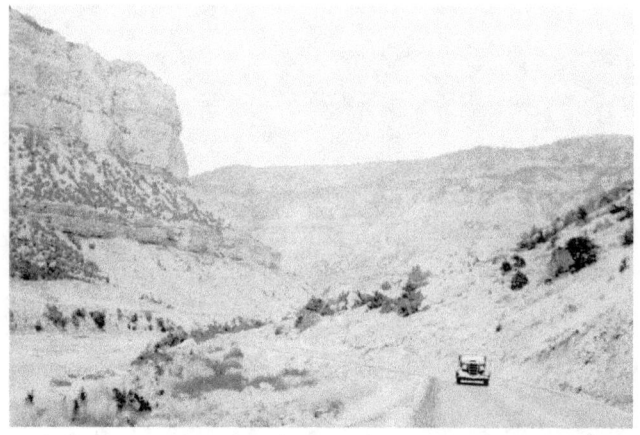

"Wind River Canyon, Wyoming...looking N...May 14, 1935"   RAD

Under President Franklin Delano Roosevelt, the Park to Park Highway system was established to link several of the early western national parks. The gravel road seen in the above photo led to Yellowstone National Park west of Cody, Wyoming. Due to snow in the higher mountain passes, this eastern entrance to the park was closed in 1935.

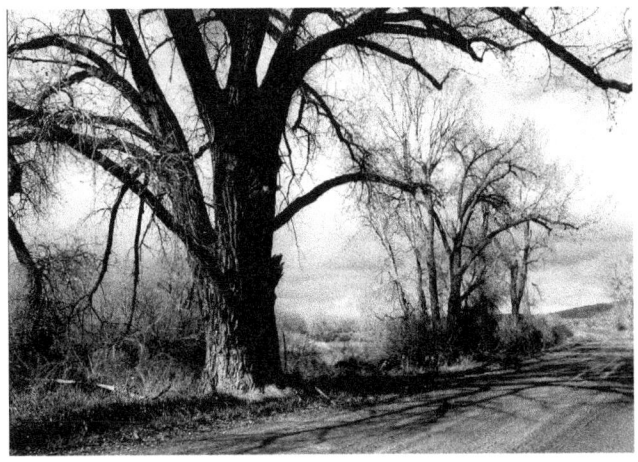

South of Bridger, Montana. 2001   JDH

During our 2000 cross-country trip, we tried several times to locate the scenery in the background of the 1935 Montana auto camp photo, but missed the location by driving route 90 from Buffalo, Wyoming, to Billings, Montana. In 2001.we drove route 120 to the Montana border. Near Bridger, Montana, cottonwood trees lined the Yellowstone River reflecting a welcome oasis.

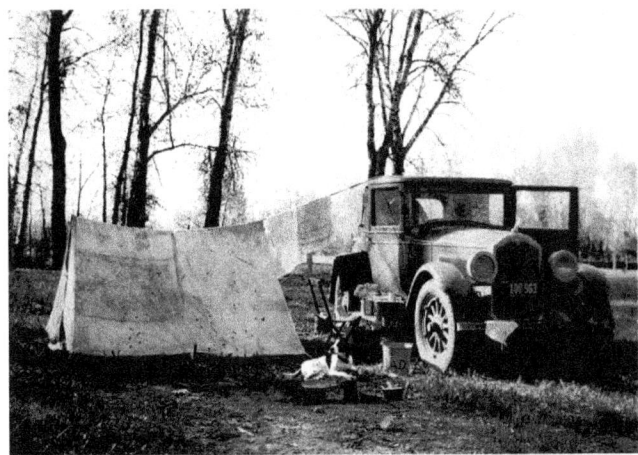

"Auto camp in Montana...dog 'Spot'...May 16, 1935"   RAD

Douglas continued north to the Montana border on a road evolved from the Bridger Trail. This trail serviced the remote ranches in the late 19th to early 20th centuries. Montana did not attain statehood until 1889. Note that the Yellowstone River is in the background of this photograph — a river that was a traveler's refuge from the hot, dusty way just south of the border.

7

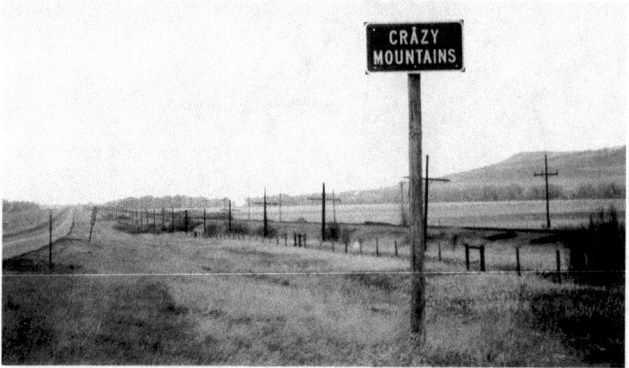

The Route just east of Big Timber, Montana. 2001   JDH

The Crazy Mountains, north of Big Timber, are home to several legends and the subject of a motion picture named "Jeremiah Johnson." The Indians called them mad mountains for their steepness and howling winds. The scenery from this area was also used in two other motion pictures, "A River Runs Through it" and "The Horse Whisperer." Big Timber is home to the Crazy Mountain Museum and a little 1912 one room school house.

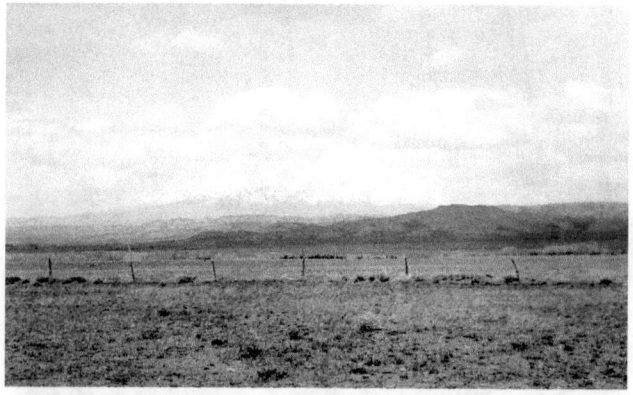

"Crazy Mountains, Montana...snow covered...May 17, 1935"   RAD

An anxious young man pulled off to the side of the road and captured the enticement of the mountain range to his right. However, even old trails and ghost towns did not turn the head of this Alaska destined gentleman. However, one brief trip down to Yellowstone National Park by way of the northern entrance, did—made before Douglas continued on to Idaho. Yellowstone was the world's first national park established in 1872 — luring many prospectors to veer south.

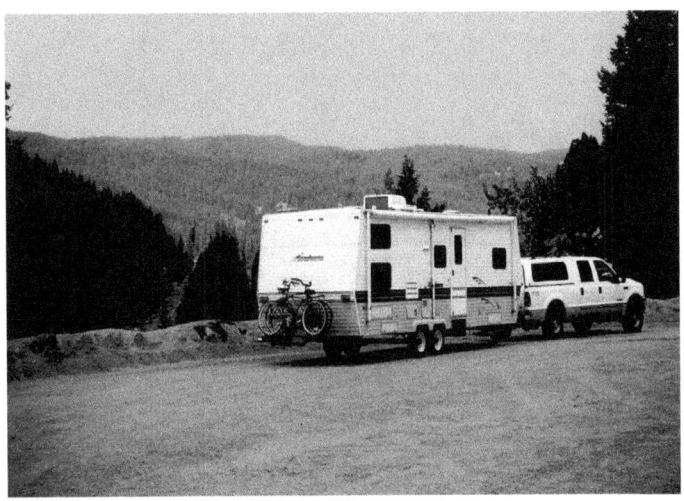

West Route 2, outside Butte, Montana. 2000   JDH

In 2000 we approached two gray-haired gentlemen in a Butte, Montana, coffee shop and asked the location of the 1935 "crossing the Rockies" photograph. They both replied that it looked like old Route 2. Our home on wheels perched on a pass posing for a photograph, while Nellie enjoyed views of the Continental Divide from inside the truck munching on a sandwich.

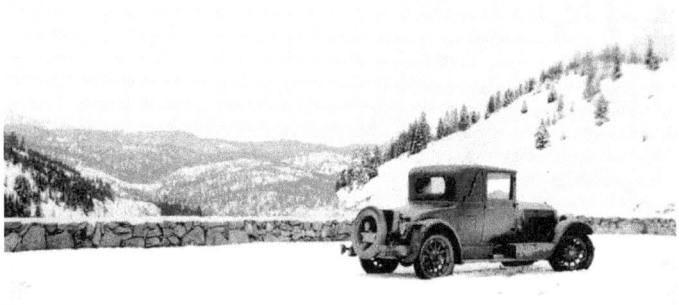

"Crossing the Rockies near Butte, Montana...three inch snowfall the previous night...May 19, 1935"   RAD

What an extraordinary journey it must have been chasing the cloud covered sun over the Bitterroot Range in Idaho on that dusty, gravel road back in nineteen thirty-five — with thoughts of Alaska becoming ever stronger in his head.

9

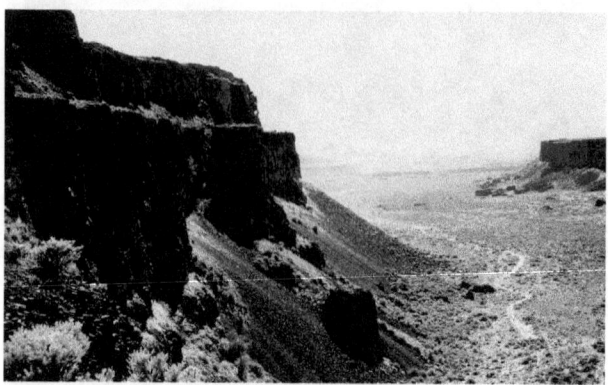

Columbia Gorge near Vantage, Washington. 1999   JDH

In an earlier trip to Washington in 1999, our very first attempt to find the exact location of two of Douglas's 1935 photographs was made. It was hot in the noonday sun in the Columbia Gorge, and we were ready to settle for that second best shot. All of a sudden Emory shouted, "I've found it." He was standing out on a craggy point off the original road. In great delight the camera clicked, perhaps motivating the entire repeat photography adventure.

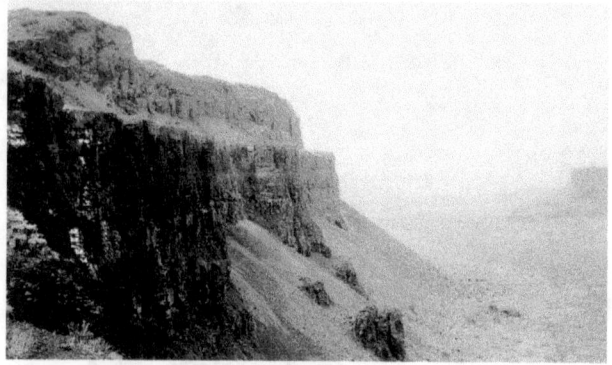

"Columbia River canyon...near Vantage, Washington...
May 20, 1935" RAD

Long after Douglas had crossed over the old Vantage Bridge, a dam was built to control flooding in the area. Sections of the old road are now covered by Wanapum Lake, a part of the Columbia River. The original bridge was built in 1927. It was relocated to Lyon's Ferry State Park in southeast Washington. A road trip was made to visit and photograph the original bridge (not included in the original book of LCA, but can be found in *Nellie's Hill* page 91).

10

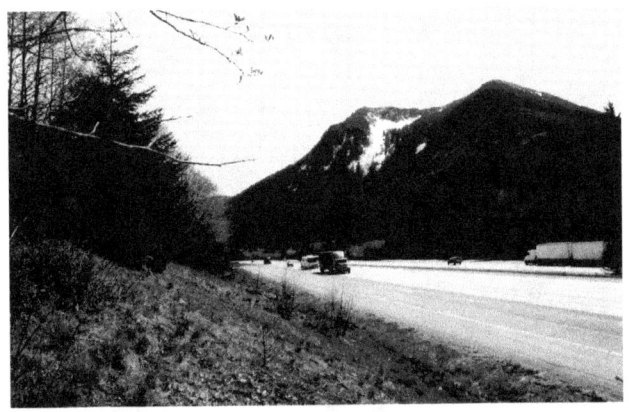

Snoqualmie Pass, Washington (looking east). 2001   JDH

Douglas's granddaughter Diane located this view of snow on the mountain — resembling an upside down check — only by chance in 1999. She held the old photo in her hand and spotted the view while looking out the back window of our rental car. We were traveling south on Route 90. The only clue had been the words "near Seattle" on the back of the 1935 photograph. The above photo was taken when the area was revisited in 2001.

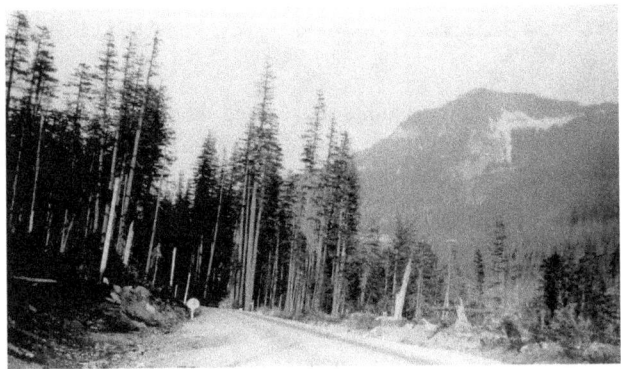

"Tall trees and high mountains near Seattle, Washington... May 21, 1935"   RAD

Seattle, Washington — known as the jumping off point to the Klondike and goldfields of Alaska — had only one more obstacle for Douglas to hurdle. This small obstacle was known as the Cascade mountain Range. The range is located inland from the Pacific Ocean on the west coast of the United States. Mount Rainier is the highest peak in the Cascades at an elevation of 14,410 feet. In 1935 the narrow, winding gravel road crossing the Cascades was called the Sunset Highway.

11

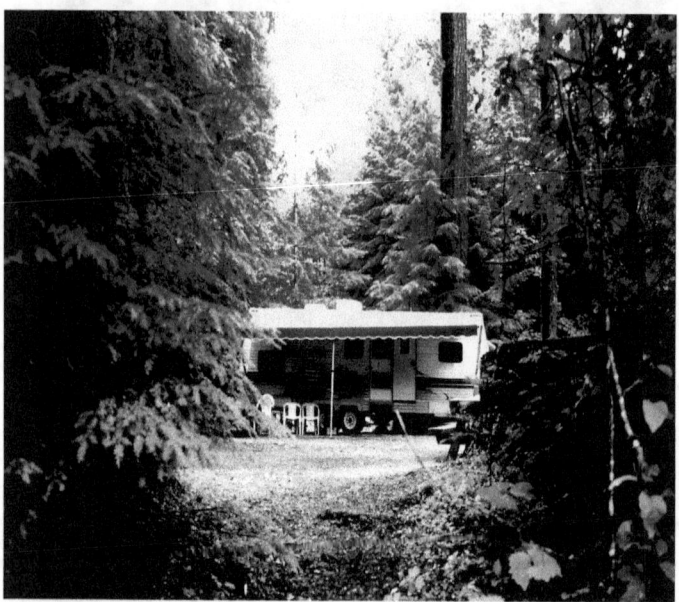

Iron Creek State Park, Washington. 2000   JDH

Arriving in Randle, Washington, seemed like we had finally made it home. In the next few days, we rented a post office box in Olympia and established a base camp at a rustic campsite in Iron Creek State Park. The site was nestled between Mount Rainier and Mount St. Helens. Emory and I had set aside one day for a drive up Mount St. Helens before Nellie and the family pet, Little Jon, were relocated to their prearranged provisional Washington homes. An "Alaska Nellie" Douglas's wife would never be.

Subsequently, we picked up three of the Ahtell Creek hikers at the Sea-Tac Airport. There was a slight mist in the air as we settled down around the campfire that last evening. All thoughts and conversation centered on the expectations of locating a little cabin in the backwoods of Alaska without being confronted by grizzlies. Later that night a multitude of gear was lined up on the camper floor as five backpacks and five suitcases were opened and scattered about. The sorting took place well into the night. Overwhelmed, Emory said, "I don't think this is going to work." It did, and the next morning everyone lined up outside of check-in at Alaska Airlines.

12

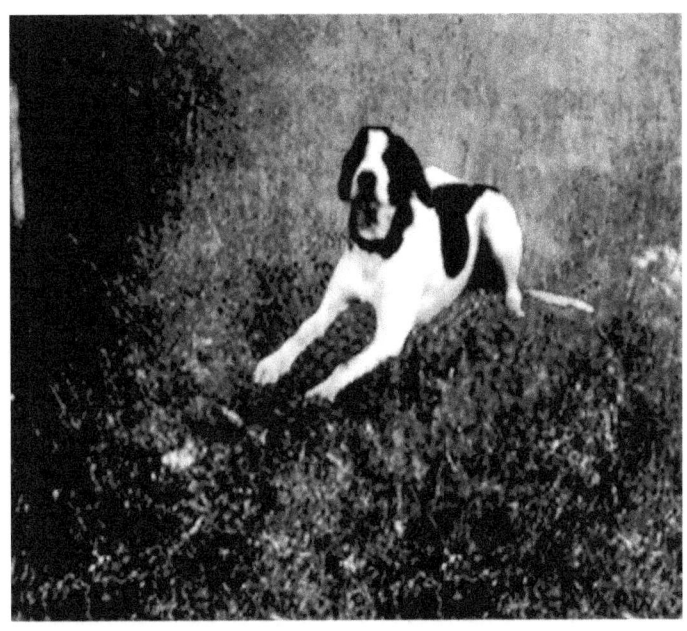

"Spot...Seattle, Washington...May 24, 1935" RAD

On Douglas's first day of travel he wrote in his diary:

> *May 8 — Did I mention the dog yet? Spot was*
> *born in Florida on May 1, 1934.*
> *He moved to North Carolina in July of 1934.*
> *His father was a setter and mother,*
> *Peg, a fox terrier. Peg is now on a farm in*
> *North Carolina where she can spend*
> *her last years in comfort.*

It was customary for prospectors during the gold rush years to have a portrait made before venturing off to the unknown. This prospector chose instead to make one of his dog Spot. Douglas had developed a special bond for this dog's mother, Peg, while prospecting for gold in Pineville, N.C.

During his stay in Seattle, Douglas recorded his last minute preparations for the untamed world of Alaska. He wrote in his diary:

> *May 22, Seattle, Washington — I stayed here in*
> *a rooming house and sold the auto for*
> *$40.00...bought pieces of equipment lacking,*
> *also supplies other than food such as shells,*
> *compass, clothes (woolen) etc. I made a*
> *reservation on the S. S. Yukon sailing June 1.*
> *Then I purchased 3 trunks and packed*
> *everything in them.*
>
> *June 1, Pier 2 — Well, so long civilization such*
> *as it is in a big city. Boat fare to Valdez, Alaska*
> *$57.50 plus $4.80 for the dog. The boat sailed*
> *at 9 a.m.*

A ship with the name S. S. Yukon stirred the imagination of prospectors everywhere preparing to leave the Seattle area for Alaska. The ship towered over this Northeasterner and his three trunks loaded with dreams and expectations from a land further north. His trunks were overflowing with undiscovered gold.

Douglas arranged to have someone help him load his trunks onto the ship. He can be seen on the gangplank in the illustration to the right carrying his suit case aboard. Also of note is a sailor on deck looking down at the activities below and Spot (roped by the three trunks) looking back at activities aboard ship.

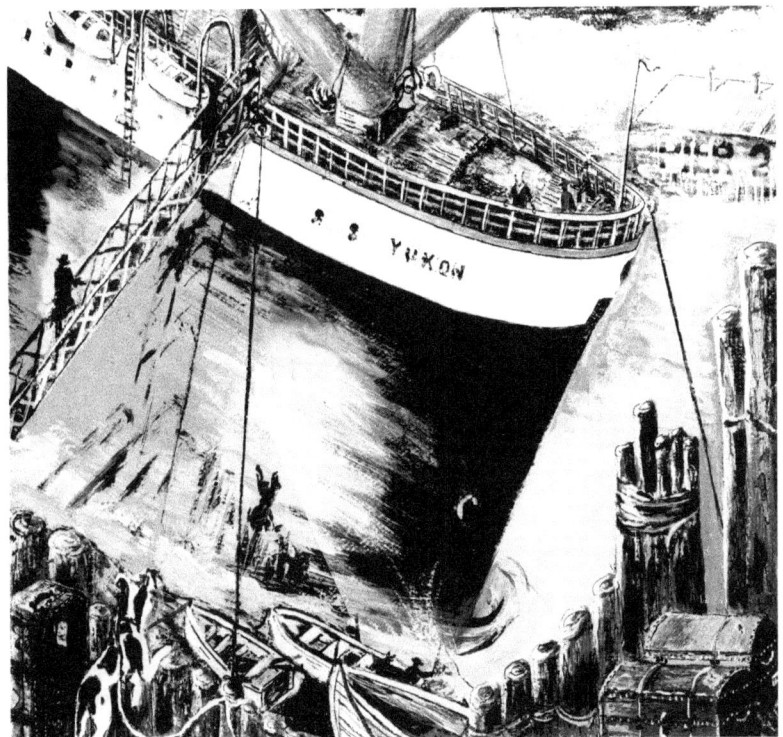

Illustration 2.   Pier 2

Once aboard, Douglas began hearing chatter of President Roosevelt's new colony in the Matanuska Valley north of Anchorage, and of a land draw that had already taken place on May 22. The first contingency of these colonists and their family pets — one cat and twelve dogs (plus a few other assorted pets) — had sailed to Alaska from San Francisco, California, on May 1, just prior to Douglas's departure.

Upon Douglas's return from Fairbanks in 1936, he photographed and spent time in the colonists' valley of rushing rivers and rugged mountain peaks during the colonists' second summer of survival. His collection of photographs of the Matanuska Colonists — repeated sixty-five years later — are featured in Chapter VI.

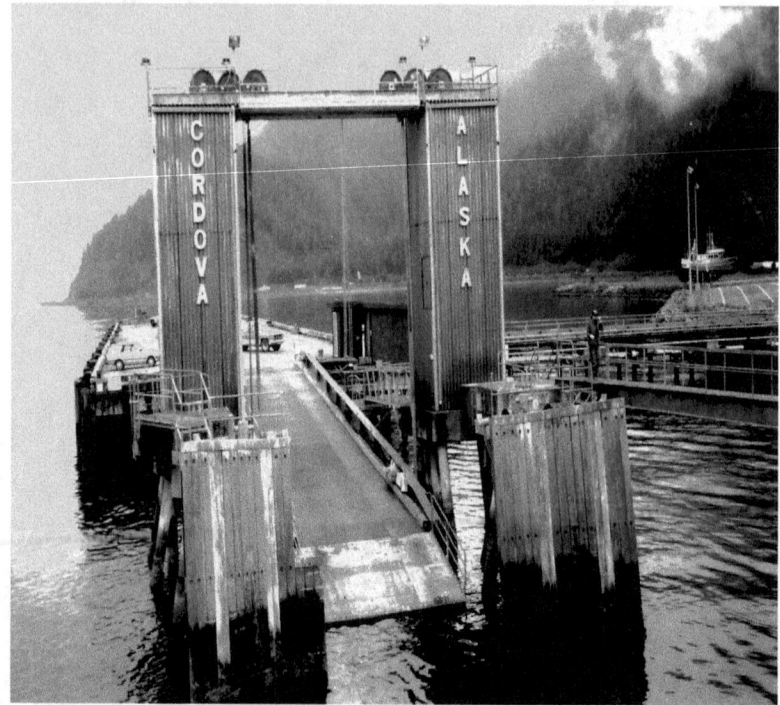

Cordova, Alaska. 2001   JDH

In late August of 2001, we booked passage for ourselves and our bikes on the Bartlett ferry heading from Valdez to Cordova with a brief stop at Tatitlek. The trip was six and a half hours one way. As the Bartlett sailed into Orca Inlet, the view of the 1935 photo was there for a repeat photograph. One hundred and ninety miles of railroad track extended into the interior from Cordova to the Kennecott-McCarthy Mine in 1911. The era ended when the last train pulled into Cordova on November 11, 1938. Due to an earlier 1900's misspelling on public records, the Kennecott Mining Company is spelled with an "e" while the river and glacier are spelled with an "i" (Kennicott).

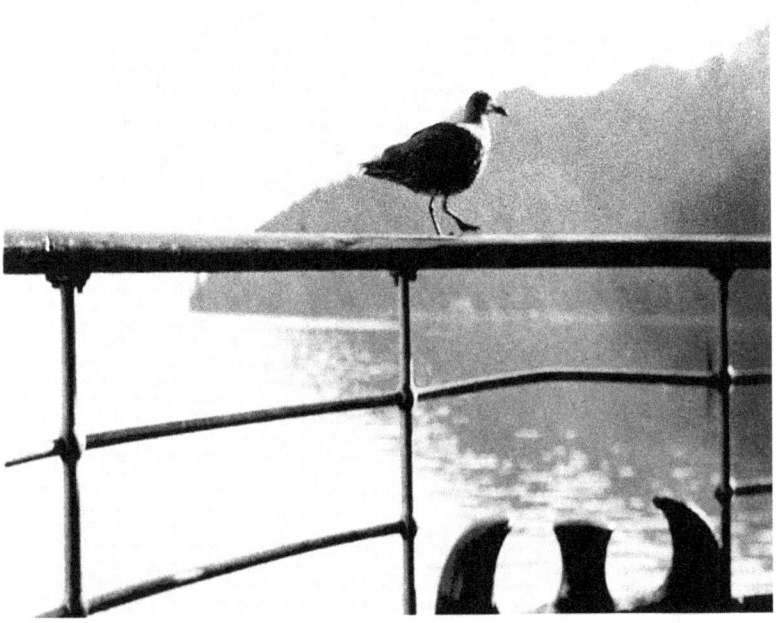

"Sea gull on the rails of the steamer Yukon in Cordova Bay...June 5, 1935"   RAD

Douglas met his first Alaska resident while docked at a fishing cannery aboard the S. S. Yukon in Cordova, Alaska — one of the many brief stops along the way to the upper mainland. Passengers not choosing Cordova as their entry point into the interior remained on board. Douglas's opening Alaska photograph was taken from the deck of the S. S. Yukon.

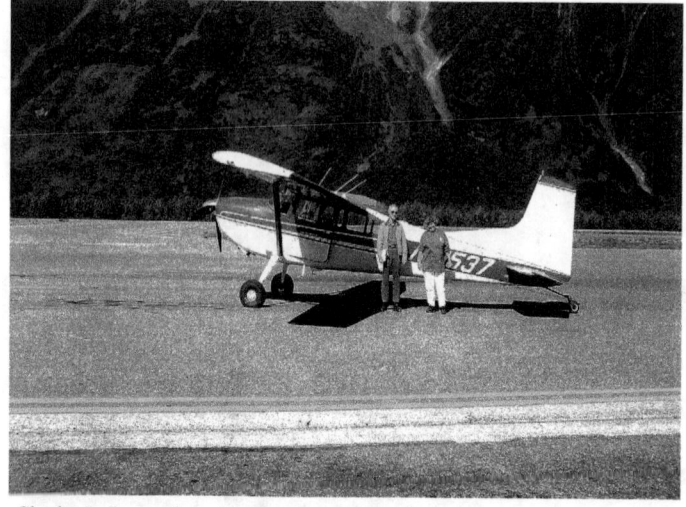

Charles LaPage, pilot with author. Valdez, AK. 2001   UEH

The weather was perfect on Monday, August 13, 2001.
We arranged a Columbia Glacier flyover with Chuck LaPage
from Alpine Aviation Adventures in Valdez. The Columbia
Glacier terminus is no longer visible from Columbia Bay due
to a rapid retreat in the early 1980's. To capture the first
branch of this glacier and vastness of such an extreme area,
wings were needed. The grounded prospectors of the early
1900's could only sense the incredible distances from
mountain peak to mountain peak, as they panned for gold
and searched in earnest for that significant strike. The
Chugach peaks have beckoned and taken the lives of
explorers journeying over the hazardous highways of ice for
centuries — mountain peaks like East Peak at 7,200 ft., West
Peak at 6,200 ft., Mount Shasta at 5,400 ft., Mount Thomas
at 4,300 ft., Mount Francis at 5,400 ft. and Meteorite
Mountain at 6,500 ft.

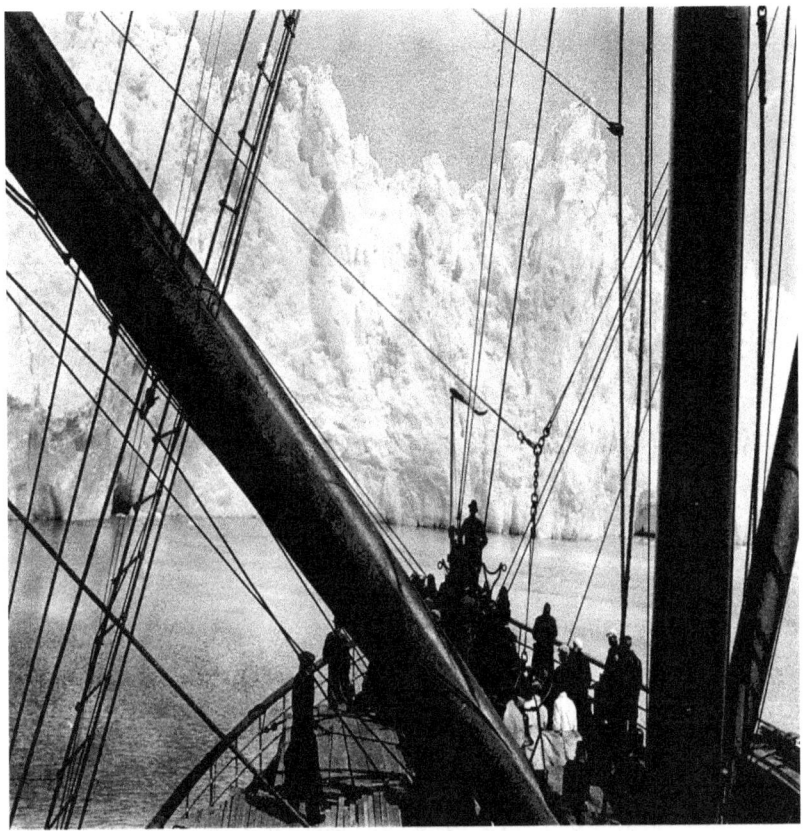

"Columbia Glacier from the steamer Yukon...June 6, 1935" RAD

Passengers aboard the S.S. Yukon were treated to this magnificent 300 foot wall of ice. The Columbia Glacier provided access to mines such as the Cameron-Johnson, Mayfield, Ruff & Tuff and Gold King in the early 1900's.

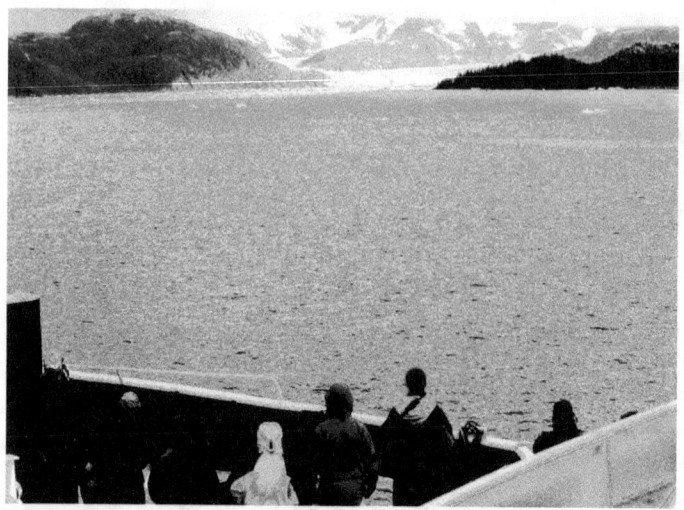

Millennium view of the Columbia Glacier, Aug. 5, 2000   JDH

Today, passengers observe what remains of the Columbia Glacier from a greater distance than the ships of yesterday. Present day breakaway ice can be large enough to create a boating hazard. This is when our interest in glacier meltdown began to bud. In 2001, on our return trip, we felt it was important to capture some of the repeat photography from the air.

In 1982 a dramatic retreat of up to 100 feet per day was recorded, leaving a floating moraine of dirty blue-gray ice from underground streams flowing inside the glacier from the upper Chugach peaks. The first non-natives to view Alaska's most famous glacier was a group of explorers from a Spanish expedition led by Lt. Salvador Fidalgo in 1790.

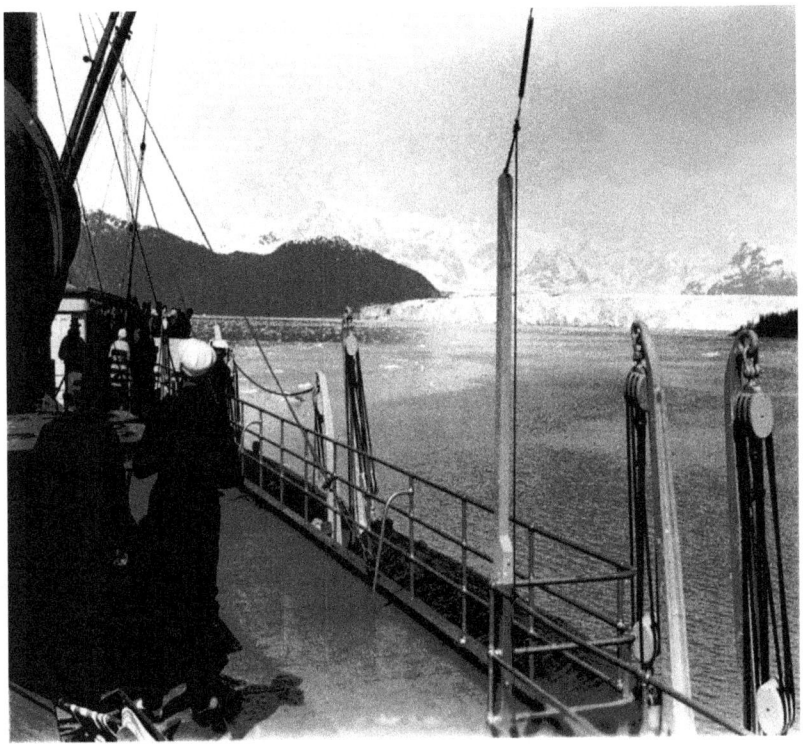

"Columbia Glacier from the S. S. Yukon, June 6, 1935" RAD

The fate of the S.S. Yukon was unknown to the passengers aboard this steamer, but it would sink in stormy seas off Cape Fairfield east of Seward on February 4, 1946. Only eleven of the five hundred passengers would be rescued. The S.S. Yukon began its service to Alaska in 1924.

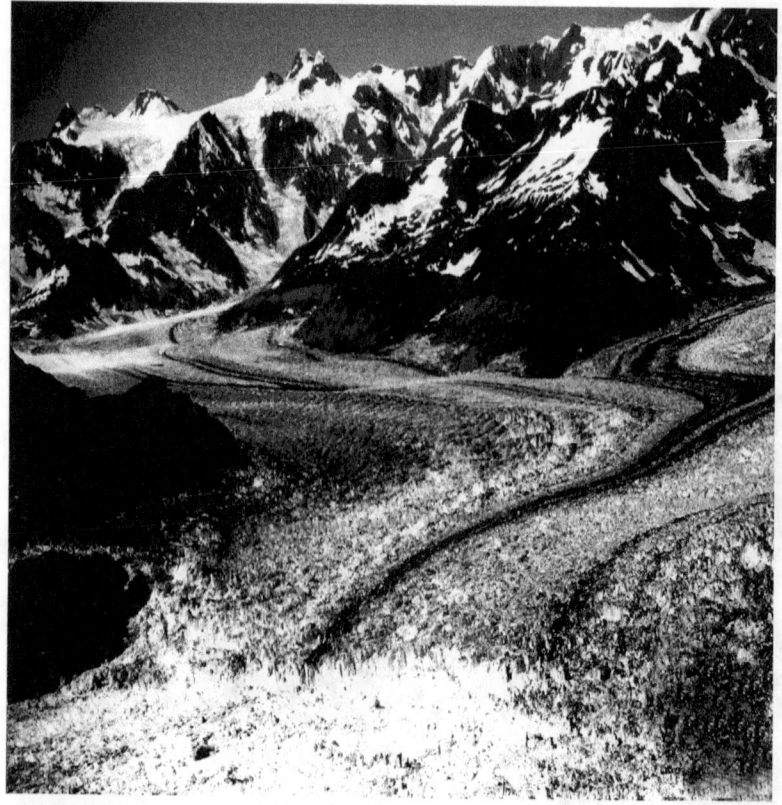

Columbia Glacier, Alaska. August 13, 2001   JDH

This 2001 aerial view is just in front of the new terminus of the Columbia Glacier. The first branch of the Columbia is located in the upper left side of the above photo.

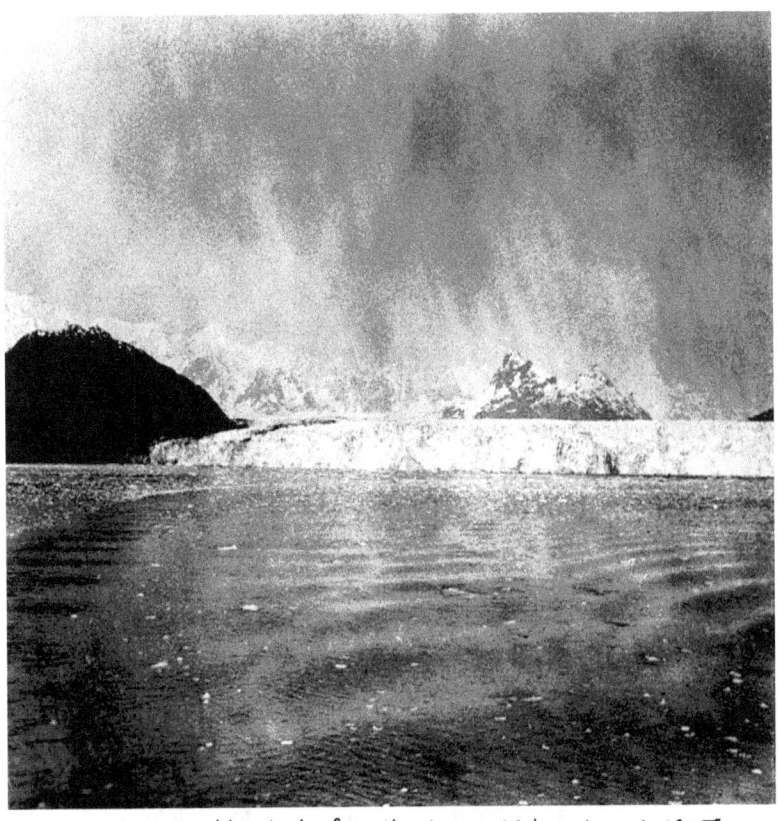

"The Columbia Glacier from the steamer Yukon, June 6, 1935" RAD

In 1935, the Columbia Glacier stretched from the mainland (left) to Heather Island (right). The glacier was named for Columbia University, New York by the Harriman Expedition in 1899.

Douglas noticed the extreme beauty of the land and waited for the 40 foot snowfall to clear on the pass. He wrote the following in his diary:

> *June 7 — I arrived in Valdez at 5 p.m.*
> *It was a small town of 200 population.*
>
> *June 8-18 — I found a small cottage*
> *and stayed here batching it with a*
> *local resident. I purchased groceries*
> *of 45 lbs. and accessory equipment,*
> *as head and bed nets and ax etc. I'm*
> *not in Seattle!!!!!!*

Valdez (pronounced Val *deez*) acquired its name from the Spanish explorer and cartographer Salvador Fidalgo in 1790, who named the Bay of Valdes after an admiral of the Spanish Marines. Later, the spelling was changed to Valdez.
  The town was surrounded by Swiss-like mountains and a glacier that you could almost reach out and touch.
  Anxious for the pass to clear and his journey into the interior to begin, Douglas and Spot spent many hours exploring in the light of the midnight sun — a phenomenon neither were accustomed to. Energized by the constant light, they trekked off on numerous hikes to nearby mountains and the area of the Valdez Glacier.

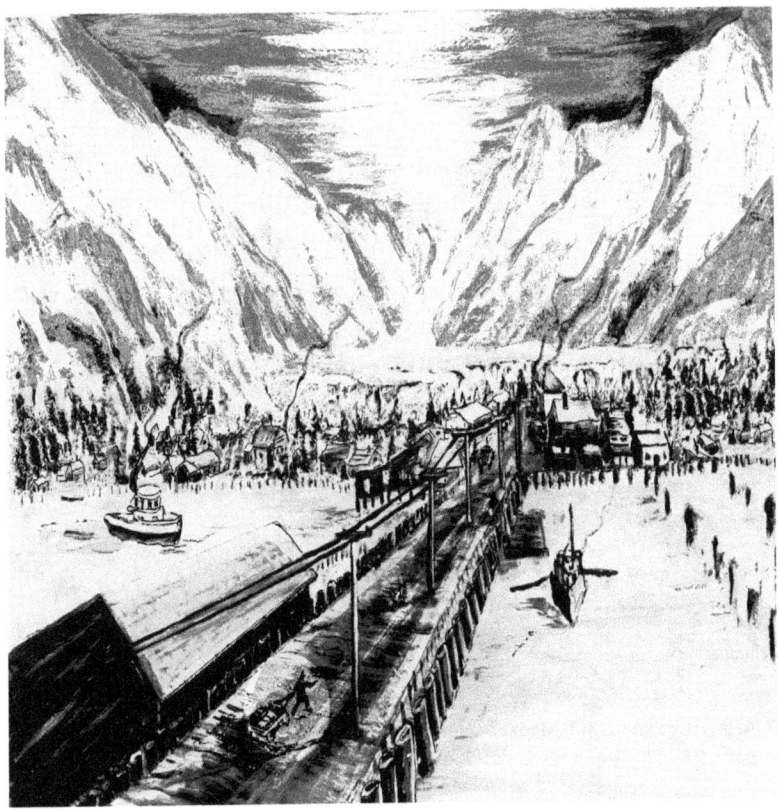

Illustration 3   First Glimpse of Paradise

Douglas eagerly walks the pier toward the small gold rush town of Valdez, pulling all of his luggage behind him. Spot runs ahead relieved to finally get off the ship. This would be Spot's home until his death.

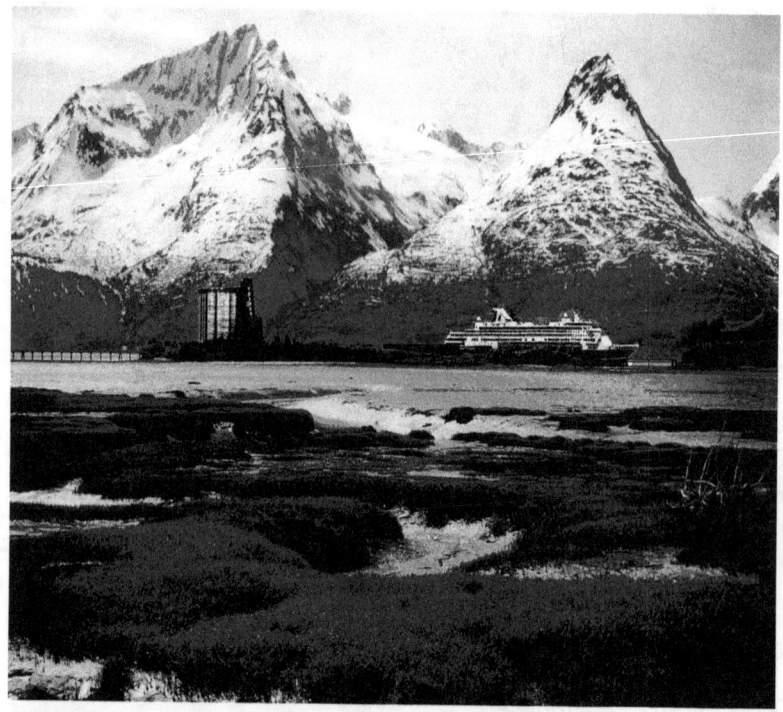

Old grainer, cruise ship, Mount Francis (left) and Sugarloaf Mountain
(right), Valdez, Alaska. 2001   JDH

What was it about Valdez? Was it the yellow dandelions
lining the streets as we entered town on the morning of
June 2, 2001? Was it the mountains covered with snow
resembling powdered sugar? Or, was it a dog named
"Fidalgo." A dog we had walked at the local animal shelter,
echoing a street and a man who had explored these waters
centuries ago? Valdez was the place we felt we had always
been.

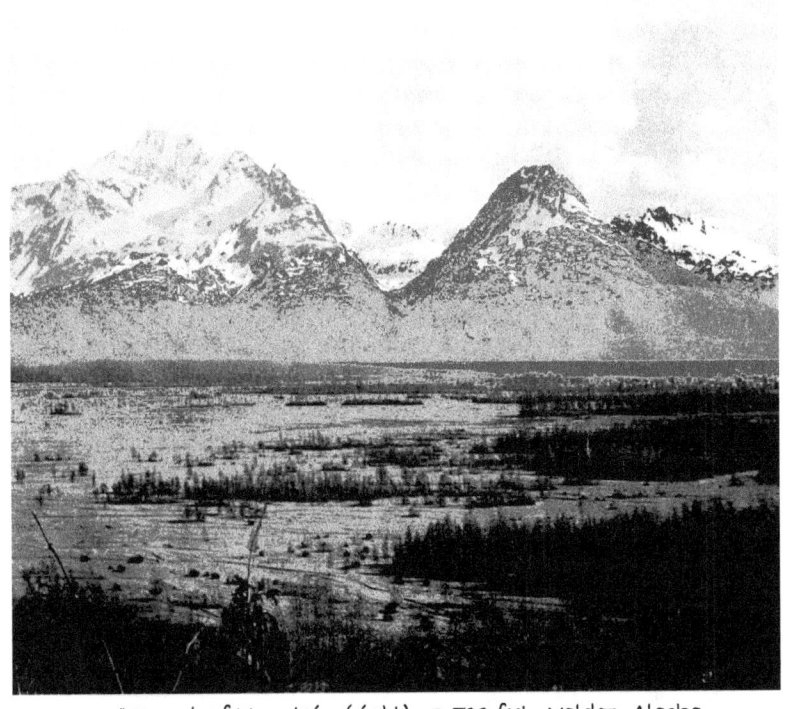

"Sugarloaf Mountain (right)...3,500 feet...Valdez, Alaska...
June 12, 1935" RAD

Douglas took only one photograph (above) during his first
eleven days on the mainland of Alaska. His film supply was
limited. It was important to save the film for that sought
after gold strike!

THE ALASKA TERRITORY
and the EAGLE-VALDEZ TRAIL

In 1896 gold was discovered on Bonanza Creek in the Yukon. A stampede town developed almost overnight on the banks of the Yukon and Klondike River's convergence. Dawson was more of a camp than a city during the early onset of the gold rush. An interior trail was established in Alaska to reach this new gold rush camp. It was called the Eagle-Valdez Trail.

In the late 19th century to the early 20th century, the Eagle-Valdez Trail connected Fort Liscum across the bay from "old" Valdez to Eagle, Alaska, on the Yukon River. A telegraph was established between the two points. The Eagle–Valdez Trail became the route of choice for many of the early prospectors. As time passed, the Eagle-Valdez Trail took on several different names. It is referred to as the "Old Military Trail" and to the local Valdezeans, "the Goat Trail" or the "Valdez-Eagle Trail." Tourists know it as the "Keystone Canyon Pack Trail."

Eventually, the trail became part of the Richardson Highway (Route 4) and a stretch of the Glenn Highway (Route 1). The Richardson Highway opened in 1919 connecting Valdez to Fairbanks. The Glenn Highway opened well past Douglas's exploring of 1935-36.

Douglas continues in his 1935-36 Alaska diary:

> *June 15 — The trail opened on the 15th. I saw Bill Ackerman, a truck driver, and arranged with him to go to Slana on his next trip. I left two trunks in storage at Dan Wilcey's store and we left on the truck Tuesday, the 18th, at 11 a.m. We arrived in Chistochina at 11 p.m. We saw a small brown bear along the road. I stayed over night in Chistochina.*
>
> *June 19 —The bridge was out 2 miles beyond Chistochina. We helped the Roadmen make temporary repairs.*

They completed repairs by 6:30 pm, had supper and Akerman went back to Valdez. The final leg of Douglas's trip was set up with a man named "Swanson." Off they went in Swanson's old pick-up—a would-be prospector, a dog and one very full trunk. They arrived in Slana at midnight— in the rain.

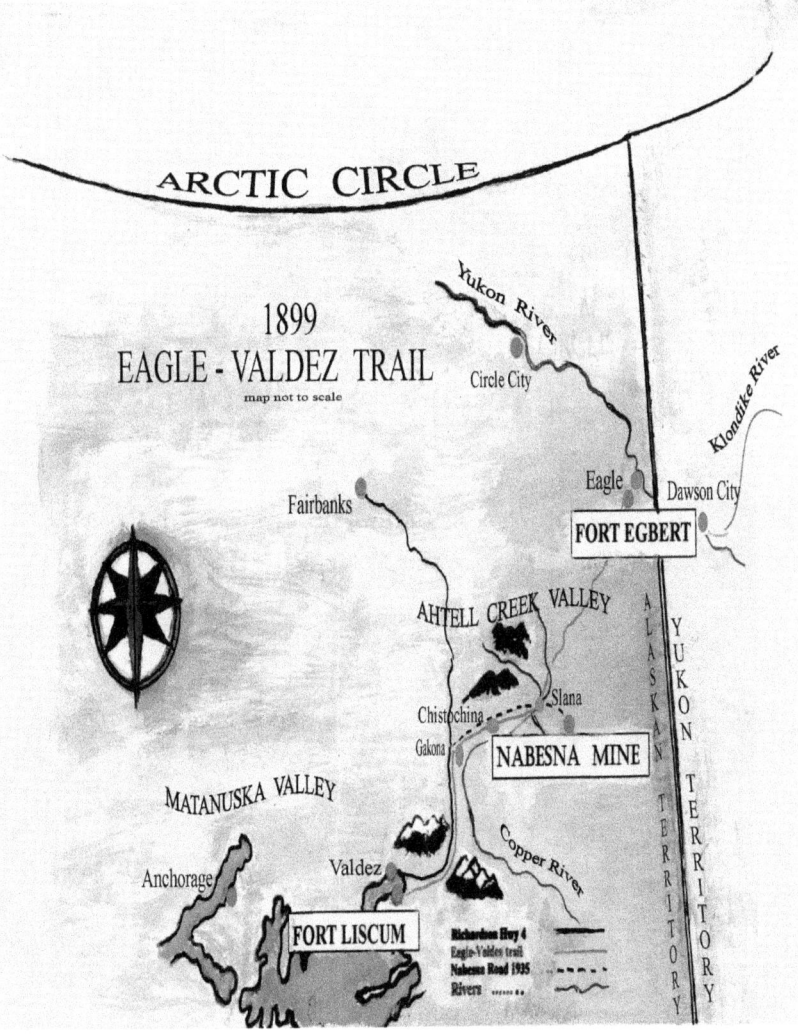

Map 4. Eagle-Valdez Trail 1899 (with the addition of the roads and towns of 1935).

  They completed repairs by 6:30 p.m., had supper and Ackerman went back to Valdez. The final leg of Douglas's trip was set up with a man named "Swanson." Off they went in Swanson's old   pick-up — a would-be prospector, one dog and one very full trunk. They arrived in Slana at midnight in the rain.

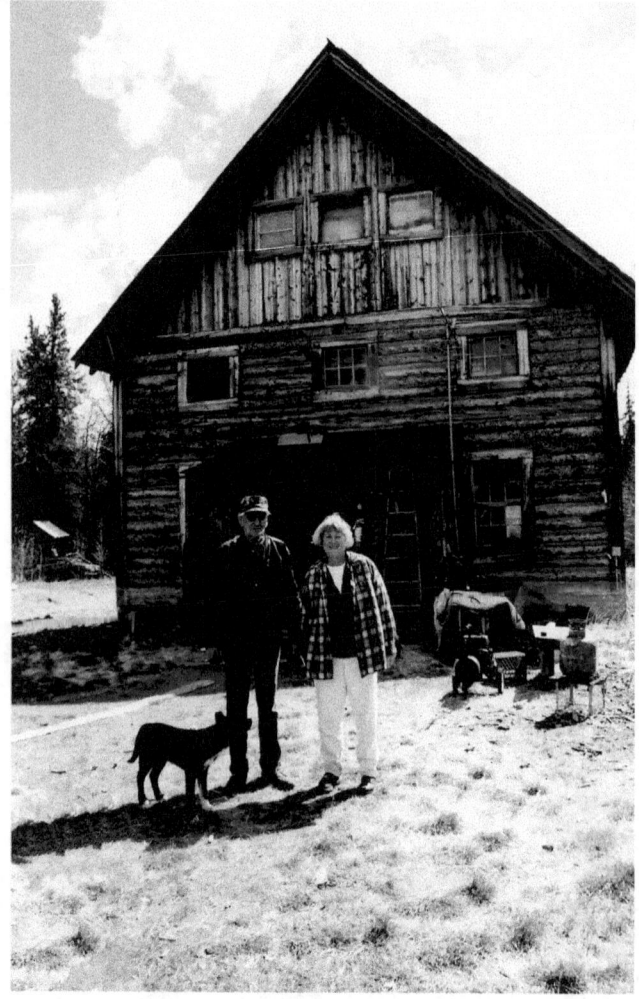

Angus DeWitt with author. Slana roadhouse, Alaska. 2001   UEH

   The old Slana roadhouse and post office (now a private residence) was built on Nabesna Road in 1932 by a Frenchman named Lawrence DeWitt. Douglas spent time here, along with other prospectors, miners and geological surveyors. Raining? It was pouring, but not enough to dampen the spirits of a man planning to pack into the wilderness in the morning to search for gold.

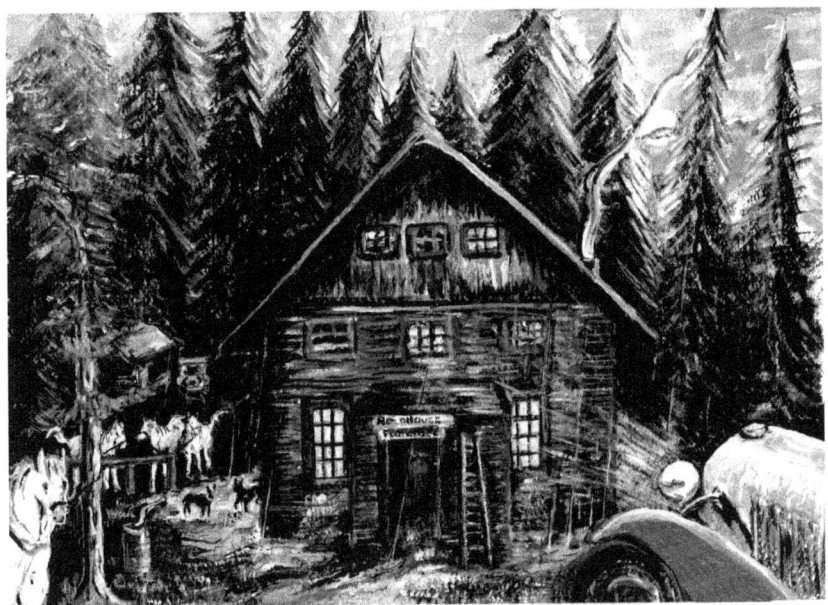

Illustration 4.   Midnight in the Rain

June 20 - Slana, Alaska —
I arranged to leave the
trunk with extra clothes
etc...I made up a pack and
started out for Ahtell
Creek. Lawrence DeWitt
has a cabin at the junction
of Flat Creek which I may
use. It came up to rain in
the afternoon. I went about
4 miles up the trail and lost
it...so rolled up in damp
blankets and lay down on
wet moss in wet clothes to
rest and sleep a little.

   Determined, but inexperienced, Douglas's first attempt to
locate the log cabin on Flat Creek was not productive. The
trail was muddy and undefined. Eventually, he returned
back to the roadhouse for his second night. Disappointed,
but still determined, in the morning he acquired the skills of
a young Athabaskan guide named Guy John, who led him
effectively to the Flat Creek cabin.

31

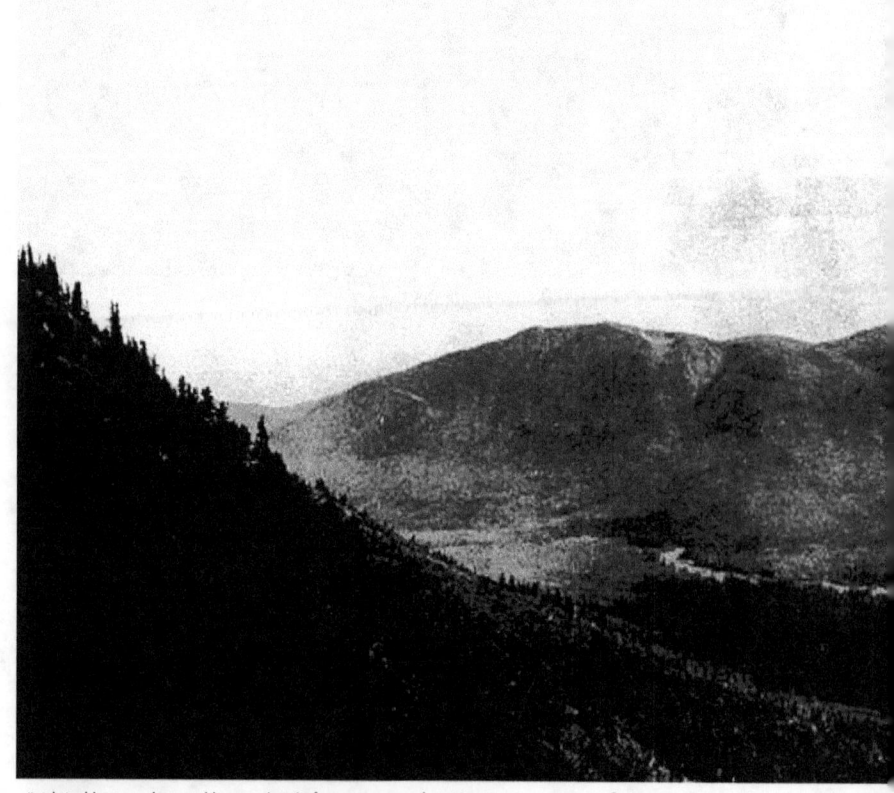

"Ahtell Creek Valley...looking west (valley el. 2,600 ft.)...
Mt. Sanford through clouds (el. 16,257 ft.).

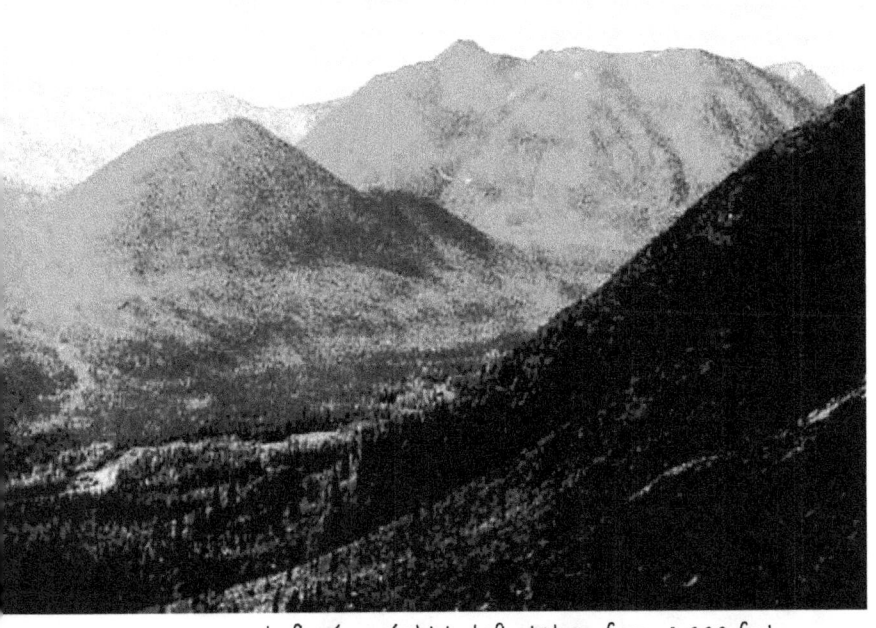

...creek flowing right to left...taken from 4,000 foot
elevation...note snow on mountains...July 7, 1935"   RAD

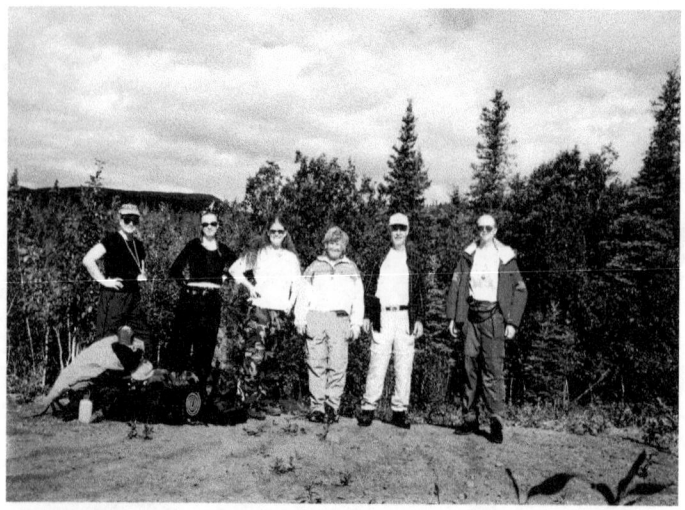

Backpackers: Diane, Heather, Alison, Jill, Emory and Ken at the Ahtell
Creek trailhead, Alaska. 2000   Timer

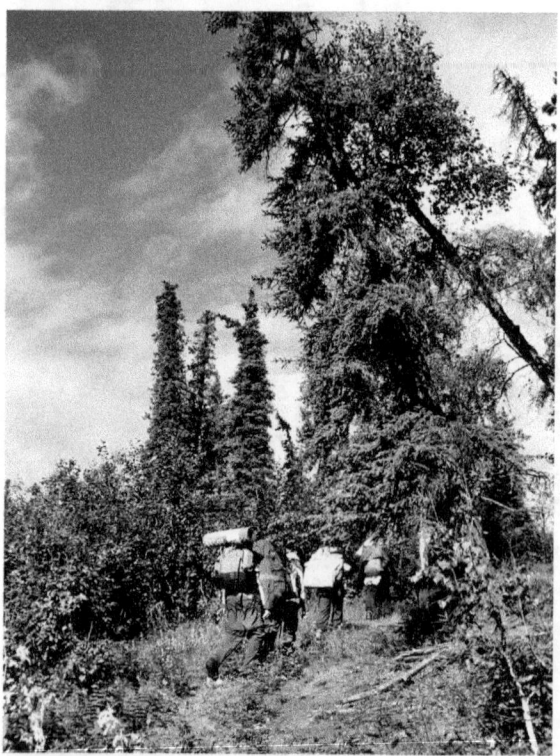

Ken, Alison, Diane and Heather hiking the Ahtell Creek Trail,
Alaska. 2000   JDH

The rustic campsite in Iron Creek State Park, Washington was now a distant memory. After gaining an hour of flight time from Seattle to Alaska, we arrived at the Anchorage International Airport late Monday, July 24, 2000.

After some days of orientation by kayaking on Eklutna Lake, ice sliding on Hatcher Pass and walking the Matanuska Glacier, the hikers were ready for the dangerous hike they were about to undertake. It was time to locate some repeat photos of an old gold mining cabin back in the Ahtell Creek wilderness — a log cabin their grandfather had lived in while prospecting for gold in the summer of 1935.

Our base camp for the Ahtell Creek hike was at the Hart-D-Ranch in Slana. It was a cloudy evening in this eastern Alaska area. Deep into the late night hours, the campers huddled. Battery chargers *blinked*, packs *clicked* and hammers *cocked* and *released* as numerous "what if" scenarios were bandied about. Neeervous? Perhaps we were. It had been reported earlier that there were an abundance of grizzlies in the valley. After all, the ultimate sacrifice was a possibility. A silent seriousness prevailed as the moment of entry drew continually nearer.

First light found our group to a great degree "sleepless in Slana." We loaded heavy packs into our van and drove to an unmarked trailhead. It was difficult to locate and was recognized only by a second phone call to the Bureau of Land Management (BLM). We entered the Ahtell Creek Valley on Monday, July 31, 2000. Rains from previous days had made trail conditions less than favorable. Mud, mosquitoes and high creeks were there to greet us. Six miles into the Alaska wilderness can quickly place an experienced hiker in harm's way. These hikers were from the east coast of the lower forty-eight and not skilled in Alaska ways. Landmarks given to them by the Glennallen BLM were all that stood between the hikers locating the little cabin on Ahtell Creek and bedding down with the grizzlies.

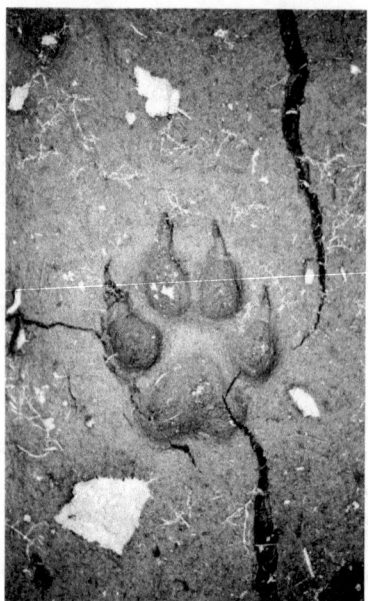

Wolf track, Ahtell Creek Trail, AK.
2000   JDH

The first bit of hiking was not so bad. The sun had come out with the temperature cool in the low 60's for good hiking. The only challenge was looking for an old car mentioned as a landmark in the blue envelope we had picked up earlier at the BLM office in Glennallen. One more little detail not previously mentioned was to be on the alert for an old prospector — a prospector who lived nearby and didn't want anyone coming near his property. He was known to tote a rifle and be accompanied by those Alaska dogs with attitude. The trail was wet and muddy and it appeared that the ATV's (four-wheelers to Alaskans) had chosen a more easterly way to enter because of this problem. "There it is," said Ken, pointing to an old car partially hidden in the brush. The trail continued up and then dipped down into an opening. This area was marshy — something like you would find in Florida. The trail was barely discernable in spots. If it were not for the tracks of the ATV's we might have been misled several times. There were not any ATV tracks back in 1935. We too, would have had to go back to Slana for a second night.

As we worked our way deeper and deeper in on the trail, the thought of bears made us increasingly uneasy. Grizzly, wolf and moose tracks were everywhere and a bear encounter on the trail ahead was a very real possibility. We stopped along the way to examine and photograph some of the prints. Soon we would be arriving at the Ahtell Creek crossing. The water was deeper than normal, but we did have waders with us. Nevertheless, the current and depth was of pressing concern. Ken was the only one with chest high waders. A slip in the cold water could turn us back.

36

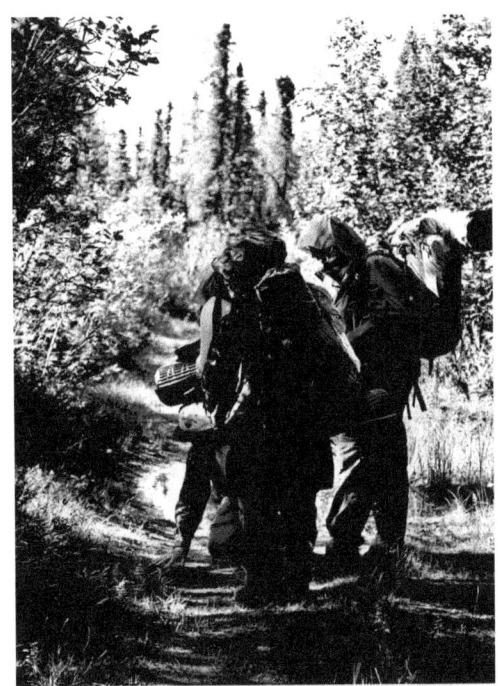

Alison, Emory and Ken examining the tracks. 2000
Photos JDH

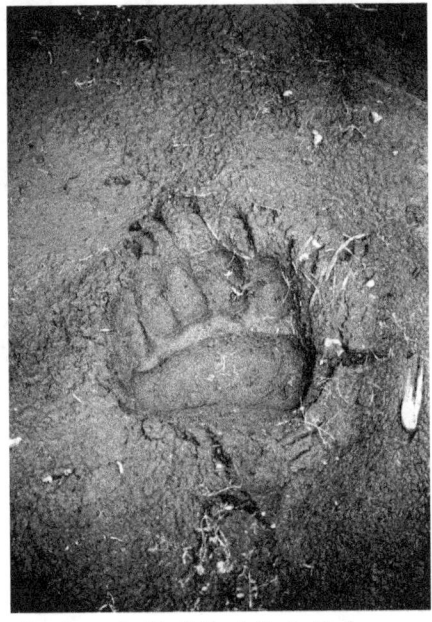

Grizzly track, Ahtell Creek Trail, Alaska.

37

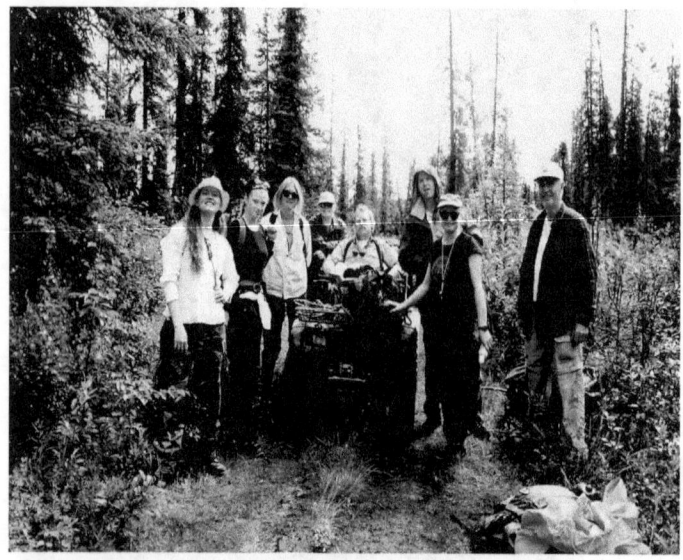

Backpackers: Alison and Heather, BLM specialists: Debbie Muenster, K. J. and David Mushovic & packers: Ken, Diane and Emory on Ahtell Creek Trail, Alaska. 2000   Photos JDH

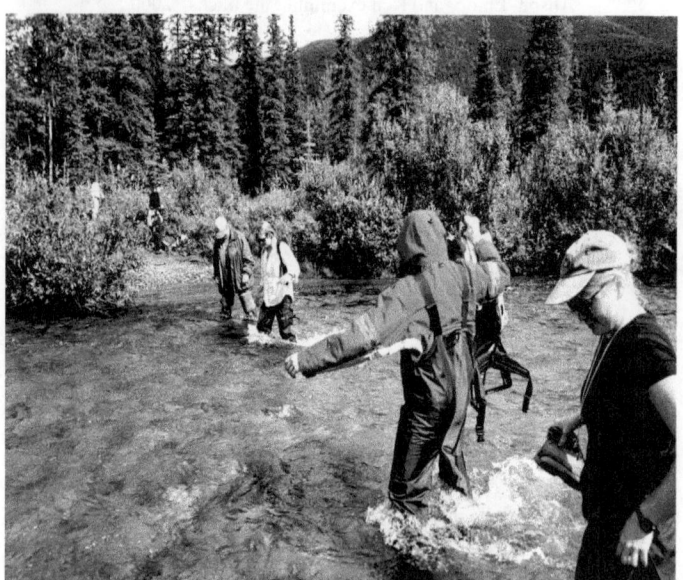

BLM specialists David, K. J. and Debbie assisted hikers Heather, Ken and Diane in fording the Ahtell Creek. 2000

After several more hours of hiking, we heard the welcome *roar* of some Alaska four-wheelers in the distance. Three BLM specialists pulled up on their way to locate GPS positions of the Ahtell Creek cabin and an old placer (surface) mine. The Ahtell Creek still needed to be crossed to reach the cabin, but we now had an escort. The 1935 small wooden bridge was no longer there.

The four-wheelers successfully rode across the swift currents of the Ahtell Creek (flowing left to right), then assisted the hikers with all their gear to the opposite bank without getting it wet. Unknown at the time, a quarter of a mile on the left off the main trail, lay the undisturbed ruins of the old Lawrence DeWitt cabin. The cabin Douglas never arrived at on his first attempt to hike the valley.

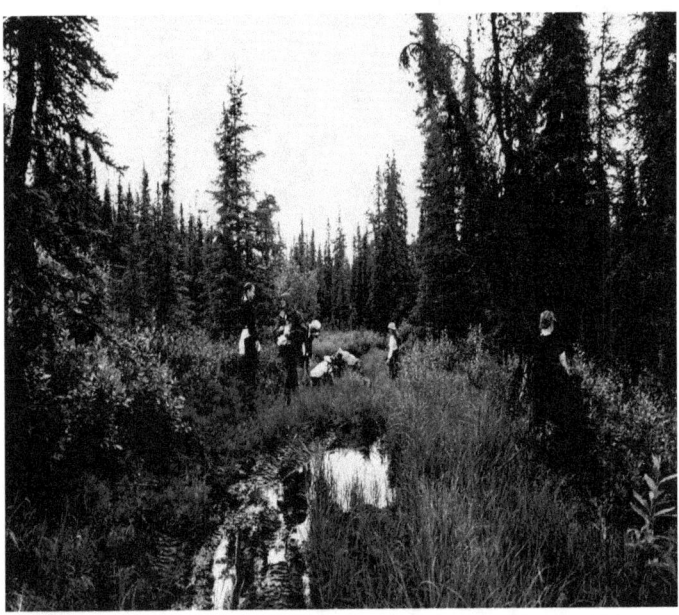

Heather, Ken, Emory, BLM specialist Debbie Muenster, Alison and Diane, Alaska. 2000   JDH

Trail conditions worsened. Trails of mud became trails of water...

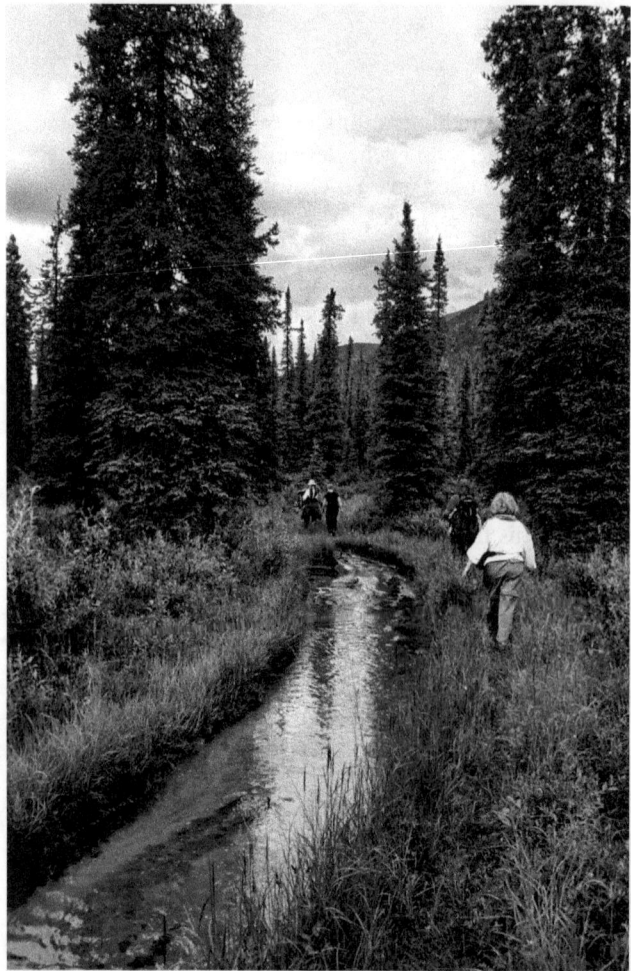

Alison, Diane, Ken and Jill hiking the Ahtell Creek Trail, Alaska. 2000

Even the four-wheelers had a hard time riding through the mud and water without getting stuck. The group was now quite scattered, and all of a sudden gunshots were heard in the distance. Immediate suspense and speculation took over as each looked around to see who was missing. We soon learned that a mother grizzly and her cubs had been startled by one of the ATV's scouting ahead. The grizzly had chased the four-wheeler down the trail until driven off as a result of warning shots fired between its ears by BLM realty specialist David Mushovic. Eventually, the mother bear and her cubs ran off into the woods.

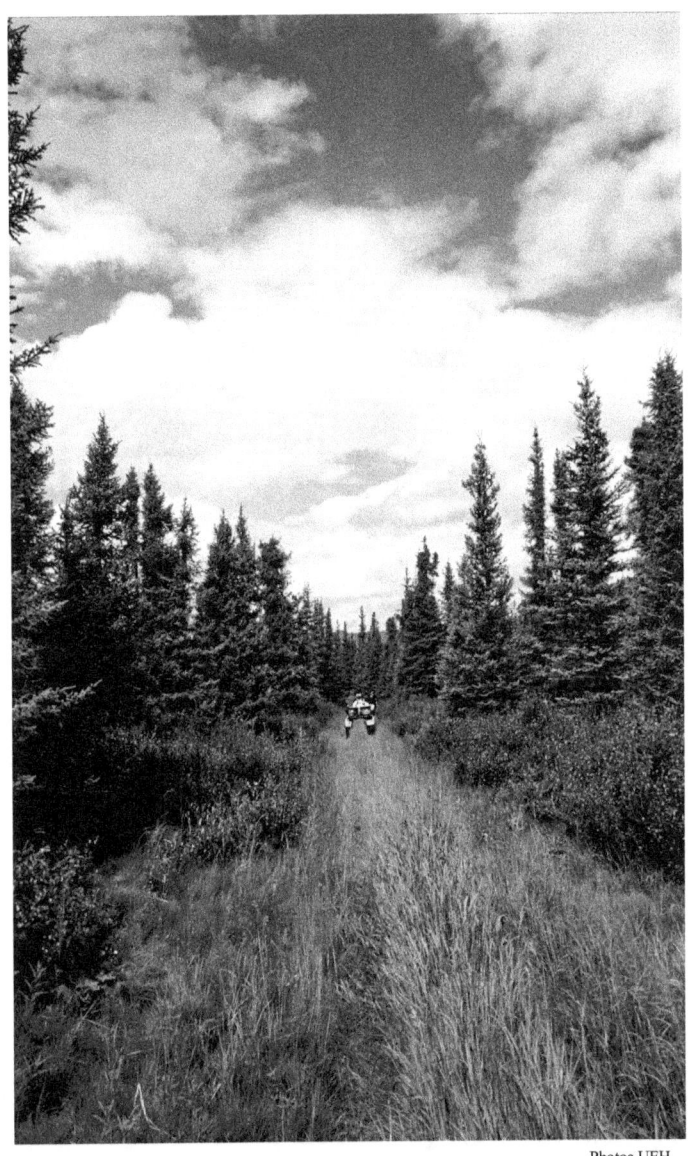

The trail finally evolved into overgrown grass and with a veer to the right there it was — our hard won goal — the cabin!

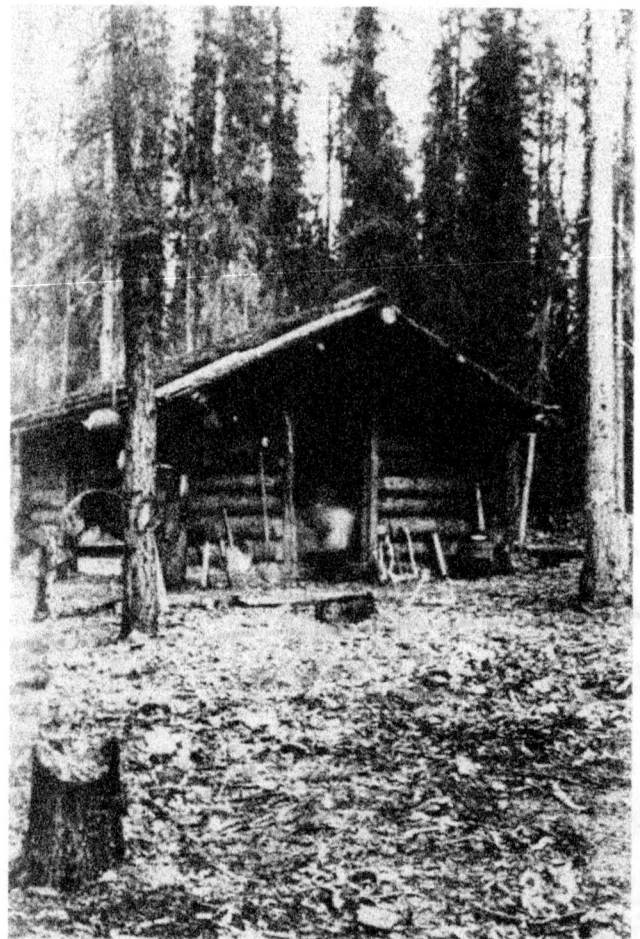

"Gus Johnson's cabin...Ahtell Creek, Alaska ...elevation 2,700..Note: dog Spot and smoke smudge in doorway to keep out mosquitoes...July 7, 1935" RAD

June 23 — A prospector named Sam Gamblin dropped in and advised me to go on another mile and a half to Gus Johnson's cabin at the foot of Grub Stake Creek. Another prospector named Ole (Olsen) was with him.

June 26 — I brought up the rest of my outfit from Lawrence's cabin.

June 28 — Sam and I went to Silver Creek
to cook and look over an old prospect of
galena. I took along my potentiometer for
a test.
June 29 —I am quite tired from packing and
hiking. I did not realize how 'soft' I was.
June 30 — Checked over minerals
from Silver King Mine on Silver
Creek. I found 3 forms of copper ore.
July 2 — Around 9 p.m. Sam came
up with Chief Nikolai, of the
Copper River Valley. He was
over 90 years old.
July 4 — I was getting ready for bed.
Spot growled and barked. There was a
noise in the back of the cabin. I went
out with my gun ready for business to
find it was Laughing Ole's dog, Spike.

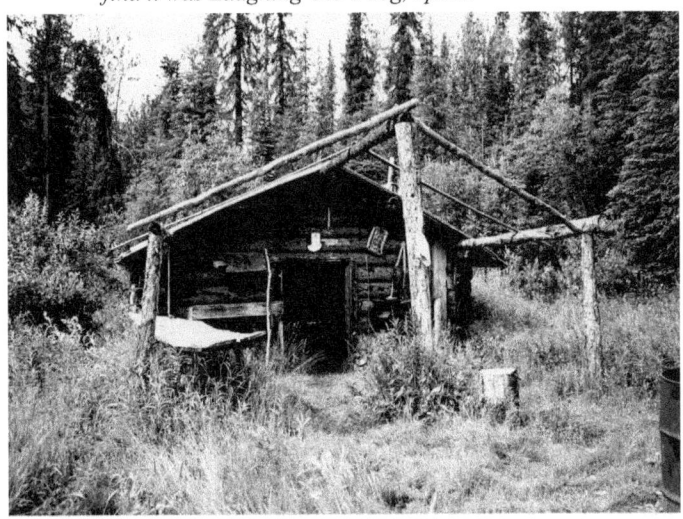

Cabin in the Ahtell Creek Valley, Alaska. 2000   JDH

This remote, reconstructed hunting cabin in the backwoods
of the Ahtell Creek Valley is all that remains of the original
old cabin used by the gold panners in the early 1900's. Although some of the previous wood and flooring are still visible "there is not enough to qualify for the historic record
books," stated BLM archeologist specialist Debbie Muenster.

43

While prospecting, Douglas had run a 3,000 foot line with his potentiometer (a device for measuring electromotive force) at 100 foot intervals at the upper end of the draw at Grub Stake Creek. He secured two good reactions. Douglas was beginning to get the attention of area notables.

> *July 13 — I went down to Flat Creek to see if the salmon were running. It started to rain. The water went over my shoe pack tops in the creek. It raised a blister on my heel and ankle from wet socks and shoes. I hiked 5 miles.*

> *July 16 — I alternate fish to rabbit. Spot gets thinner every day. He must have worms.*

> *July 17 — I stayed in camp to salt and smoke fish. Spot eats plenty, but gets thinner.*

> *July 20 — I hiked out to Slana for grub. While I was there I met War-ren Taylor, the assistant district attorney and his friend George. They came back to the cabin to stay for a week. These were friends of Olsen's.*

Why this area was selected by Douglas to seek his fortune, one can only speculate. Maybe it was talk aboard ship, or maybe it was reading about two earlier gold discoveries at Fortymile in 1881 (or 1886 depending on source) and at Nabesna in 1899. These two major discoveries placed the Ahtell Creek Valley in the spotlight and away from the mayhem. This valley may have appeared less claimed to a prospector determined to track down his own Eldorado.

Prospectors also had aches and pains in the early 1900's from arduous hikes over passes to creeks whose names are no longer on any maps, or never had been — names such as: Rainbow, Slope, Dome, Gamblin, Silver and we must not forget Grub Stake.

Douglas referred several times in his diary to the troubles of being a prospector (and of being a dog) in the rough bush of Alaska.

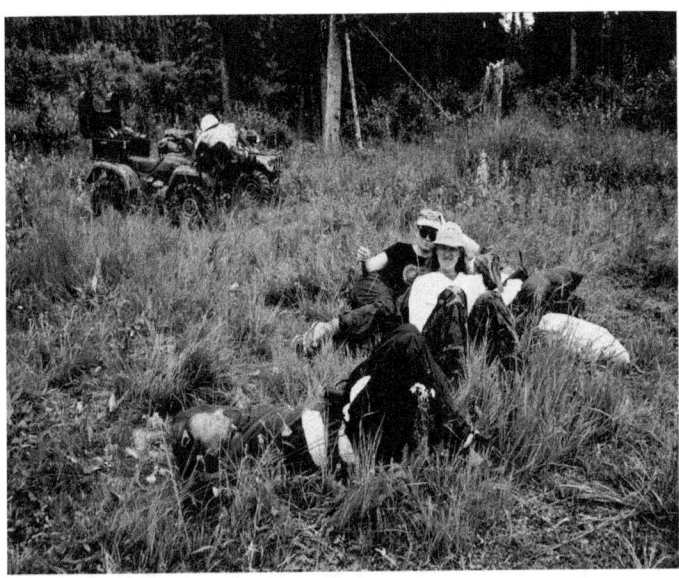

Hikers: Heather, Alison and Diane in the front area of the cabin, Ahtell Creek Valley, Alaska. 2000   JDH

Aches and pains in 2000 left the backpackers worn out after a daunting six-mile hike up the rough Ahtell Creek Trail. The BLM, on the other hand, went busily about their work. Realty specialist David Mushovic activated the GPS to determine land status, while BLM archeologist Debbie Muenster measured and photographed the old cabin to determine its authenticity. Public affairs specialist K. J. Mushovic asked for three volunteers to go up to the placer mine on Grub Stake Creek. Instantly, fatigue was replaced with curious energy. Ken, Heather and the author prepared to leave.

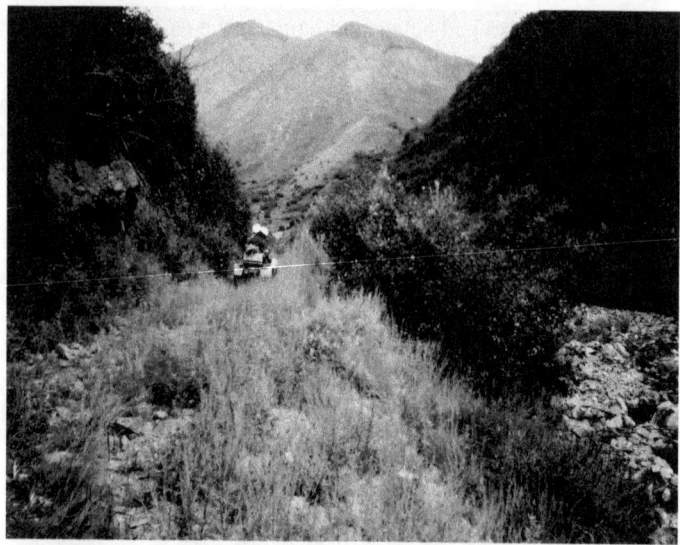

Grub Stake Creek Trail, Ahtell Creek Valley, Alaska. 2000   HDV

Like a force of nature, the group propelled forward on a steep trail of overgrown alder, towards mountains that once dwarfed a man in the mid-thirties as he stood on the divide photographing the Copper River Valley.

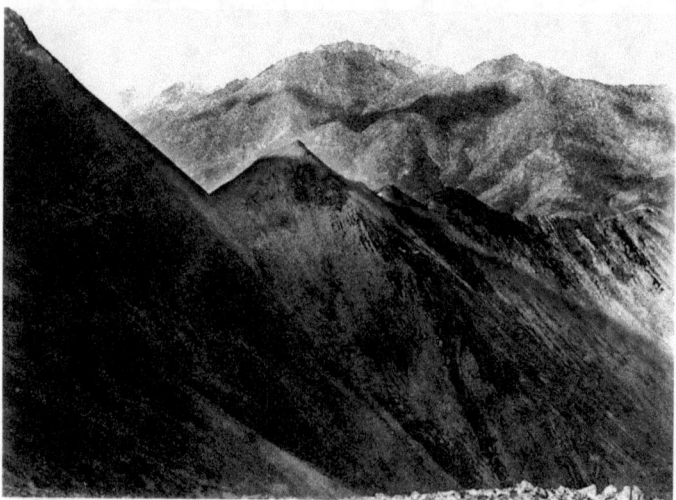

"On the divide...elevation 5,500 feet...between Grub Stake Creek (not shown) and Slope Creek (not shown)...Note: rugged character of mountains...all showing in the view well above the timberline...looking east...view of Copper River Valley for over 50 miles both ways...Alaska...July 12, 1935" RAD

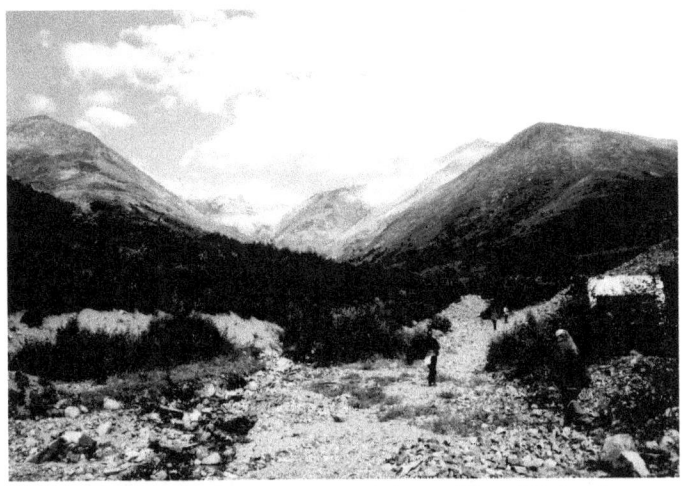

Hikers: Heather and Ken with BLM specialists Debbie and K. J. at the placer mine on Grub Stake Creek, Alaska. 2000   JDH

We arrived at the old placer mining camp on Grub Stake Creek to find an aged mining cabin and various rusty pieces of mining equipment. BLM realty specialist David Mushovic examined the campsite for hazardous materials and took a GPS reading. Later, this was described by Heather as "my favorite part of the hike."

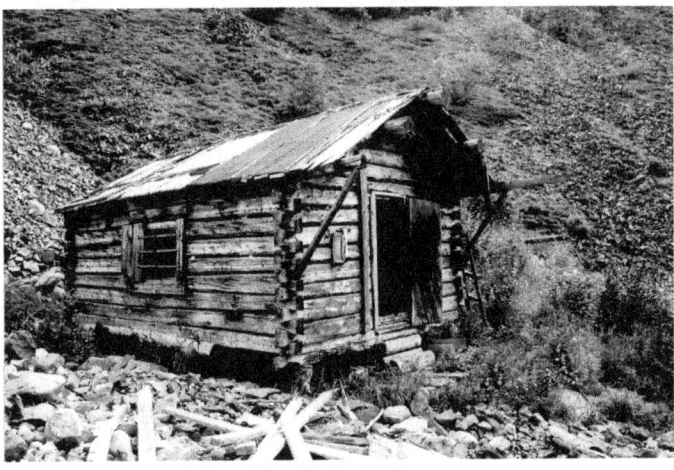

Grub Stake Creek mining cabin, Alaska. 2000   JDH

The cabin was measured and photographed for its historic merit. The BLM concluded that this old cabin was built after the prospector had come and gone in 1935. The evidence was in Douglas's old photograph of the mining site with mention of four tents halfway down Grub Stake Creek and no visible presence of a cabin.

47

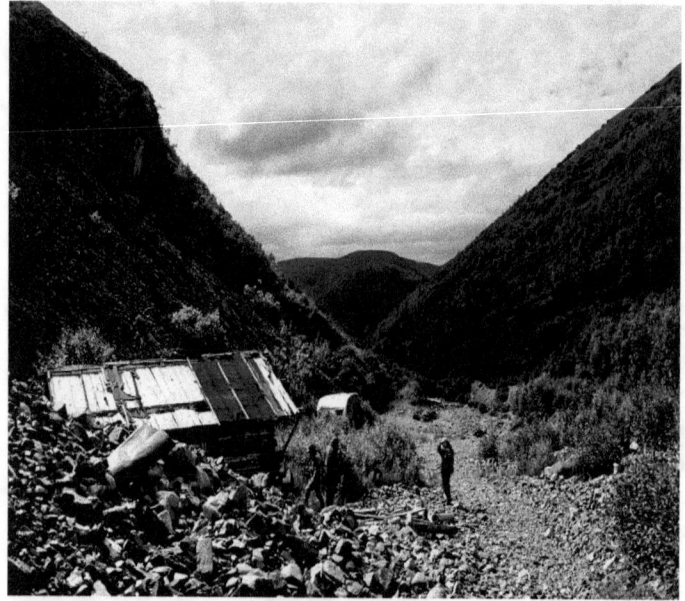

BLM specialists Debbie Muenster, David and K. J. Mushovic and Ken at the
Grub Stake Creek mining camp, Alaska. 2000   JDH

A last look around and the group headed back down the
overgrown trail to the Ahtell Creek Cabin. The three hikers
left behind were busy preparing the campsite for their
overnight stay. As the Alaska night slowly began to fall,
the BLM personnel warned us to stay close together and
make plenty of noise on the way out. We waved good-bye
as they *vroomed* off down the trail.

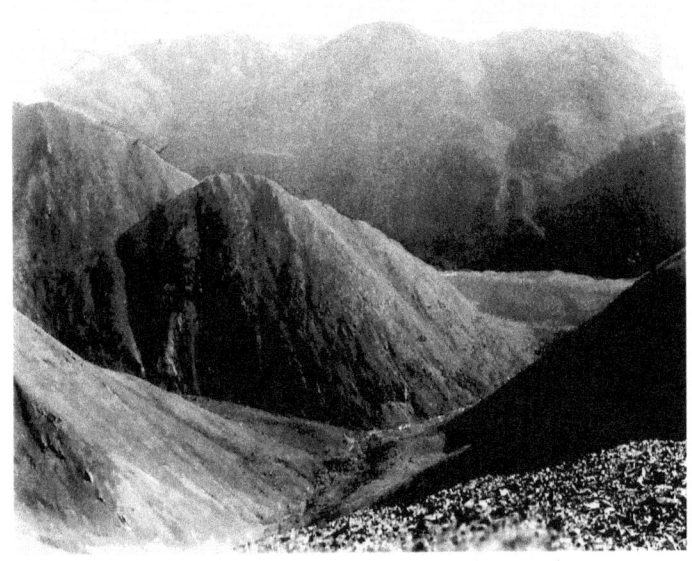

"On the divide...white dots halfway down Grub Stake Creek
(lower center right) are four tents at placer mine...Ahtell Creek
(center right) EL 2,600 feet...looking west...July 12, 1935" RAD

Douglas left an important piece of equipment behind at the
Robinson camp and wrote:

> *July 22 — The three of us (Warren, George
> and Douglas) went over to Slope Creek to
> Vern Robinson's camp. It was a very steep
> climb going up Rainbow Creek to the pass
> about 4,500 feet.*

> *July 31 — I left my camera at Robinson's
> camp the other day...went over after it...
> 10 miles.*

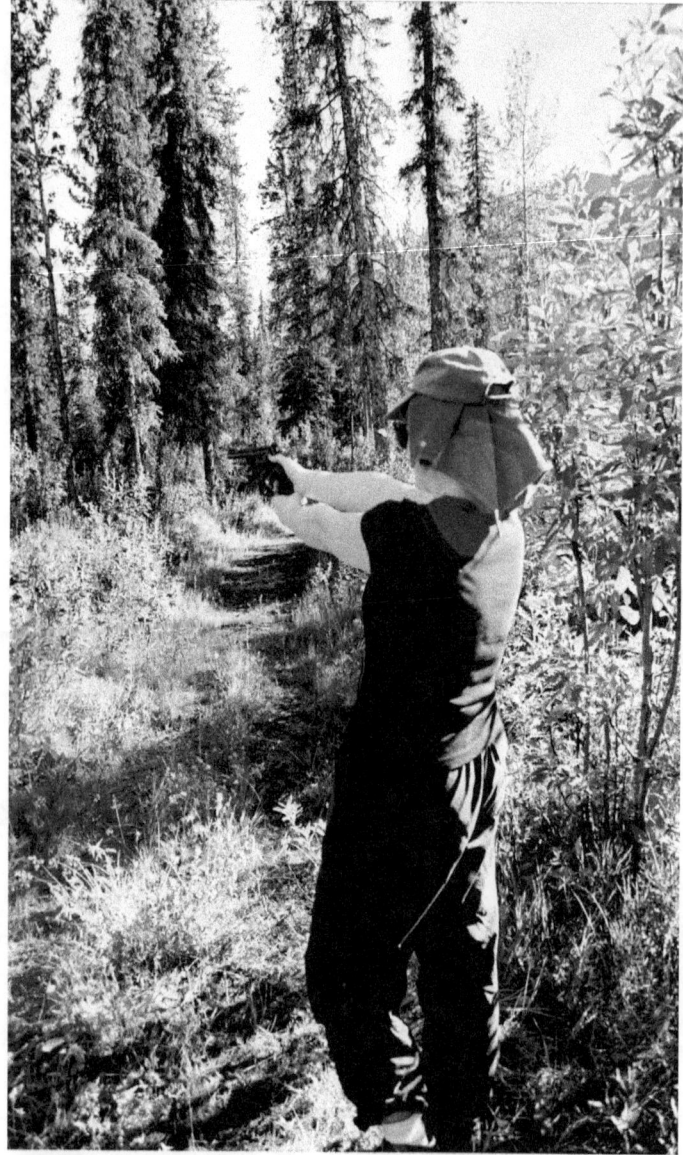

Diane outside the cabin, Ahtell Creek Valley, AK. 2000   JDH

We were alone now. Target practice began and Diane was hoping to send the bears deeper into the woods and away from the cabin. Ever present were the words of BLM specialist David Mushovic, "If you could see one set of bear eyes, there are fifty more out there you can't see."

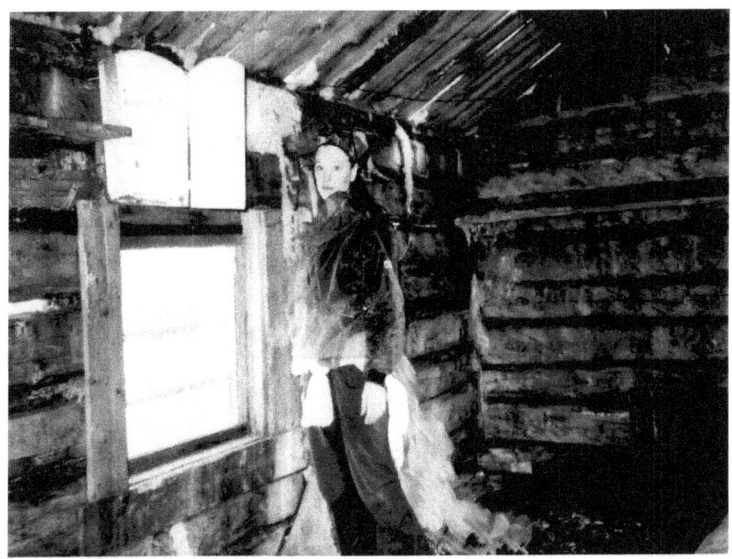

Heather inside the Ahtell Creek cabin, Alaska. July 31, 2000   JDH

Inside the cabin, Heather stood wrapped in mosquito netting, while two tents were pitched between the bonfire and a so called lean-two. It was getting chilly and we knew we would need heat and protection. Light from the sun was slowly fading.

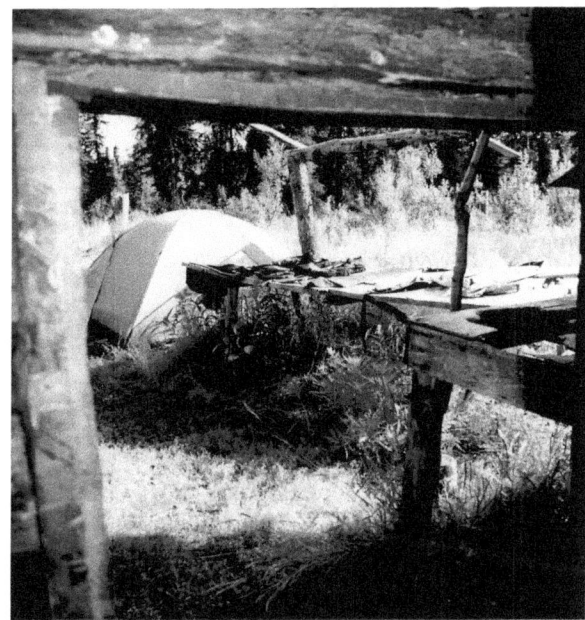

Tents were pitched outside the cabin. 2000   JDH

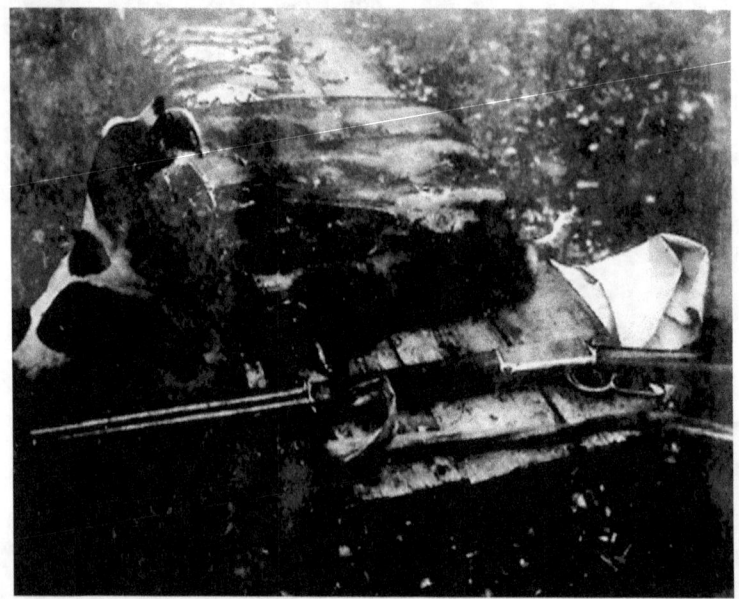

"Ahtell Creek Valley, Alaska...Note: dog Spot with a two hour catch on Flat Creek...three king salmon with heads and tails removed (3 feet 12 inches long), five grayling (10 to 12 inches long), one rabbit...July 16, 1935"   RAD

Food gathering was an important part of everyday existence. It was referred to often in writing:

> *July 16 — Sunday, I went to Flat Creek*
> *with George and got 50 lbs. of fish.*

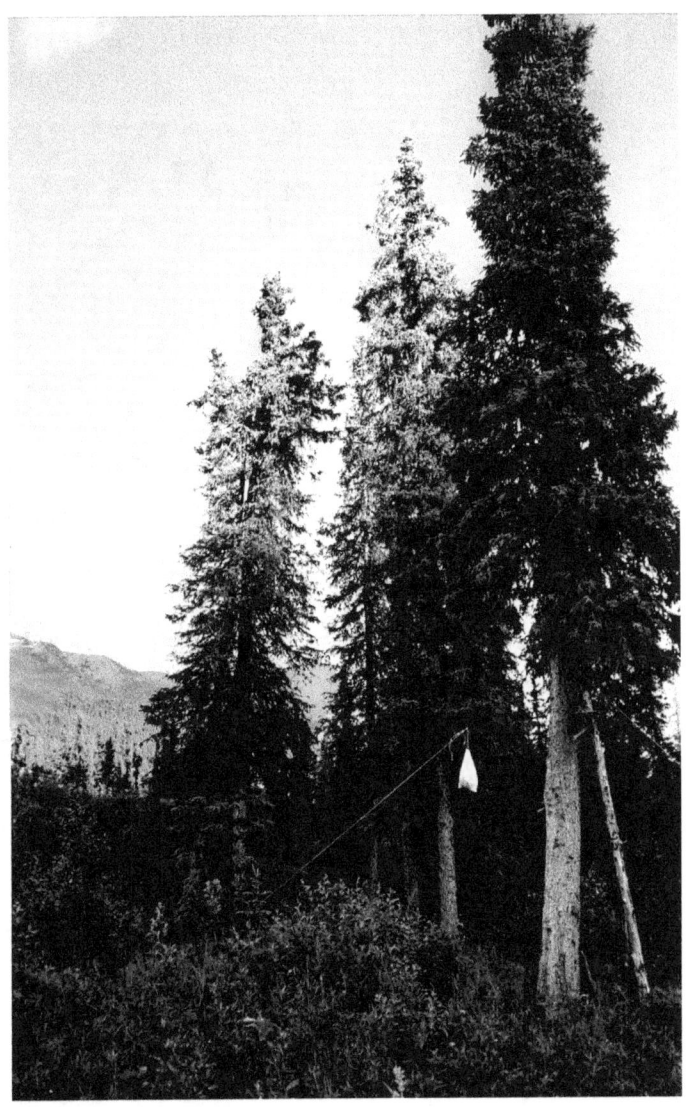

Outside the cabin, Ahtell Creek Valley. 2000   JDH

There wasn't really time to reminisce about what it might have been like in 1935. There was work to be done before darkness set in. After eating, Emory suspended our food supply between two black spruce trees. I stored the film inside the cabin which was dirty at best. A fire was enhanced to last all night by chopping more wood. Water needed to be hauled from a stream that was way too far away. Tents were put up. Emergency equipment was placed on the outside table so as to access it quickly in darkness.

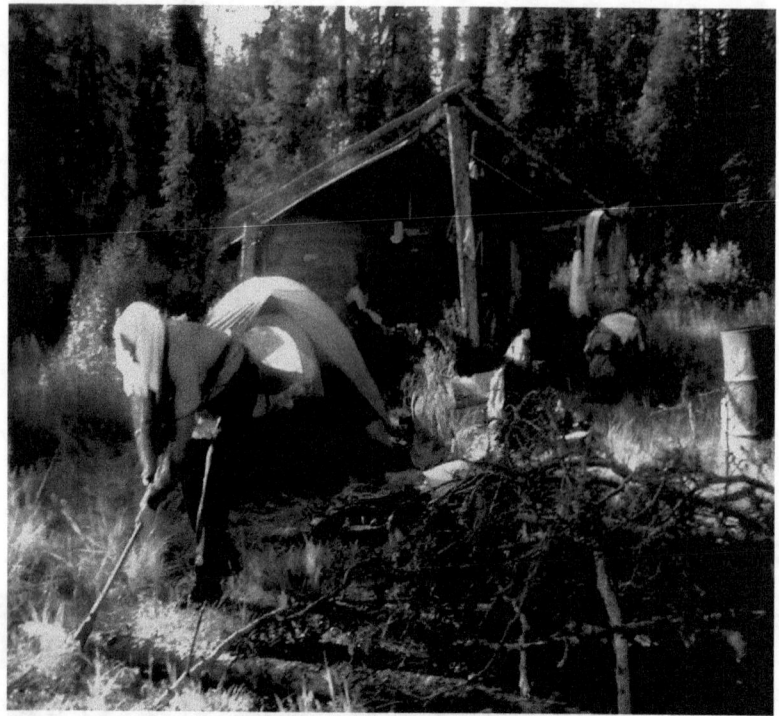

Ken preparing for nightfall at the Ahtell Valley cabin. 2000   JDH

Ken chopped and chopped as wood piled up in front of the cabin. Other hikers assembled branches and kindling for an all-night bonfire vigil. Ken and Diane took the first watch while four of us attempted sleep in the tents by the cabin. At 1:00 a.m. Emory and I volunteered a shift. Suddenly, we heard something very large coming through the woods in a straight line for the cabin. Was this the eminent bear attack? "Come out of your tent, Ken!" I shouted. Ken had one of the larger caliber weapons. I took a position with my back against the cabin door ready to enter into our last place of retreat. Emory paced the perimeter for at least an hour until eventually, the heavy tracking noises trailed off into the distance. To be honest, there was not much time to recall Douglas's experiences here. That evening in the Ahtell Valley darkness was "our" moment of truth and perhaps we were never more removed from the events of 1935 than at this time.

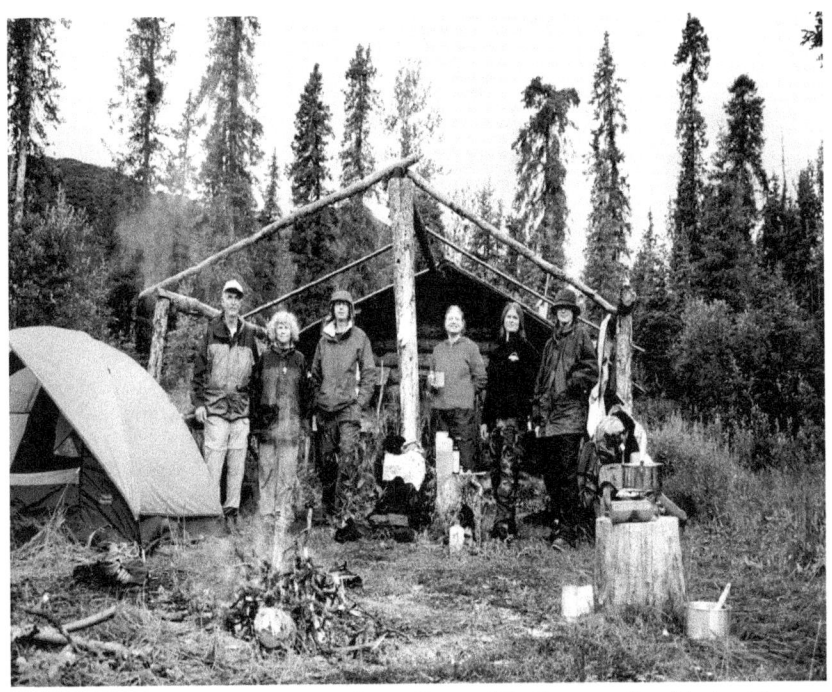

Hikers: Emory, Jill, Ken, Diane, Alison and Heather pause for a "daybreak" portrait in front of the cabin. August 1, 2000 Timer

The temperature dipped to 42 degrees. After breakfast around the campfire we remembered being warned by the BLM to make plenty of noise hiking out. It was time to break camp.

Before leaving I videoed and photographed all around and in the cabin. The rotten floor boards and door threshold may have been the only thing left of the original cabin from 1935. We were informed that the cabin is now referred to as the "Angus" cabin.

The hikers, just like the prospector, would later reflect in wonderment of those days back in the raw untamed land of the grizzlies — now, just a lingering memory of a place very far away.

The prospector, too, prepares to leave the area. There was a chill in the air and talk of better areas to try down in Valdez before his prospecting window closed which led to his decision.

On July 7, 1935, Douglas took a portrait of himself and his dog Spot, by holding a string in his left hand attached to the camera shutter, as he stood along the northwest side of the cabin.

Earlier that day, he went up the second draw east of Grub Stake Creek on the north side of the Ahtell Valley, and tried out the potentiometer again just one more time, around some

Douglas's mind was made up:

> *July 15 — It rained. Harry*
> *(Ole's nephew) brought up*
> *some mail. There were 11 letters.*
> *This was the first batch since*
> *leaving Valdez.*
>
> *July 27 — It rained most of the*
> *day. George and Taylor went back*
> *to Slana...then on to Valdez.*
>
> *July 30 — Harry went down to Slana*
> *with 3 dogs, so he took some of my*
> *things down. I have given up finding*
> *anything in this section. I have de-*
> *cided to go to Valdez.*
>
> *August 1 — I took a load of stuff out*
> *to the road and came back to the*
> *cabin. It was 12 miles round trip.*
>
> *August 2 — I took the balance of my*
> *outfit to the road and piled things all*
> *together and covered it with a tent.*

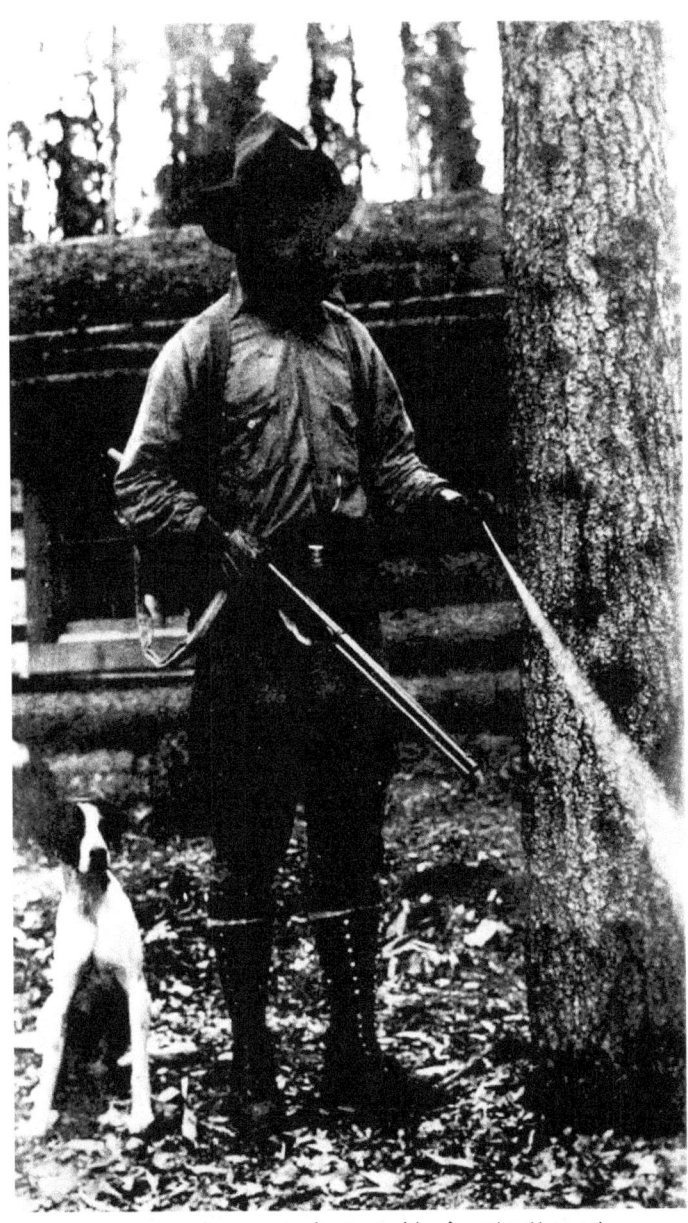

"R. A. Douglas (prospector), Spot (dog)...Ahtell Creek,
Alaska...Note: head net and gloves for mosquitoes...
July 7, 1935"   RAD

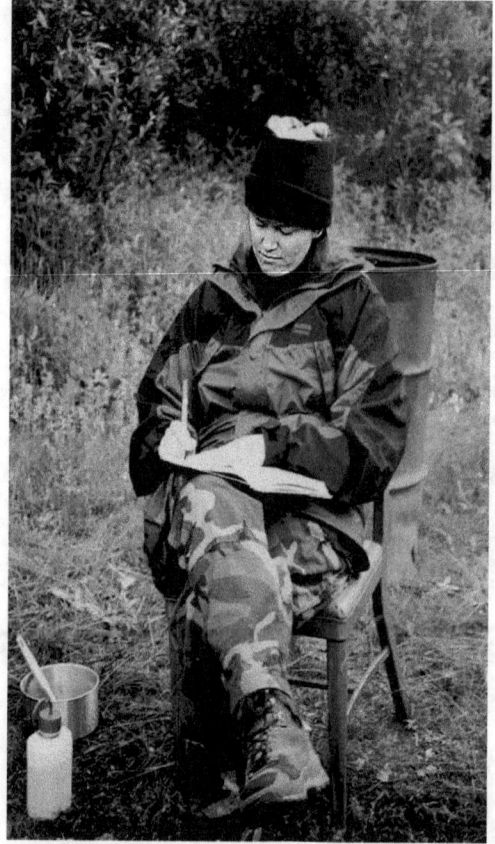

Alison, sitting in front of the cabin on Ahtell Creek,
Alaska. 2000   JDH

DREAMER'S PEAK

I want to stay in Alaska
Loose myself so deep in the forest that even the wild
animals won't know where I am
become a tree among the like
grow above the rest to view the world from a dreamer's peak
precious flowers at my roots and birds in my branches

I fear I may even tremble in the winds
human populations continue to grow, stealing the wild that
surrounds them

One day, I may be the only tree left
        until someone takes a saw to me
        and makes a table from my knee
        a toothpick from my arm
        press board from my heart
        wooden frames from my dreamer's peak!

        My pieces cut up and sold.

I want to go to Alaska
lose myself so deep in the forest that even the wild animals
won't know where I am
become a tree among the like
grow above the rest to view the world from a dreamer's peak

I want to be a tree
but I want to keep my knee
        my arm
        my heart
        my dreamer's peak

I want to stay in Alaska
to be a lost tree
        no where to be found
but free

AMV

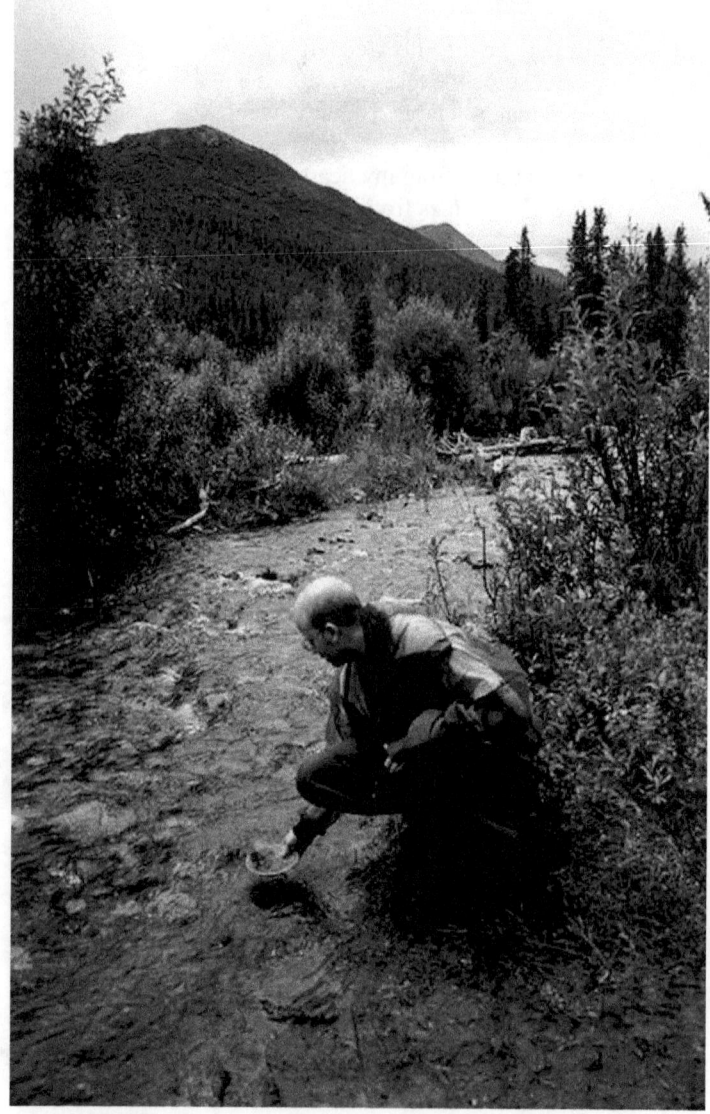

Ken panning in Ahtell Creek (looking north), Alaska. 2000   JDH

A last chance dip into the Ahtell Creek along side the cabin on August 1, 2000 before we packed up our gear, put on our bear bells and hiked out. The mother bear and her cubs were still somewhere down the trail, but they stayed away — and upon reaching the trailhead, Ken dropped his pack and hiked an additional couple of miles to our parked van.

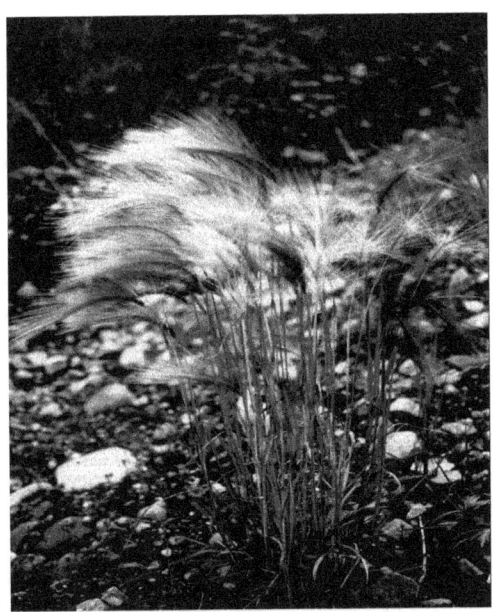

Foxtail along the Nabesna Rd. 2001

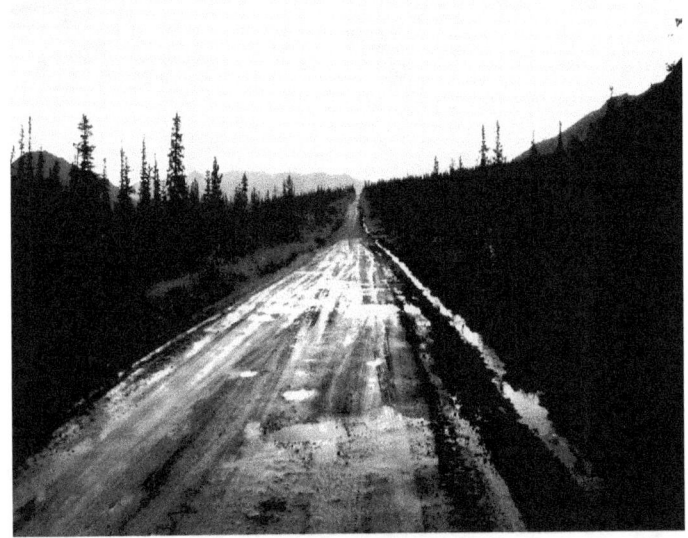

Nabesna Road (looking southeast), Slana, Alaska. 2001

At the end of this forty-six mile gravel road called Nabesna is the famed Nabesna Mine. The backpackers left the Hart-D-Ranch on the morning of August 2, 2000, and headed for Thompson Pass. Not much has changed. This region is still as beautiful and unforgiving as it was in 1935.

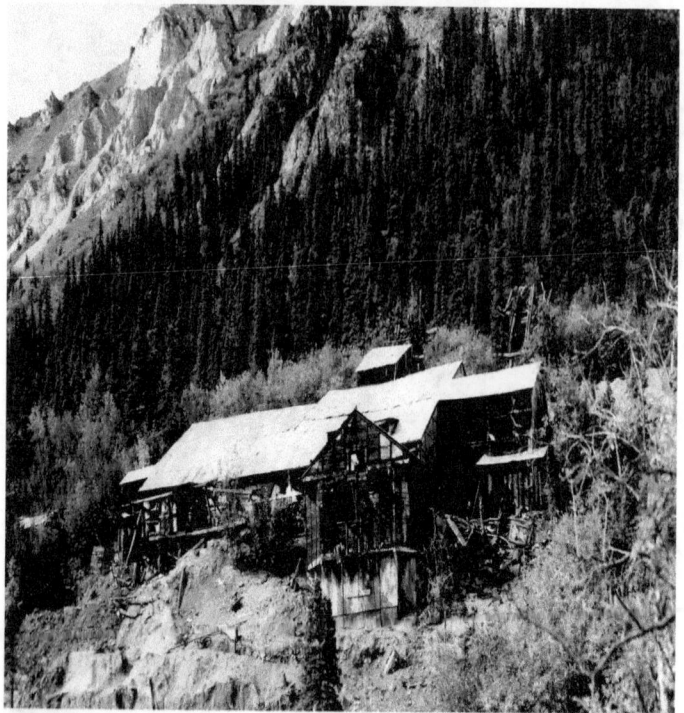

Nabesna Mine, Alaska. August 28, 2001   Photos JDH

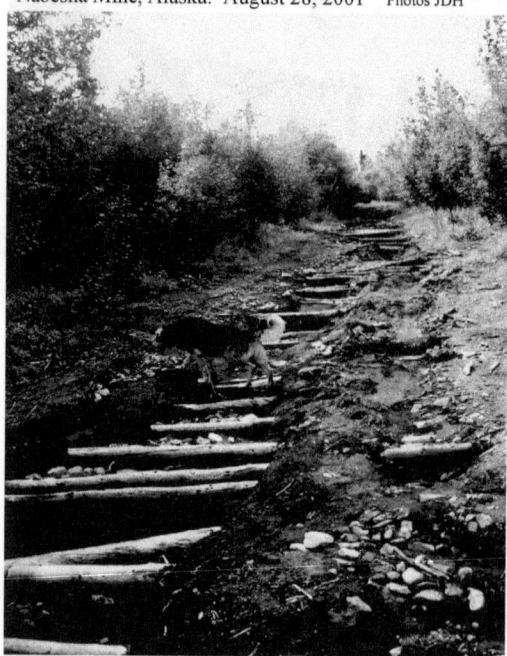

Duke, the family pet and escort to the mine.

A year after our 2000 hike to the cabin we revisited Slana. We drove to the end of the forty-six mile Nabesna Road. The road was gravel and creeks were not bridged. Road closings were common due to rain. Upon reaching the end, we parked our truck at a friendly bed and breakfast, located next to the old Reeves Field airstrip. The road to the mine was closed, so we hiked the final miles to the Nabesna Mine escorted by "Duke," the B & B's family pet. The Nabesna Mine is now privately owned. It ceased operation in 1940.

Soon we would be leaving this rugged area scattered with homesteaders, just like we did a year ago. Local Athabaskan refer to the prospectors and people who frequent the area as "Nondlae" meaning people who always come and go.

Back in 1935, Douglas wanted to visit the Nabesna Mine before leaving for Valdez. He wrote in his diary:

August 2 — I decided to go to the
Nabesna Mine, so caught a truck with
Erikson (driver) at 10 p.m. We arrived
at Nabesna at 3:30 a.m. Nine miles in,
we had to stop and put chains on the truck.

August 3 — I looked over the Nabesna Mine.
I came back after lunch with Erikson. We
arrived in Slana for supper. We learned the
Chistochina Bridge was out so we had to
layover in Slana. There was 2 inches of
snow in the morning.

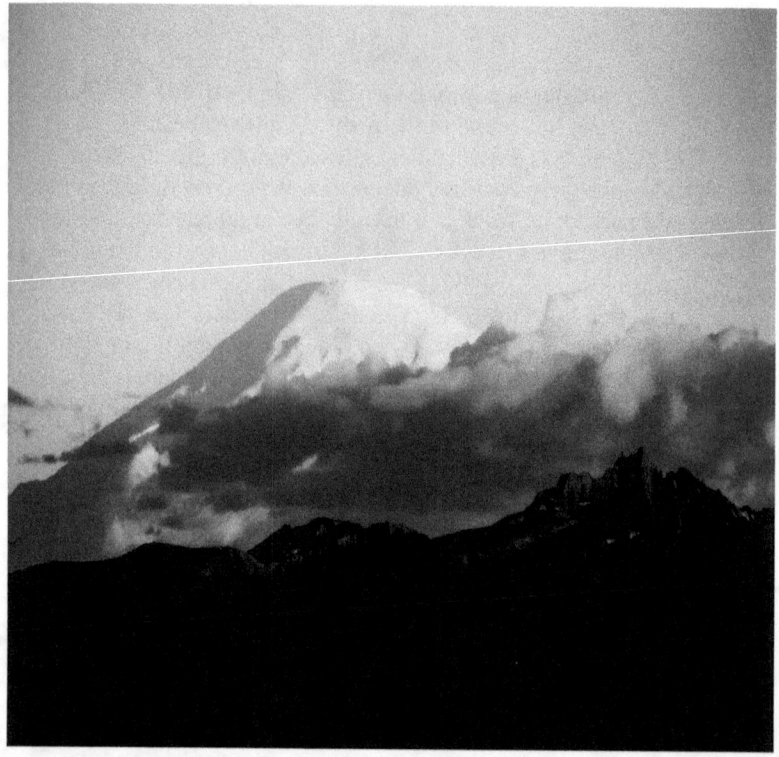

Mount Sanford (16,257 feet), Slana, Alaska. 2000   JDH

The mighty Mount Sanford was casting its shadow over the land long before gold was discovered at Nabesna. It was casting its shadow long before the mere two thousand years of known recorded history of the headwater people.

Douglas left behind the foreboding *howl* of wolves, the lonesome *call* of loons and a valley full of unfulfilled dreams:

> *August 5 — We picked up my outfit along*
> *the road and went as far as the bridge.*
> *I packed my outfit over the bridge which*
> *could be walked over, but no vehicles.*
> *Swanson took me in to Chistochina —*
> *about 4 miles. I stayed there overnight.*

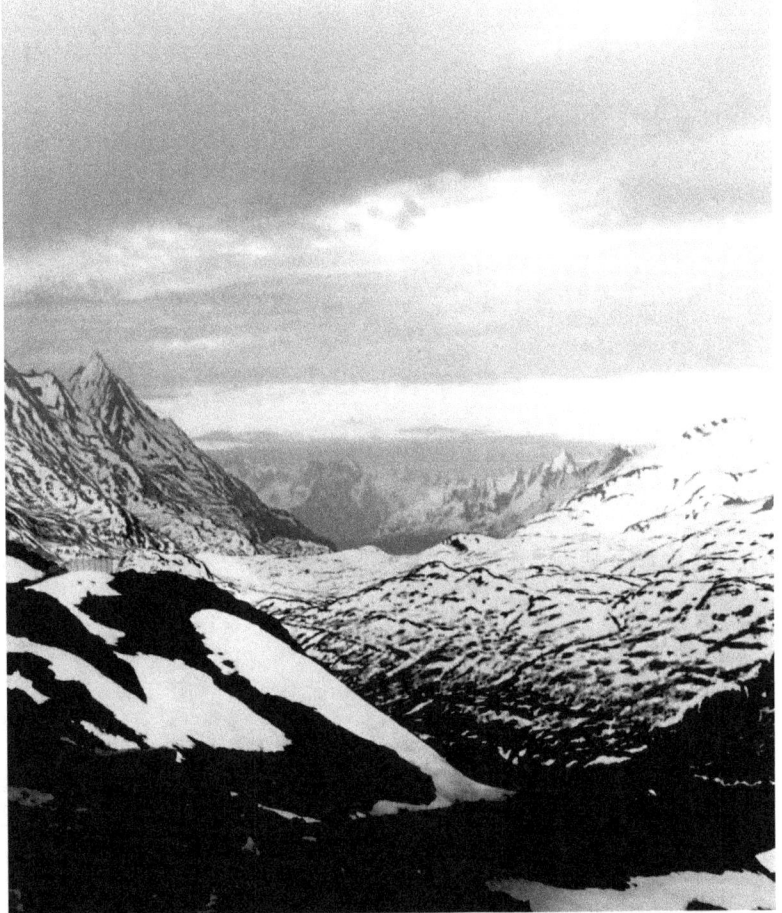

Summer solstice (sunrise recorded at 3:07 a.m.), Thompson Pass, Alaska.
June 21, 2001   JDH

A truck, driver, prospector and a dog broke this
absolute quiet solitude in the early morning hours of
August 7, 1935. They headed south toward the little post
gold rush town of Valdez and Douglas later wrote:

> *August 6 — I got a lift with a road commission*
> *truck as far as the Copper Center ...and*
> *had two meals there ...then at 10 p.m. 'Max'*
> *came thru from Fairbanks. We started for*
> *Valdez arriving at 3 a.m. I put up at a hotel.*

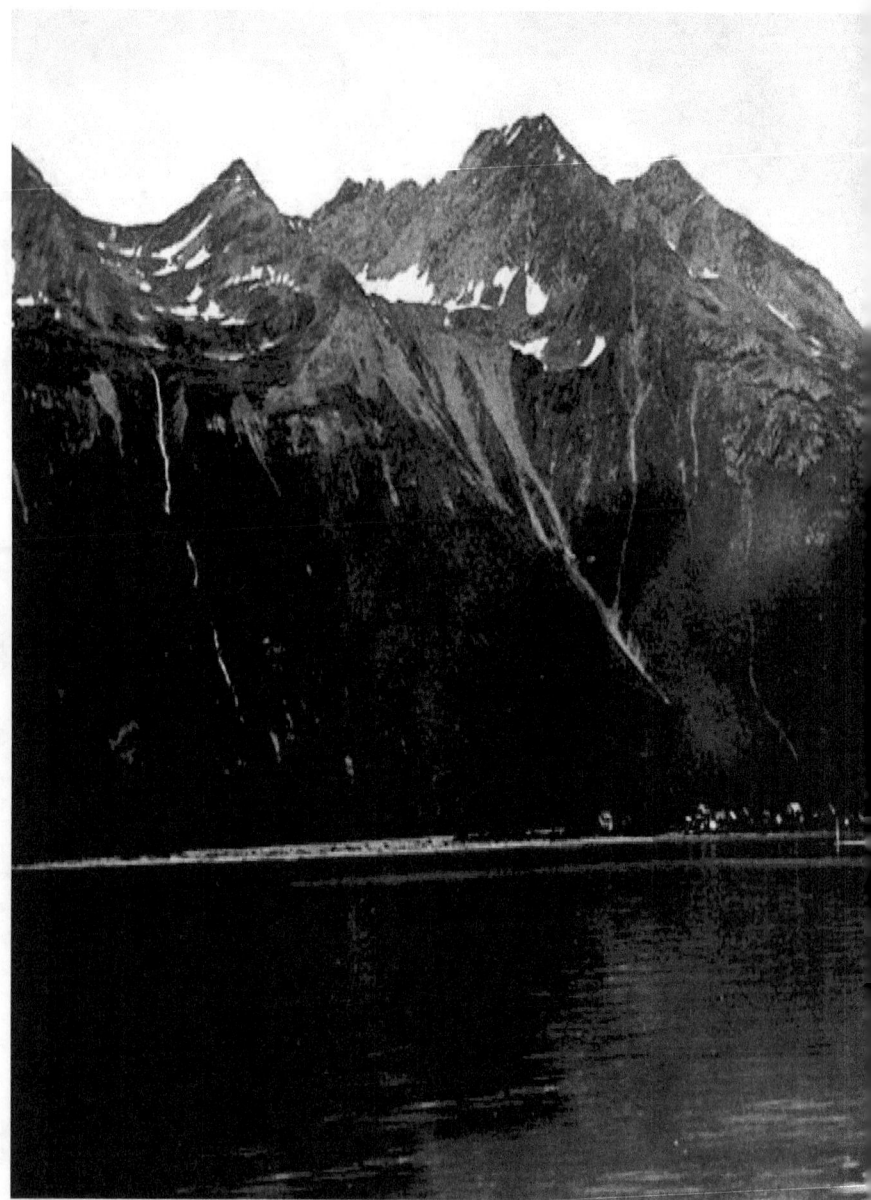

*Valdez, Alaska...Valdez Glacier 8 miles from town center)...

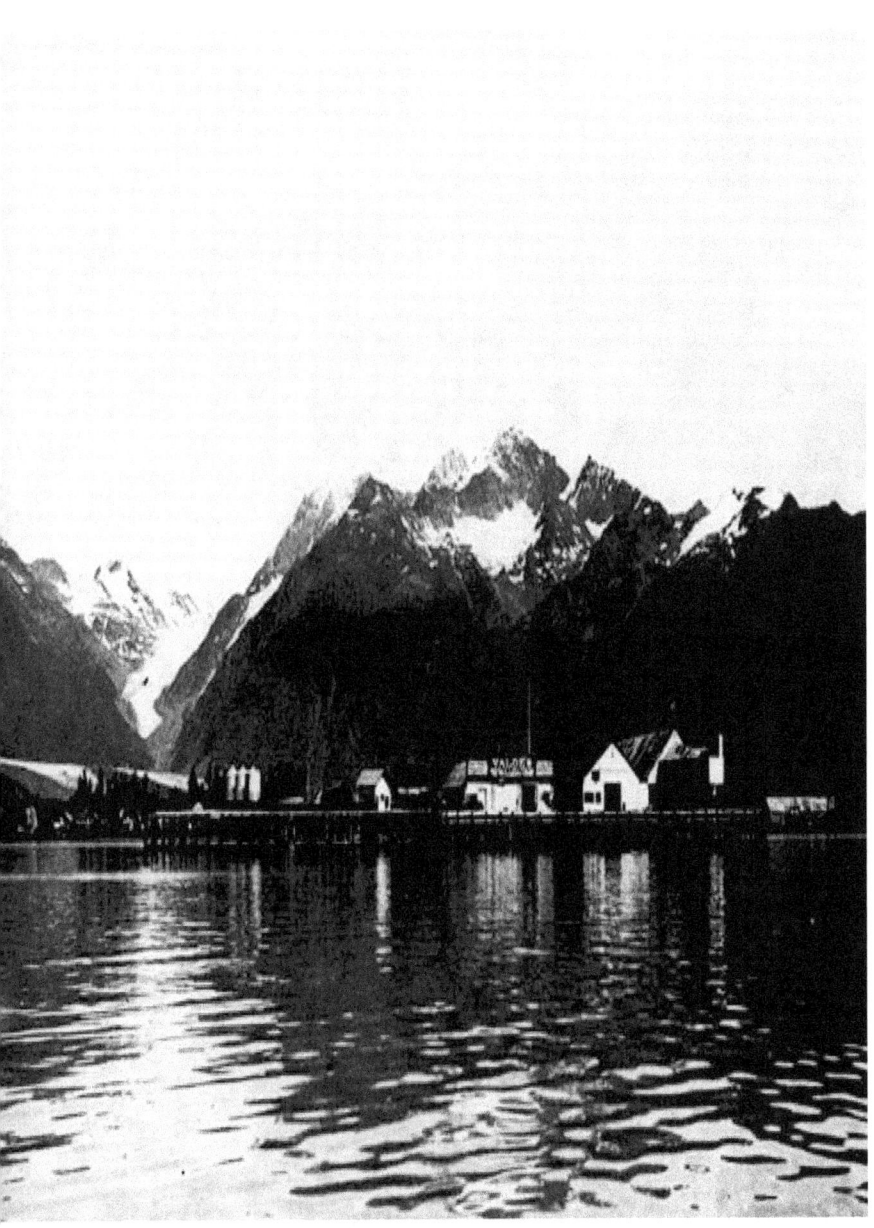

mountains (5,000 ft)...looking northeast...August 14, 1935." RAD

In 1964, time ran out for the little gold rush town of Valdez. A sudden earthquake of giant proportion hit just north of Prince William Sound. The epicenter was only 45 miles west of Valdez. Seismic activity of 8.6 (or 9.2 depending on source) was recorded on the Richter scale.

A massive tsunami visited this small town sinking the earth's crust and forever changing the dock area.

Thirty-three people lost their lives. Large fissures developed throughout the region. With the possibility of further slides and continued settling along a temporary dock constructed by the Corps of Engineers, relocating the town was advised.

An area of land four miles west of old Valdez was selected. Fifty-two of the original buildings were relocated to this new town site in 1967.

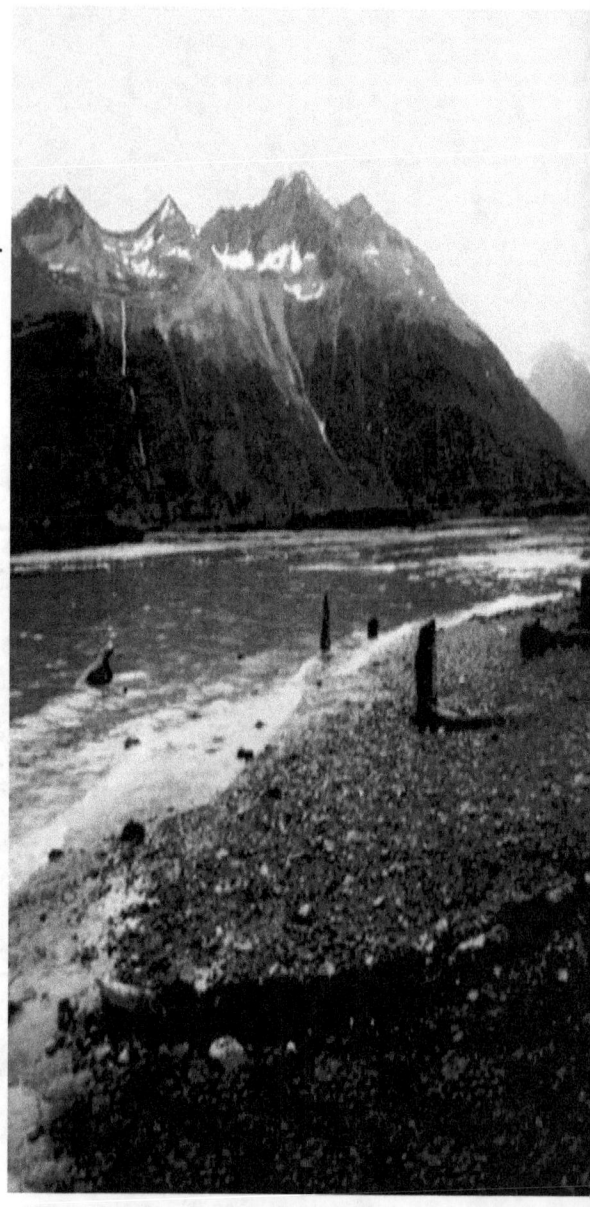

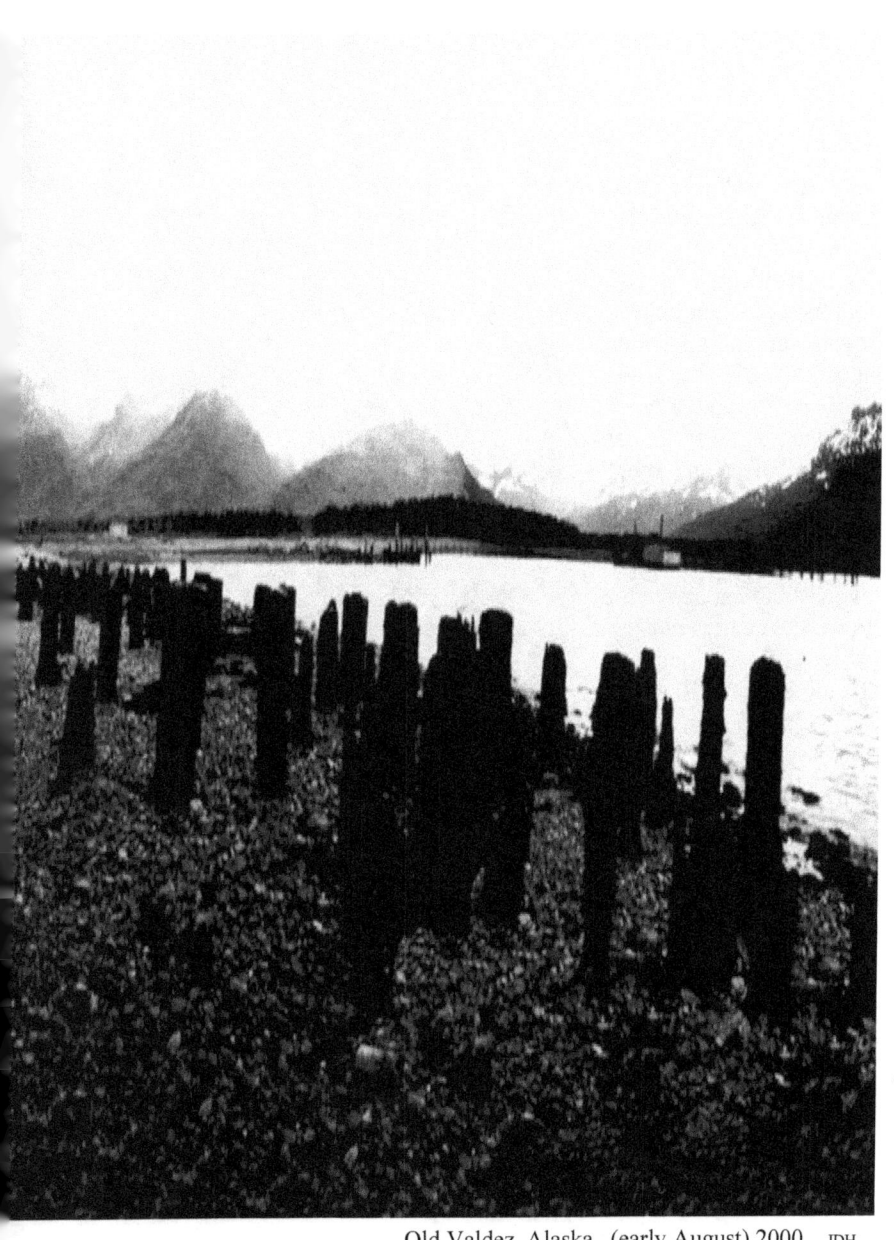

Old Valdez, Alaska. (early August) 2000   <small>JDH</small>

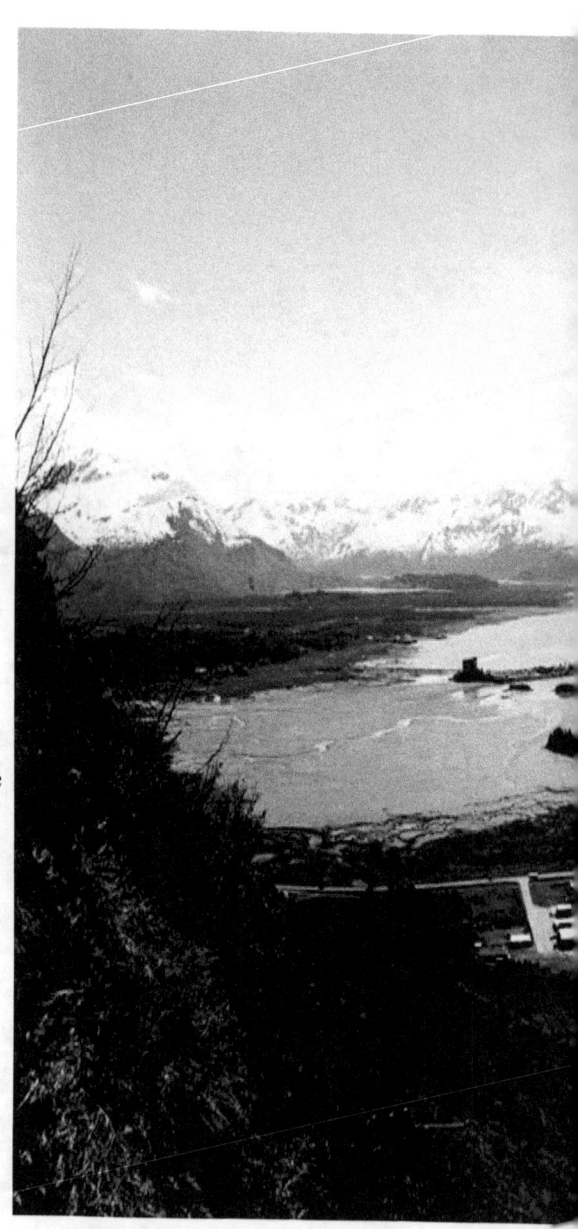

The year is 2001. In the distance (center left) old pilings sit silently reminding its residents of a wave that battered their small town over a half a century ago.

Cries of "grab the rope" are heard as we try to capture the before and after town photograph of "new" Valdez. With my feet dangling off a ledge over 1,000 feet above the town, the camera *clicks*.

The Alyeska Pipeline Terminal, established in 1973, can be seen across the bay.

As Alaska became a state in 1959, a native Valdezean named William A. Egan became the state's first governor. He served two terms.

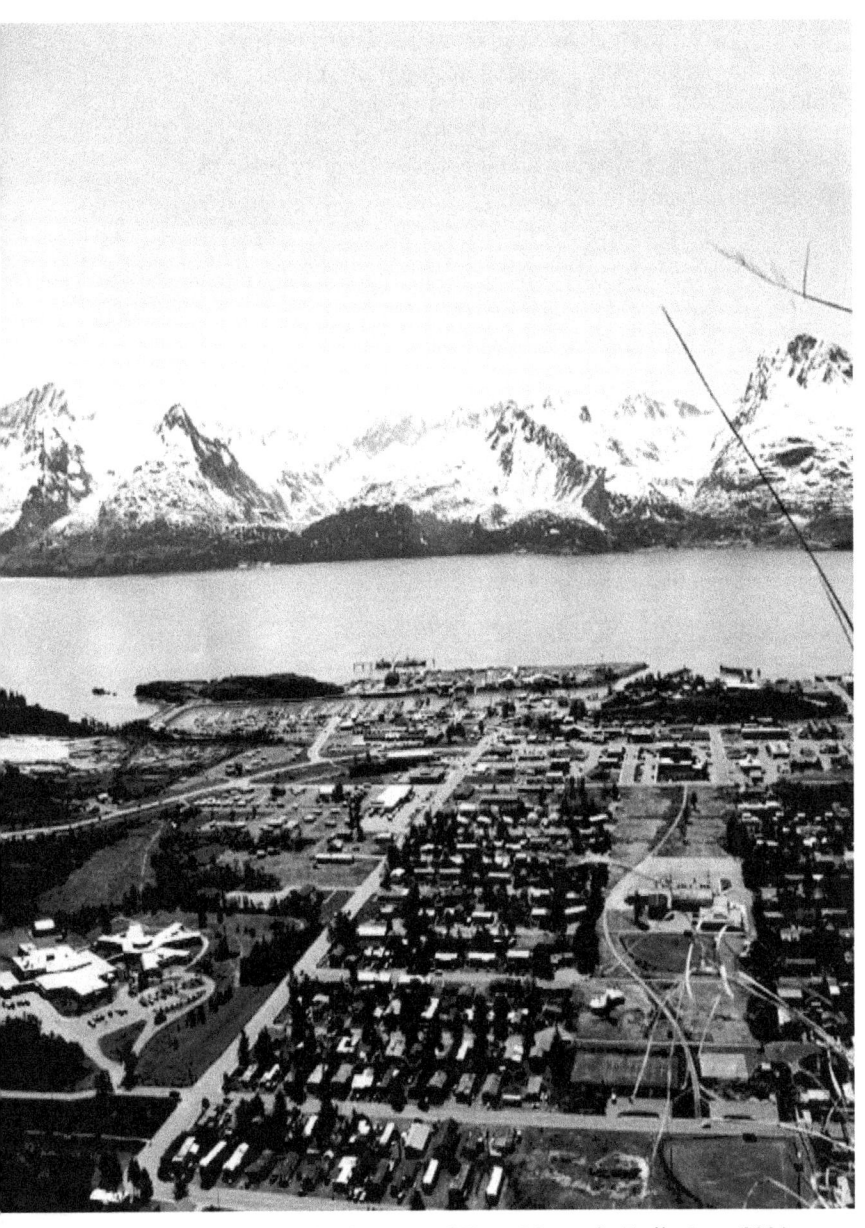

Valdez, Alaska from top of Town Mountain Trail. June, 2001 JDH

We turn back the clock to when Douglas arrived for the second time in the little bustling gold rush town of "Old Valdez." It was a two day journey from Slana.

Highlights from his arrival and the following next few days are described below in his diary:

August 7 — I got up at 8 a.m., ate breakfast and rented a two bedroom cottage from Dan Wilcey I took my stuff off the truck and began building up my supplies for a run down the bay. The next few days I continued gearing up my equipment with a Monday departure in mind. I rented a boat and went to a movie show in town.

August 11 — Spot is hit by a car. He does not move. Although there doesn't seem to be any broken bones, I can't leave the sick dog yet.

August 16 — I climbed up the mountain due north of town. I slipped crossing a rock slide and cut my head, but it was not serious. Later...up on top (about 4,000 feet) while crossing a small glacier, one leg broke through the crust and into a crevice. I escaped without injury.

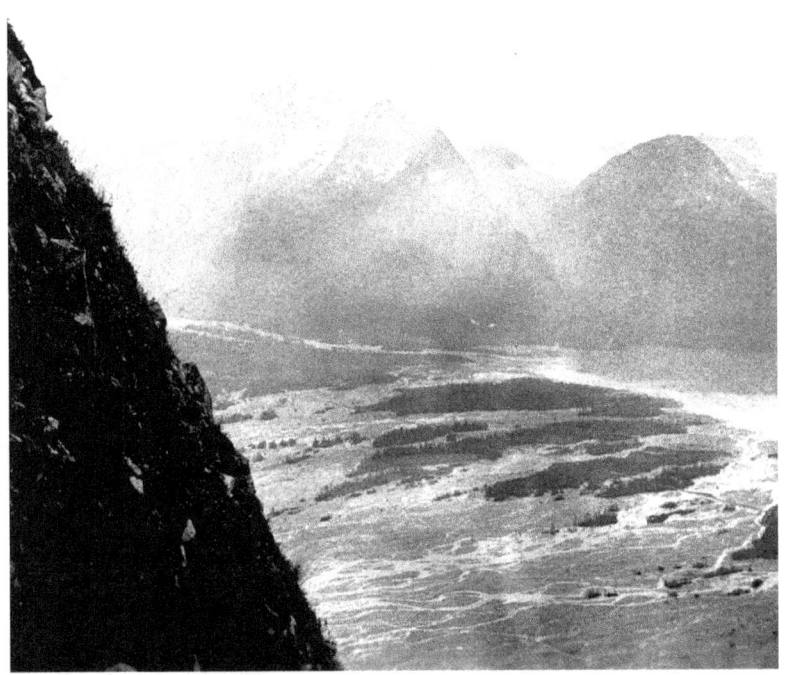

"A tough bit of climbing...elevation 4,000 ft...Valdez, Alaska
(extreme right) straight line (center) ...Richardson Highway to
Fairbanks...looking east (from Mile High)...
August 16, 1935"....RAD

Because of this unexpected delay, and the fact that he had
retrieved his camera from Robinson's camp, six additional
photos were taken in the Valdez area. Two 1935 photographs of old Valdez were captured from out in the water
and digitally fused in 2002 by Miracle Photo in Titusville,
FL. These photo areas may not have been otherwise
captured. Douglas stayed fairly close to home while his dog
convalesced. He rowed to nearby islands and down the
Valdez Arm to Shoup Bay, always glancing longingly at
those coveted places of interest existing in the mountains of
the canyon. The mountain due north of town, Douglas could
see from his cottage window. This mountain is known to
locals as Mile High Regretfully, we were unable to repeat the
photography for this area.

Douglas made a trek back to the Valdez Glacier for an
added two photographs before packing up once again to
enter the canyon. The two 1935 Valdez Glacier photographs
were also digitally fused in 2002.

Why was the town of Valdez built in the path of this sleeping giant? Gold. Valdez incorporated in 1901, just after the biggest gold rush in history. The quickest way to the interior of Alaska at the end of the nineteenth century was over the Valdez Glacier. The trail became known as the All-American Trail.

Three to five thousand gold rushers crossed the Valdez Glacier in 1877-99. It took some prospectors over two months to haul their equipment over this intimidating block of ice. It was soon learned that those arriving in early spring would have an easier time carrying their gear over snow that was still held together by cooler weather. Backtracking was required due to the large quantity of supplies needed to sustain them for extended periods of time. Some prospectors continued all the way to the Klondike.

The Ramsey-Rutherford mine, situated 3,500 feet above the Valdez Glacier, began operating in 1911 — closing off and on until 1925. In 1934 the mine reopened, closing for good in 1939. This mine and several others were operating while Douglas spent the summer in 1935.

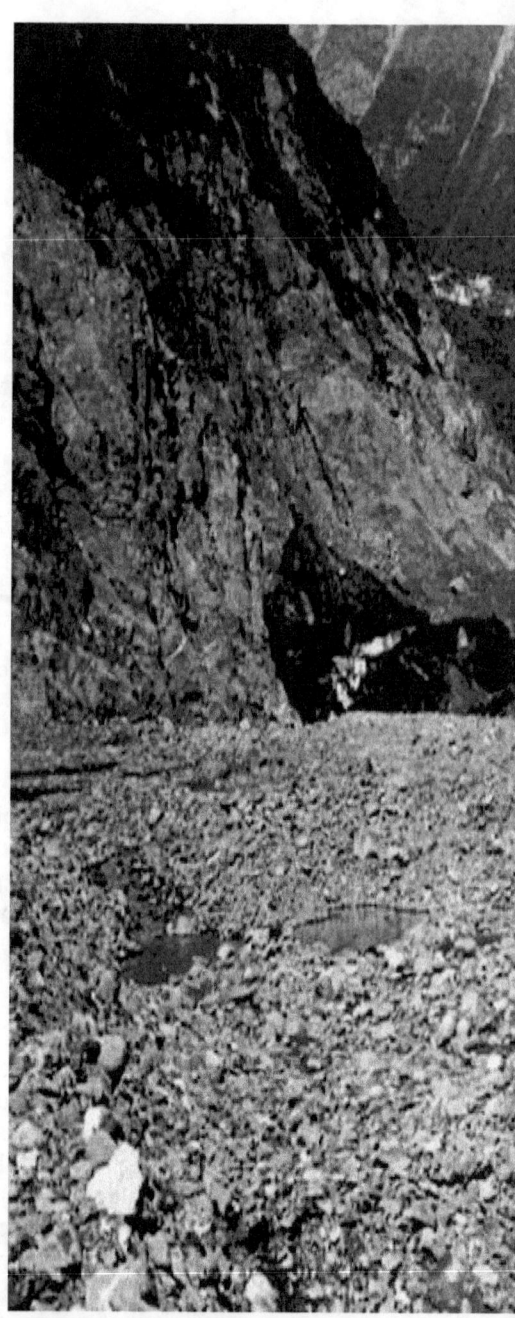

"Terminal, Valdez Glacier...AK.

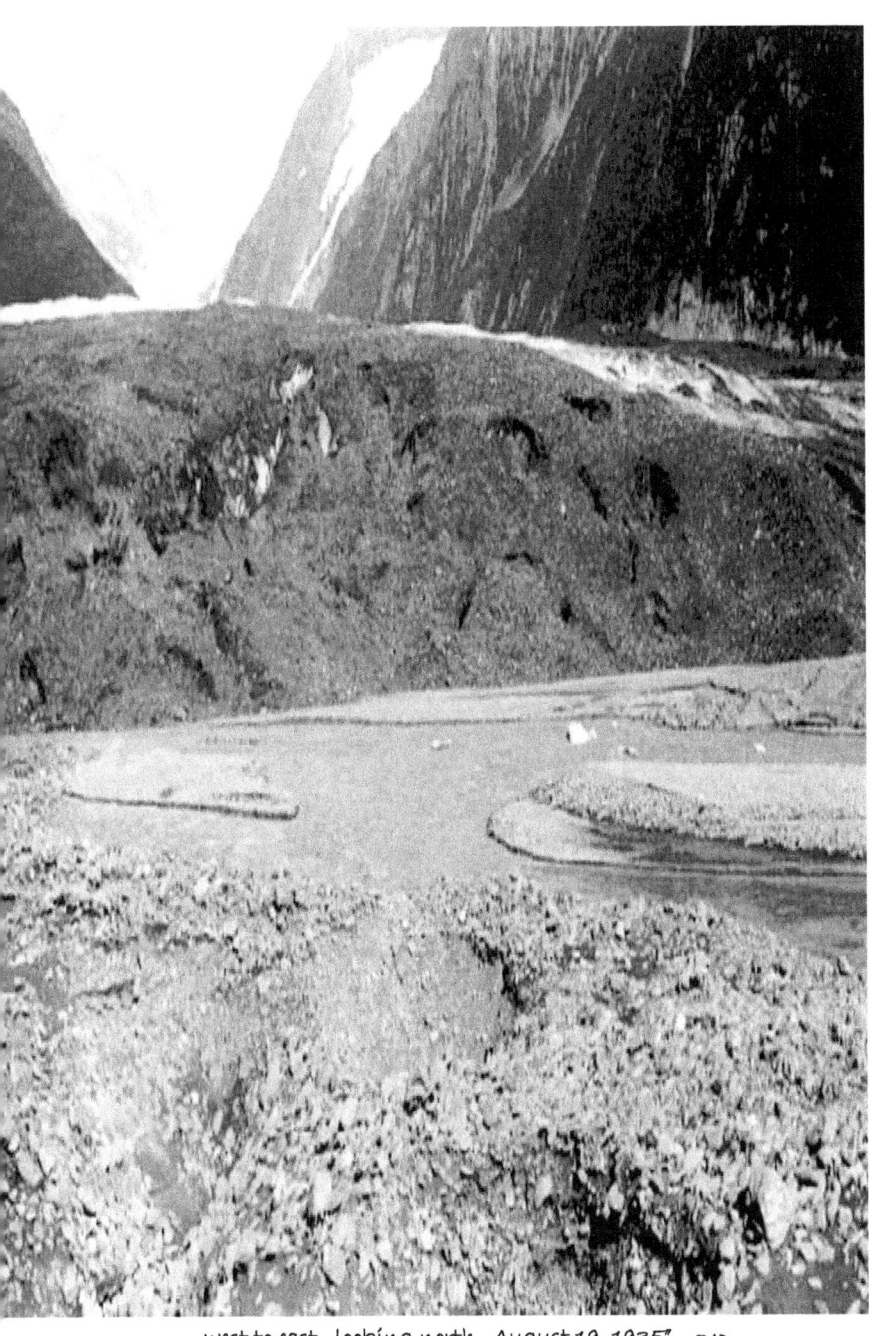

west to east...looking north...August 19, 1935" RAD

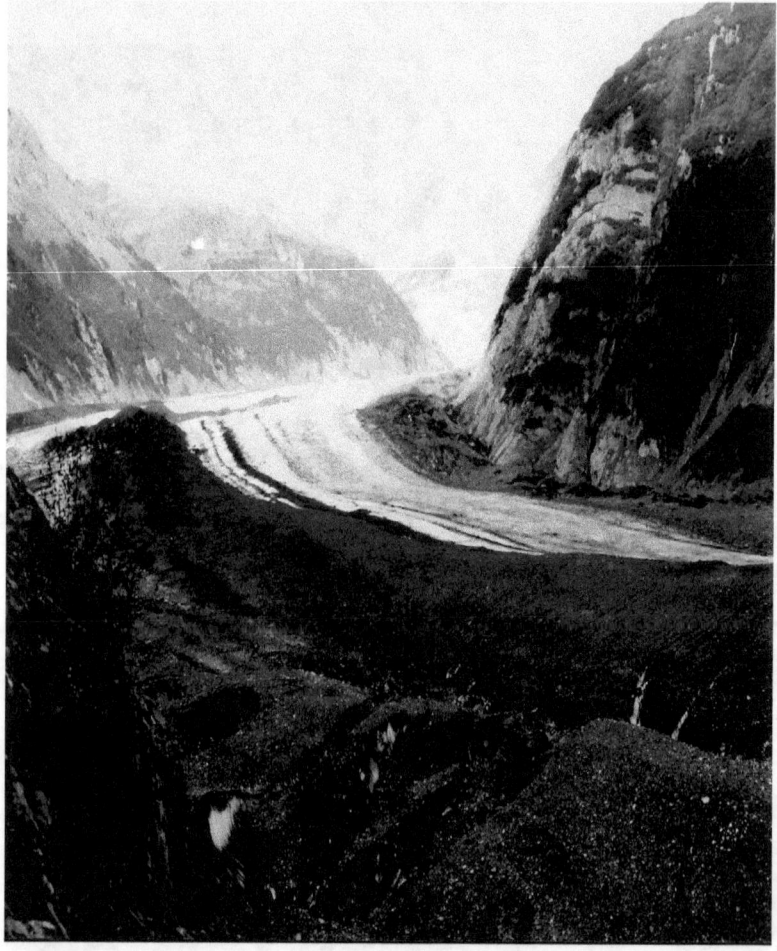

Valdez Glacier, Alaska. August 22, 2001   Photos JDH

   After four attempts, we finally located the terminal moraine
of the Valdez Glacier. We sat high on a westside bluff,
listened to the sound of ice *cracking* and photographed the
glacier snaking its way from the ice fields of the Chugach
Range. The scruffy trail to this glacier was difficult to
locate and impossible to hike on in certain areas due to high
water levels. Eventually, we had to bush whack through
heavy alder to arrive at the bluff above (lower left).

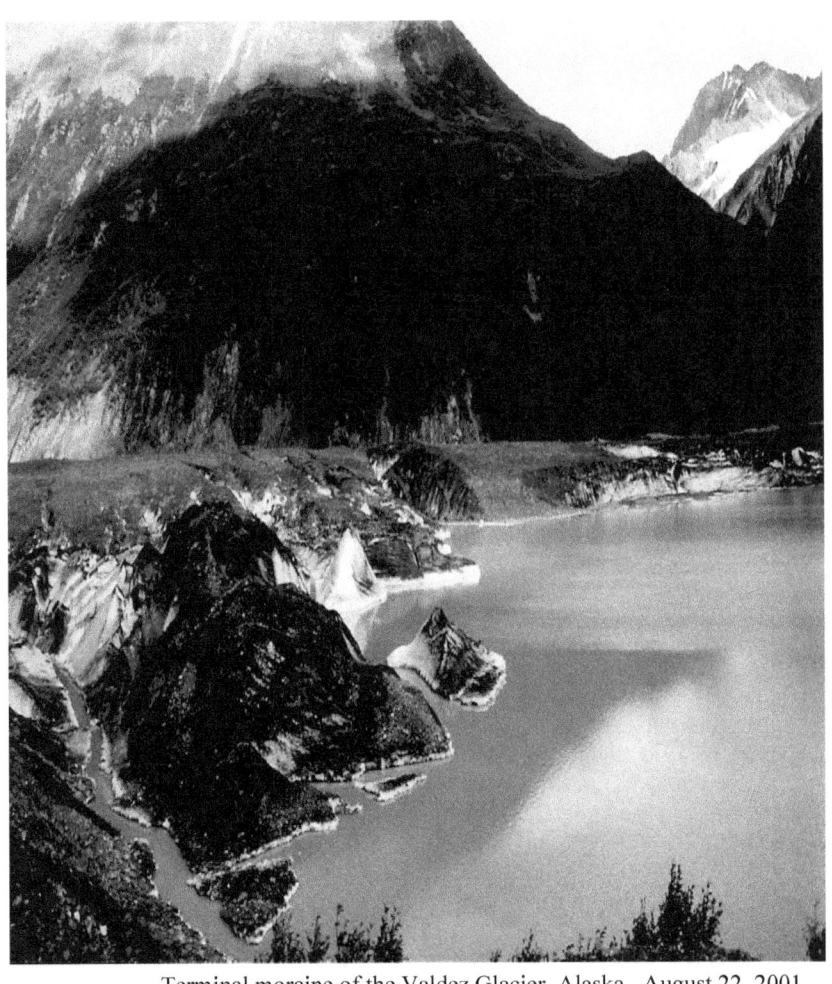

Terminal moraine of the Valdez Glacier, Alaska. August 22, 2001

A small terminal lake has established itself between the Valdez Glacier (left) and the Camicia Glacier (upper right) fed by years of retreating ice. The terminal moraine of the Valdez Glacier has relocated itself significantly around the corner to the left of the original 1935 photo. During winter months some enthusiastic Valdez locals have been known to ride their snow machines over the Valdez Glacier and Chugach ice fields to the town of Eureka on Glenn Highway 1.

77

OLD MINE SITE LISTINGS — courtesy of Charles LaPage and Alpine Aviation, Valdez, Alaska

Valdez Glacier: Donahue Mine
                       Ramsey Rutherford Mine

Mineral Creek: McIntosh Mine
                       Giant Mine
                       Cash Mine—Smith Mill
                       Hercules Mine
                       Big Four Mine—Johnson Mill

Shoup Glacier: Cliff Mine
                       Cameron Johnson Mine (south of
                       Mount Cameron at 5,360 feet)

Columbia Glacier: Mayfield Mine (Lake 1 Lobe, N)
                       Ruff & Tuff Mine (north of Mayfield)
                       Gold King Mine (east of Ruff & Tuff,
                       1.5 miles at 4,000 feet)

Great Nunatak (geological term for mountain
surrounded by ice)
Twin Peaks (at 3,652 feet W and 3,412 feet E)

OLD MINE SITE LISTINGS courtesy of Nancy Lund

Boulder Bay – East of Tatitlek, 20 miles South of Valdez:

Northwest side   *Northeast side*

Wagner Mine   Copper Mountain
Rua Mine   Group
                         Copper Crown Mine
                         Lone Hand Mine
                         Sunnyside Mine
                         Starvation Mine
                         Vesuvius Mine

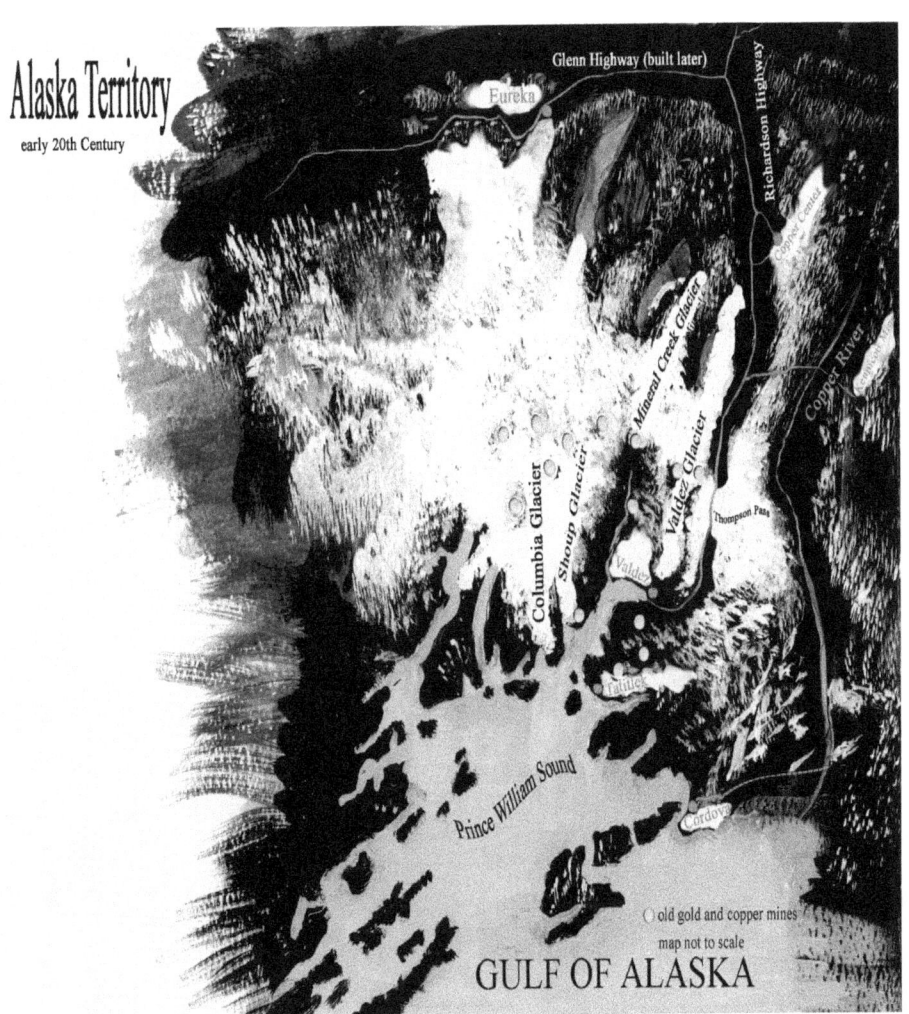

Map 4. Selected old gold and copper mine sites from the
Prince William Sound area circa. early 1900's.

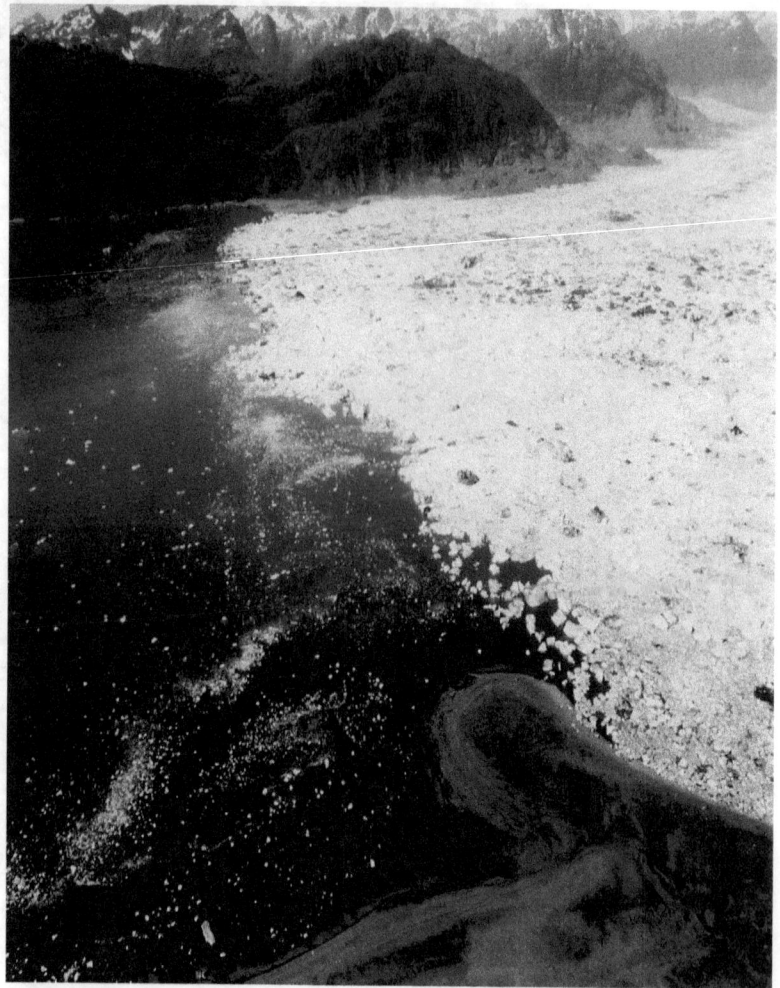

Heather Island (lower right), Columbia Bay, Alaska.
August 13, 2001   aerial photo JDH

Gold was scattered in this area like the stars of the Alaska
flag. The call of the canyon and its surrounding areas was
brutally powerful. In early times, access to the mines of the
icefields had to be made by dog sled or mule from Shoup
Bay.

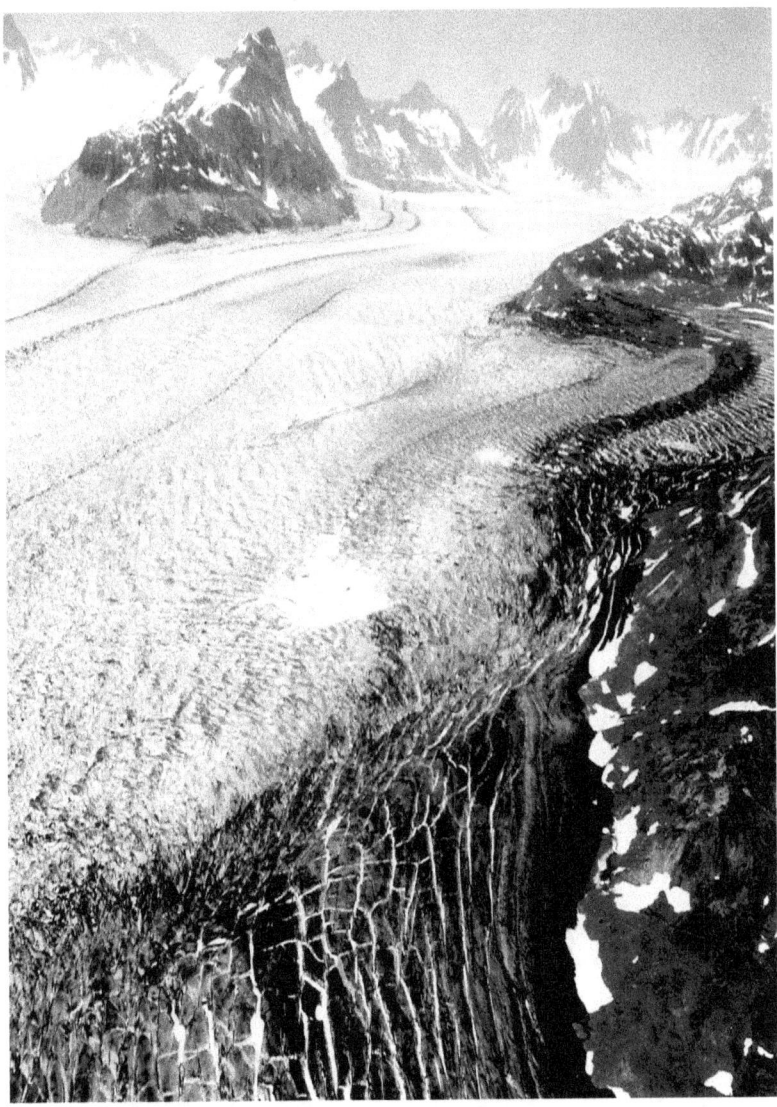

Chugach Icefields, Alaska. August 13, 2001   aerial photo JDH

The Ruff & Tuff Mine site is located on the upper, second land mass (above right). This ridge runs from the west side of Mount Cameron. The land mass in the lower right hand corner, on the east side of the Columbia Glacier, is the end of a ridge extending from Anderson Pass.

81

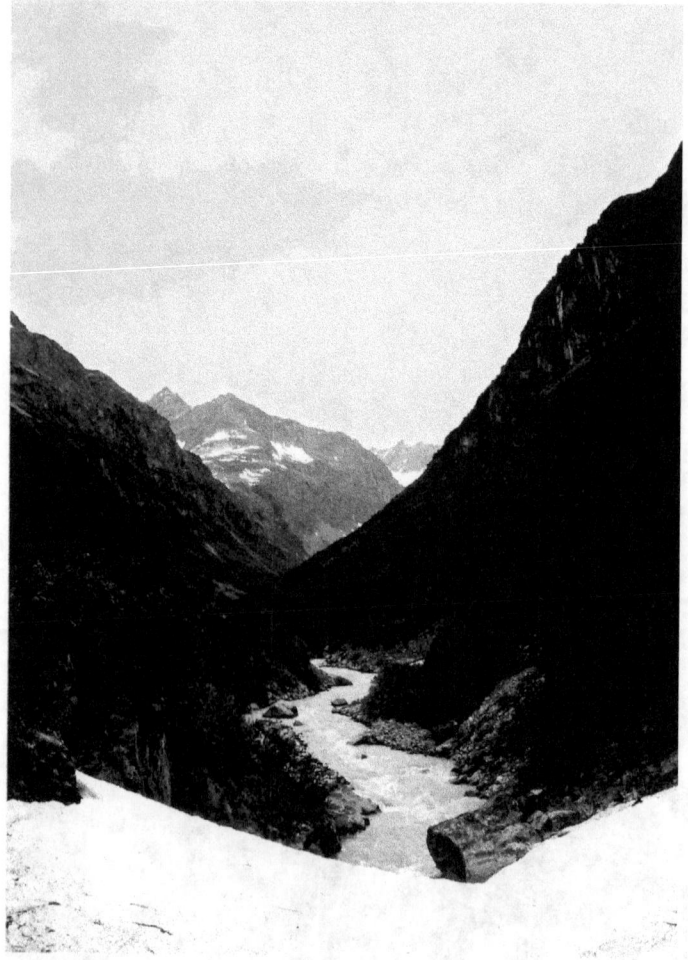

Mineral Creek Canyon. August 15, 2000   JDH

Back in 1935, this canyon of glitter was beckoning all those with gold in their eyes. It had caught Douglas's attention when he had first arrived. He entered the Mineral Creek Canyon on August 27, 1935. His Alaska window was dangerously close to closing and he knew it.
He wrote:

August 26 — It was raining again.
I picked up acid at the dock.

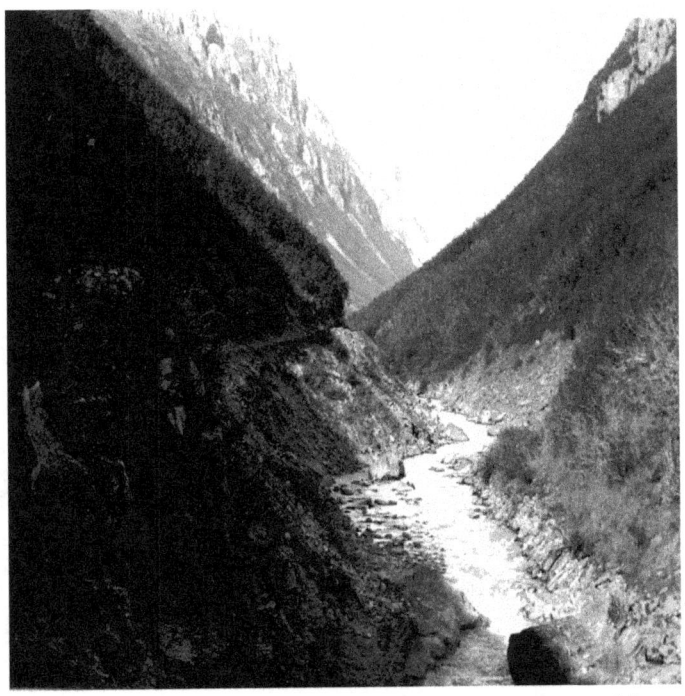

"Looking north from seven mile on mineral creek... near Valdez, Alaska...road on left hand side... boulder in foreground is 15 feet across...late summer, 1935" RAD

August 27 — There was a slight rain.
I rowed to Mineral Creek with the dog.
We stopped at a cabin at an old town
site a quarter of a mile from the beach.

August 28 — It rained hard all day.

August 29 — I hiked up Mineral Creek
Road three and a half miles. I made
some bread and saw a large black bear
at the three mile waterfall. He ran
into the bushes before I could get a
shot off.

Rain had plagued nineteen of Douglas's gold seeking days in the canyon, as he continued to photograph his adventure. Six of his Mineral Creek photographs are displayed on the following pages with repeat photography.

83

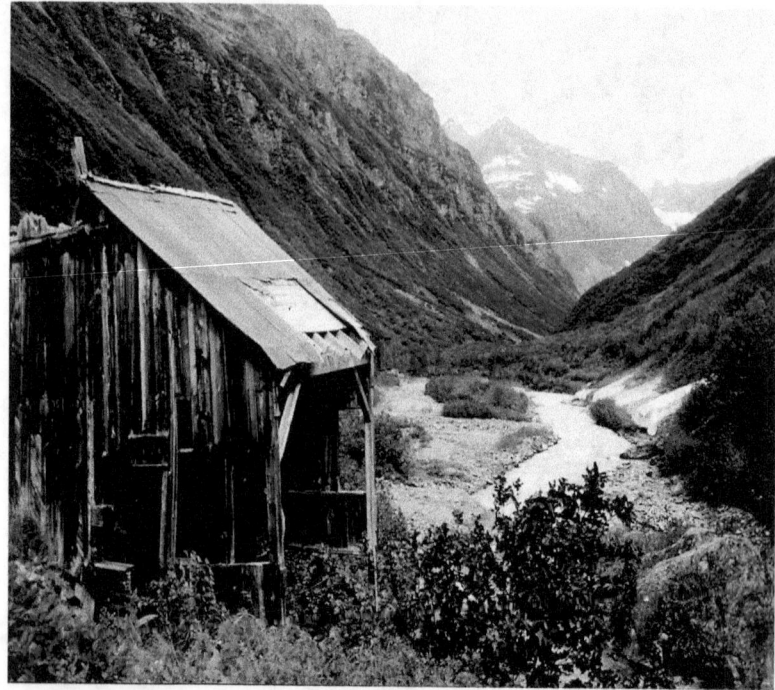

Smith Stamp Mill off upper end of Mineral Creek Road, Valdez, Alaska.
August 15, 2000   JDH

    The Smith Stamp Mill was built by W. L. Smith in 1915 to process ore from his mine. The mine was located at the 3,000 foot level, a mile east of Brevier Creek. The mine was named Eldorado.
    There once was a wooden bridge behind the old stamp mill crossing waters too deep to safely cross by foot. The bridge led to dirt roads winding steeply up to mining areas higher and further into the canyon.
    Activity beyond the stamp mill was mentioned several times in Douglas's diary:

> *September 11 — I helped a*
> *prospector extricate his car out*
> *of the mud in p.m. then went*
> *to the end of the road with him to*
> *a cabin on Brevier Creek...3miles*

> *September 12 — It rained... I went*
> *1/2 a mile further up Mineral*
> *Creek, then turned left 1/2 mile up*
> *the first creek north of Brevier Creek.*

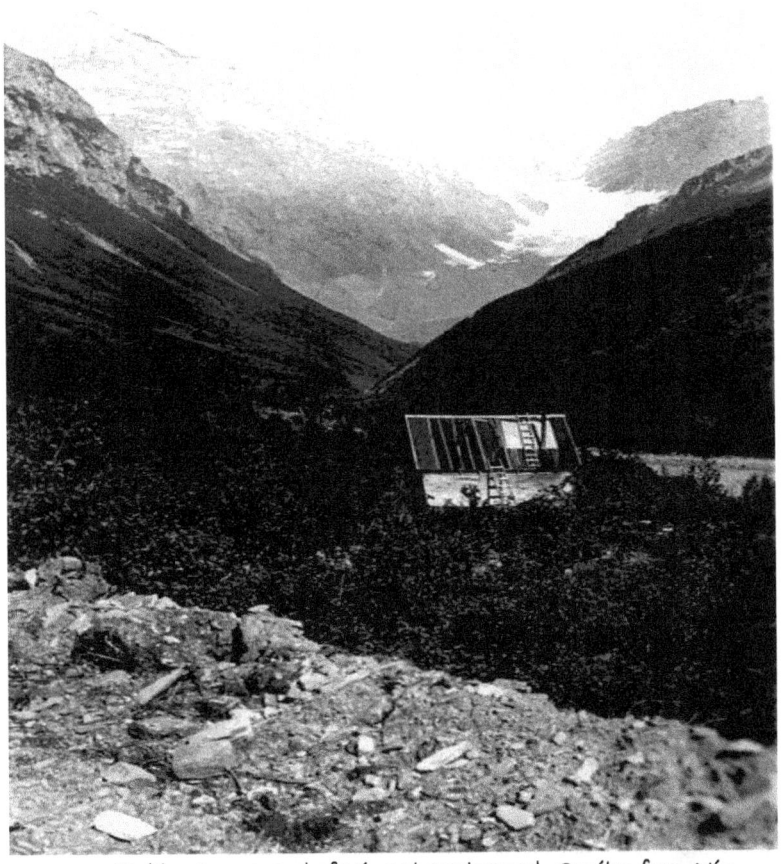

"Cabin at upper end of Mineral Creek Road...8 miles from Mineral Creek Glacier (background)...near Valdez, Alaska... September 14, 1935." RAD

September 13 — I made bread then went up Brevier Creek 1/2 a mile to test Samples. I met Ted Johnson on his way up to his mine at the top of the hill... 2 miles...

September 14 — I went back down the road 6 miles then up a rock slide 3/4 of a mile. It was a total of 4 miles...

It is on this day that Douglas captures the stamp mill photo and his final photo of Spot.

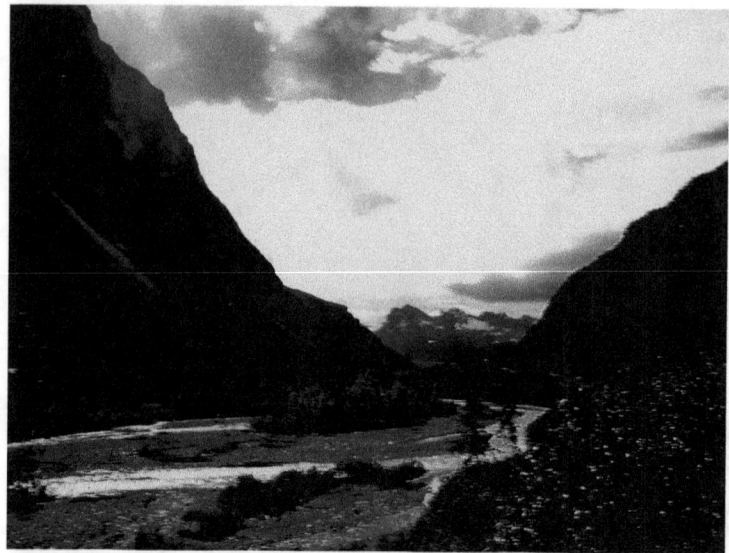

Mineral Creek looking south, Valdez, Alaska. August 15, 2000   JDH

In years past a small tram was used to service the McIntosh Roadhouse midway on Mineral Creek around 1912. Today, both the tram and roadhouse remain only in old photographs.

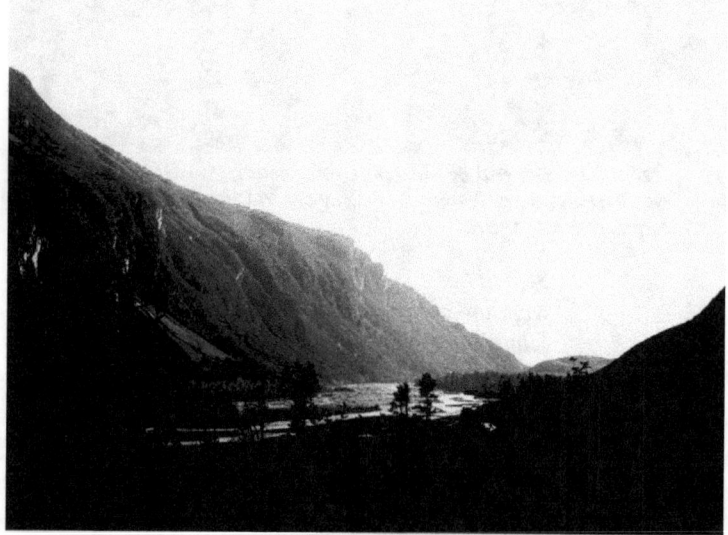

"Looking south from three mile on Mineral Creek...near Valdez, Alaska,....September 28, 1935" RAD

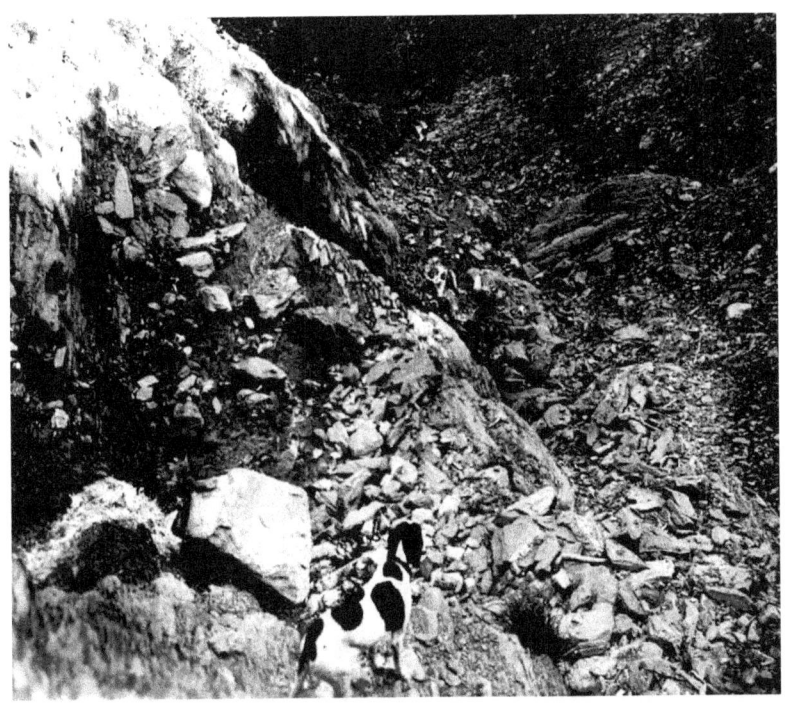

"Rock slide at 6 mile...Mineral Creek, Alaska....Spot, dog...looking west up the slide...elevation 1,000 feet...September 14, 1935" RAD

It was late, and some tough decisions had to be made. A local family offered to give the convalescing dog a home in Valdez. Douglas wrote in his diary on October 3, 1935, *"I left the dog with Lee Albin."*

The Albin family was highly regarded by the local old-timers when interviewed in 2001. One old-time Valdez resident — while recalling the 1930's in a phone interview said, " I remember seeing a black and white dog riding around in the back of a pickup truck through the streets of old town Valdez when I was a little girl."

Today, if you look very carefully along the streets of town, you can see some little, and some not so little, black and white canine faces peeking out from some of the houses and businesses there.

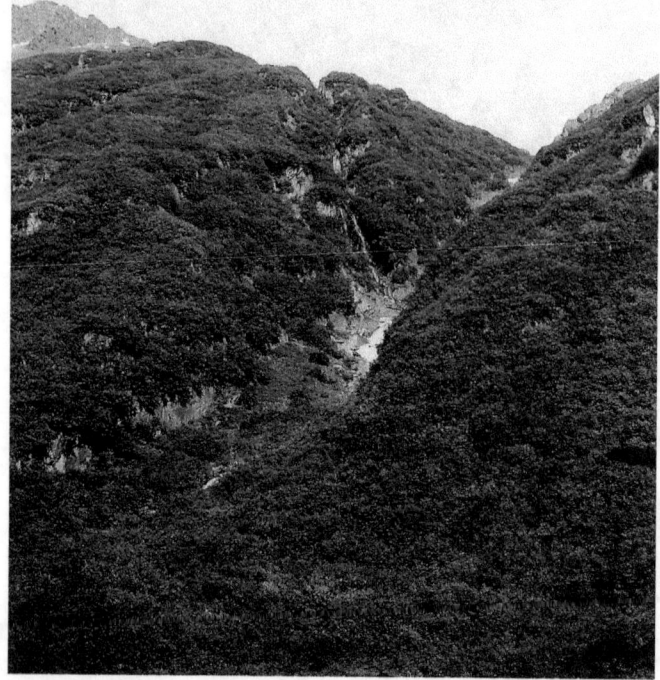

East side of Mineral Creek above 3,000 feet, Valdez, Alaska. 2001   JDH

We stood on the west bank of Mineral Creek with
a telephoto lens, elated to have located still another one of
the more difficult 1935 photos of the RAD "Alaska trip"
Photo Collection. An east bank shot was unattainable due to
the high waters of Mineral Creek. A record snowfall that
previous winter was now melting. We were not able to enter
the Mineral Creek Road until August because of avalanches.

Both of us pondered what life must have been like above
the 3,000 foot level, where most of the gold was located.
Names such as the Hercules Mine lends one's imagination as
to earlier gold mining activities taking place, north and west
up Brevier Creek.

Some distance past the Smith Stamp Mill are the Johnson
Mill ruins at the 2,500 foot level and the Big Four Mine,
continuing production until 1941. Eventually, overgrown
dirt roads reach distant mines and the Johnson Glacier area.
The Johnson Glacier and its western neighbors Shoup and
Columbia were home to several other mines of record. The
Little Giant, one of a group of mines located at the foot of
the Mineral Creek Glacier, operated off and on until 1955.

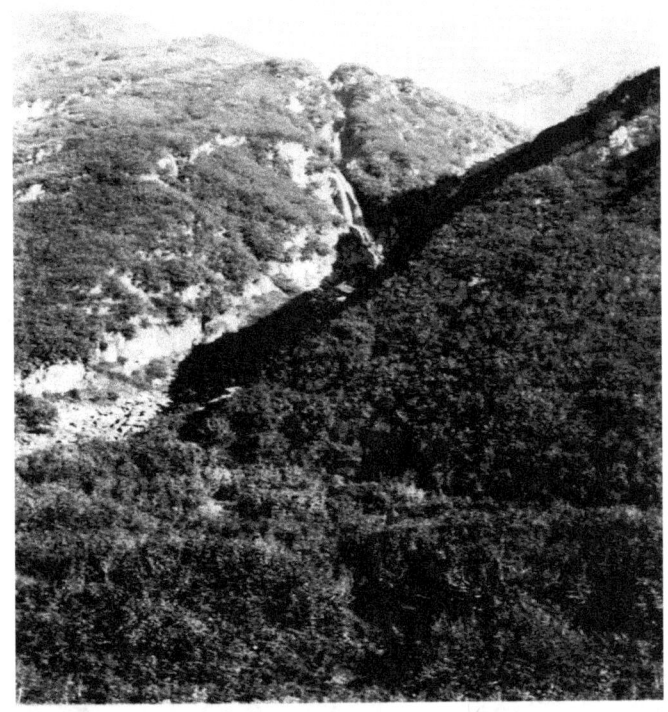

"Opposite Brevier Creek...east side of Mineral Creek...near Valdez, Alaska...Note: dense underbrush...September 26, 1935" RAD

In late September Douglas noted unremitting days of cold, wet weather in his diary:

> September 24 — I went up
> Brevier Creek 1 mile. It was
> hard going. There was ice
> on the creek. The hike
> totaled 2 miles.
>
> September 25 — It rained.
>
> September 26 — More rain.
>
> September 27 — The same.

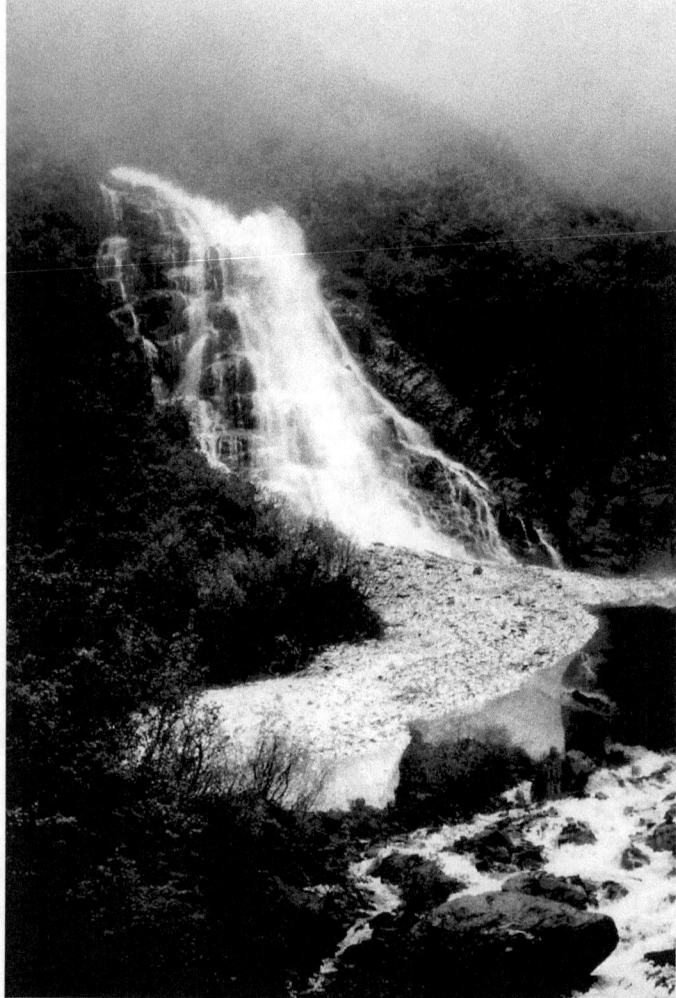

Three Mile Falls off Mineral Creek Road, Valdez, Alaska.
August 4, 2000   JDH

It is a wild, raw land back in the canyon of Mineral Creek
and now Douglas was equipped with the knowledge that
Alaska glitters only to those with time and endurance to meet
the elements of the terrain.
  One year? A lifetime is more like it.

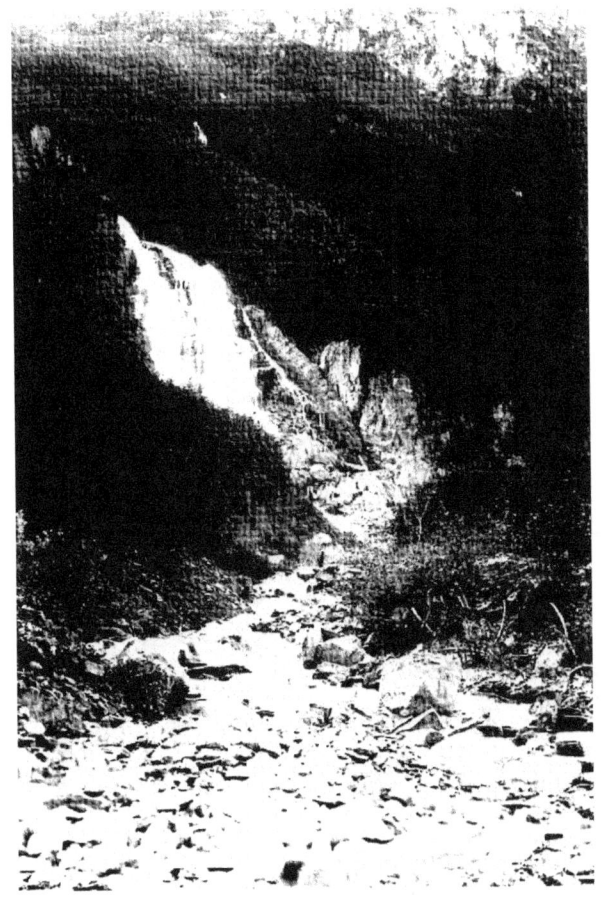

"Falls at 3 mile...near Valdez, AK...September 28, 1935" RAD

The summer sun had long since lost its warmth and the cold winds of winter were upon him. On September 28, Douglas took his last Valdez photograph of the falls at three mile. He wrote in his diary:

> *September 28 — I took my load to the lower cabin. The hike was 8 miles...*
>
> *September 29 — I hiked back and brought down the balance of my equipment. A hike of 16 miles...*
>
> *September 30 — I rowed to Valdez.*

91

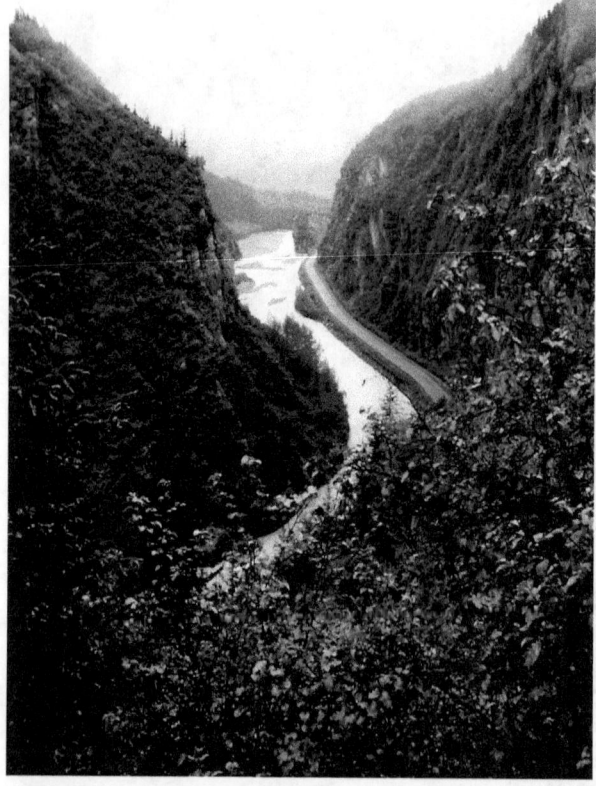

Keystone Canyon, Alaska. 2001   JDH

Another notable 2001 photo adventure, this time not to repeat photographs, was the Eagle-Valdez Trail hike from Valdez up through Keystone Canyon. On June 14, we followed the gold rushers' footsteps of 100 years ago, up switchbacks to a narrow cliff trail above Horse Tail Falls.

The old Eagle-Valdez Trail lay abandoned for ninety years until 1997-98 when re-clearing began. Using hand tools to maintain the spirit of the original trail, a group of dedicated trail clearing enthusiasts went to work. Now hikers can make their way up the steep mountain trails and over cliff areas wide enough for one human foot to step. A sign on top reflecting the turn of the 19th century reads, "Use as little dynamite as possible — just enough for the horses' hoofs."

This photograph was taken from the top of Horse Tail Falls along the renovated Eagle-Valdez 'gold rush' Trail. The Richardson Hwy can be seen heading south toward Valdez. The Lowe River runs left of the highway, flowing south.

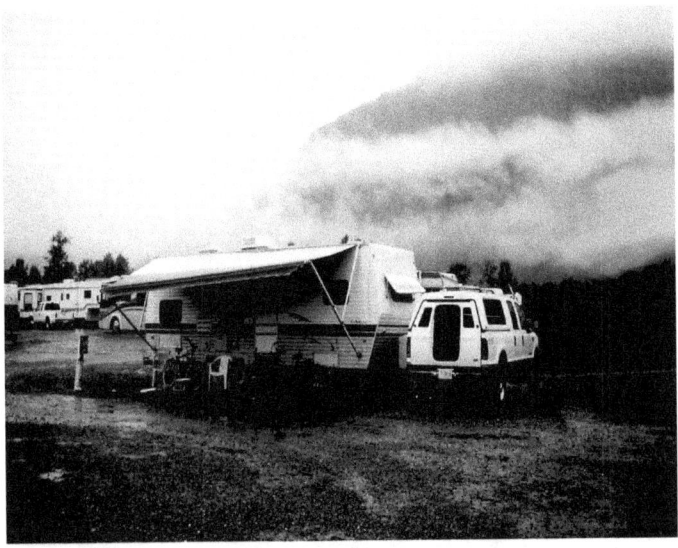

Eagle's Rest RV Park, Valdez, AK. 2001   JDH

Our 2001 summer base camp was at Eagle's Rest RV Park in Valdez. A clockwise loop trip was made in late June as the last of the once bright yellow dandelions were being mowed down along the roadside. By now, we had become ardent adventurers and it was time to complete the last of the Alaska repeat photography.

In the early morning hours of June 29, 2001, the Tustumena Ferry pulled away from the Valdez dock in heavy fog. Our 4 x 4 white diesel Ford was also booked for passage. The truck, normally used for towing, would now serve for our transportation and overnights. The ferry crossed Prince William Sound uneventfully and arrived in Seward during early evening light. We located a campsite and were amused to find that by sleeping in the bed of our truck, we were too comfortable for the tent campers, but not comfortable enough for the motor homes.

Misfits, but happy and unfaltering misfits, we hiked the trails of the old gold rush days. We drove our truck down into and up into places it was not really suppose to be — to accomplish that perfect shot. Discovering the old photo sites had become a relentless endeavor. We traveled north to Anchorage, Palmer, Hatcher Pass and Fairbanks. Prior to our final leg south through the delta on the Richardson Highway, we made an additional trip east on the Steese Highway to Circle and the Yukon River.

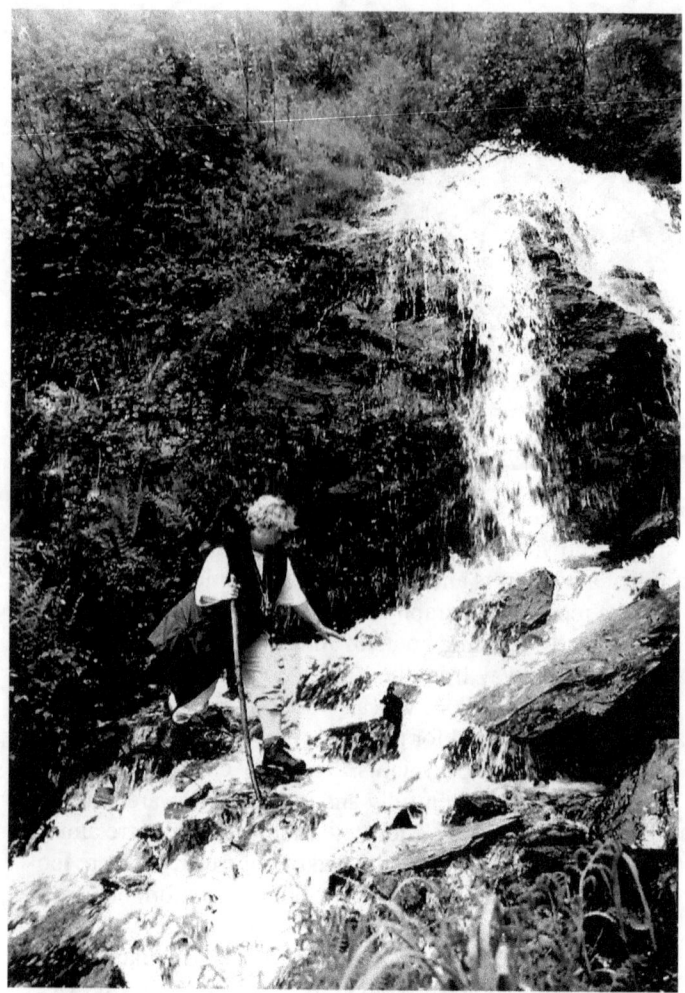

Jill hiking the Shoup Bay Trail, Alaska. 2001   UEH

Upon arriving back to base camp from our loop trip in late July 2001, we decided to explore areas mentioned in the Douglas diary, but not photographed in 1935:

RAD wrote the following:

> *September 7 — I rowed to*
> *a falls east of Gold Creek*
> *to test gravel and examine*
> *rocks. It was 6 miles.*

Gold Creek can be reached by hiking the Shoup Bay Trail along the north bank of Port Valdez. This trail takes hikers deep into bear country. Of course, we were already prepared for that and pulled out our Ahtell Creek bear bells.

The first leg of the Shoup Bay Trail led us vigorously through a waterfall with a thirty foot drop below. After several miles of hiking, we descended steeply into the old Gold Creek mining area to photograph and film. In 1914, the Budd Mining Company made plans to start up a hydraulic operation there.

This 2001 aerial view of Gold Creek depicts how rich the
land was north of Prince William Sound. Waterfalls abound.
They are fed by creeks from the upper Chugach Range.

The Cliff Mine, west of Gold Creek and east of Shoup Bay
and the Columbia Glacier, was the richest gold deposit claim
made in Prince William Sound. This claim was made in
1906. In 1936, the upper levels were reopened, so it appears
this mine was not in operation while Douglas was spending
time here in the summer of 1935. Later, the lower buildings
of the mine were destroyed by the 1964 tsunami. Over one
hundred claims were staked between Valdez and the
Columbia Glacier in earlier times.

Douglas mentioned in his diary before leaving Mineral
Creek and wrote:

> *September 10 — I rowed four and*
> *a half miles down the bay near*
> *Gold Creek to look over a greywork*
> *dike. I then took some gravel and*
> *rock samples back to a cabin at the*
> *old town site on Mineral Creek and*
> *rowed back to Valdez for the night.*
> *It was a total of 12 miles.*

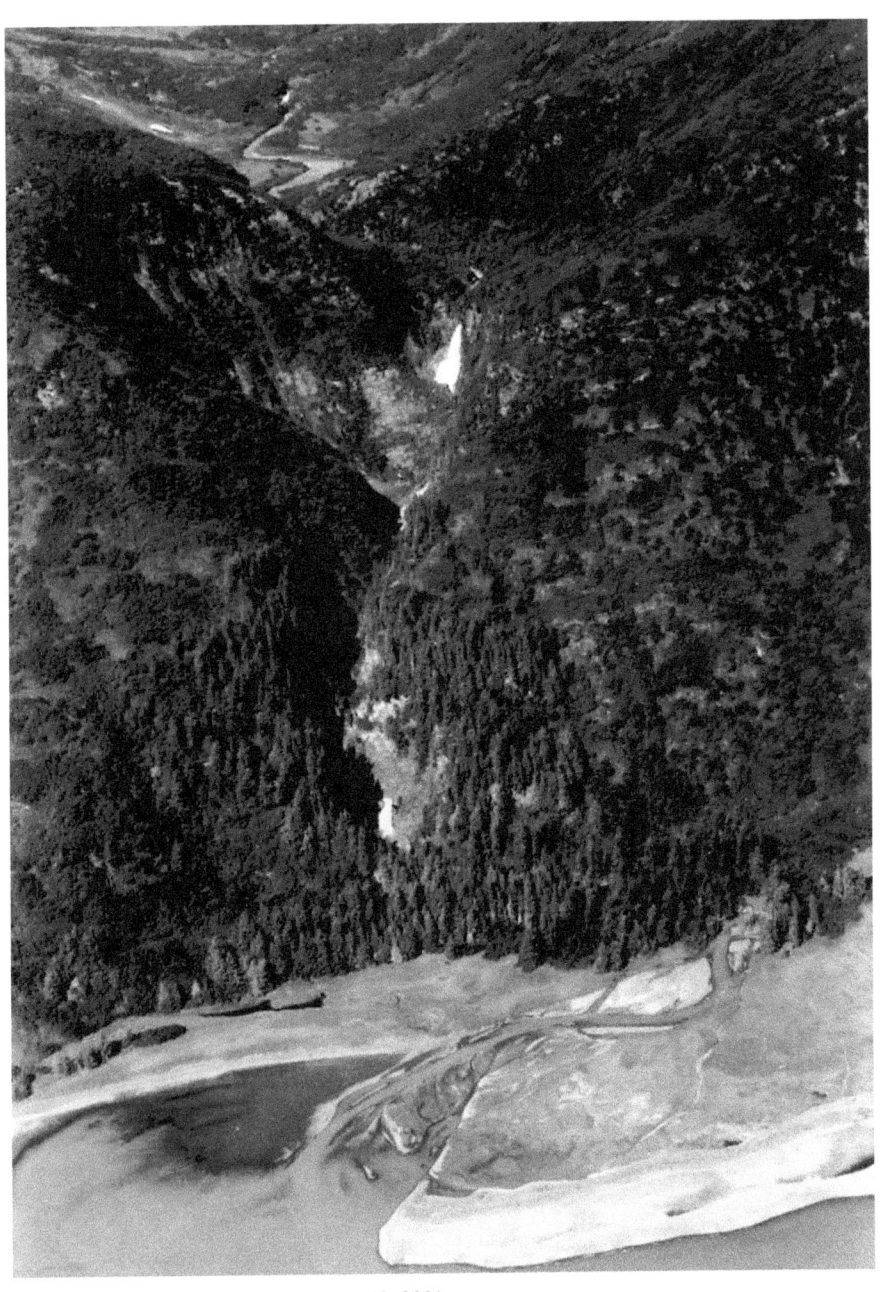

Gold Creek, Alaska. August 13, 2001....aerial photo JDH

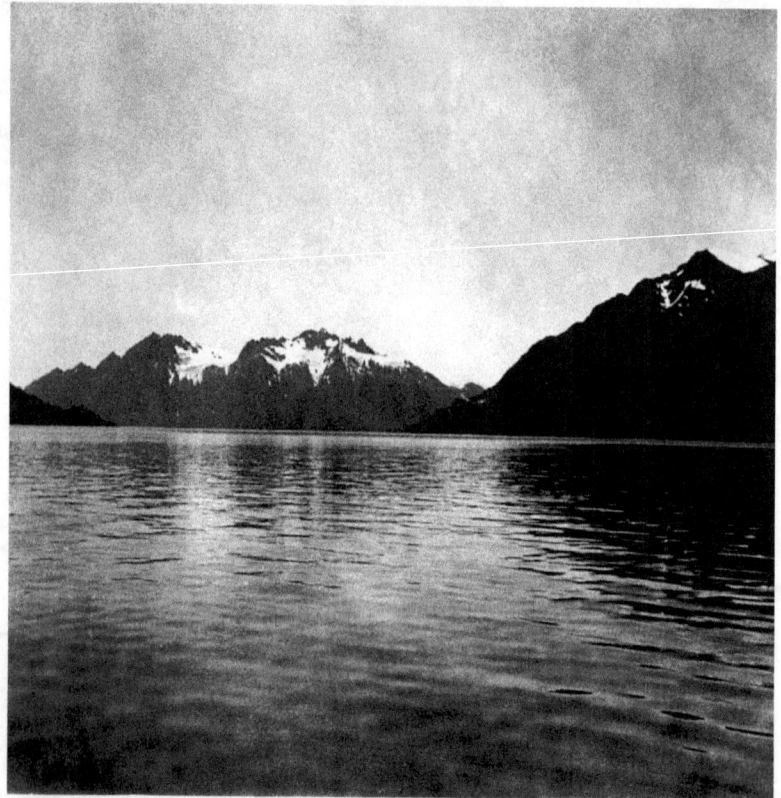

"Shoup Bay area in center...Mineral Creek comes in just behind island (out of photo right)...looking northwest... Valdez, Alaska...August 13, 1935" RAD

Today, a Trail continues on from Gold Creek. It makes its way west through undefined, muddy switchbacks. After a steep descent running along a divide on the east side of Shoup Bay and a series of stairs and cairns (trail markers), the trail enters the inner bay of the Shoup Glacier. The Shoup Bay Trail is approximately 12 miles round trip from Valdez.

After securing a boat and returning from the Shoup Bay area, Douglas wrote:

> *August 13 — I rowed to first*
> *island...4 foot layer of grey*
> *wacki. On 2nd island is quartz*
> *dike...it is hard to define its*
> *limits. About 4 Miles.*

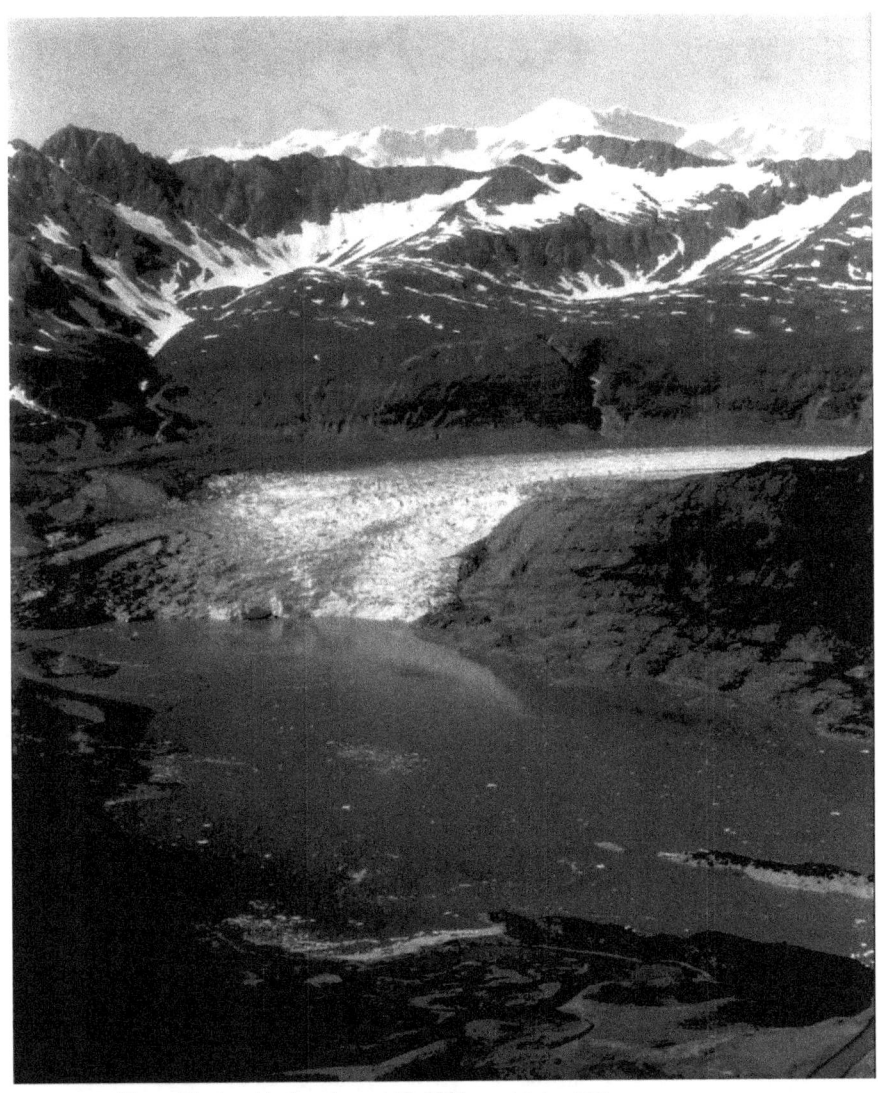

Shoup Glacier, Alaska. August 13, 2001....aerial photo JDH

This aerial photo of the Shoup Glacier terminus was taken by the author on August 13, 2001. Aerial photography of glaciers only began in the late 1930's. The Columbia and Shoup glaciers were among the first recorded. USGS maps published in the 1950's were the earliest to show contours on the glaciers. The icefields were also recorded at that time.

99

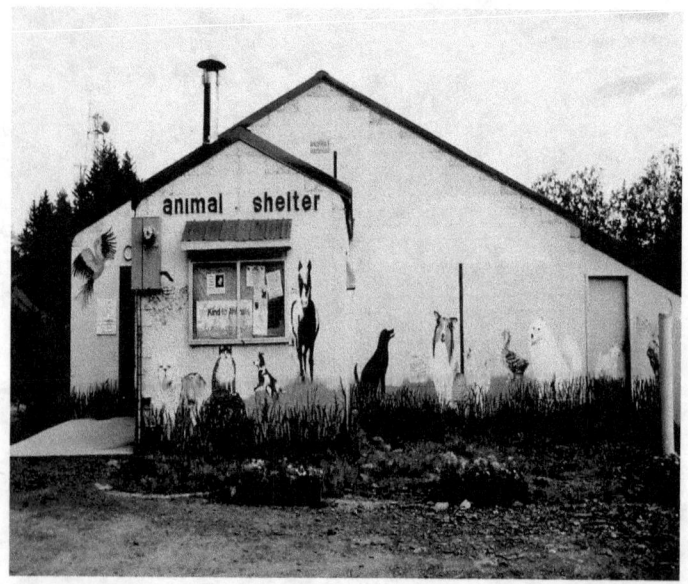

Animal Shelter of Valdez, Alaska. 2001   JDH

After the 1964 tsunami, the first building built over in the bay to the west of old town was a treatment plant. In 1979 a wooden addition was built to house unwanted dogs and cats from Valdez and neighboring communities — some as far away as Glennallen and Slana. A veterinarian arrived in town in the early 1990's.

The last building seen in our rear view mirror in late August, 2001 was the Valdez Animal Shelter. Spot's 1935 Seattle portrait hung proudly on the reception room wall.

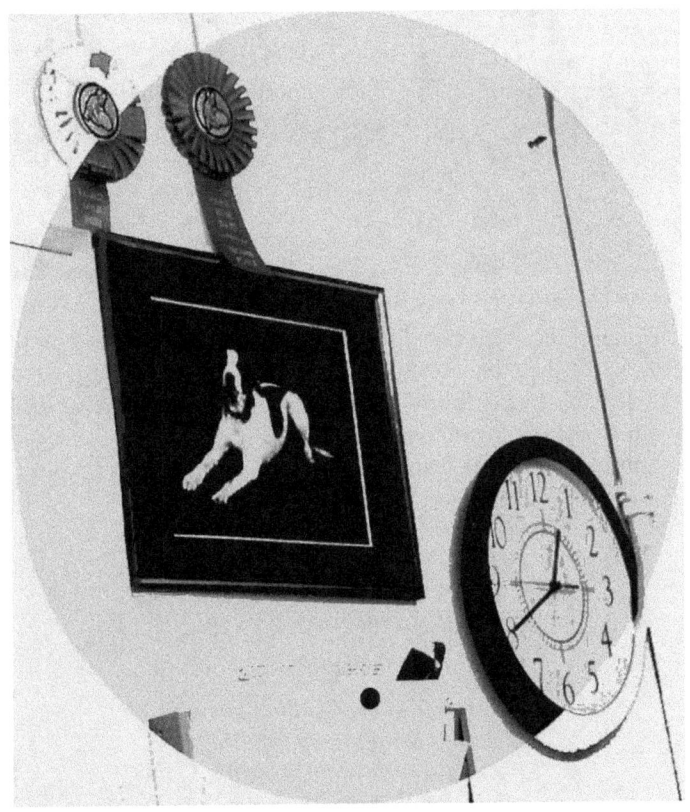

Reception room at the Valdez Animal Shelter, Alaska. 2001   JDH

In 2001, under the leadership of the local Boy Scouts we helped paint the inside walls of the Valdez Animal Shelter a happy dandelion yellow.

Where else but in Valdez does a cruise ship offer as an excursion option a chance to walk a dog at the local animal shelter.

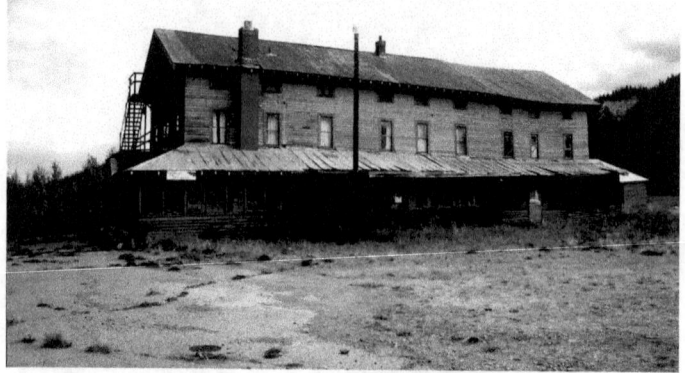

Tonsina Lodge (privately owned), Tonsina, Alaska. 2001 JDH

Douglas recorded very little in his diary after October 8, 1935. On the other hand, he did not stop photographing. This enabled us to follow his journey all the way to Seward with repeat photography.
Subsequent entries below:

October 4 — I arranged to go with Bill Egan to Fairbanks. The number 2 bridge had already washed out just east of Valdez.

October 5 — I waited.

October 6 — We left Sunday noon. The road temporarily repaired. We had supper at the Tonsina Lodge (above) and drove on to Paxson. The temperature was +15 degrees. We arrived in Paxson at 3 a.m....got word of a 4 foot Snow in Rapids...

October 7 — Again, we started out at noon. A cat came through from Fairbanks clearing the way. Five trucks and three cars lined up waiting to get through. The lead truck slid off the edge of the road getting around a rock slide. We did not go off...and later helped push all the trucks and cars up a bank where a stream had washed out another bridge. Supper at Rapids...drive on...

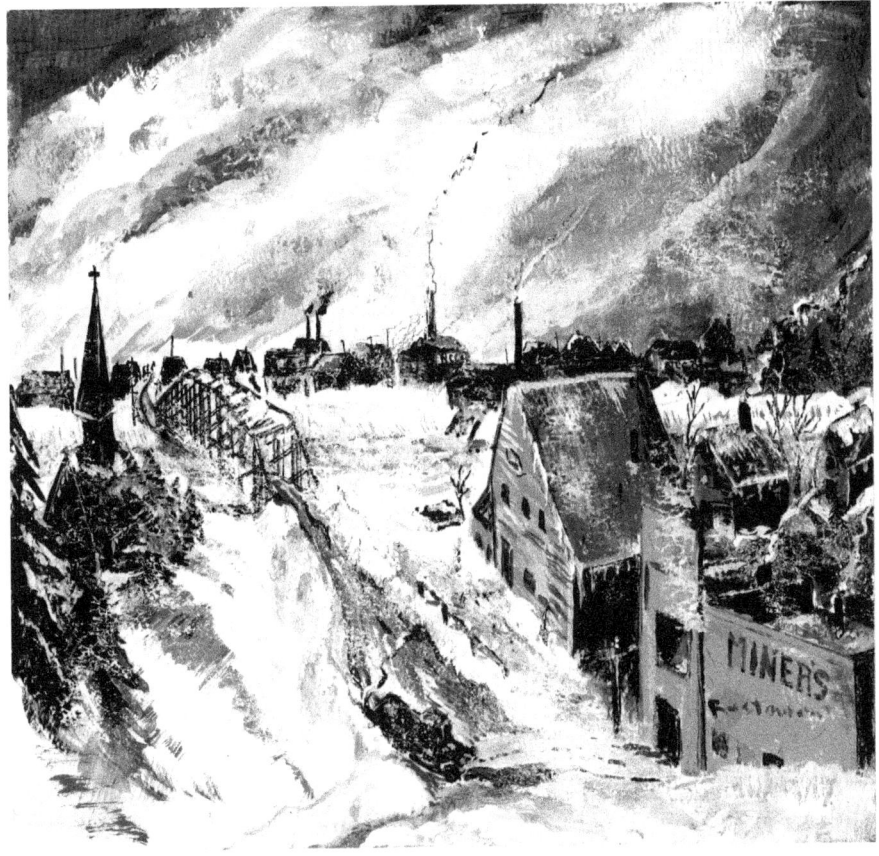

Illustration 5.   End of the Line

Everything was darker and colder than Douglas had imagined. There was a light coming from a building across the Cushman Bridge on the north side of the Chena River.

To appreciate some of the earlier history and logistics of the old gold rush town called Fairbanks, one needs to see where these locations are placed on a map. There were three points of entry to the Klondike Gold Rush at the end of the nineteenth century: the treacherous "Chilkoot Trail" from Skagway, the very dangerous "All-American Trail" over the Valdez Glacier from Valdez, and the risky one thousand mile voyage up the Yukon River by boat from Saint Michael (south of Nome across Norton Bay). The Yukon River was known as the rich man's entrance into the interior. E.T. Barnette, a 1897 Klondike stampeder and founder of Fairbanks, chose the Yukon River as his first entry point to the Klondike Gold Rush. He traveled up the river from Saint Michael on a ship named "Cleveland," past Galena, Ruby, Tanana, Rampart (known as the halfway mark), Steven's Village, Beaver, Fort Yukon and Circle City (later, renamed Circle) where his ship became frozen in for the winter. A river of very thick ice flow presented itself to the crew that year. In the spring, Barnette reached Dawson (later, renamed Dawson City). The small Alaska villages along the Yukon River with very little infrastructure did not go unnoticed to the businesslike mind of Barnett.

Four years would go by. In 1901, loaded with supplies and an Irish wife named Isabelle (maiden name of Cleary), Barnette started out once again from Saint Michael. This time he planned to open a trading post at Tanana Crossing (Tanacross). Ill-advised, he chose a route up the Chena Slough to save time and avoid the Bates Rapids. Unfortunately, the Chena Slough had a low water level that year, and Barnette's ship became stuck near the shore.

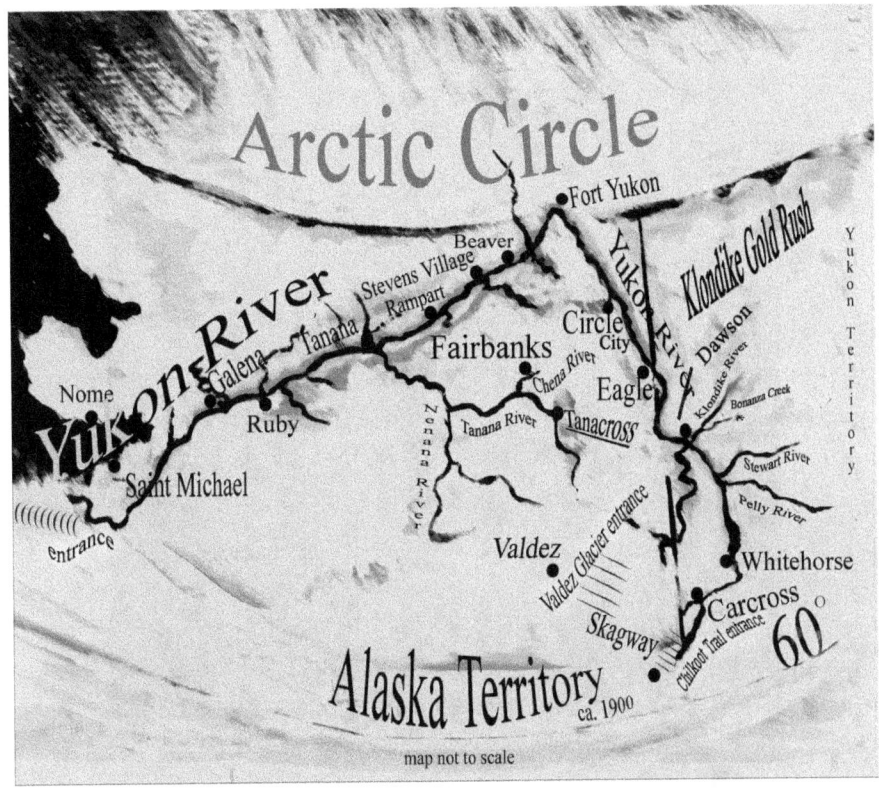

Map 5. Three points of entry to the Klondike Gold Rush. This map
reflects the present day names of cities, towns and villages.

He soon established a small trading post. A year later
(in 1902) gold was discovered by Felix Pedro, just north of
this shore area. A "Fairbanks Stampede" followed. Without
this event, Fairbanks might be just another bend in the Chena
River. This discovery expanded E. T. Barnette's little rustic
trading post into the Northern Commercial Company known
as N.C.CO.

The towns of Circle and Eagle are the only towns along the
Yukon River that can be reached by car. The Steese Highway connects Circle to Fairbanks and the Taylor Highway
connects Eagle to Tok. In earlier times, Circle was reached
by the 162 mile Circle-Fairbanks Trail.

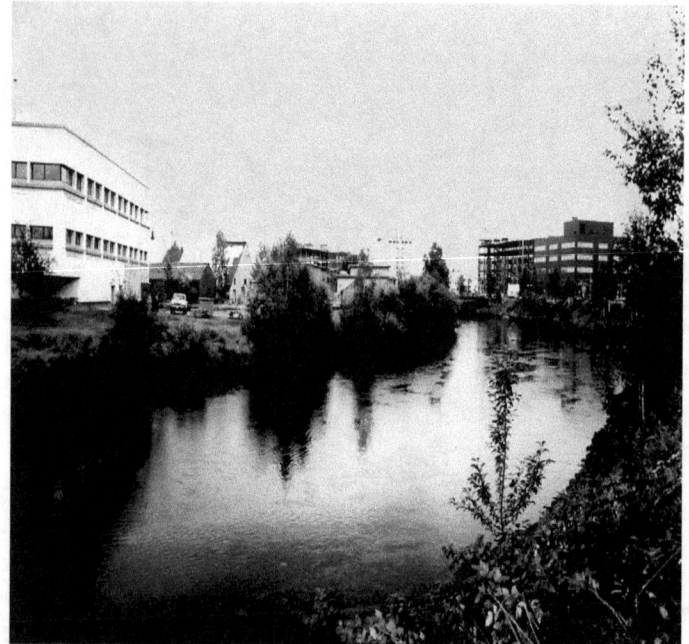

From the south bank of the Chena River, Fairbanks, AK. 2000   JDH

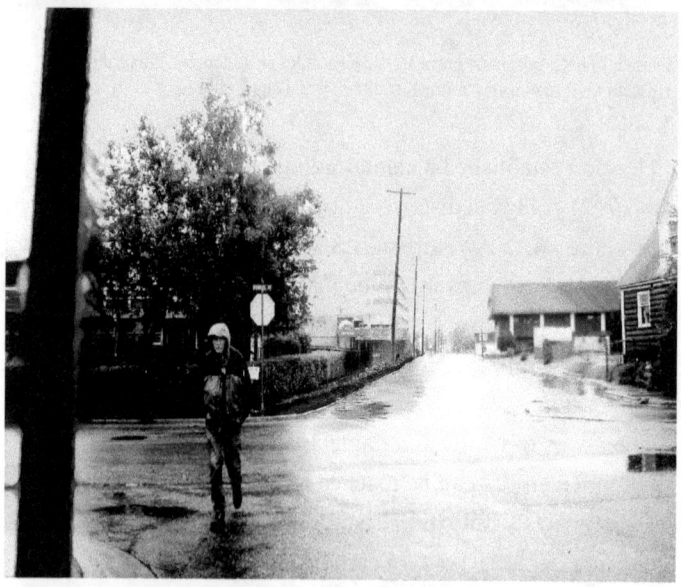

Ulys Emory Hopper. First Avenue, Fairbanks, Alaska. August, 2000   JDH

A parking lot now replaces the Mitchell house where Douglas stayed—located between two buildings on R of photo.

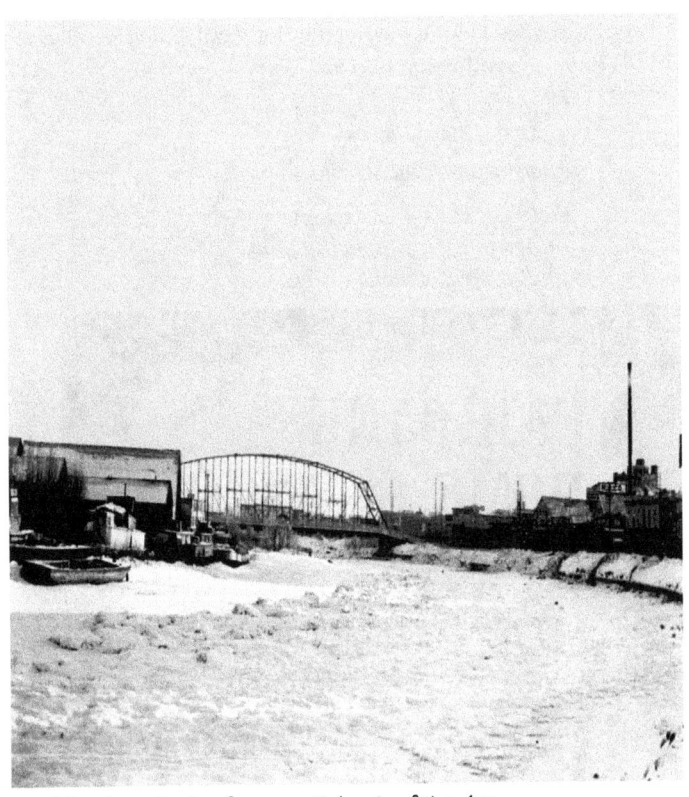

"Fairbanks, Alaska from south bank of the river
(right)...completely frozen over...October 18, 1935" RAD

The first 1935 photograph taken in the Fairbanks area by
Douglas was of the frozen Chena River. It was easily
repeated in 2000. "A" frame buildings on the north bank of
the Chena River are the same ones seen in the 1935
photograph. Samson Hardware (built in 1905) sits just beyond the "A" frame buildings. A new Marriott Hotel (right)
is in progress. The original bridge (above) crossing the
Chena river in Fairbanks was relocated to Nome. The bridge
now crosses the Kuzitrin River on the Nome-Taylor
Highway at mile marker 67.4.
    Barnett's trading post, N.R.C.C., can be seen on the
south side of the Chena River.

Five days after Douglas arrived in Fairbanks, he recorded in his diary the following two entries:

> *October 14 — The temperature*
> *is +20 degrees Fahrenheit.*
> *There was 10 inches of snowfall.*

> *October 15 — I moved my*
> *things to Mrs. Mitchell's house*
> *at 208 First Avenue on Tuesday.*

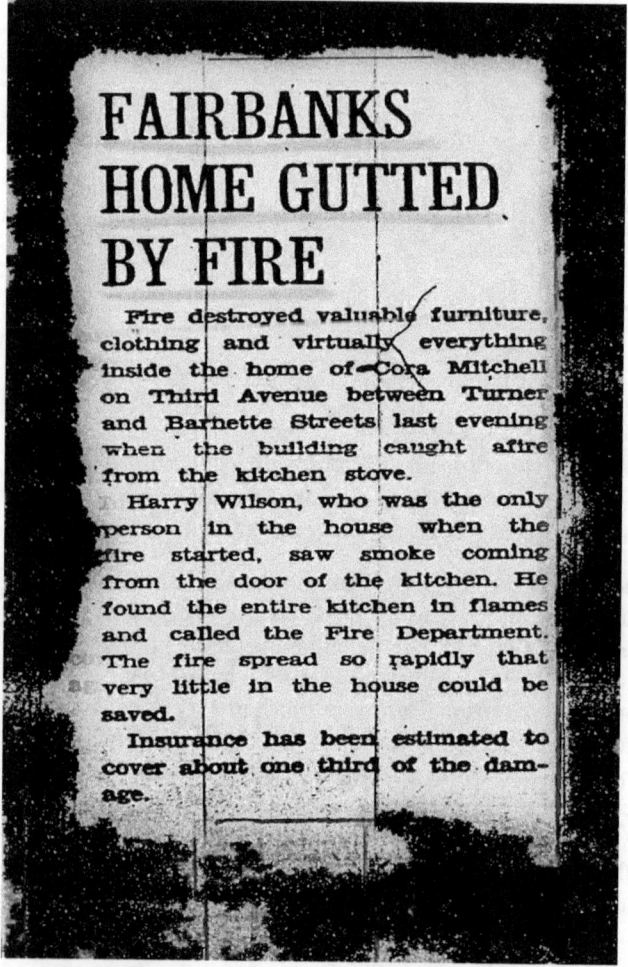

FAIRBANKS HOME GUTTED BY FIRE

Fire destroyed valuable furniture, clothing and virtually everything inside the home of Cora Mitchell on Third Avenue between Turner and Barnette Streets last evening when the building caught afire from the kitchen stove.

Harry Wilson, who was the only person in the house when the fire started, saw smoke coming from the door of the kitchen. He found the entire kitchen in flames and called the Fire Department. The fire spread so rapidly that very little in the house could be saved.

Insurance has been estimated to cover about one third of the damage.

Courtesy of the FAIRBANKS DAILY NEWS-MINER

On Monday, October 21, 1935, this article appeared in the FAIRBANKS DAILY NEWS-MINER.

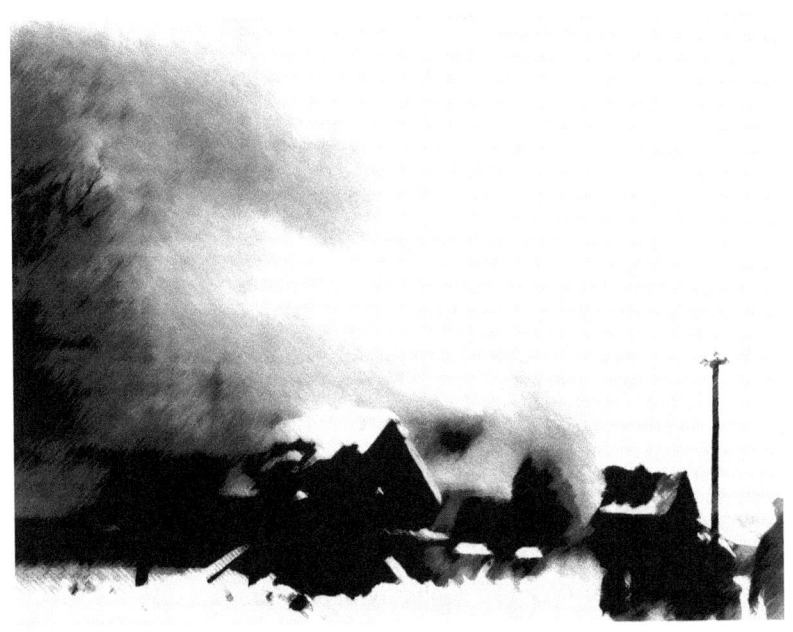

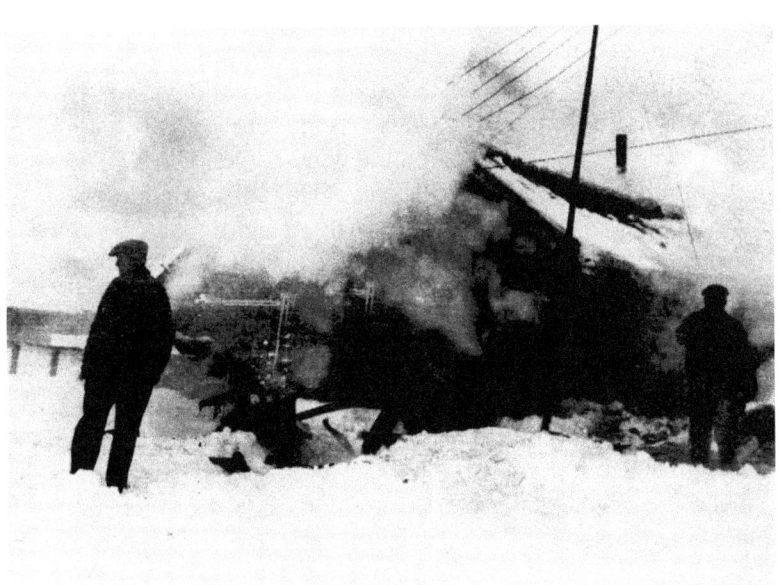

"Cabin fire...Fairbanks, AK. October 20, 1935." RAD

  On Sunday, October 20, 1935, the home of Cora Mitchell on Third Avenue between Turner and Barnett Streets was gutted by fire. The temperature on Sunday was -20 degrees Fahrenheit. Two of Douglas's most compelling photos were taken on this day.

The final entry in Douglas's diary was on November 5, 1935. He had turned a cold eye on the prospect of returning home. He braced for the frigid Fairbanks winter and waited for spring. Alaska was a land requiring tolerance.

Today, photographing a house fire could easily make use of well over 100 digital photos, but Douglas was living in the mid-thirties and had to frame all of his photographs painfully well thought-out.

During the oppressive time of winter when daylight lasted only three hours of each day, it was the season of shafts and tunnels. Work was available to some by tunneling into the frozen soil and hauling gold bearing dirt to the surface through shafts. In spite of this, prospectors everywhere preferred the season of never ending light and the paydirt days of summer.

On December 21, he captured the winter solstice at a gold mining area north of Fairbanks. He took a single photograph to capture the solstice and an additional one further down the road, before what could only have been a bleak holiday season.

If it were not for the quotes on the backs of all of his 1935-36 photographs, the written extension of his journey up to Fairbanks and down to the Matanuska Valley, would not have been recorded.

The prospector always told his family to date and label all photos. As the years passed on, some laughed, and some labeled.

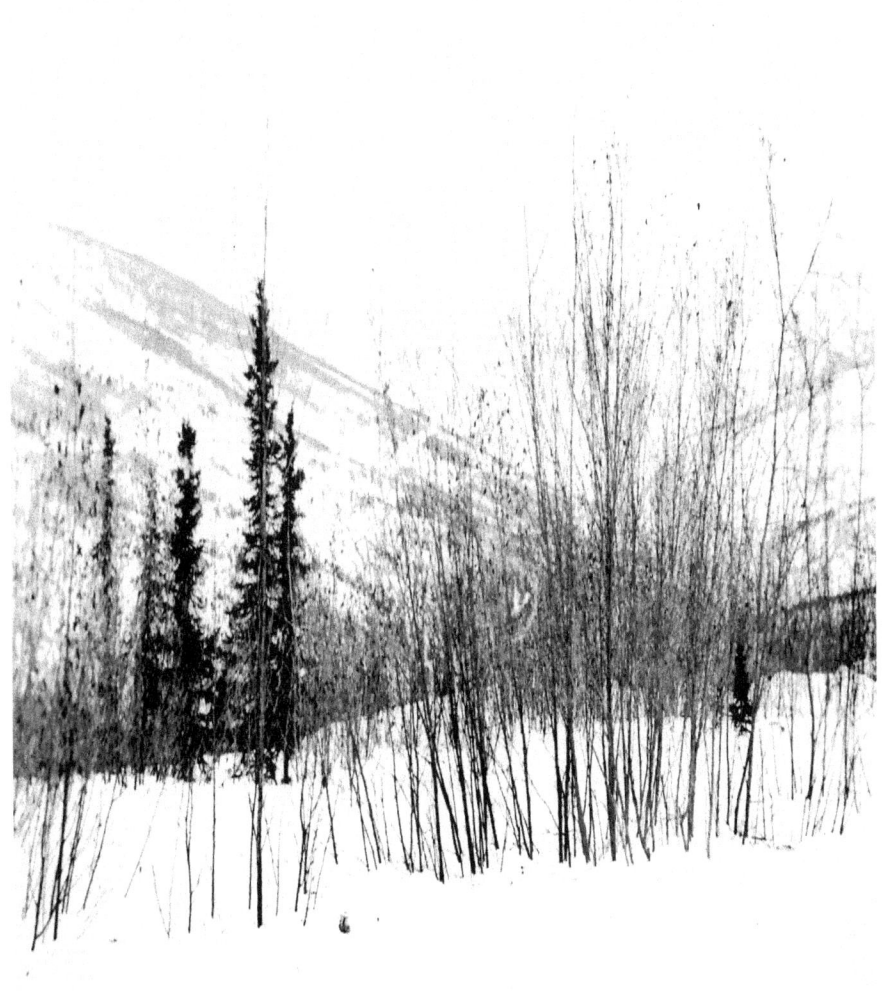

"Shortest day of the year...time exactly 15 seconds at noon...Cleary Creek from the Newsboy Mine...Fairbanks, Alaska...looking north...December 21, 1935" RAD

All writing from here on by RAD was from the back of his photographs — continuing in the Bradley font.

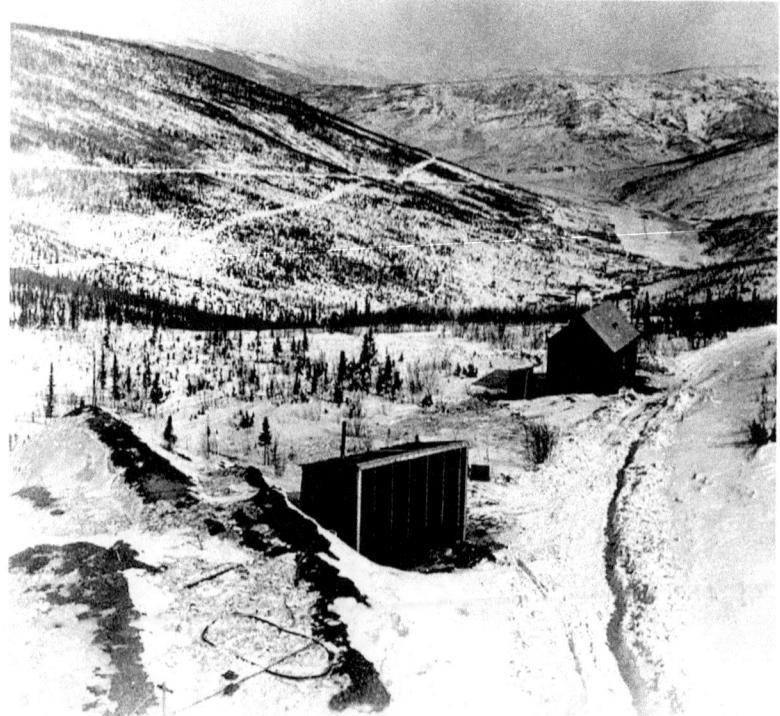

"Looking north...Newsboy Mine area...22 miles north of Fairbanks, Alaska...December 21, 1935" RAD

Three months had gone by. Tomorrow would be the first day of spring. Douglas took out his camera once more. He had three pictures left to complete his roll and the sun was brighter now. Where did he go to photograph those valued three photographs in Fairbanks?

On March 20, 1936, Douglas chose the Newsboy Mine area yet again, where he captured the first of the additional photos of this mining site in the Little Eldorado Creek Valley.

But, where is all the repeat photography?

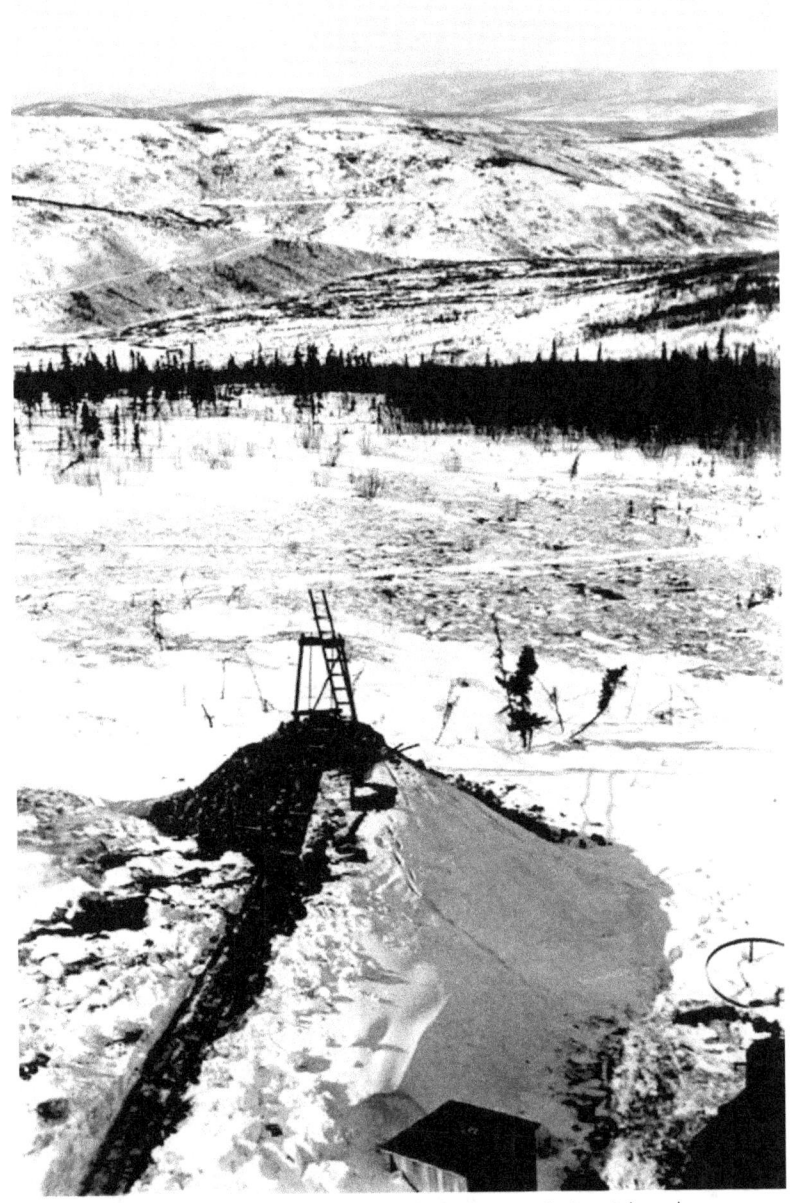

"Newsboy Mine area...looking down Little Eldorado
Creek...22 miles north of Fairbanks, Alaska...
March 20, 1936" RAD

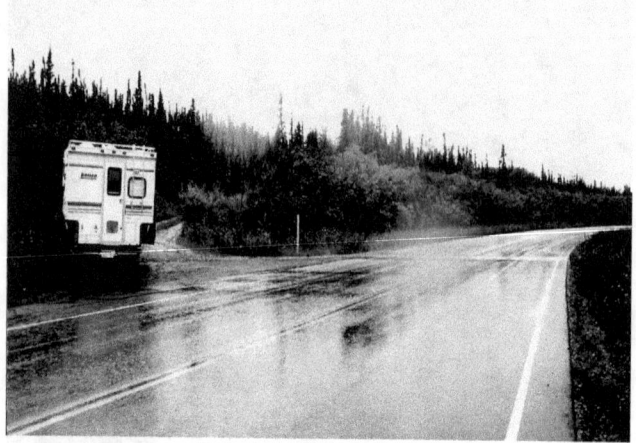

Steese Highway, Alaska. 2000   JDH

   Deteriorating weather conditions in the Fairbanks area
made our repeat photography attempt on Cleary Summit in
2000 a disappointment. We knew we would be returning.
Those old 1935-36 Fairbanks photos held some obvious
clues that were only noticed upon returning home from our
second Alaska summer in the fall of 2001 — after all the
film had been developed. This was a clue that the green of
summer had camouflaged.

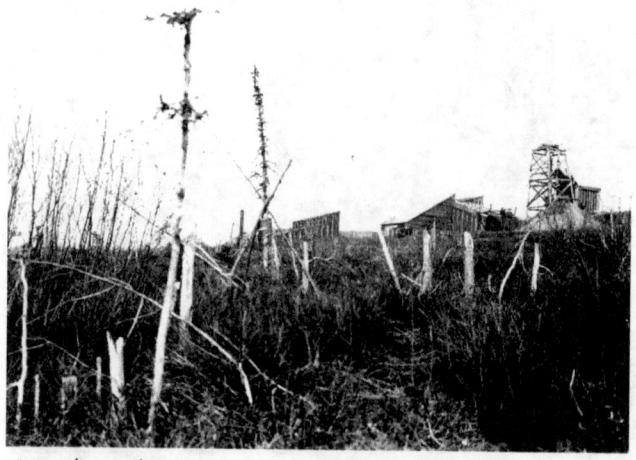

"Newsboy Mine, looking E, Fairbanks, April 25, 1936." RAD

   One of the five "Newsboy Mine area" photos left off the
word *area* in the writing recorded on the back of the photo.
This led us to believe the only record of the actual Newsboy
Mine was captured in the above photo.

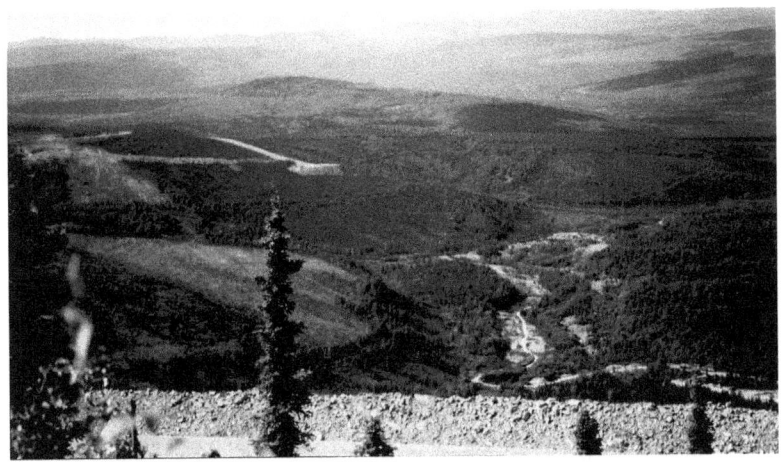

Little Elderado Creek Valley from Pedro Dome, N of Fairbanks. 2001   JDH

We tried one last time to locate just one of those elusive "Newsboy Mine area" photos. Everything seemed right as we drove up the winding Pedro Dome Road. There were signs reading "keep out" and large trucks carrying heavy loads of paydirt traveling at forceful speeds on the road just below. On top of this dome, an image was taken of the Little Eldorado Creek Valley. Later, by magnifying it up, all the lines matched on four of the five 1935-36 "Newsboy mine area" photos. A large sideways "X" was defined in the distant hills — and we had found *our* Eldorado! This valley was open to prospectors in the mid-thirties, but presently it is not accessible to the public.

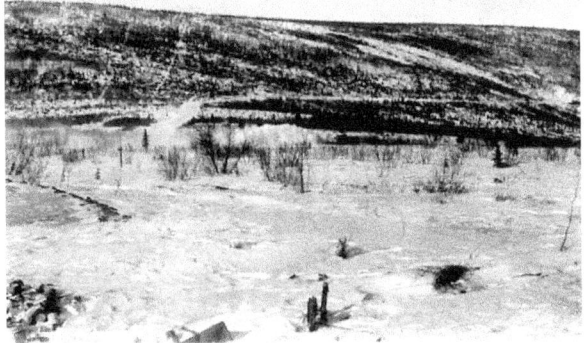

"Rotary snow plow...Newsboy Mine area...Fairbanks, AK. April 30, 1936" RAD

The old railroad began servicing the gold camps between Fairbanks and Chatanika in the mid-twenties. Claims were not required to be registered with the federal government until 1979.

115

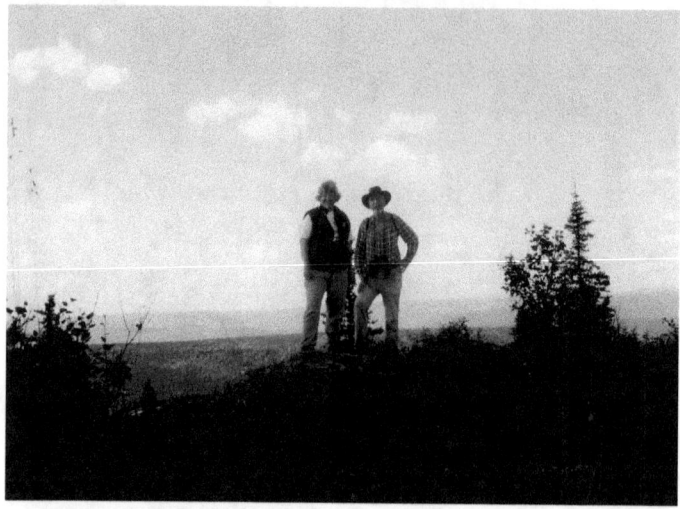

Jill and Emory on Cleary Summit, north of Fairbanks, AK. 2001   Timer

In late summer, before leaving the Fairbanks area, we climbed a steep hill north of Cleary Summit and looked down on the Steese Highway winding its way through the goldfields of former times. We silently absorbed the immensity of the gold rush saga. Just down the hill to the left was "Last Chance Creek" and the "Newsboy Mine." A piece of old mining equipment, a rotted out wooden mine shaft and the snort of a grizzly in nearby bushes was all that was left of the bustling Newsboy Mine that Douglas had photographed in 1936

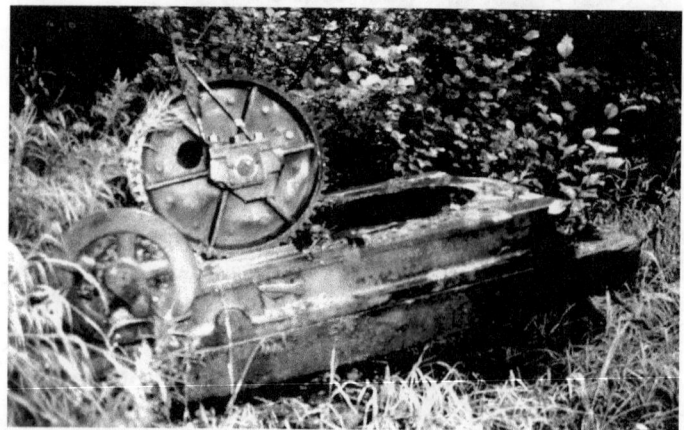

Cold, rainy, wet...looking for Newsboy Mine, Cleary Summit, AK. 2000   JDH

The closest we ever came to four of those five prized "Newsboy Mine area" photo locations was from afar. What is now a restricted area, was open land to a 1936 prospector with a camera in his hands.

Whether or not Douglas ever made it to the Arctic Circle Gold Rush Camp is pure speculation. He was out of film and money. Regardless of that though, by now he had a serious case of gold bug fever and a propensity for arranging rides in this harsh land above the 60.

We decided to turn *our* truck wheels northeast and travel to the end of the Steese Highway — totally unprepared for the breathtaking scenery that waited for us up ahead.

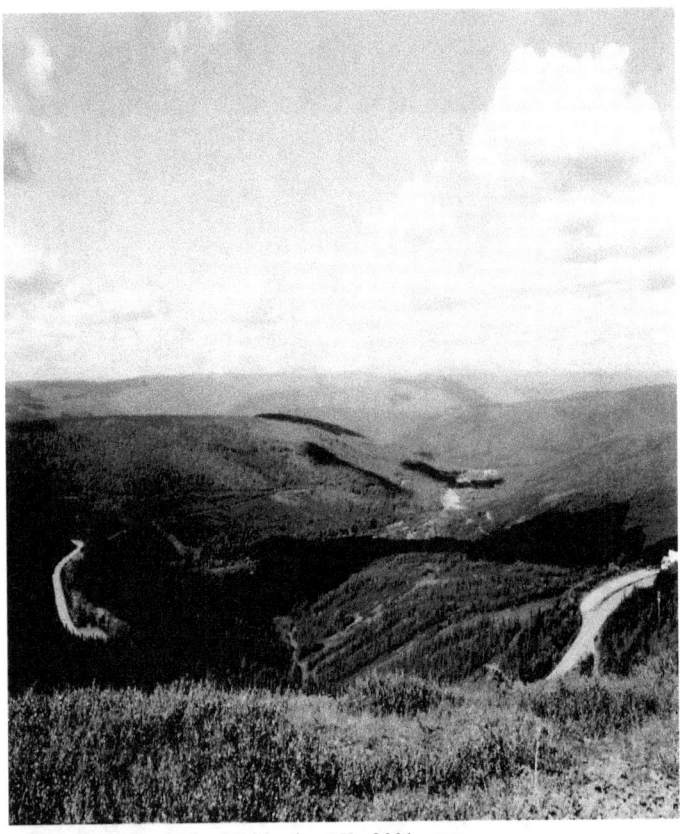

Cleary Summit, north of Fairbanks, AK. 2001   JDH

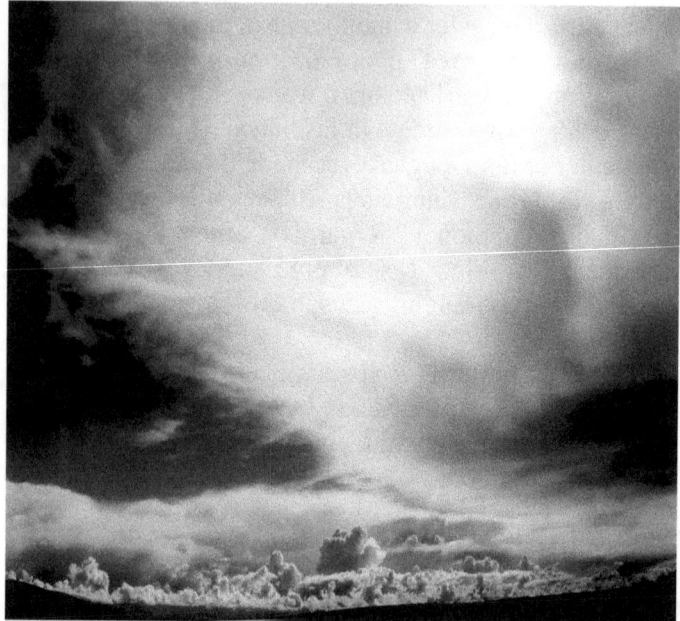

Steese Highway, Alaska. 2001   JDH

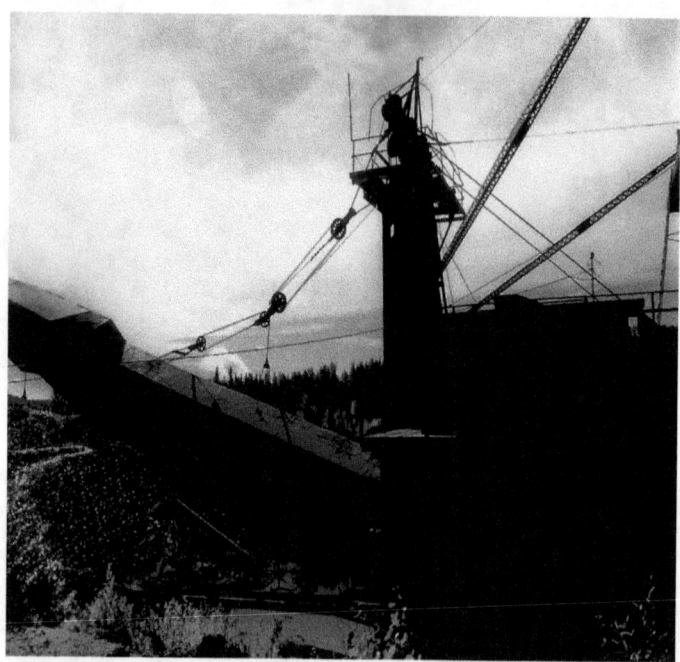

Goldstream Dredge No. 8...Fairbanks, AK. 2001   JDH

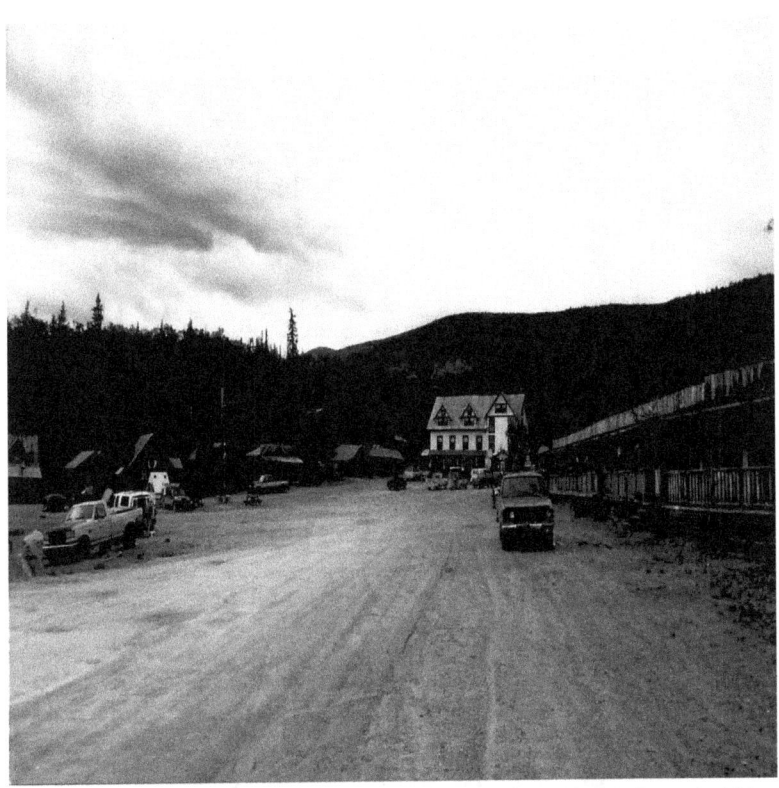

Arctic Circle Gold Rush Camp, Circle Hot Springs, Alaska. Our overnight truck can be seen to the L with Emory loading items. 2001 JDH

The one hundred and sixty-two mile journey to the Yukon River took us beyond the Chatanika gold Camp where the streets still sparkled in the midnight sun. The road took us past the ominous Davidson Ditch built in 1925 to carry water to float the monster dredges now abandoned, or used as tourist attractions.

The *droning* of our truck was not the only sound heard as we traveled through this incredibly desolate area to reach the old Arctic Circle Gold Rush Camp. The sounds of mining equipment tediously operating in the distant hills could be heard echoing the sounds of days gone by.

It was like driving back in time. The 1890's camp was used by prospectors involved in mining activities in the Steese Highway area. A natural hot springs made this a gathering place for "earlier" Athabaskans and a get away "today" for locals and tourists. We were fortunate to be able to visit with Harry Hughes, who lived in the left hand cabin to the main lodge. Hughes had a box of old tapes (a gold mine of history surprises) of *sounds* and *voices* from early Alaska.

119

Cushman St. Bridge (just after Midnight) Fairbanks, AK. July 20, 2001   JDH

Douglas took his three trunks over the old bridge, crossing the Chena River for the last time in the summer of 1936. The trunks were heavy with rocks from his gold seeking efforts. This time, no dog was by his side. He headed north past the Catholic church to the old train depot. This was an area known to many as the end of the line. Even though summer had just arrived, there was a coolness in the air, reminding him of the long, cold winter that would soon be coming again to this land 120 miles south of the Arctic Circle. By enduring an Alaska winter, Douglas had earned himself the title of "sourdough" replacing the lesser acquired title of cheechako (newcomer).

The chapter closed on this prospector's Fairbanks gold seeking quest. He left behind beckoning hills and creeks and a land overflowing with dreams and dreamers. A mere thirteen years earlier (1923), a train from the Alaska Railroad Company traveled its maiden voyage from Seward to Fairbanks, completing access to the western interior for the first time. In 1936 the mode of travel by auto from Nenana to Fairbanks was non existent. Dog sled, river travel and old trails were there for the robust travelers. The George Parks Highway did not reach completion until 1971.

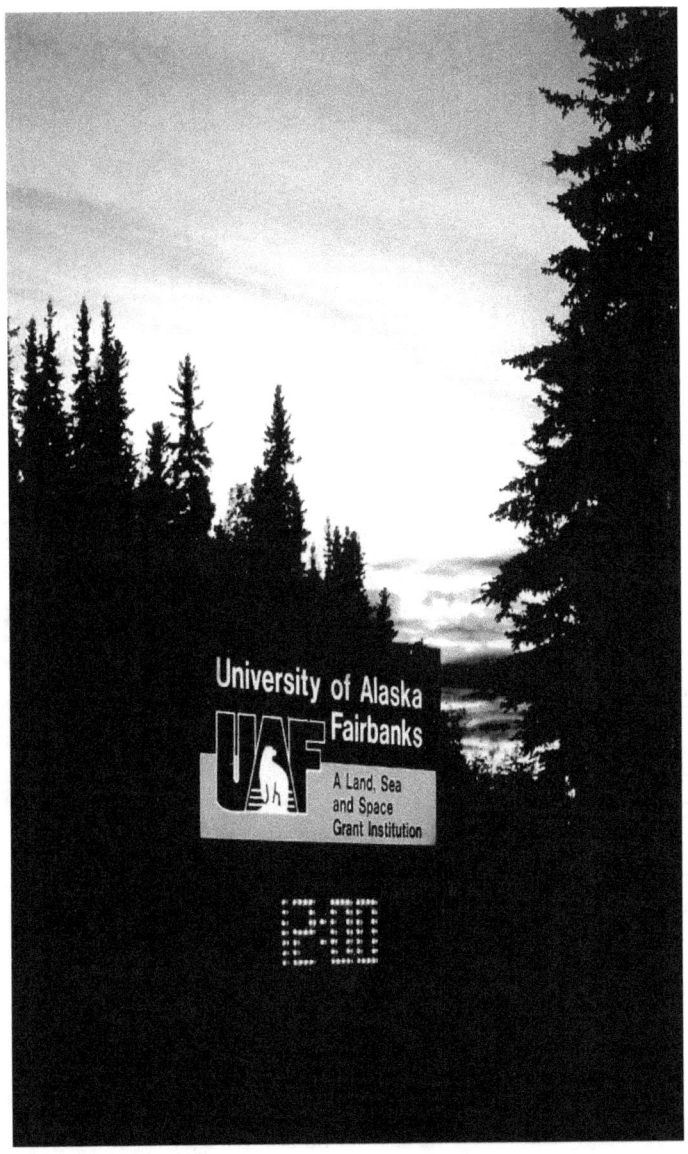

University of Alaska-Fairbanks (midnight). July 20, 2001   JDH

The present Cushman Street Bridge is made of concrete and steel. It flies the flags of all fifty states. In the distance can be seen the (relocated) Catholic church that once was positioned on the south banks of the Chena River in the early 1900's.

121

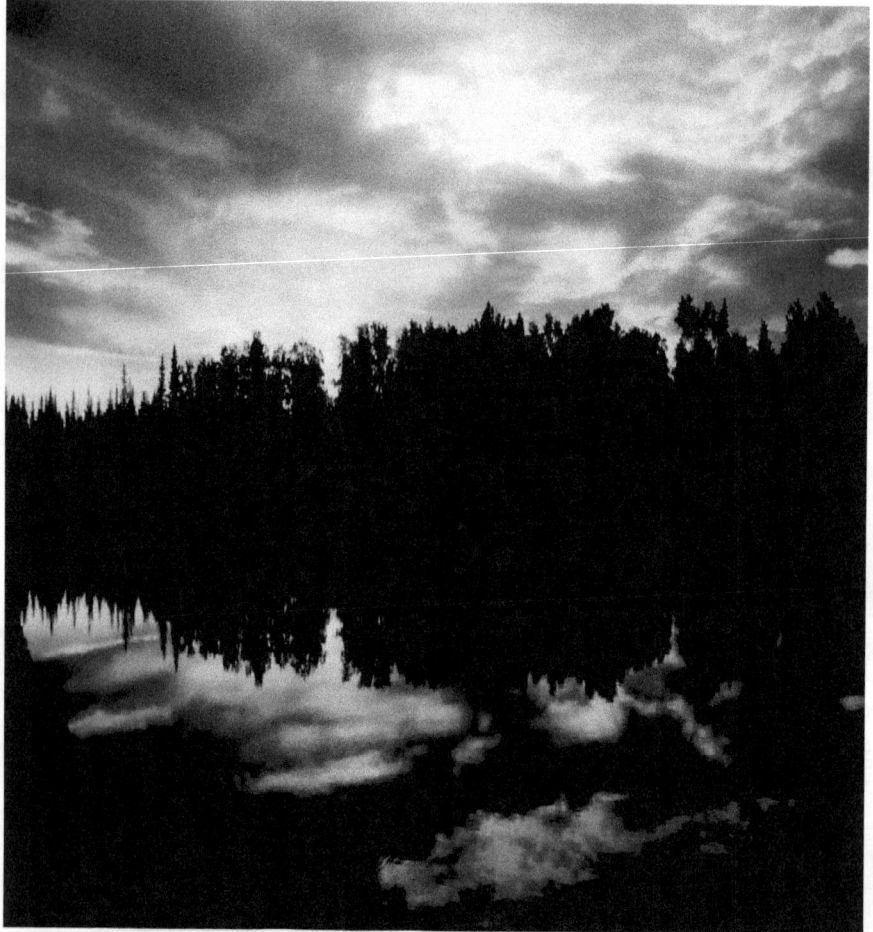

Chena River at Riverview RV Park, Fairbanks, Alaska. 2001   JDH

In 2001 the Chena River mirrored a sunset as golden as the hills and valleys it prevailed over. This land has been an enticement through the decades of brighter days to come. We left the skies of the midnight sun and turned south, as regretfully as did the prospector named Douglas in 1936.

The sourdough's head was still burning with "gold fever." Now he was surrounded by gold discoveries from the east, west, north and south as he prepared to enter the hopeful world of the Matanuska colonists he had heard so much about on his boat trip up to Valdez a year ago. There were canyons in Lazy Mountain that needed exploring and that Independence Mine on Hatcher Pass was most intriguing.

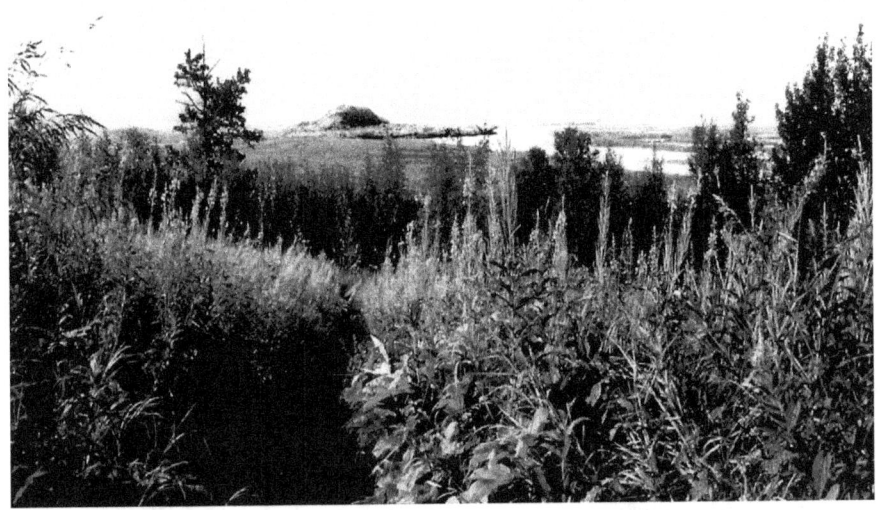

Matanuska Valley from Lazy Mountain (looking S), Palmer, AK. 2000 JDH

The Matanuska River (above) winds its way through the valley of Palmer into the Knik Arm. The water continues down past the Cook Inlet, eventually reaching the Gulf of Alaska and the open waters of the Pacific Ocean. The Bodenburg Butte (above) — raised land in the distance — we eventually climbed and photographed on July 4, 2001.

Less than six months prior, "Camp Palmer" was a tent city, while selected colonists from Wisconsin, Michigan and Minnesota waited for their houses to be built. Bingle tokens were used as a money source at the local commissary during the first half year of the colony's existence. Bingles were soon replaced by a work-credit system. Today, Bingle sets are worth several thousand dollars each.

Douglas most likely picked up some temporary work with the CCC (Civilian Conservation Corps), or perhaps the A.R.R.C. (Alaska Rural Rehabilitation Corporation) and began life in the fledgling community of the Matanuska Valley. Only one hundred miles of road connected the Matanuska and Susitna areas at that time. Infrastructure was still all but nonexistent. Electricity came to the valley in 1942. Douglas recorded mid-thirties Alaska with his camera until his ship sailed from Seward in late fall of 1936. The last two chapters have repeat photographs when possible.

123

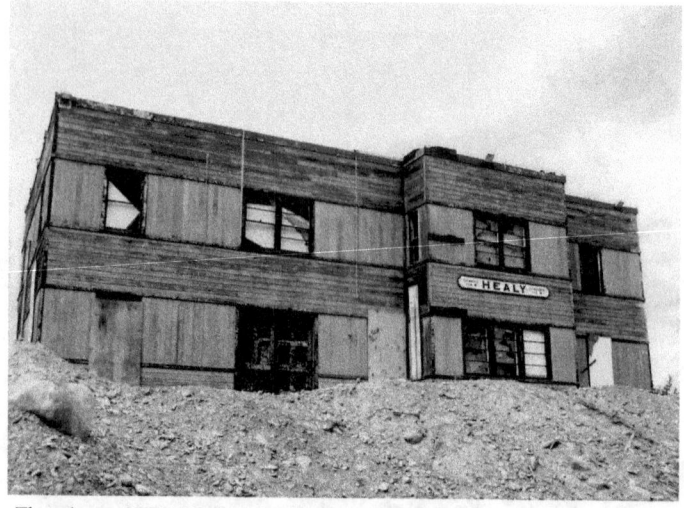

The relocated HEALY DEPOT, Healy, Alaska. 2001   JDH

The Healy depot sat stoically on top of a hill awaiting its renovation. The depot was once located close to the "old" Alaska Railroad tracks. In 1936, a train stopped en route to the Matanuska Valley and a few passengers disembarked. Was the sun shining on Mount McKinley (20,320 feet) that day, as the train continued south?

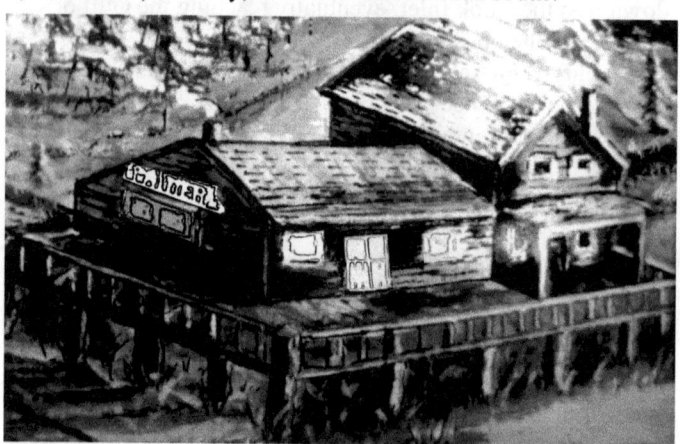

Illustration 6. The "new" MATANUSKA VALLEY DEPOT. 1936.

A steam train from Fairbanks *clattered* to a halt at the original Matanuska depot, not yet a year old. The train stopped long enough for a few passengers to disembark. Local goods such as vegetables and products from the creamery were loaded aboard and the train disappeared down the tracks toward Anchorage.

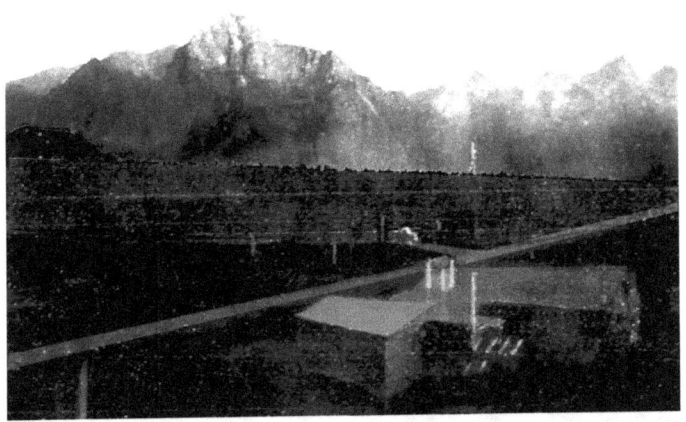

"Mountain southeast of Palmer, Alaska is Mount Pioneer, elevation 7,400 feet... (note the Butte at center left and an old truck at the cross roads)...June 15, 1936" RAD

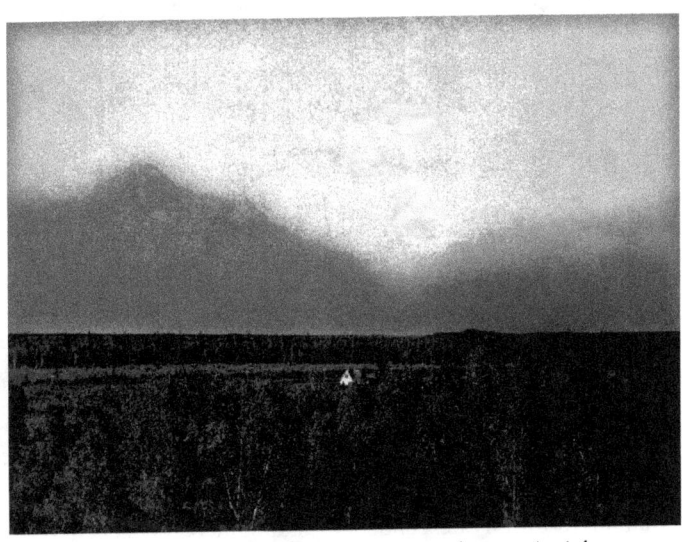

"A Matanuska colonist farm...Mount Pioneer, looking southeast in Palmer, Alaska...June 15, 1936" RAD

Mount Pioneer is barely visible under the veil of early, minimal quality photography. The Bodenburg Butte can be seen low on the horizon (center right).

125

2001 Palmer, Alaska

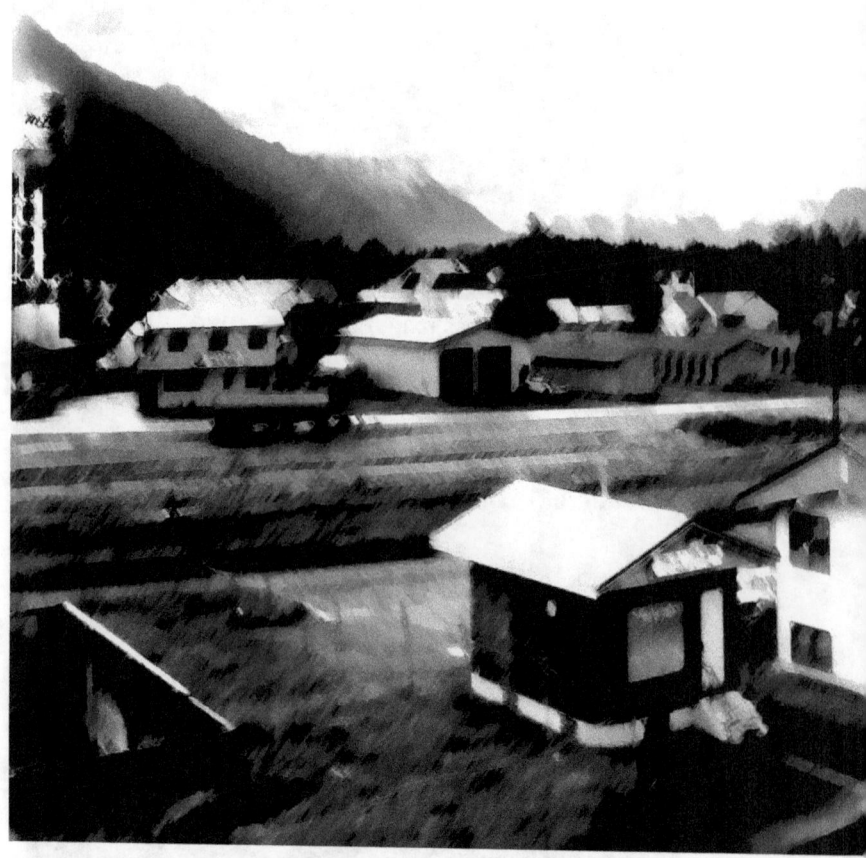

   Palmer still remains a small town with many of the original Matanuska Colony descendents residing there. This active community — located northeast of Anchorage — is known for its valley peas and roadside stands. Vegetables grow unusually large due to a growing season of 80 to 110 days of almost constant light. Musk ox, descending from the ice age, still survive well in this area.

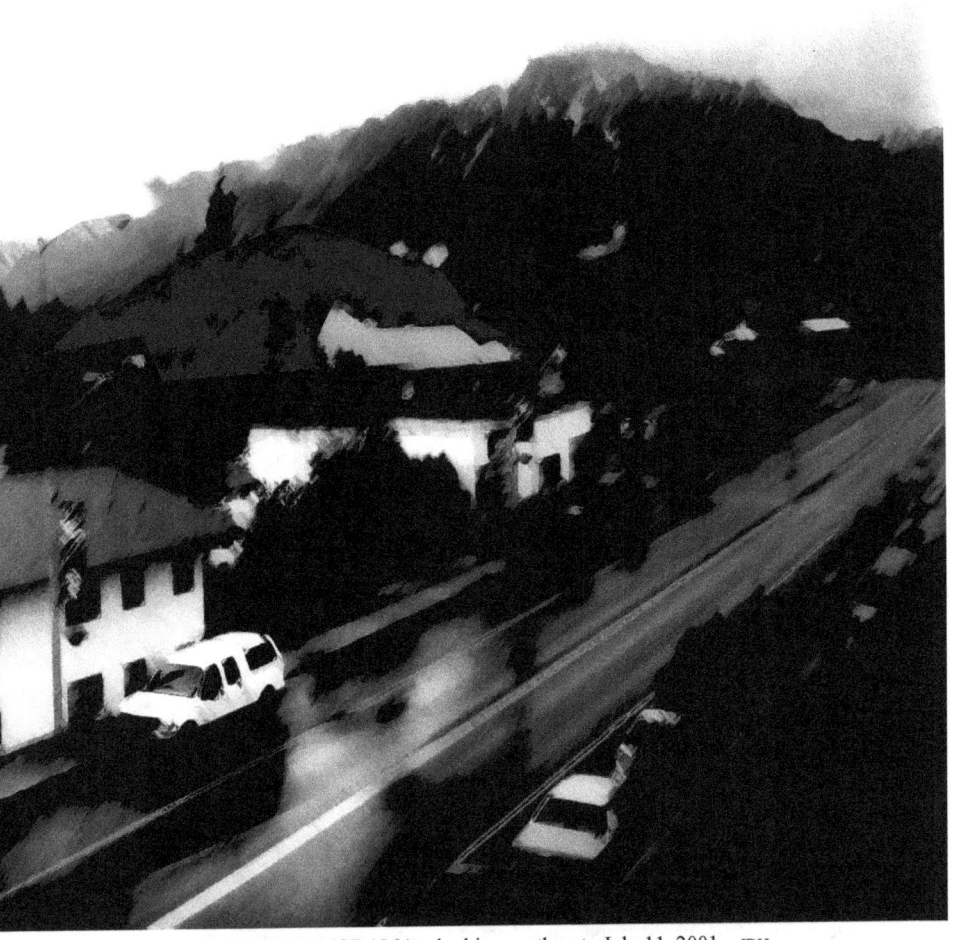

PALMER PANORAMA…looking southeast…July 11, 2001   JDH

Courtesy of the Palmer Hotel, we were able to position ourselves on the roof for an exclusive 2001 Palmer Pano-rama. This time, the water tower (upper left) that Douglas may have climbed in 1936 to achieve *his* Palmer Panorama, was included in this photograph. In the distance (upper right center) is the Bodenburg Butte above the old train depot.

127

The isolated 1936 colonist farm on page 125 demonstrates the richness of land, lack of roads and remoteness of location. The absence of electricity during the extended daylight hours of summer, before 1942, were not as much of a hardship as were the long, dark cold days of winter.

There was a variation of floor plans to choose from. While the colonists waited in tents for their homes to be constructed, they selected one of five designs — alterations were allowed according to budget.

Even the promise of a nice home was not enough to entice some of the typically tough Scandinavian farmers to stay. These were farmers who had been through the Midwest dust bowl years, a period of high winds, no rain and relentless heat in the early 1930's. They had also just been through the beginning years of the great depression. There was not a doctor or hospital facility set up in the colony yet. Three children had already died and six families had returned to the lower forty-eight. Eventually, sixty percent of the original colonists left. Replacements were selected through 1940.

Douglas's 1936 Matanuska Valley photos indicated that he climbed up Lazy Mountain on July 4th, alone. Soon after, the photographs begin to reveal social activities as Douglas befriended a replacement colony family and their friends. Alaska residents were now the focus of his photography. The photographs created a brief, but fascinating, pictorial account of the lives and times of various colonists in the Matanuska Valley, during their second summer of existence.

The first and most popular manager of the Alaska project was Don L. Irwin. He and his family made their home in the Matanuska Valley. Before coming to Alaska, Irwin was Wyoming's state agricultural planner for nineteen years. Through patience and encouragement, he held the colony together during the early months of its infancy. He cherished the valley and wrote music and lyrics to reflect it. The music was titled "Where the Matanuska Flows." Irwin referred to the area in lyrics as "happy valley." He was also an established author.

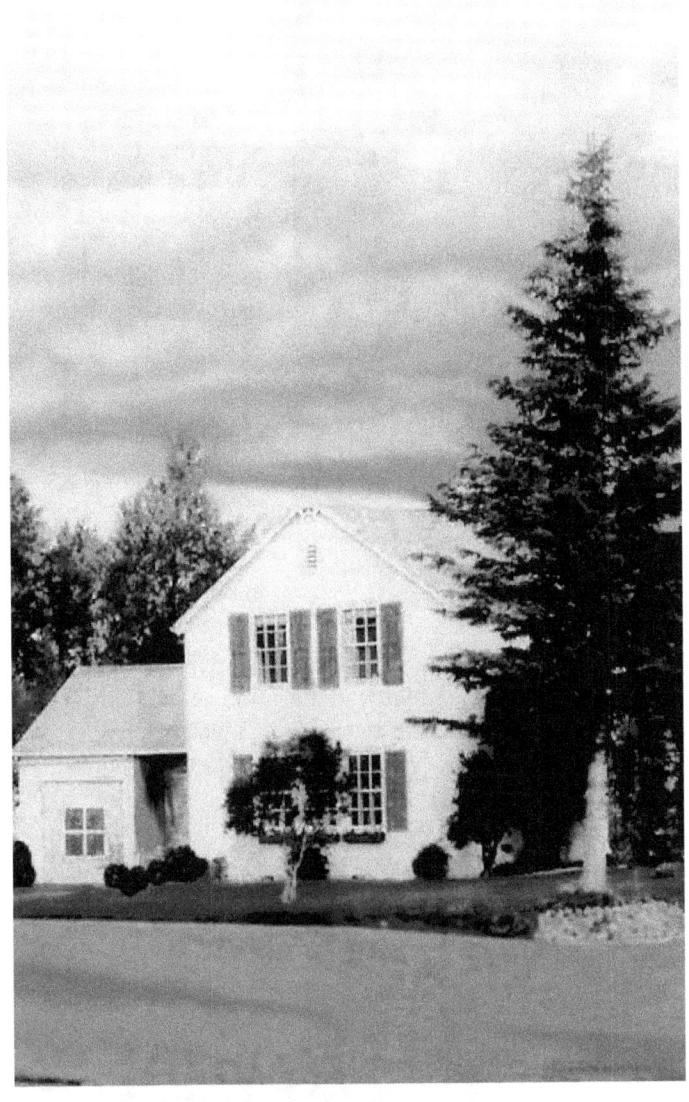
A 2001 view of the colony manager's house, Palmer, AK.   JDH

Imagine the way it was on a little dirt street across from the dormitory building in 1936. The colony manager's house stood taller than other staff houses. It was the only two story plan constructed at that time. It housed the A.R.R.C. managers through the years and is now privately owned.

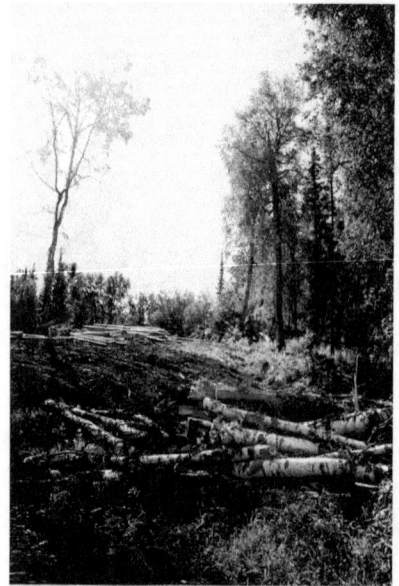

Farm Loop Road, Palmer, Alaska.
August 7, 2000   JDH

In the early thirties the population of Alaska was about sixty thousand. This was an area of land considerably larger than Norway, Finland and Sweden combined. The total population in these three countries was roughly thirteen million. Was it privately envisioned to send a million families up to Alaska? Military defense was very much interested in populating and securing the land. Two thousand families from Texas wanting to become Alaska pioneers were ignored, while two hundred families from the north central lower-forty eight were chosen — states with a much harsher climate. The success of the first colony was of the utmost importance.

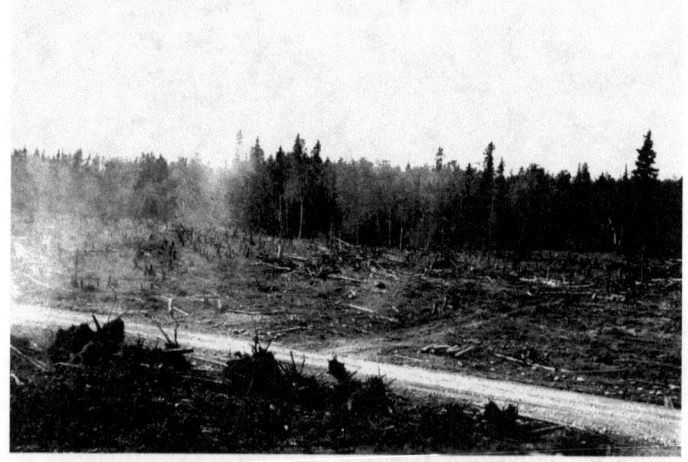

"A Matanuska stump ranch...clearing land for a farmer...Palmer, Alaska...June 15, 1936" RAD

130

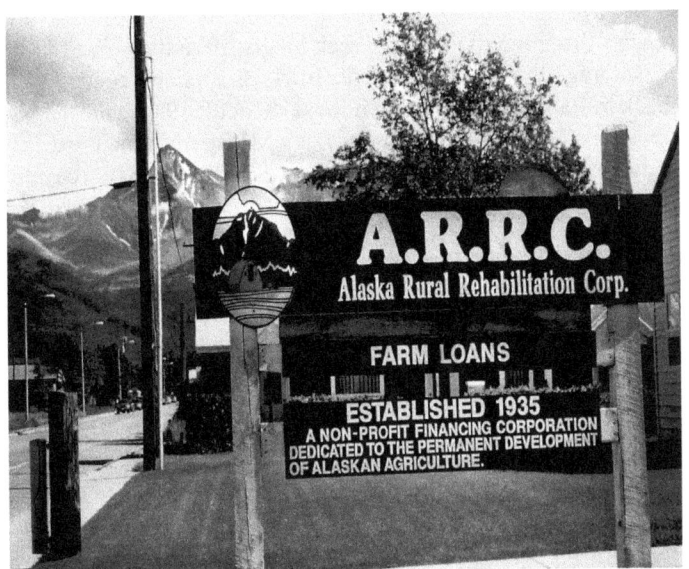

The relocated Alaska Rural Rehabilitation Corp., Palmer, AK. 2000   JDH

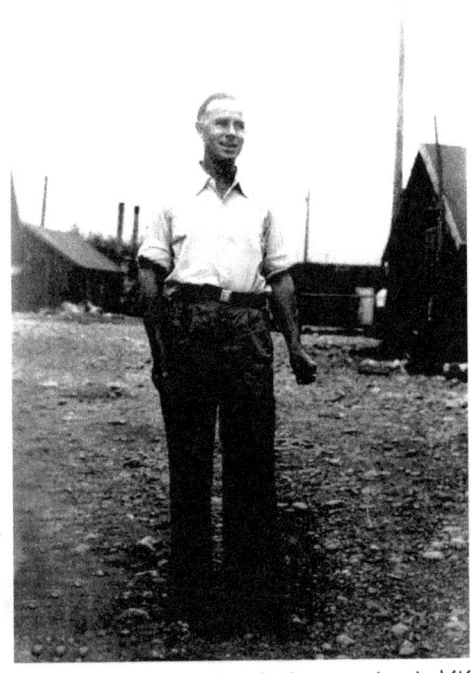

Randolph Angus Douglas at the Alaska Rural Rehabilitation
Corp., Palmer AK...June 15, 1936   RAD

After dropping the Ahtell Creek hikers off at the airport in Anchorage in 2000, we rented a truck camper and headed back to Palmer to photograph those difficult 1936 photo locations on the three ridges of Lazy Mountain. The third ridge had an elevation of 3,720 feet (depending on source).

The trailhead began a short drive up from the town of Palmer (approximately 800 feet elevation). The air traffic control center in Palmer is 248 feet above sea level.

After achieving repeat photography on the first ridge, turning back was discussed. It was a steep climb up a slippery, unpredictable trail. We used tree branches as handholds to keep from sliding back down the vertical muddy incline.

Bad weather was closing in and we had no guarantee of a photo opportunity on the third ridge, but we continued on. The last ridge I climbed alone throwing caution to the wind — rationalizing, who would want to climb up that first, extremely steep, muddy embankment
for a second attempt?

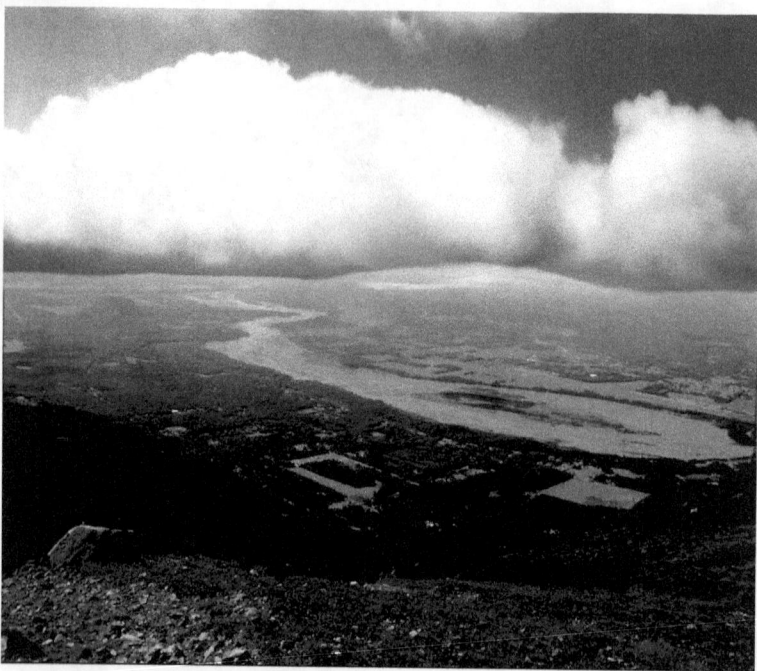

First ridge of Lazy Mountain, Palmer, Alaska. August 8, 2000   JDH

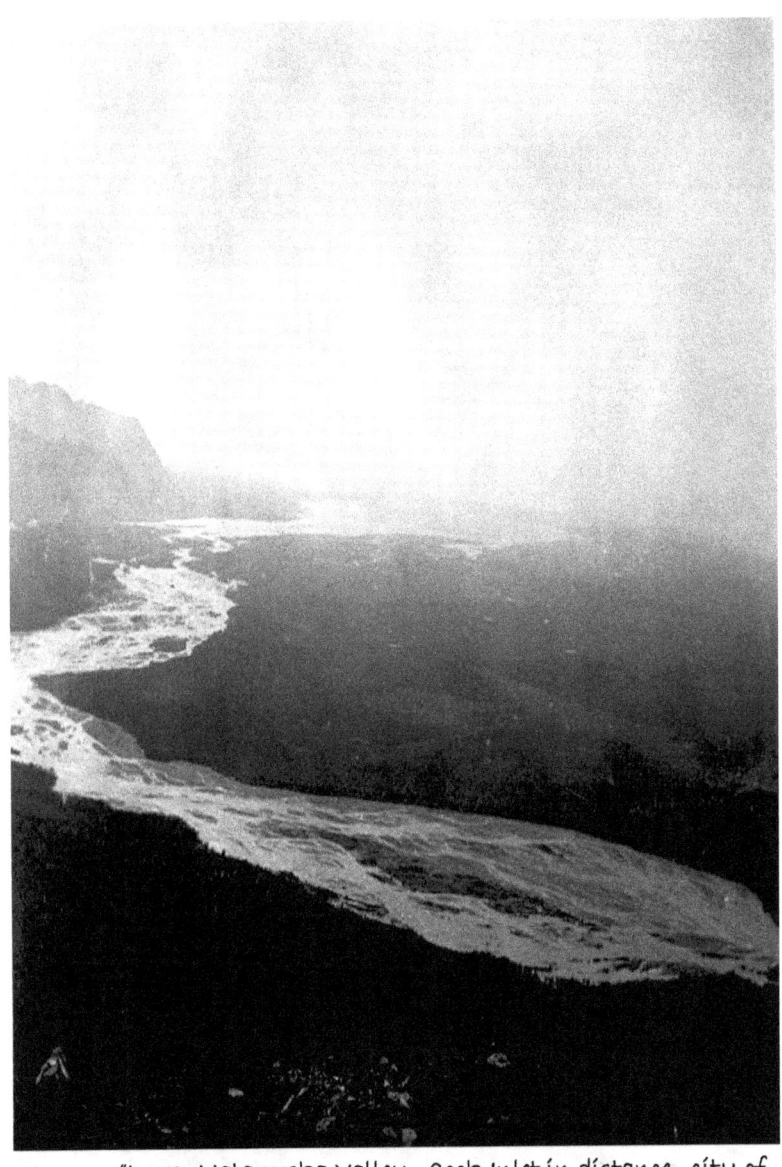

"Lower Matanuska Valley...Cook Inlet in distance...city of
Anchorage just before farthest mountains...photo taken
from Lazy Mountain looking south...Palmer, Alaska...
July 4, 1936" RAD

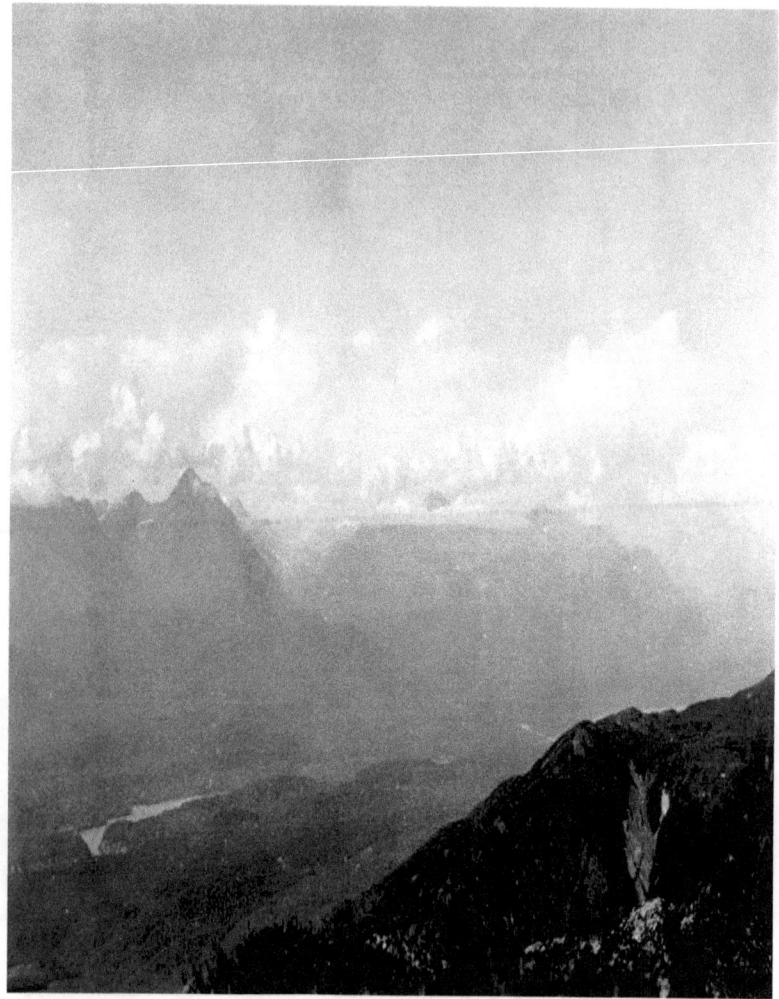

"Upper Matanuska River Valley...Alaska...photo taken
from top of Lazy Mountain...looking north"   RAD

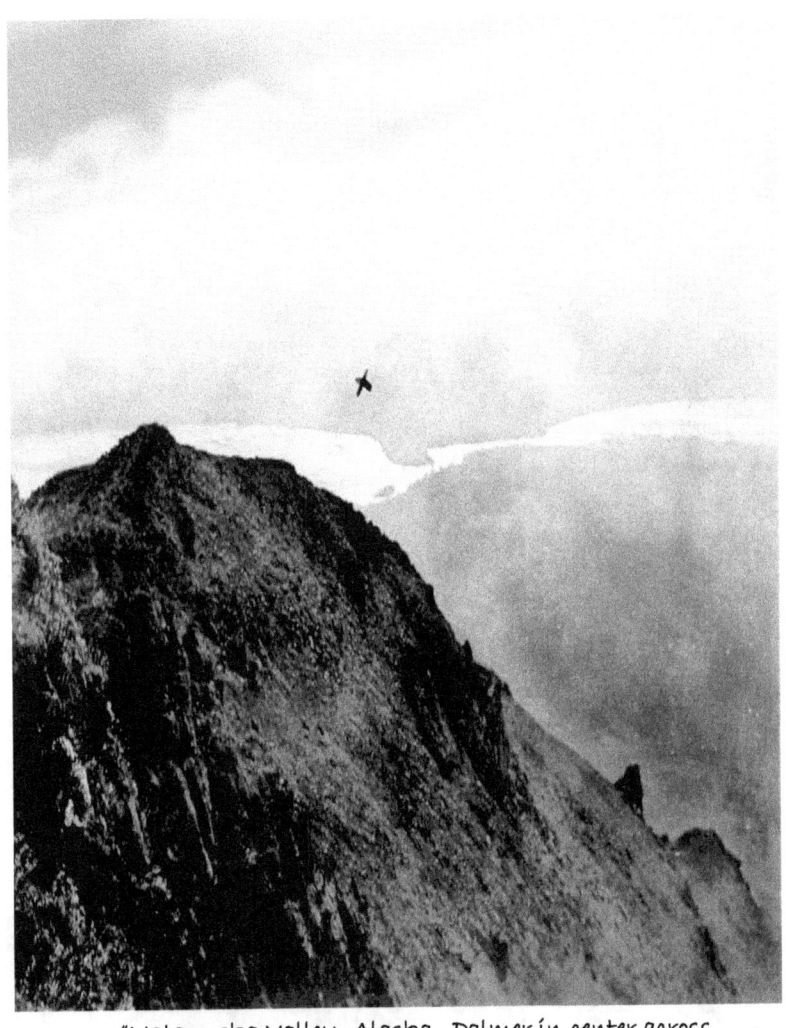

"Matanuska Valley, Alaska...Palmer in center across river...July 4, 1936" RAD

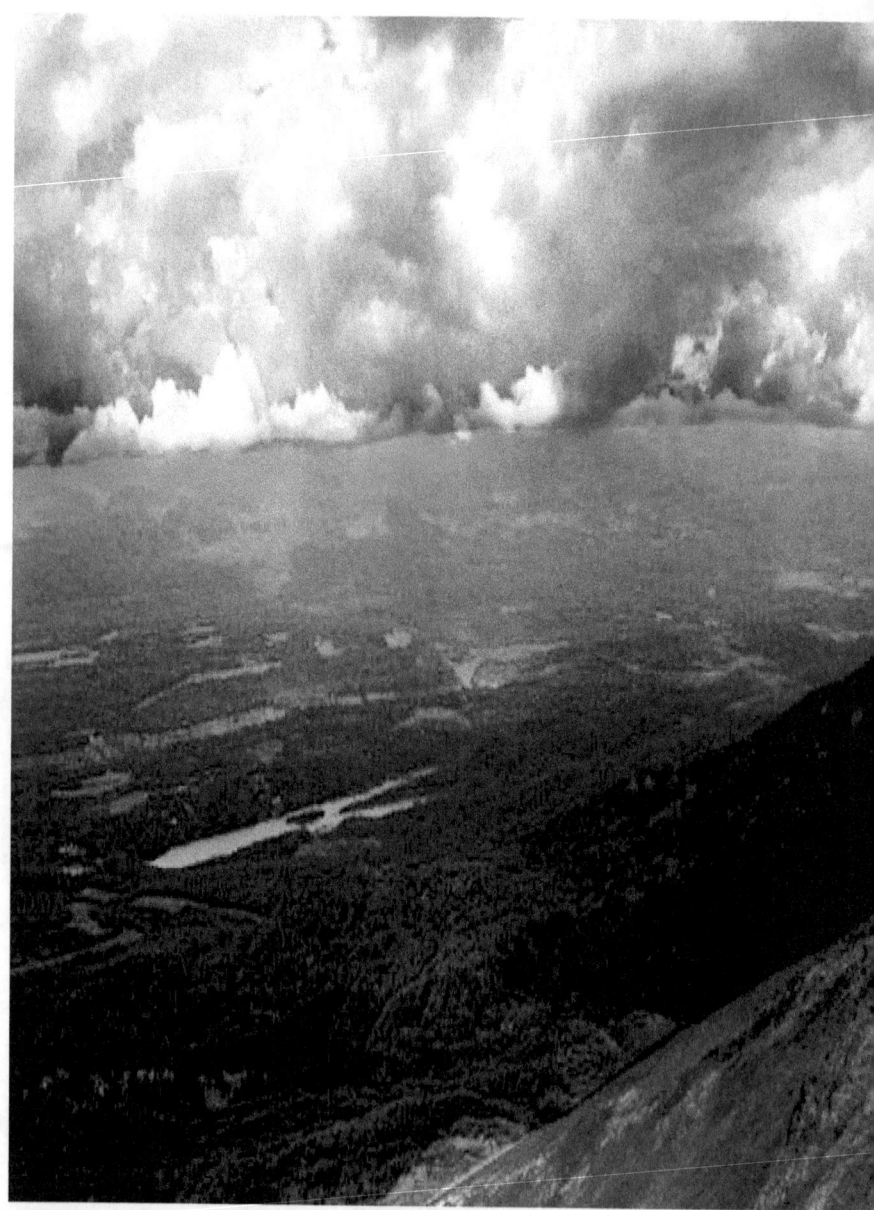

Lazy Mountain looking north (third ridge), Palmer, Alaska.
August 8, 2000   JDH

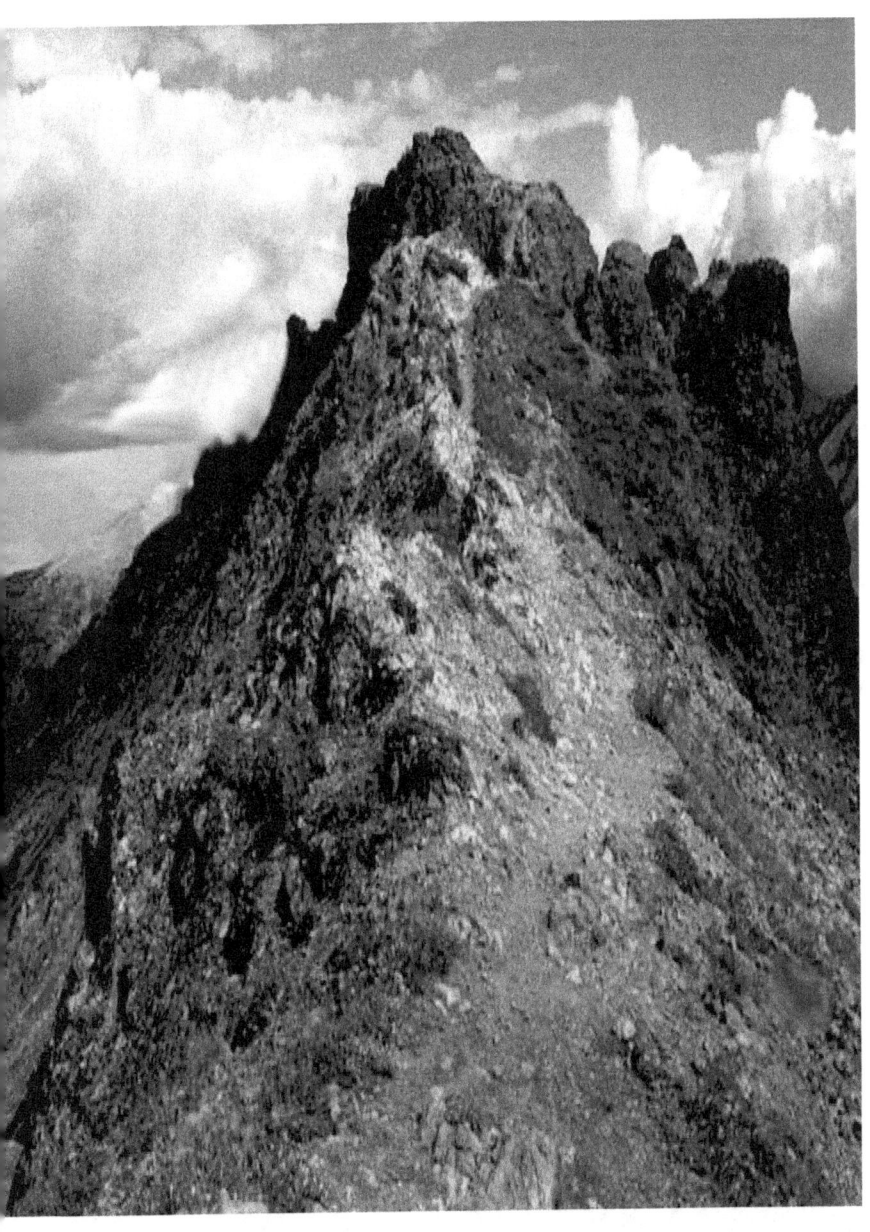

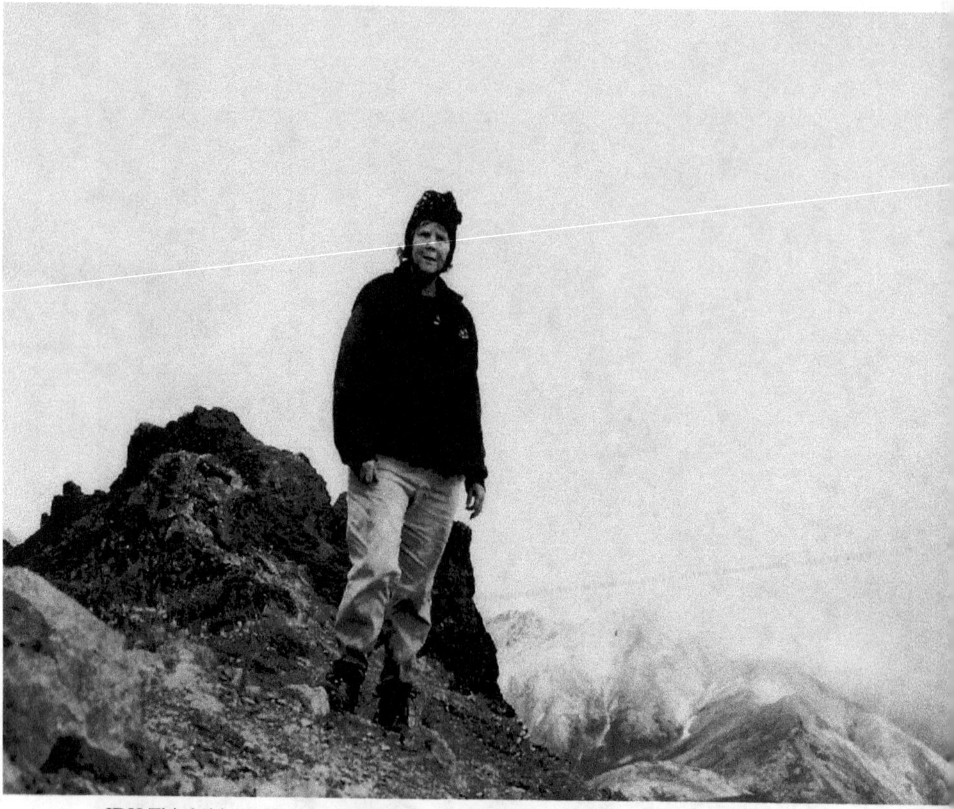

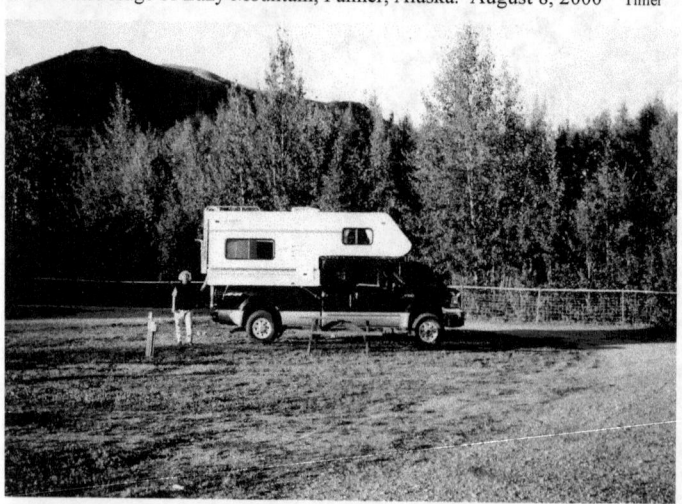

JDH Third ridge of Lazy Mountain, Palmer, Alaska. August 8, 2000   Timer

Author by truck camper at Mountain View RV Park. Lazy Mt. in
background. 2000   UEH

138

2000—The trail narrowed on the final ascent. I steadied the camera with shaking hands and pushed the timer button. Standing high atop the third ridge of Lazy Mountain, unaccompanied and shrouded in clouds, I waited for the *click*. It is hard to explain, but for a moment I became one with the prospector.

Down below unbeknown to us at the time, a young couple sat in their car and waited for us to return. This mountain came with a reputation...peaking at 3,720 feet.

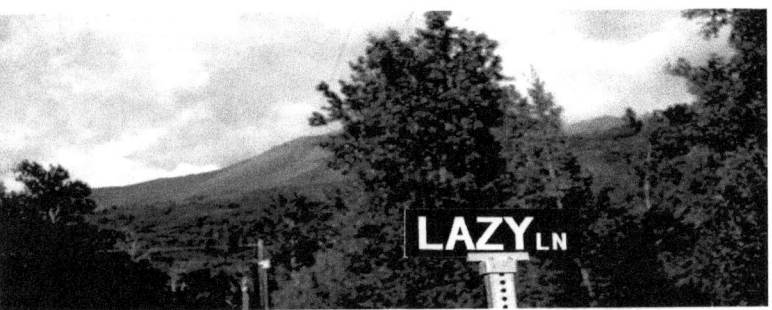

1936—Within weeks of the prospector's 1936 fourth of July climb up Lazy Mountain, he befriended a newly arrived "replacement" family. Douglas genuinely enjoyed their company and was getting used to his new social life in the valley. Even if only for a moment, he had entertained thoughts of returning to this area one day.

Maybe he could talk some of his gold mining friends in North Carolina into joining him for a future trip to Alaska. How would he describe this land of wonder "above the 60," as Alaskans say it? Photographs? Unfortunately, the images of yesterday are not what they are today, and his words did not adequately describe the awe he had just witnessed.

Like prospectors through the decades, the reality of relocating back to the lower forty-eight was upon him.

Gold was not found in Douglas's pan in the rushing creeks of the Ahtell Creek Valley, north of Slana. His pan remained empty in the deep, dark canyons of Mineral Creek in Valdez and the limitless stretch of goldfields north of Fairbanks. His expectations for discovering gold were left unfulfilled in the canyons of Lazy Mountain in the Matanuska Valley.

In spite of this, Douglas left behind a notable trail of intriguing photographs for all adventurous spirits to follow, a trail for the footsteps of tomorrow. This was *his* gold — left for all to mine.

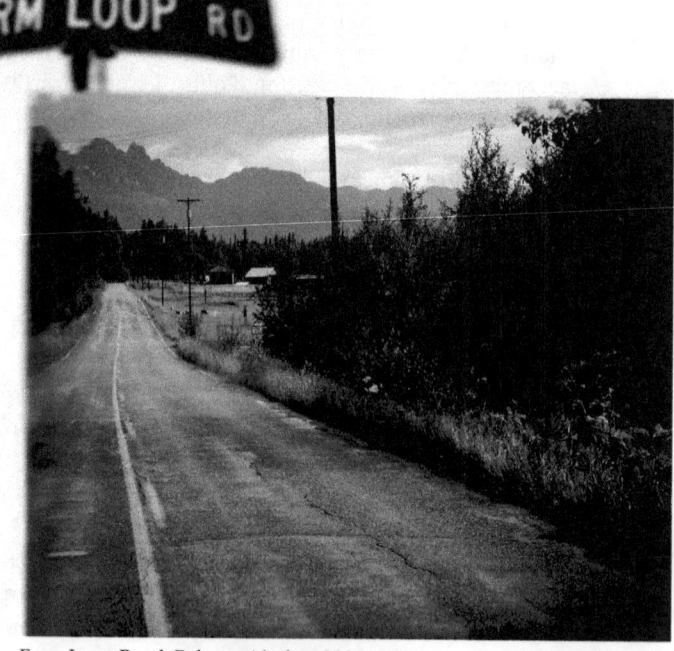

Farm Loop Road, Palmer, Alaska. 2001   JDH

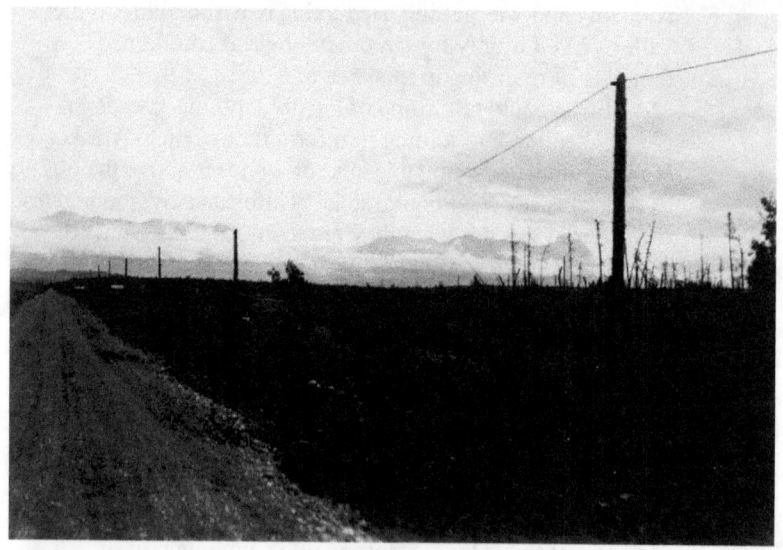

"Farm Road...Palmer, Alaska...1936"   RAD

"I had walked that road a good many times," said an elderly replacement colonist in an interview in Oregon. 2001   JDH

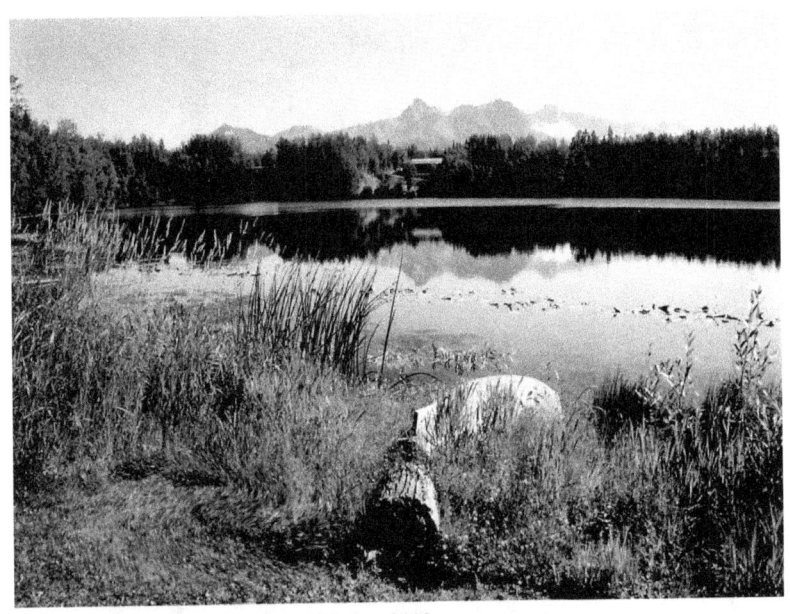

Meier's Lake, Palmer, Alaska. 2000   JDH

A long time ago *voices*, *splashes* and *laughter* could be heard from the shores of this now silent lake. Douglas integrated into the valley life, working and joining in on the merriment of off days—and the grass was so green.

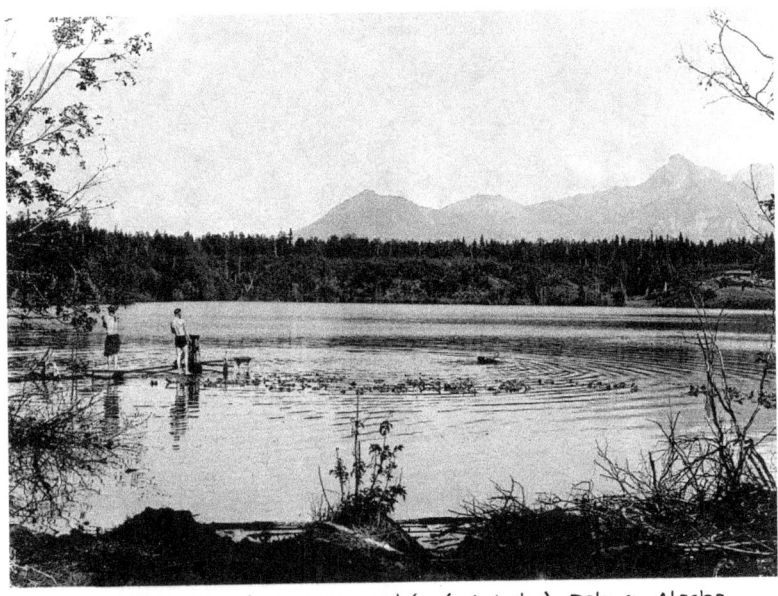

"Swimming in Myer's Pond (Meier's Lake)...Palmer, Alaska ...July 19, 1936" RAD

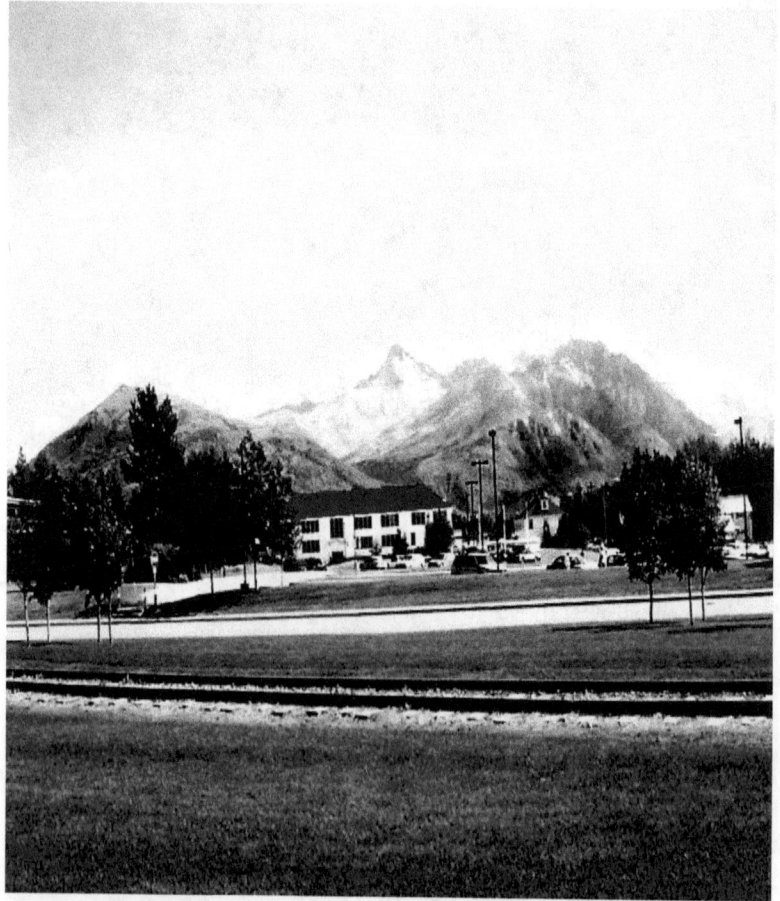

Original schoolhouse and civic center, Palmer, Alaska. 2000   JDH

   The three story building (center) is now the Mat-Su
Borough office building. The dormitory building, (right of
center) is a privately owned inn and restaurant. It used to
house the school teachers and travelers needing a temporary
place to stay. The two-story colony manager's house can be
seen in the distance (right).

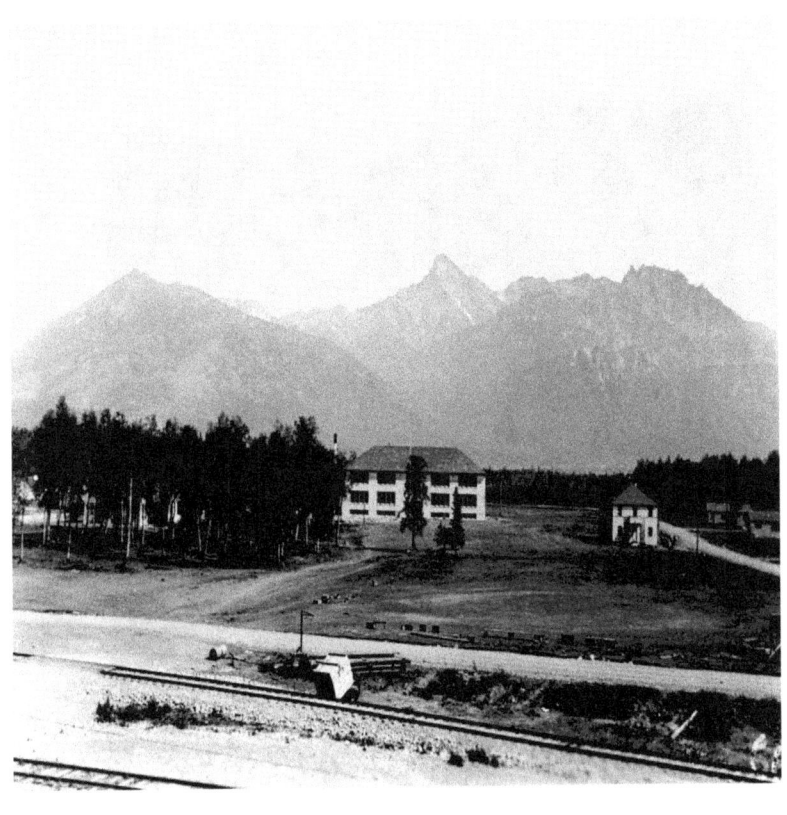

"Civic center (center)...colonist school ball diamond (right front)...Lazy Mountain (distant upper left) ...Matanuska Peak (Buyer's Ridge, distant center)...Palmer, Alaska... July 19, 1936" RAD

The first year colony children were under the direction of traveling teachers until their school (above center) was completed by the A.R.R.C. in 1935-36. This was the first territorial school in Palmer serving elementary through high school students. The school operated from 1935 to 1975.

Palmer acquired its name from a Pennsylvanian named George Palmer. He was the first white resident to arrive in the Mat-Su Valley in 1875. He established a trading post around 1890 along the Matanuska River and in 1903 Palmer's Store" was constructed in old Knik. It was not until 1951 that the "city" of Palmer was established.

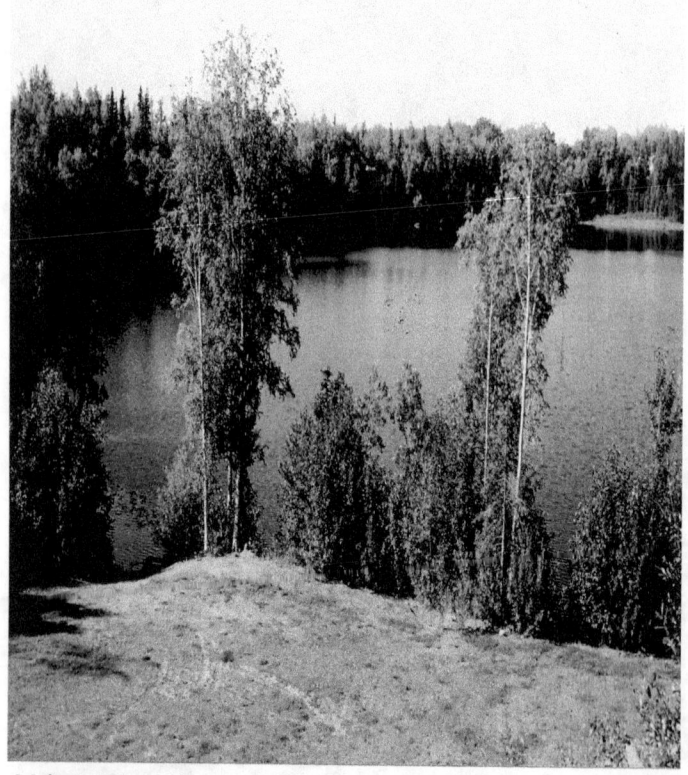

Meier's Lake, Palmer, Alaska. 2000   JDH

A soundless picnic ground on the northeast side of Meier's Lake is all that remains of the joyful gatherings of the early Matanuska Valley colonists.

Meeting with some of the original colonists and several replacement colonists in 2001 was like dabbling in time travel. Young voices that were conversing in 1936 were now happily chatting to me through aged bodies about earlier times. I had not anticipated meeting any of the actual Fish Creek picnickers. How fortunate to be able to contact some of the early valley homesteaders — colonists that were in the early pictures and others that were not.

Interviewing "colony kids", including the first born baby, the youngest one to arrive and the girl whose father told her to jump off the train so that she would be the first colonist to arrive in the Mantanuska Valley was a great honor.

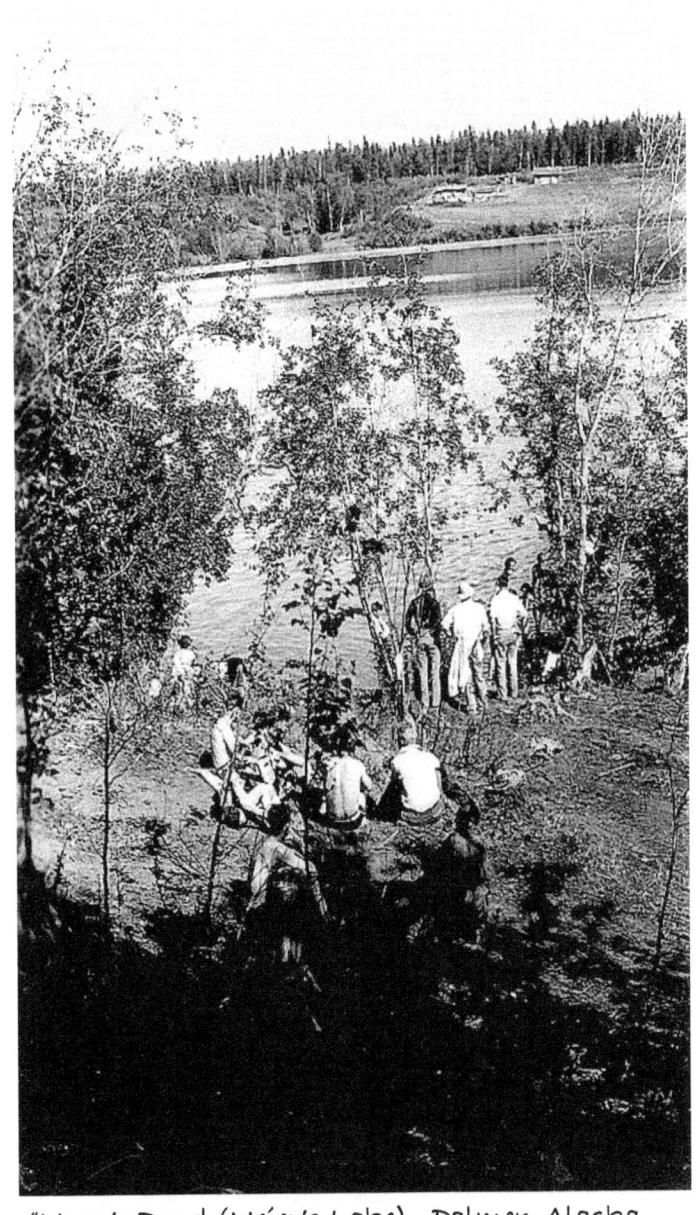

"Myer's Pond (Meier's Lake)...Palmer, Alaska...
July 19, 1936"   RAD

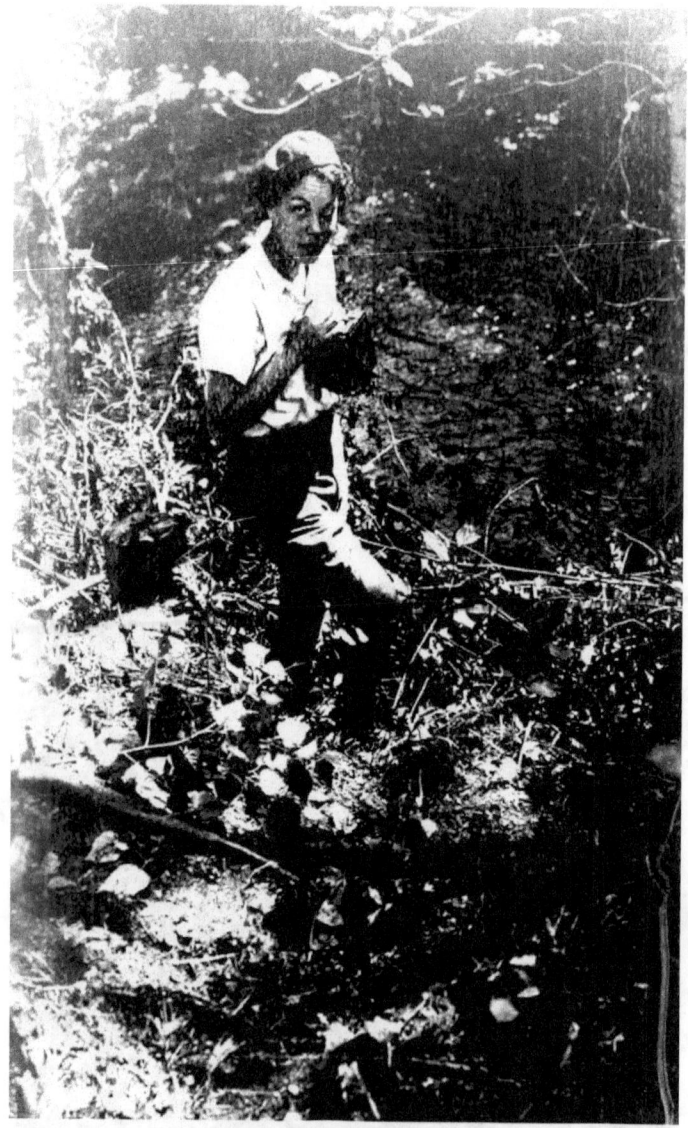

"Virginia Broostrom (replacement coloist)...Fish
Creek near old Knik...Matanuska Valley,
Alaska...July 26, 1936"   RAD

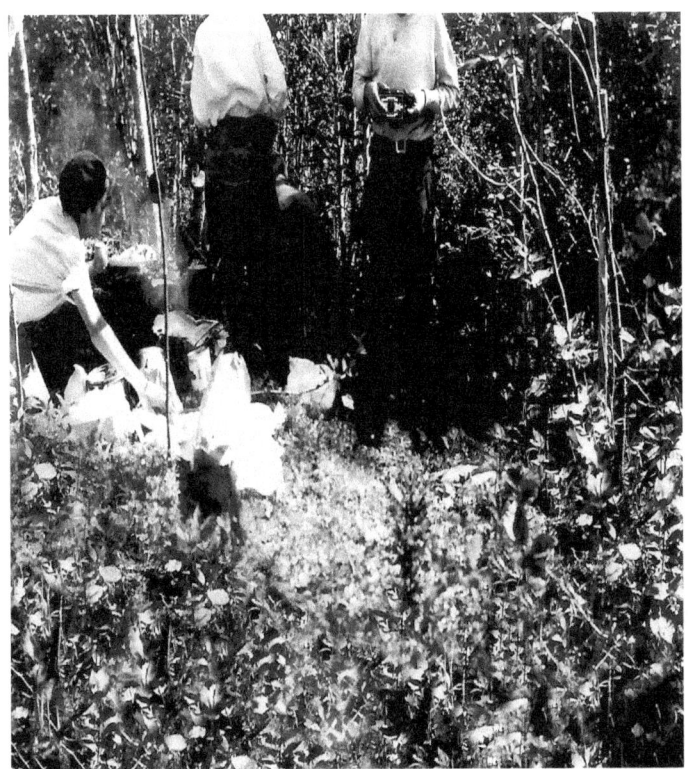

"Hotdogs and coffee (with Matanuska Colonists)
...Fish Creek near old Knik...Matanuska Valley,
Alaska...July 26, 1936" RAD

There are many "Fish Creeks" in Alaska, but only one
traveled to by a group of enthusiastic Matanuska colonists
on July 26, 1936. They drove on a stretch of unpaved road
traveling south from Wasilla to old Knik. The town is now
hidden in the folds of an Alaska topographic map. *This* Fish
Creek is located just west of Knik.

Travel to Knik would have been an all-day adventure. The
creek's reputation for fish was the obvious attraction. What
a refreshing change of menu to compliment all those large,
tasty vegetables being grown!

The word Knik is derived from a Tanaina Indian Village
name meaning "fire." Originally the name was spelled
"Kinik" which explains its present day pronunciation. The
town of Knik developed with the beginning of the gold rush
years in 1898.

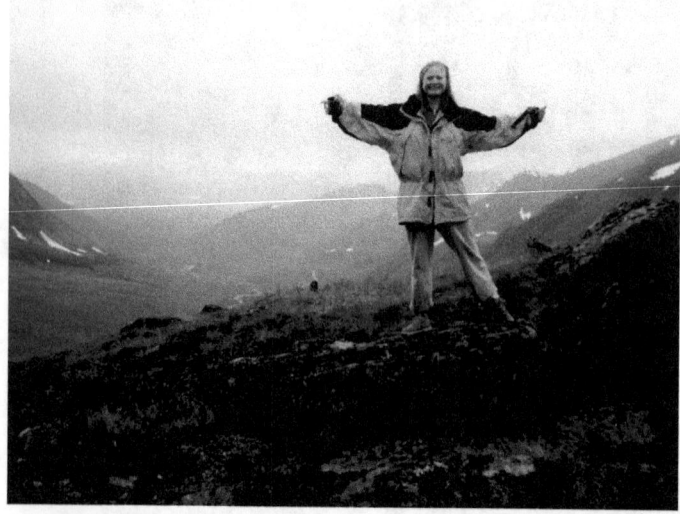

Diane heading up to Hatcher Pass. 2000   HDV

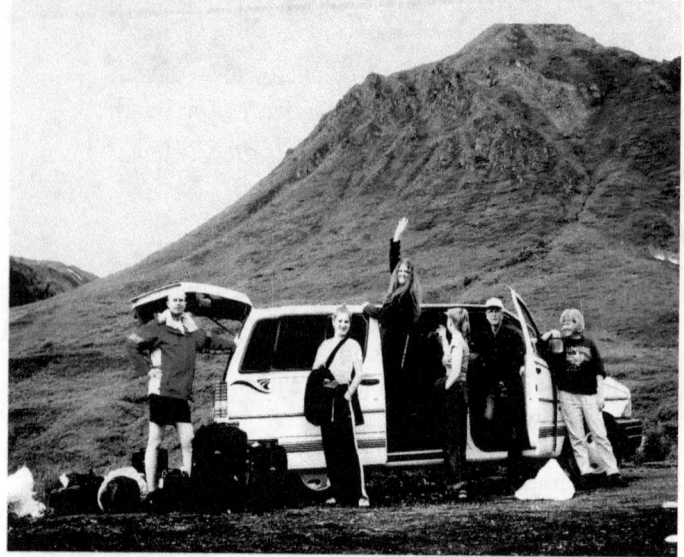

Ken, Heather, Alison, Diane, Emory and Jill en route to the summit
of Hatcher Pass, Alaska. 2000   Timer

The mountains were kicking and the road was jagged, as
fog moved in on this "van" load of fun. It was July 29, 2000,
and it was time to celebrate. Today was Douglas's birthday.
He would have been 99 years old.

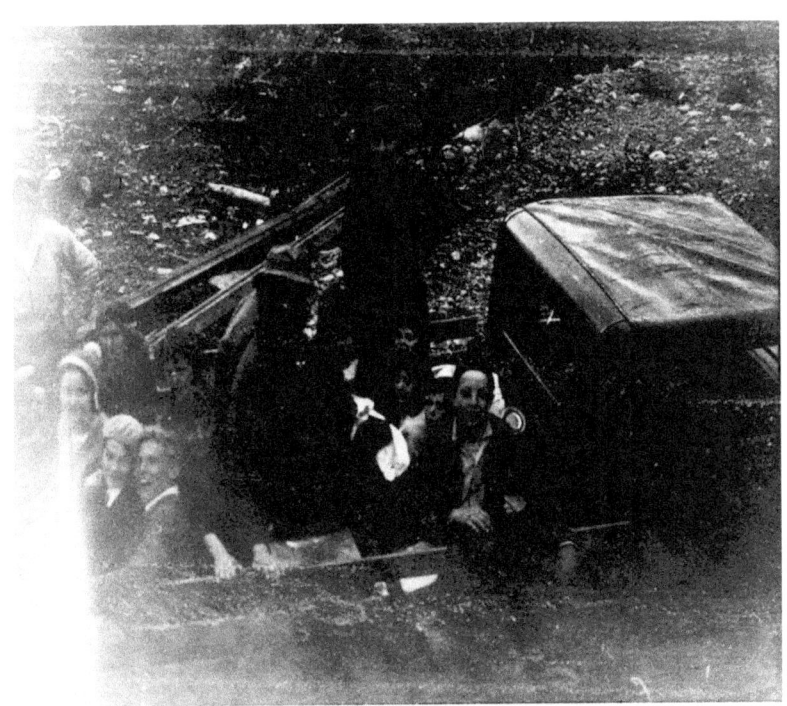

"A truck load of fun heads to Lucky Shot Mine
(Matanuska colonists)...Palmer, Alaska...
August 9, 1936" RAD

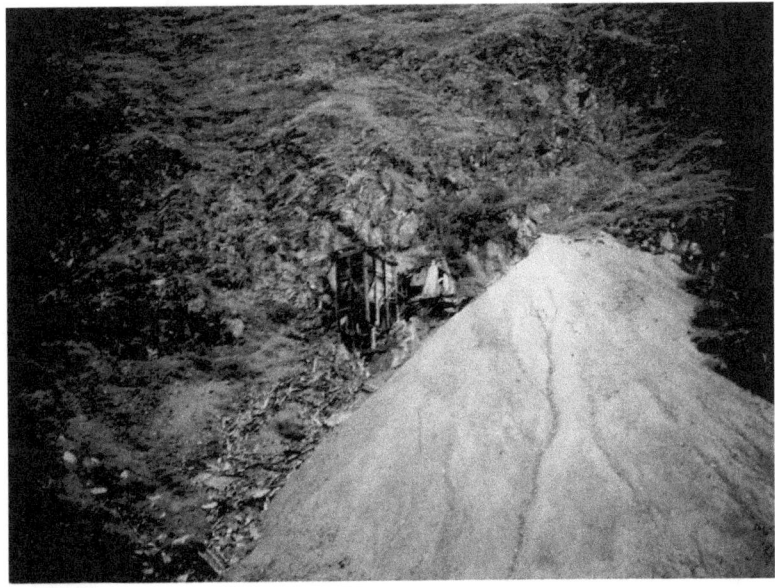

Lucky Shot Mine, Hatcher Pass, Alaska. 2000   JDH

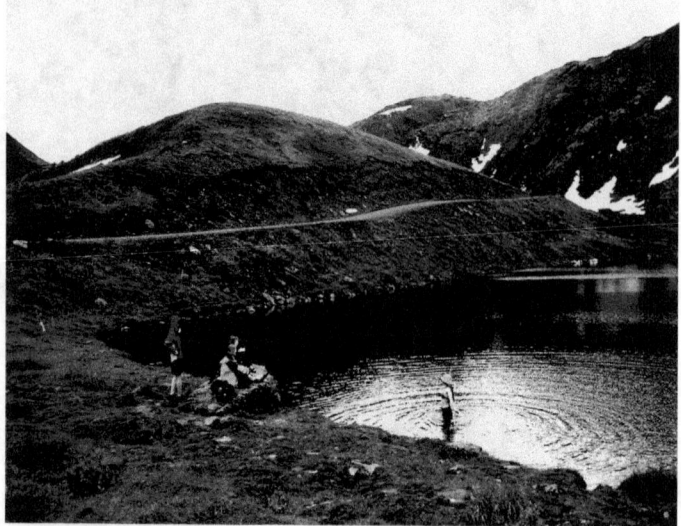

Ken, Diane, Heather and Alison at Summit Lake on Hatcher Pass,
(north of) Palmer, Alaska. 2000   JDH

Like a polar bear in the Arctic, Alison tested the ice-fed
water at Summit Lake on Hatcher Pass. To be a member of
the Summit Lake Polar Bear Club you had to submerge
completely under. In 2000 Alison and the author took the
challenge while others preferred to be spectators.

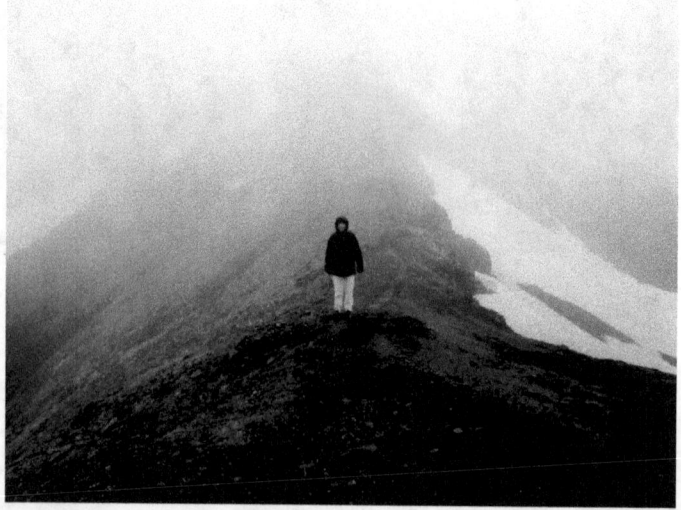

Author on the Hatcher Pass Ridge trail, AK...above Summit Lake.
July 8, 2001   UEH

150

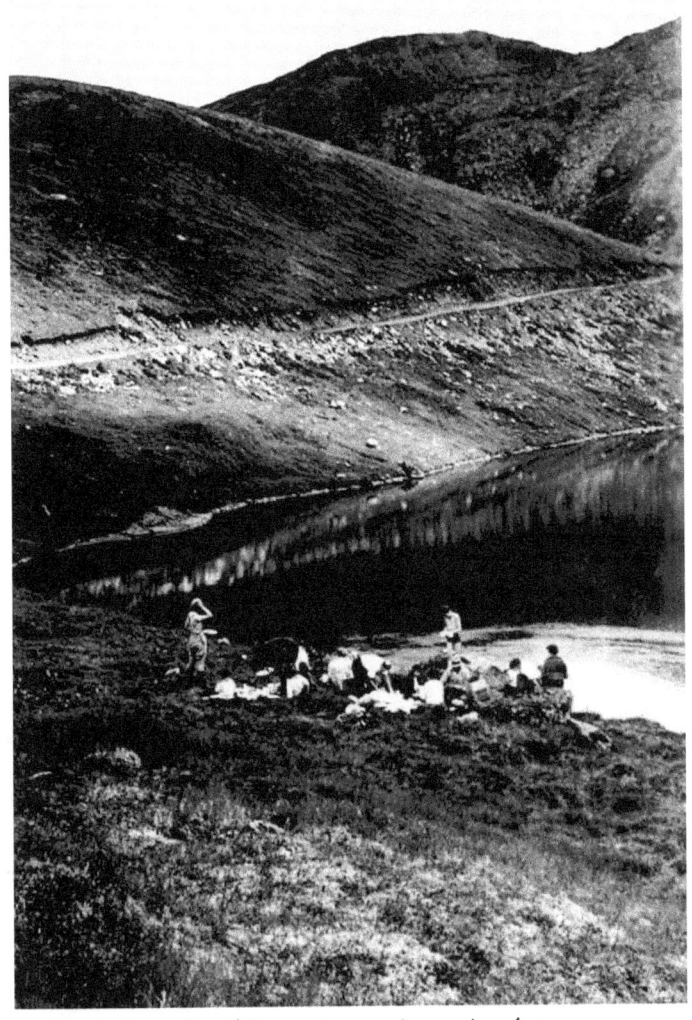

"Picnic lunch with Matanuska colonists on mountain pass on way to Lucky Shot Mine... elevation about 4,000 feet...near Palmer, Alaska ...August 9, 1936....RAD

An elderly Matanuska placement colonist from 1936 recollected in 2001 in an interview that "it was very cold, but we did not care and swam it anyway."

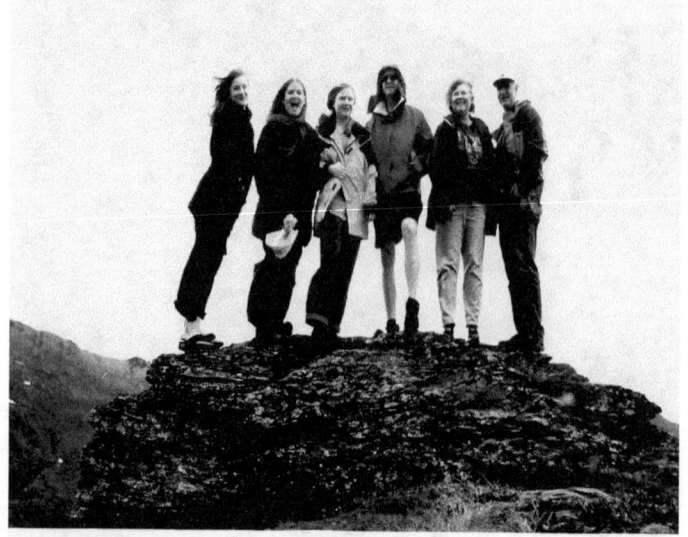

Heather, Alison, Diane, Ken, Jill and Emory on top of summit rock, Hatcher Pass, (north of) Palmer, Alaska. July 29, 2000   Timer

We, too, got to stand on the Summit Lake rock. We used the background to establish its location.

Thanks to the Colony House in Palmer, contact was made with Ina Belle Irwin. What a day it was! An unexpected moment to actually meet the young lady on the right in the Hatcher Pass summit rock photo. After all, it had only been 65 years ago that the prospector took this picture. Her blue eyes sparkled as she remembered back fondly to the good old days of Hatcher Pass and the activities in the Matanuska Valley. She was on a visit from the lower forty-eight when we made our lucky call.

It was hard saying goodbye after our visit in Wasilla. We looked back to see them waving from their porch, knowing we would never see them again. How fortunate just to get that one day, and how very much a wayward prospector from earlier days would like to have been there.

Eventually, we got to meet the lady on the left down in the lower forty-eight on our way back home in the fall of 2001.

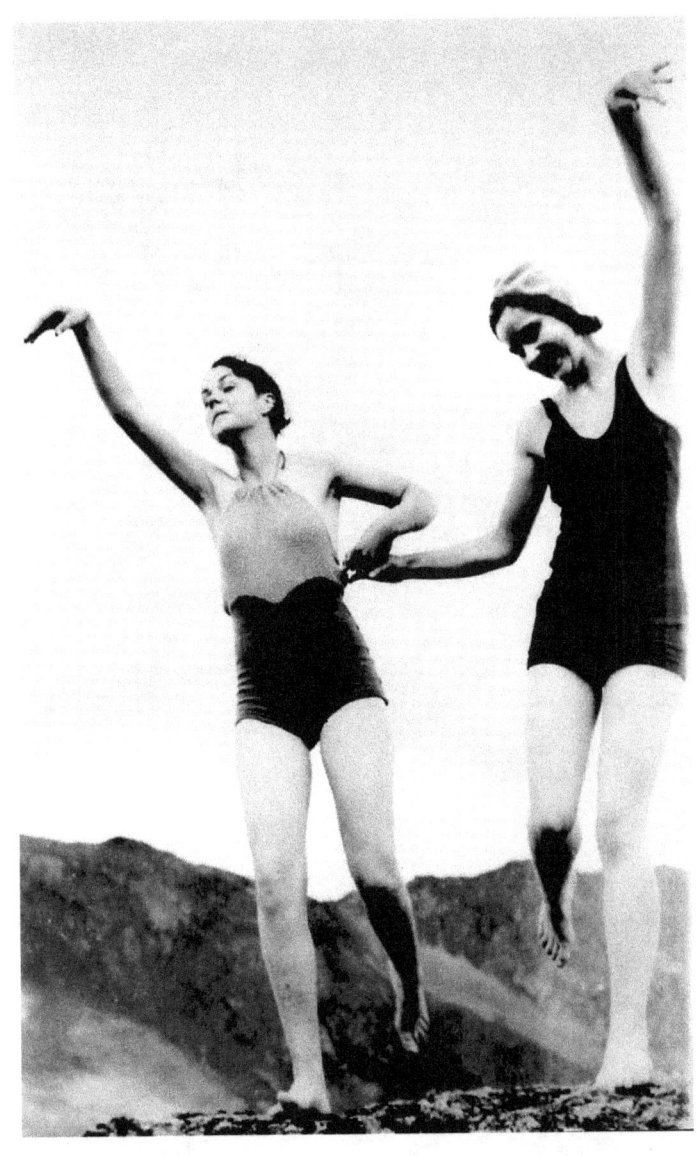

"Mountain Pass on way to Lucky Shot Mine
...near Palmer, Alaska...Virginia Broostrom
(replacement colonist, left) and Ina Belle Irwin
(first colony manager's youngest daughter,
right)...August 9, 1936"   RAD

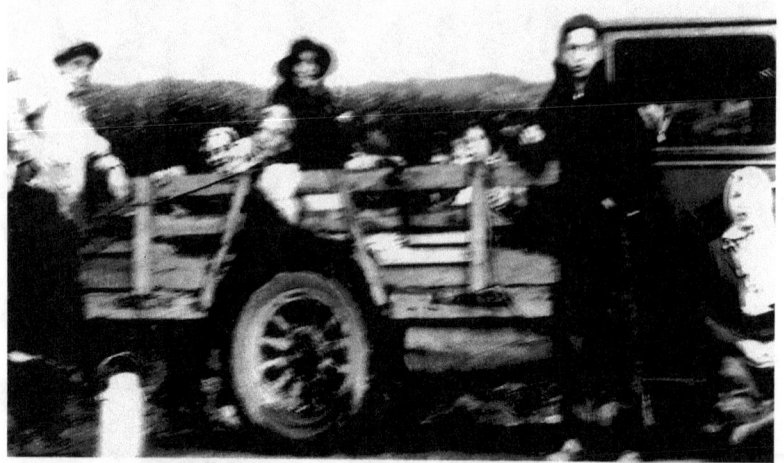

"Cooling the brakes on the way back from Lucky Shot Mine
(Matanuska colonists)...som'in moved...near Palmer,
Alaska...August 9, 1936"   RAD

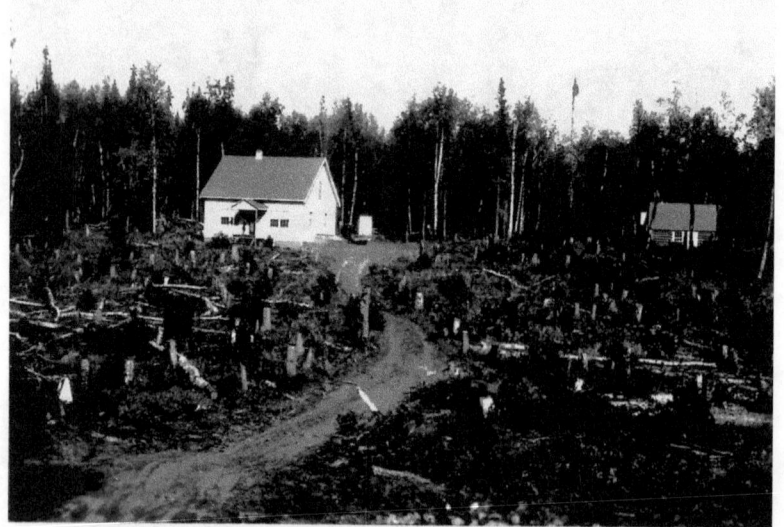

"Tract number 146...Matanuska colony house...Palmer,
Alaska...August 23, 1936" (chicken coop to R)   RAD

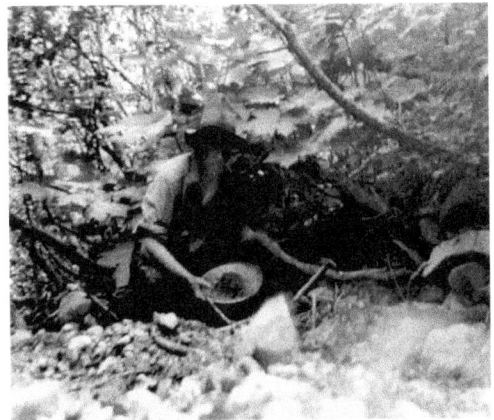

Randolph Angus Douglas holds a string attached to the camera
Shutter to achieve a self-portrait while prospecting on Lazy MT.,
Palmer AK., 1936.

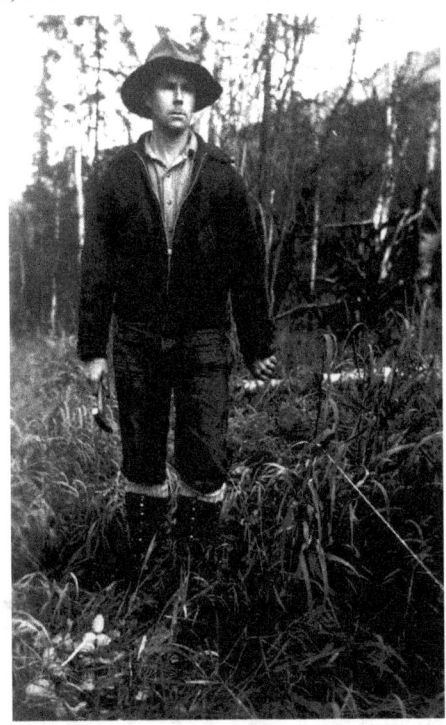

"Twenty miles west of Palmer, AK...September 20, 1936" RAD
Again, a fourth self-portrait was taken by Douglas while
holding a string in his left hand attached to the shutter of the camera.
This was his last photograph taken in the Palmer area just before
leaving.

155

1930's GOLD MINING RESUMPTION
  Third largest lode-gold producing district in Alaska was the Independence Mine/Hatcher Pass District. Also known as the Willow Creek Mining District.

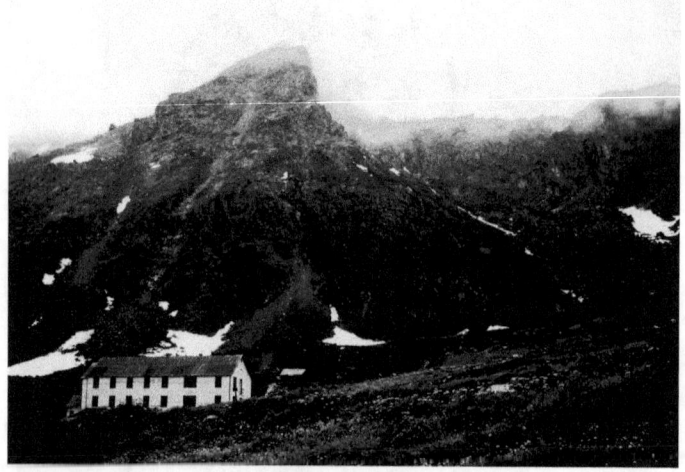

Independence Mine State Historic Park. 2000   JDH

  The Alaska Free Mine on Skyscraper Mountain and the Indpendence Mine on Granite Mountain were brought together into one company in 1938 for war efforts. Now known as the APC (AK Pacific Consolidated Mining CO.)

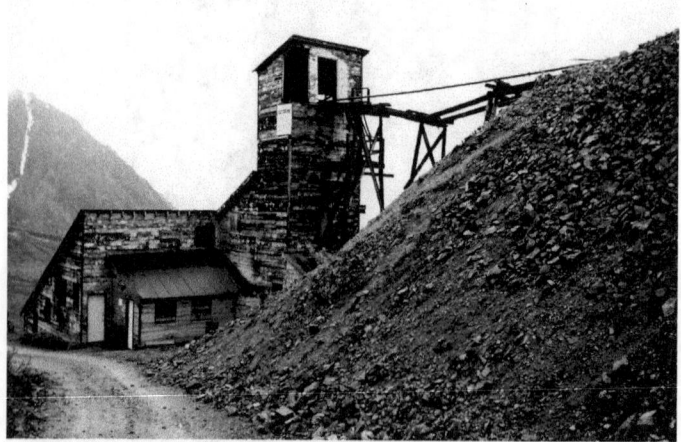

The mill at the Gold Cord Mine. Operating in 2000. JDH

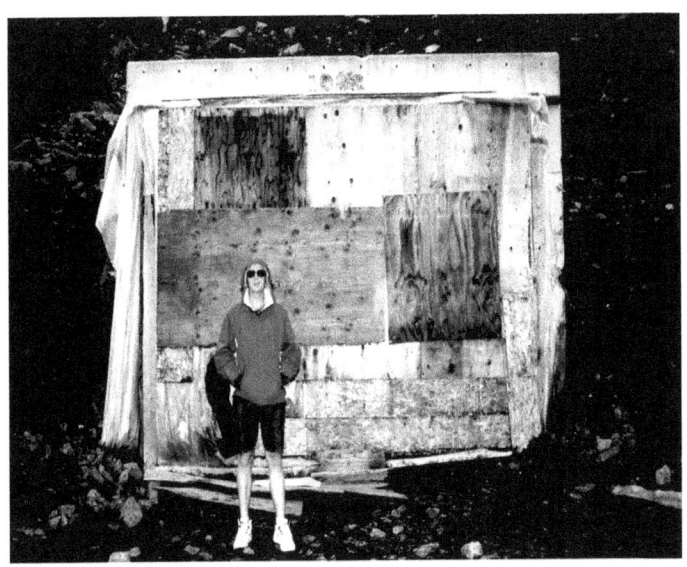

Ken in front of the Willow Creek Mine
entrance, Hatcher Pass, AK. 2000   JDH

In 1942 gold mining in the US (including the Alaska
Territory) came to a halt.

Other notable lode-gold producing mines in the area were:
Lucky Shot Mine, Gold Bullion Mine, Martin Mine, Fern
Mine, War Baby Mine and others not mentioned — mines
that produced Gold, Copper, Mercury, Tungsten, Tellurium
Zinc and lead.

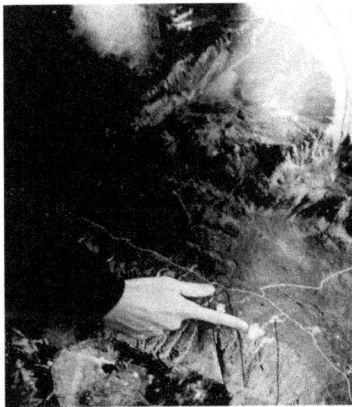

For nearly a decade the
Lucky Shot Mine supported
a small bustling town with a
post office, houses, camp,
and office buildings. The
mine operated until 1942.

The Lucky Shot Mine got
its name in the early 1900's
when a man aiming at a
ptarmigan (a game bird)
missed and found gold
where his bullet struck.

Dan Renshaw of the Gold Cord Mine points to location of
the Lucky Shot Mine. 2000   JDH

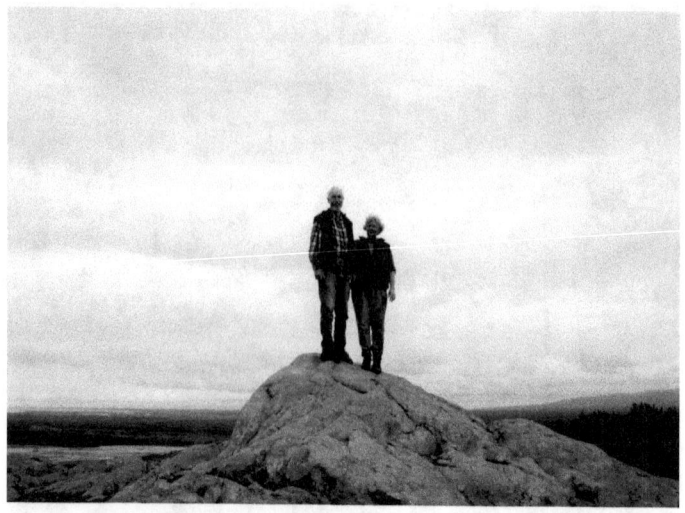

Emory with author on top of the Butte, Palmer, AK. 2001   Timer

   On July 4, 2001, we hiked up the Bodenburg Butte
(elevation 881 feet). At the top there were views of the
Knik Glacier, the Knik River-arm and the Matanuska River.
Also, we noticed a ridge road leading to Anchorage.
Farmland below belonged to Henry Bodenburg in 1917,
more than a decade before the colonists arrived in 1935.

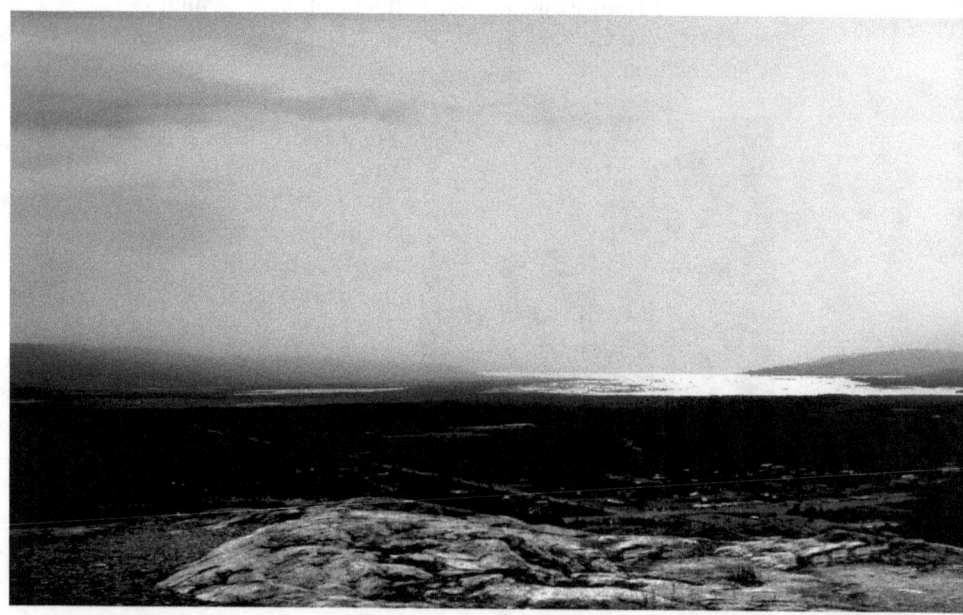

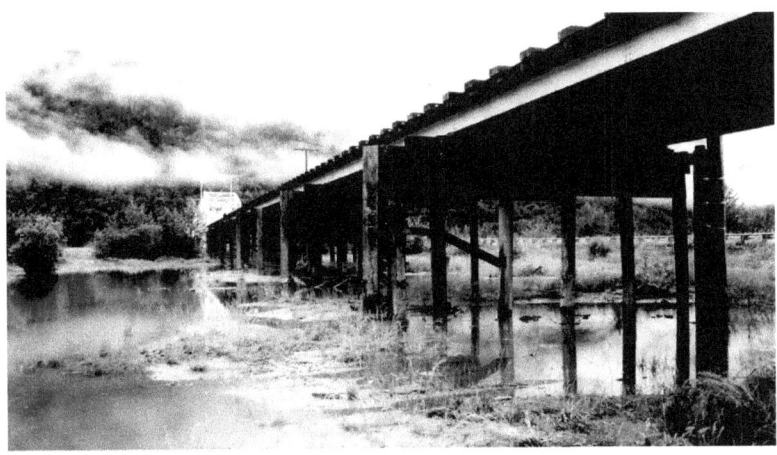

Old Knik River bridge and new replacement bridge (in distance),
Palmer, AK. 2001   BUTTE PANORAMA and bridge photo by Author

The Anchorage-Palmer Highway (now known as the Old
Glenn Highway) was completed in 1936. This opened up
travel between Palmer and Anchorage. The Matanuska and
Knik Glaciers used to cover this valley. Over time they
retreated leaving the remnant of the Butte.

Periodic flooding during the breakup of Lake George into
the Knik River each year ended as the 1964 earthquake made
lasting changes to the height of the land.

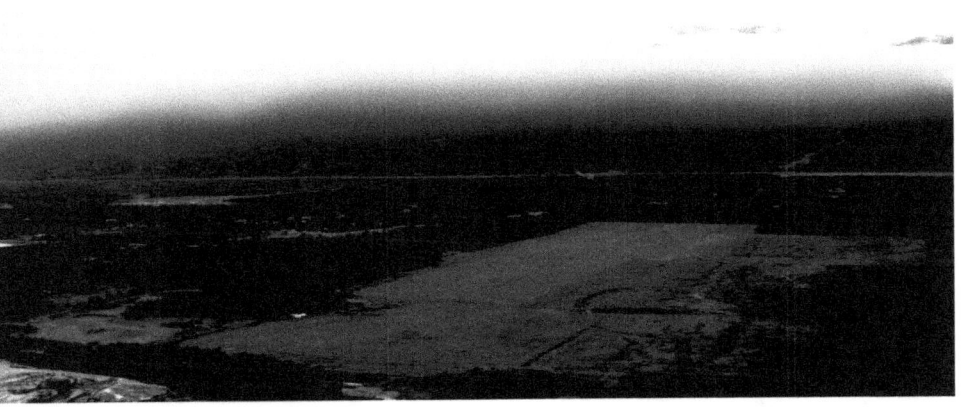

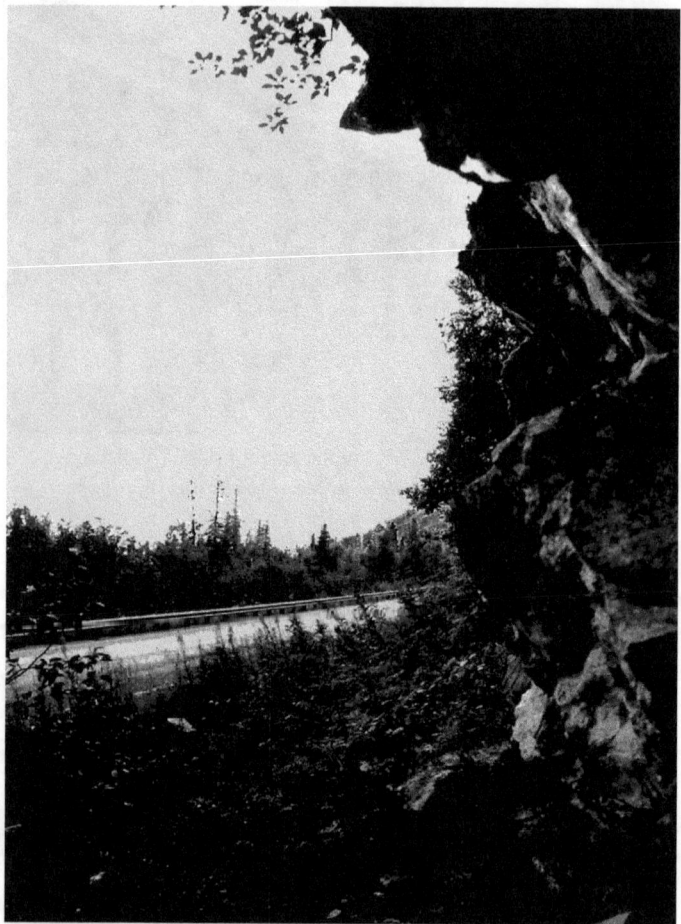

Old Glenn Highway (looking east), Palmer, Alaska. 2000   JDH

It was difficult locating repeat photography for the two 1936 Anchorage-Palmer Highway photos. The road was narrow and without any shoulders. Curves made it awkward to notice oncoming vehicles while the photographs were being taken.

The old Anchorage-Palmer Highway (now called the Old Glenn Highway) curves left to the Knik River bridges and the town of Palmer. Unfortunately, Douglas was no longer recording in his diary, but thanks to his photographic efforts (R), his journey takes us to the new Anchorage-Palmer Highway for a view of what it would have been like for the colonists to have traveled down to Anchorage for the very first time.

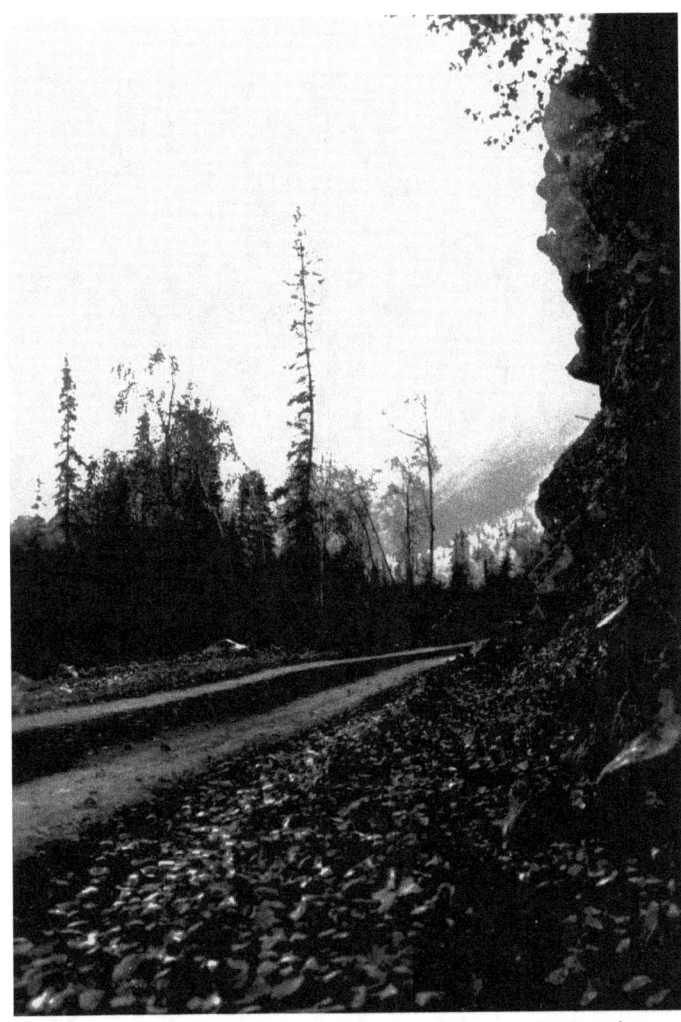

"Anchorage-Palmer Highway...mile 36...Pioneer Peak elevation
6,398 ft seen in distance...looking E...September 20, 1936" RAD

Douglas most likely walked to these two photo locations
from the town of Palmer. It was only a few miles away
across the "new-1936" Knik River bridge — and walking
was a way of life to him now, as it was for many back in the
wooded areas of Alaska.

At this point, Douglas's thoughts were focused south. He
made a brief trip down to Anchorage with one (or some) of
his newly acquired colonist friends before leaving Palmer for
Seward. Two 1936 photos were taken at the southern end of
this historic highway in the developing town of Anchorage.

161

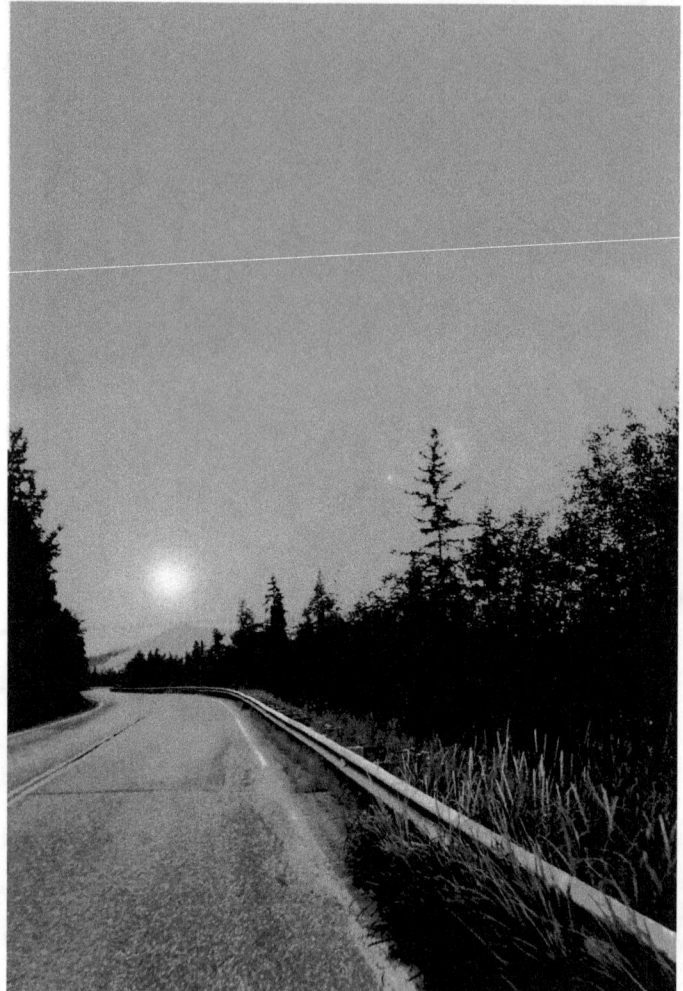

Old Glenn Highway (looking west), Palmer, Alaska. 2000   JDH

   This repeat photograph of the Old Glenn Highway looking
west can only make a start to reflect the road between Palmer
and Anchorage during that earlier time period. The elevation
of the land around this bend had clearly been altered by the
earthquake of 1964.

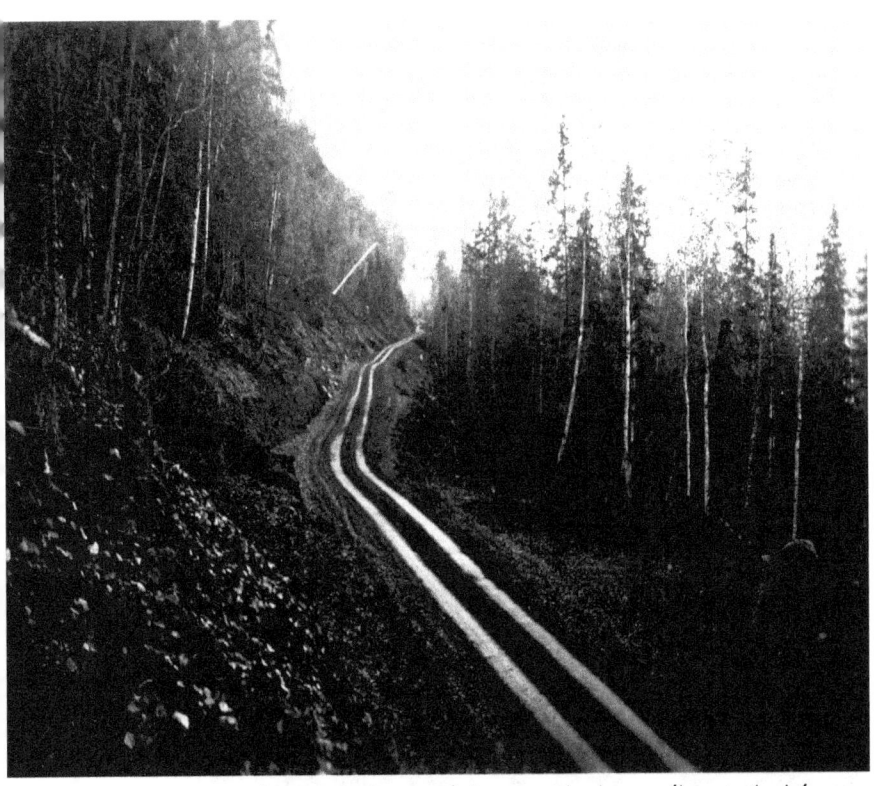

"Anchorage-Palmer Highway, Alaska...mile 36...looking west...September 20, 1936" RAD

Glancing back at Douglas's rough and amazing journey through the ALASKA INTERIOR can only be summed up as follows:

AHTELL CREEK was his passion.

VALDEZ was his first home in Alaska.

FAIRBANKS was his challenge.

PALMER was his reward *and*

SEWARD was his place of discontent.

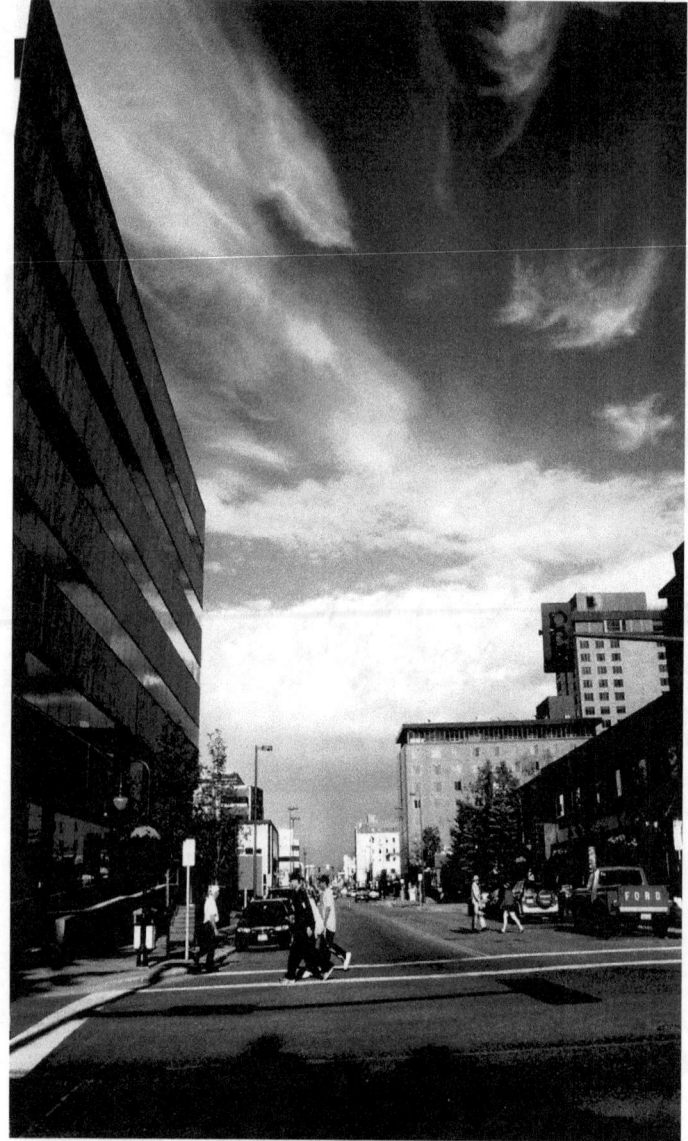

Emory, Ken and Diane crossing Fourth Avenue, Anchorage, Alaska. 2000   JDH

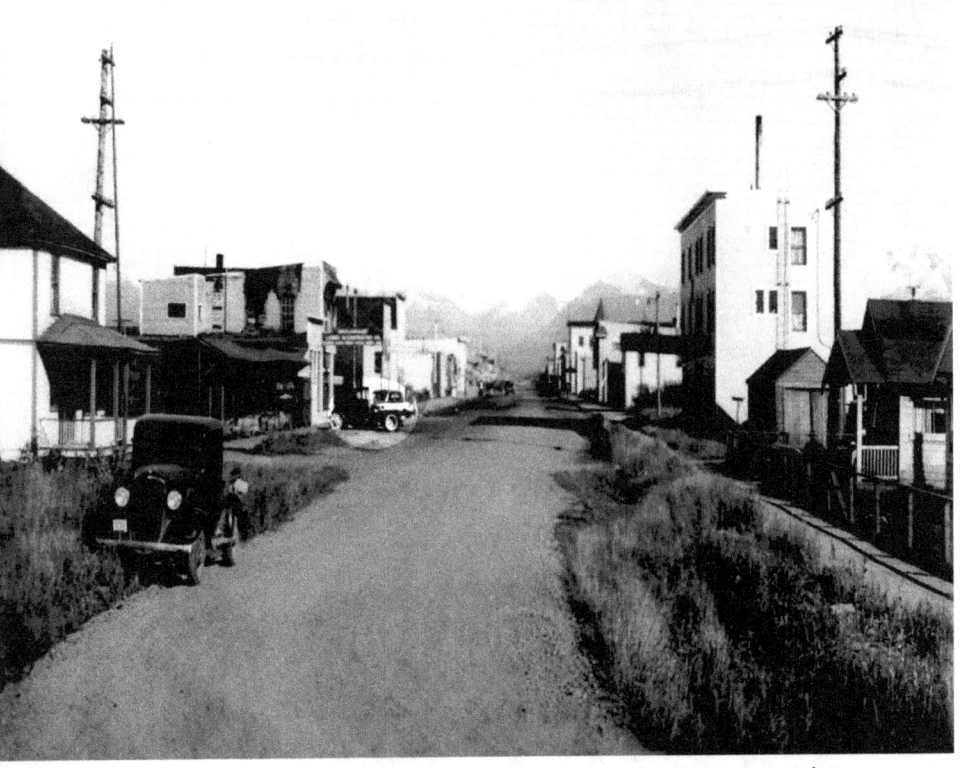

"Fourth Avenue...main stem...Anchorage, Alaska...looking east...note: truck (middle left)...September 15, 1936" RAD

In 1915 the post office gave Anchorage its name. The waters were deeper at Ship Creek which enabled steamers laden with heavy railway and mining equipment to anchor and unload their goods to skiffs without running aground. The skiffs then sailed across the Knik Arm to the town of Knik, the main trading area of the times.

Formerly, in order to save transportation costs by rail, homesteaders would transport their products in all-day boat trips. Colonists traveled from Palmer down the Knik Arm to Ship Creek in Anchorage.

165

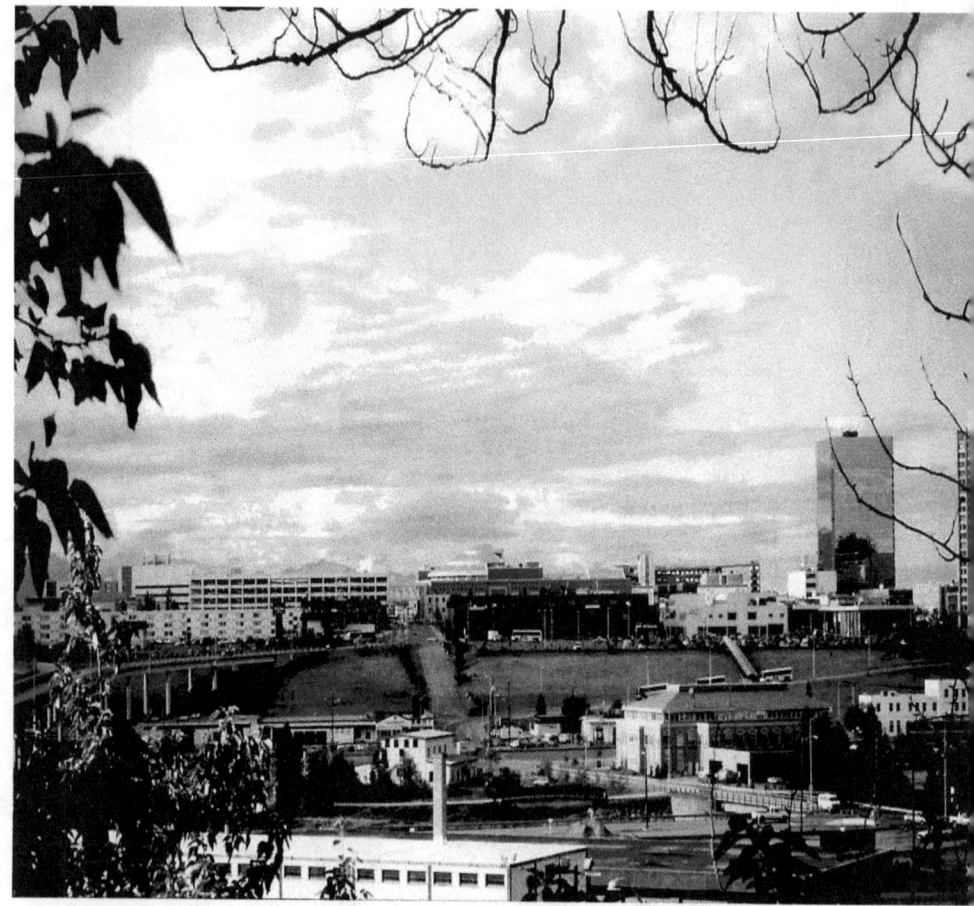

Top of Government Hill, Anchorage, Alaska. 2000   JDH

Looking south from Government Hill, one can only imagine the tent city erected on the muddy banks of Ship Creek the first year of the town's history. Anchorage was laid out by railroad engineers in 1915, like the rails of a track. Statehood was in 1959. The steep hill — seen in both the 2000 and 1936 photos — was lowered in the two minute and fifty-six second earthquake of 1964.

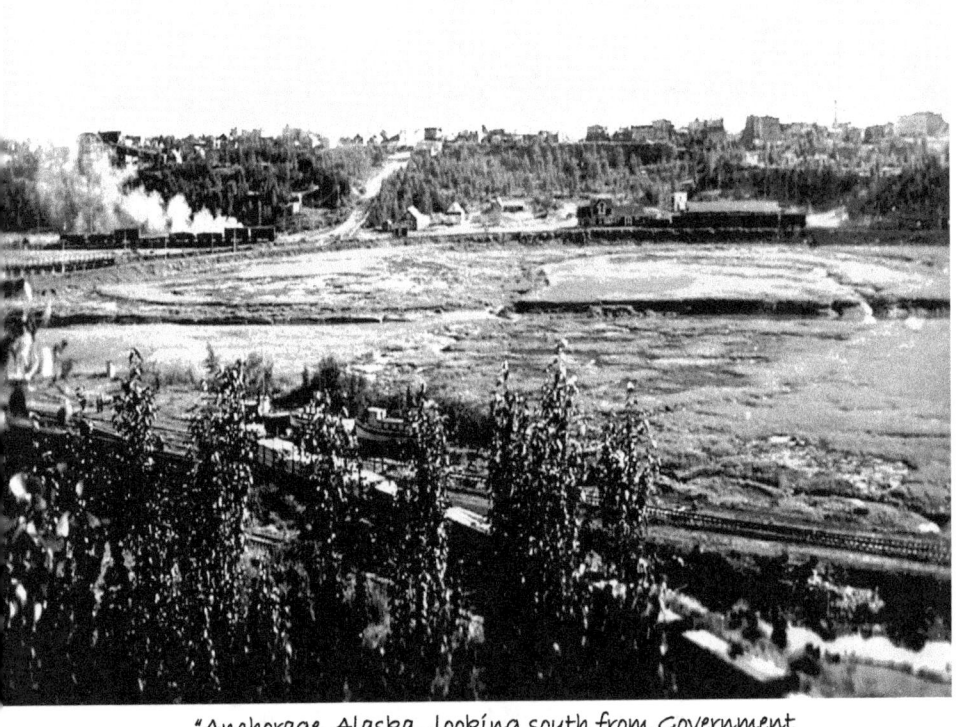

"Anchorage, Alaska...looking south from Government Hill...September 15, 1936"   RAD

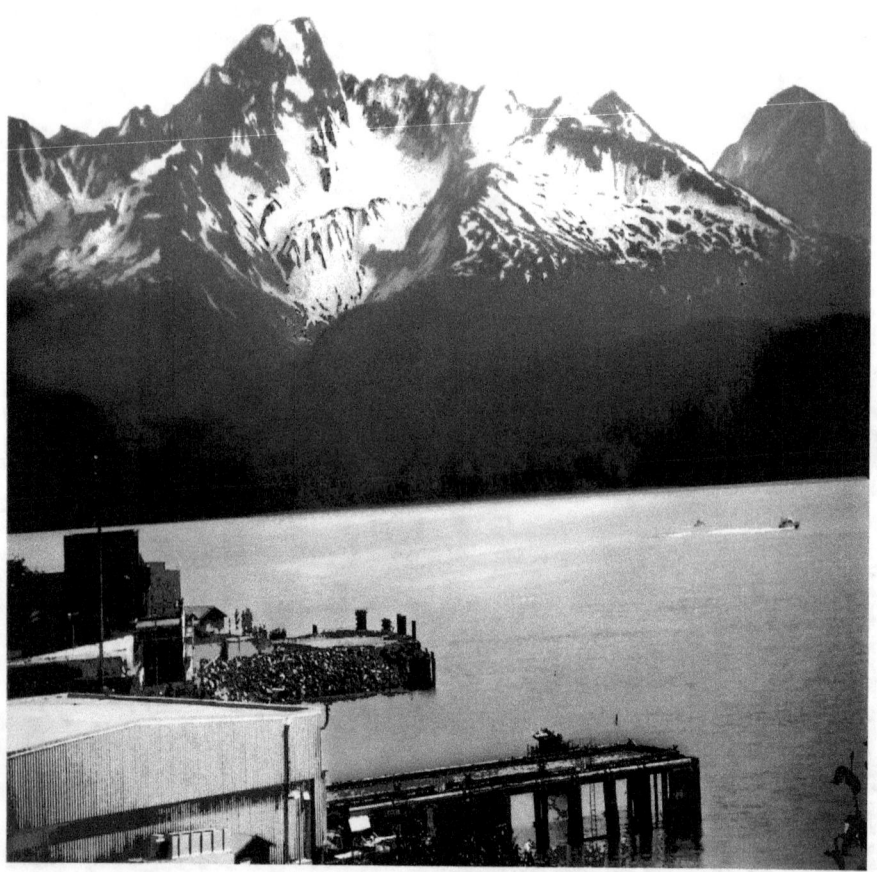

Mount Alice (center) and the old dock area, Seward, AK. 2001   JDH

    The old dock area (lower center) was photographed from the top of Lowell Creek Waterfall at Bear Mountain. The new Sea Life Center (lower left) was built from Exxon Valdez oil spill funds.

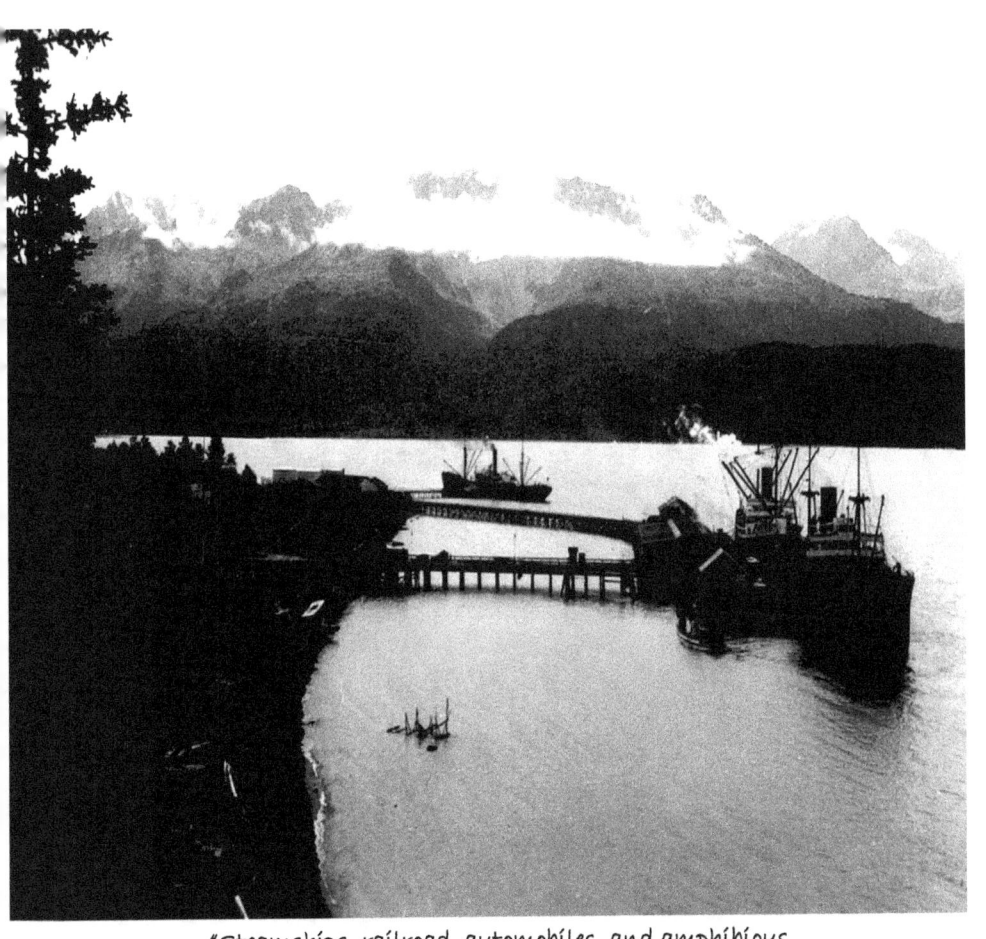

"Steamships, railroad, automobiles, and amphibious
plane...Seward, Alaska...October 3, 1936"   RAD

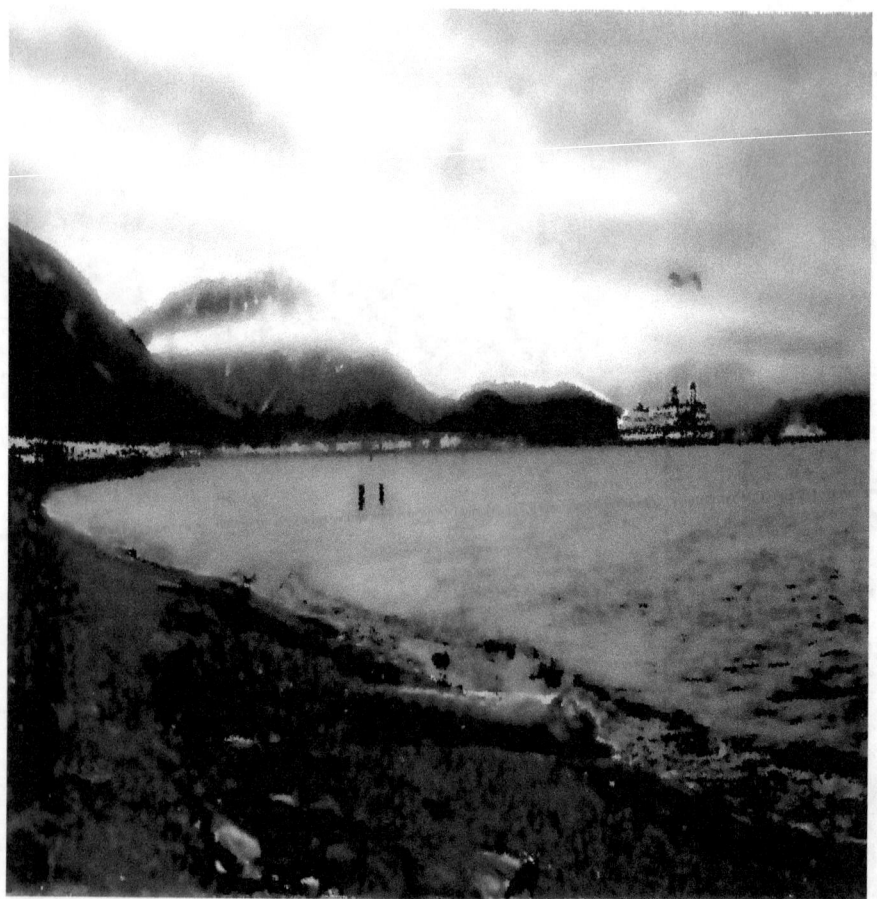

Resurrection Bay, Seward, Alaska. 2001   JDH

Past meets present in the above photo. Notice old pilings in
the water standing silently against a shoreline of
motorhomes, travel trailers, tents and cruise ships. In spite
of the encroachment of modern civilization, Seward still
remains a very rugged land where seagulls fly and fog hangs
in the mountain valleys. Seward was founded in 1903 and
named for William H. Seward, who in 1867, negotiated the
purchase of the Alaska Territory from Russia for a mere 7.2
million dollars.

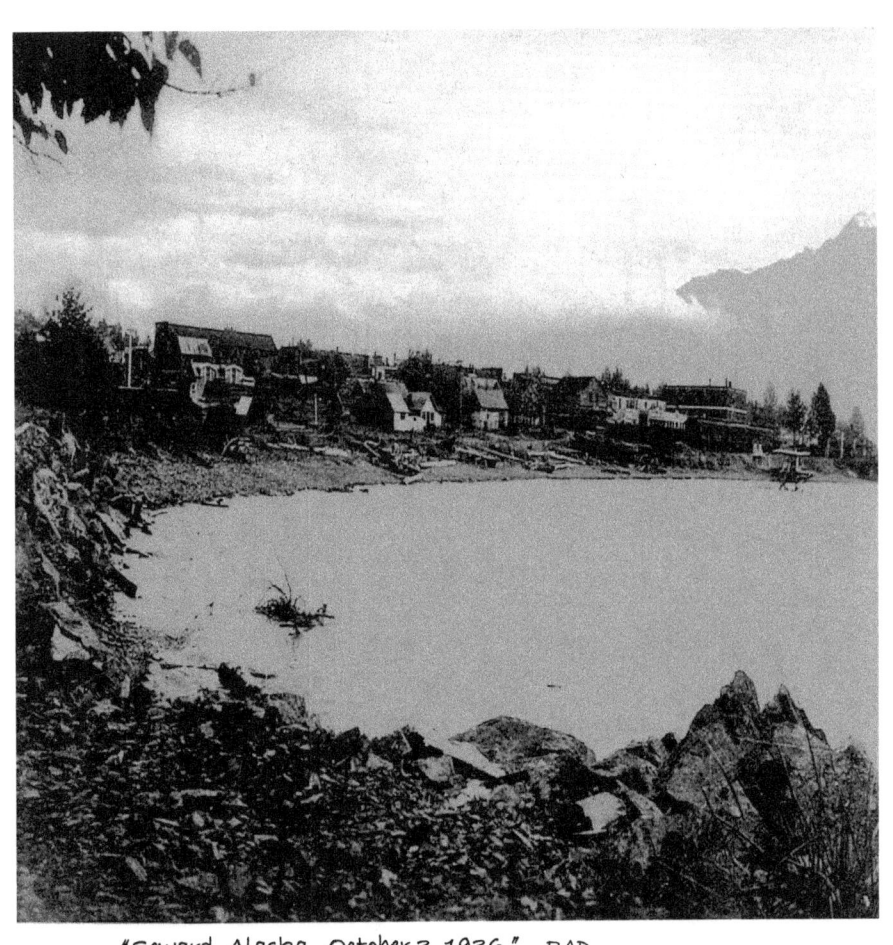

"Seward, Alaska...October 3, 1936."   RAD

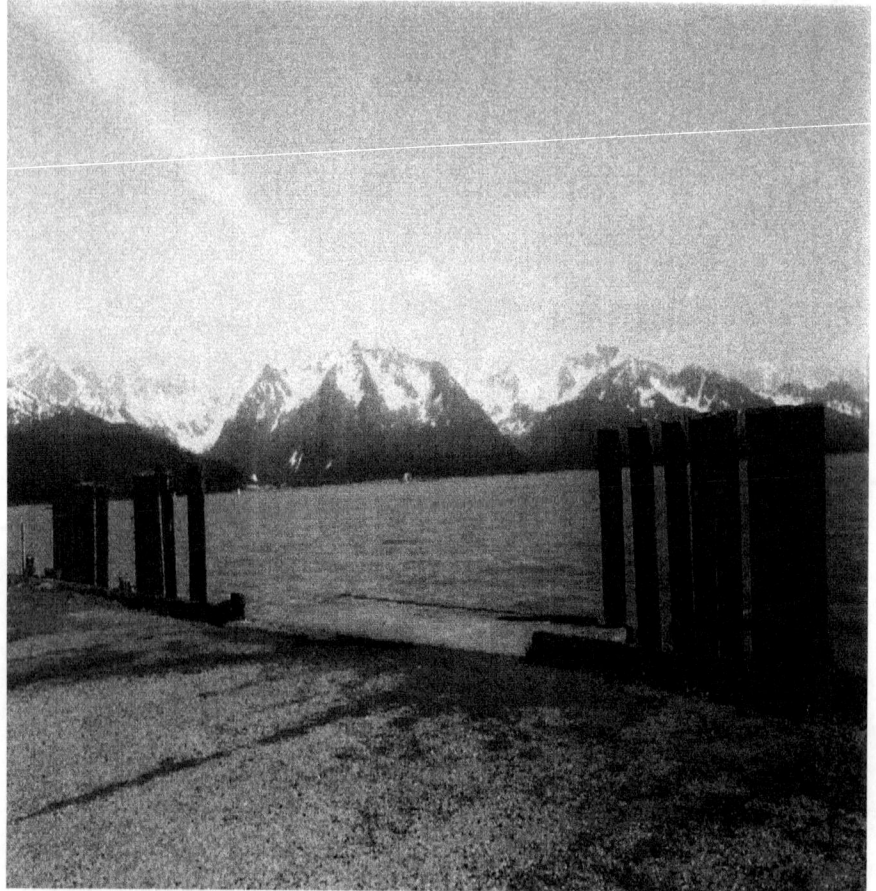

Old dock area with Mount Alice in distance, Seward, AK. 2001 JDH

A Russian named Alexander Baranov sailed into the bay on Easter morning in the late 1700's giving it the title of Resurrection Bay. In 1799 the Russian American Company, managed by Baranov, was given control over all of Alaska by the Tsar of Russia.

Mount Alice (upper center) was named for Frank and Mary's daughter, Alice. These earlier settlers made their home at the head of Resurrection Bay in 1884, after the Russian colony had left the area.

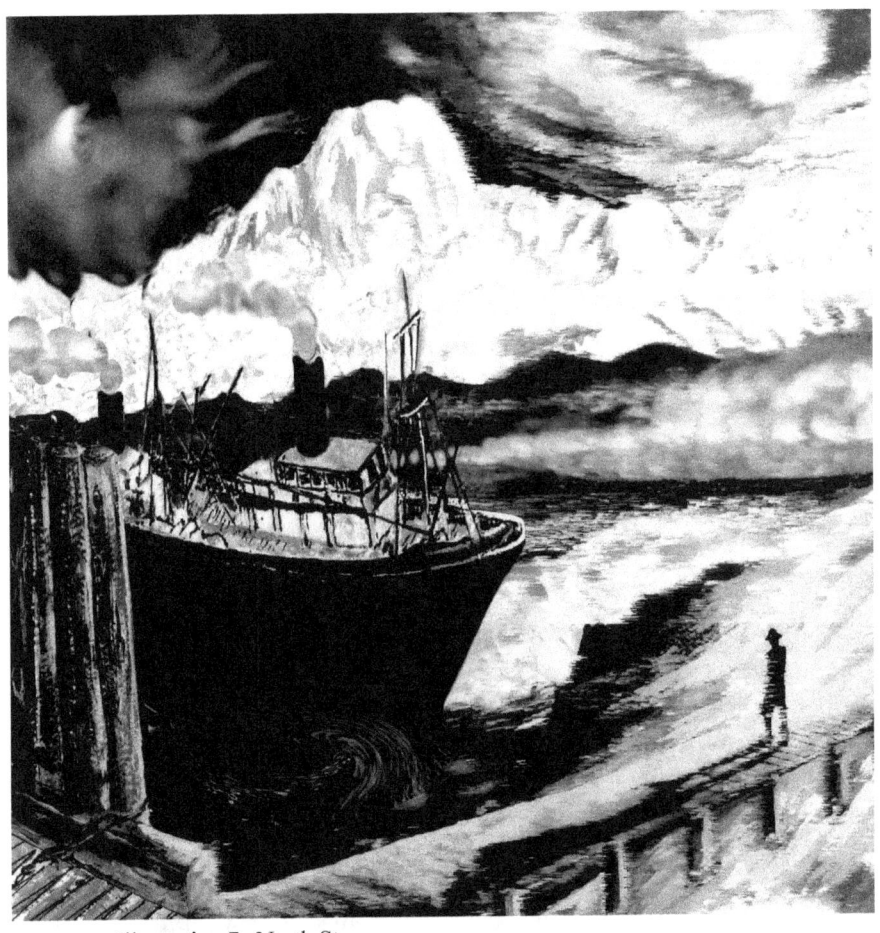

Illustration 7. North Star

Rustling like pages in a book caught by the wind, years
would come and go and Alaska would not come again for the
prospector — nor would he ever have another dog. The
heavy steamer made its way down the narrow, dark
passageway of Resurrection Bay in October of 1936.
Douglas glanced north toward the mainland of Alaska for the
last time, from the deck of a southbound ship.

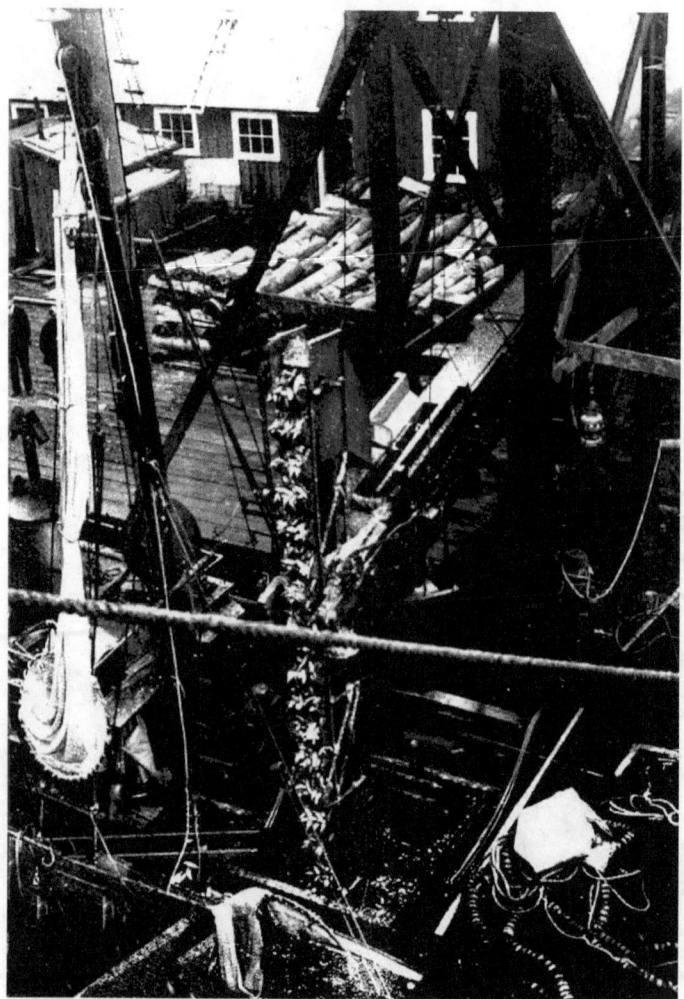

"Mechanical conveyer unloading herring at an Alaska
cannery near Valdez... (from aboard ship)...
October, 1936"   RAD

Logistically we were unable to achieve repeat photography
on the last two photos in the RAD Photo Collection.
  Douglas completed his roll of film at Evans Island, after
leaving Resurrection Bay. The area was located to the east
of Seward.
  Actually, the prospector was no where near Valdez, but
perhaps his heart was.

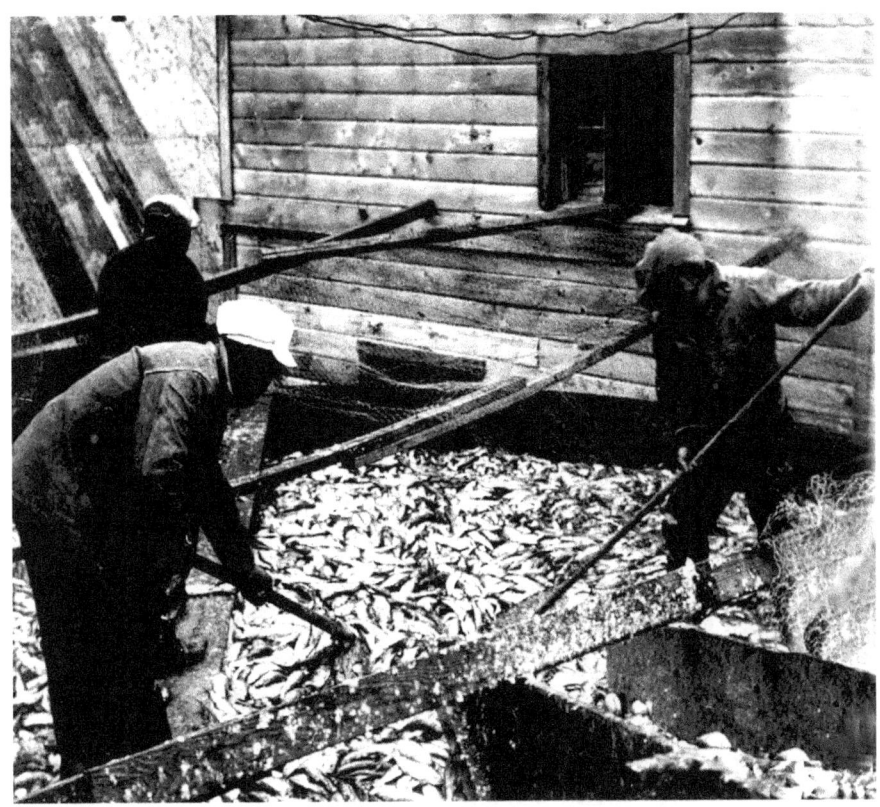

"Herring in vat for fertilizer...Crab Bay...near Valdez, Alaska...October, 1936" RAD

We read some interesting facts about Evans Island in some ship literature aboard the Tustumena Ferry from Valdez to Seward in 2001. In 1964 a thirty-five foot tsunami nearly wiped out an Aleutian village on the south side of Chanega Island. Survivors were relocated to Anchorage, Valdez, Tatitlek and Cordova for twenty years, until the site of "Crab Bay" was chosen for its deep, safe harbor.

In 1989 the Exxon Valdez pulled away from the pipeline terminal in the port of Valdez and struck Bligh Reef, ripping open eight of its thirteen cargo tanks. Nine hundred square miles of oil slick blanketed the area in a period of a week. The struggling village of Crab Bay was completely surrounded by the oil slick and once again had to consider the option of relocation. Located across Sawmill Bay is an abandoned herring cannery.

ACKNOWLEDGEMENTS

ORIGINAL PRINTING *LAST CHANCE ALASKA*

WRITING CONSULTANT
SUSAN LAROSE

PHOTOSHOP CONSULTANT
SUE TOWNSEND

PHOTOGRAPHY CREDITS:
HEATHER VAN ARSDEL, ULYS EMORY HOPPER
and AUTHOR

SUPPORT
ULYS EMORY HOPPER Emory logged over 20,000 miles of safe driving

ALISON M.VAN ARSDEL Alison wrote the Foreword & contributed the poem, *DREAMER'S PEAK* in Chapter III.

NELLIE CLARKE DOUGLAS Nellie authenticated the first leg of our 2000 cross-country road trip from Florida to Washington State.

A SPECIAL THANK YOU TO MY BROTHER,
DANIEL RANDOLPH DOUGLAS who transcribed and shared the original RAD Alaska diary whose quotes enhanced many of the 1935-36 photographs.

A BIG THANK YOU TO ALL THE
PROOFREADEERS and READERS WHO MADE
LAST CHANCE ALASKA **a SUCCESS:**

SUE TOWNSAND, HOWARD and SUSAN LAROSE,
KAY PEARSON, ROGER and SALLIE RIBREAU,
LINDA BATICK, ALISON M. VAN ARSDEL, CONNIE PIPER,
FRED K.VAN ARSDEL, GLORIA CRAMPTON,
CHUCK and NAN HIGGINS

OTHER UNNAMED RELATIVES, FRIENDS and NEIGHBORS
who encouraged, aided and shared maps Thank you.

LOWER FORTY-EIGHT SOURCES
All contacts between 2000 and 2001

STATE MUSEUM OF PENNSYLVANIA: Harrisburg, Pennsylvania

FORT PITT MUSEUM: Pittsburgh, Pennsylvania

WYOMING PIONEER MEMORIAL MUSEUM:
Douglas, Wyoming
HELL'S HALF ACRE: Natrona County, Wyoming
CRAZY MOUNTAIN MUSEUM: Big Timber, Montana
GINKO INTERPRETIVE CENTER: Vantage, Washington
SNOQUALMIE VALLEY HISTORICAL MUSEUM:
North Bend, Washington

VALDEZ SOURCES
All contacts between 2000 and 2001.

FRIENDS of the VALDEZ ANIMAL SHELTER
    SHANA ANDERSON, Animal Control Officer
    COLETTE DU CHARME, Manager
EAGLE'S REST RV PARK
VALDEZ CONSORTIUM LIBRARY
    ROBERT KELSEY
OLD EDGERTON PHOTOGRAPHY
STAN STEPHENS CRUISES
UNITED STATED FORESTRY SERVICE of CROOKED CREEK
ALPINE AVIATION ADVENTURES
    CHARLES LAPAGE, Pilot   Endorsed Last Chance Alaska
PRINCE WILLIAM SOUND COMMUNITY COLLEGE
    NANCY LUND
VALDEZ MUSEUM and ANNEX

GLENNALLEN SOURCES
All contacts between 2000 and 2001.

UNITED STATES DEPT. of the INTERIOR BUREAU of
LAND MANAGEMENT, Glennallen
    BLM Specialists: DAVID MUSHOVIC,
    K. J. MUSHOVIC and DEBBIE MUENSTER

SLANA AREA SOURCES
All contacts between 2000 and 2001

MARY FRANCES DEHART Slana Post office and Hart D
Ranch Complex
WRANGELL-SAINT ELIAS NATIONAL PARK and
PRESERVE RANGER STATION
ANGUS DEWITT
KATIE JOHN Mentasta Village
GRIZZLY LAKE RANCH

FAIRBANKS AREA SOURCES
All contacts between 2000 and 2001.

FAIRBANKS DAILY NEW-MINER
UNIVERSITY of ALASKA FAIRBANKS
DR. EARL H. BEISLINE
HARRY HUGHES Circle Hot Springs Resort
ALASKALAND
CIRCLE DISTRICT HISTORICAL SOCIETY MUSEUM
STATE RECORDS OFFICE
UNITED STATES GEOLOGICAL SURVEY
ALASKA PUBLIC LANDS INFORMATION CENTER
GOLD DREDGE NO. 8 Historic landmark on Steese Highway
VISITOR INFORMATION CENTER
NOEL WEIN LIBRARY
ELDORADO GOLD MINE

PALMER SOURCES
All contacts between 2000 and 2001.

COLONY INN
PALMER HISTORIC SOCIETY

178

INA BELLE IRWIN BOSS KENNEDY Youngest
Matanuska Valley colony manager's daughter

GLENN BROOSTROM FAMILY 1936 replacement colonists
in the Matanuska Valley

Original "Colony Kids" of Palmer:

GERRY KINDGREN KEELING

ROSE MARY (TINY) VICKARYOUS DEPRIEST

PATTY HEMMER WEISENBERGER

VALLEY HOTEL

JACKIE DE JONG A.A.R.C
Alaska Rural Rehabilitation Corp.

HATCHER PASS LODGE

DAN RENSHAW Gold Cord Mine

GOLD MINER'S HOTEL

AMERICAN LEGION POST 15

MOUNTAIN VIEW RV PARK

COLONY CURIO

HOMESTEAD RV PARK

TOWN AND COUNTRY RV PARK

ANCHORAGE, SEWARD and CORDOVA SOURCES

All contacts between 2000 and 2001.

ROBERT KING United States Department of the Interior Bureau
of Land Management

ANCHORAGE MUSEUM OF HISTORY AND ART
ARCHIVES

RESURRECTION BAY HISTORICAL SOCIETY
MUSEUM

CORDOVA MUSEUM AND HISTORICAL SOCIETY

ALASKA MARINE HIGHWAY

Douglas was born in Plainfield, New Jersey in 1901. He arrived on Alaska soil to stake his claim in 1935. Regretfully, he returned home empty-handed in 1937 and did not make the long trip again. Although this Northeasterner did not strike it rich, he was a player in the early aftermath of one of the world's greatest sagas. Douglas recorded what he saw through writing and film. Today, that *plink* in the pan is still being heard through the mountains and valleys of the Alaska interior.

Unable to establish shafts and tunnels to veins of gold in Alaska, as he had so hoped, he began creating a board game of gold mining in the basement of his New Jersey home. "Gold Bug" enriched the lives of his three children and brought pleasure to all those who were invited to play.

His final, cold northeastern nights were spent sitting in front of the fireplace with a far off look in his eyes. Alas Alaska, not to have returned to your northern latitudes above the 60.

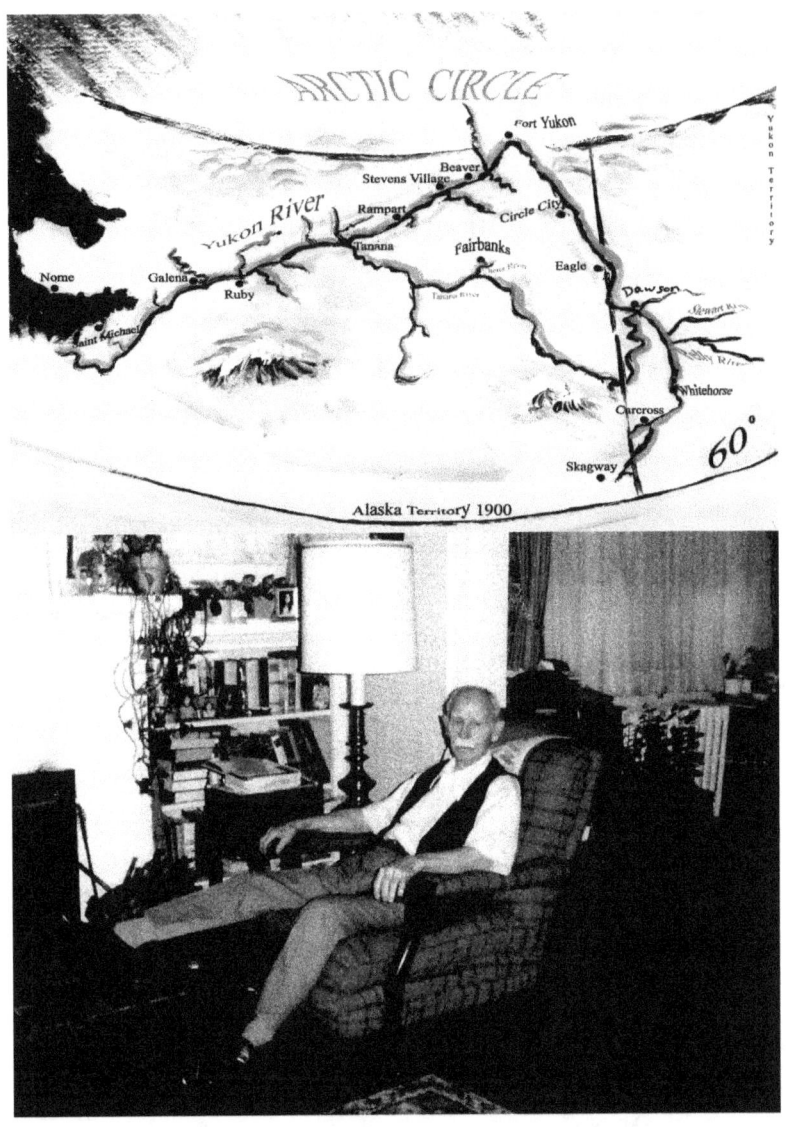

Randolph Angus Douglas, Pompton Plains, N. J. Circa 1980's

As his legacy, Douglas left behind a diary, an assortment
of letters and an unforgettable photo collection of a 1935
cross-country rode trip and a 1935-36 adventure to
discover gold in Alaska.

181

CONTENTS

  All photography from Behind the Scenes 2000
was taken by the hikers: Heather, Diane, Alison,
Ken, Author and Emory, but not disclosed.

  All photography from Behind the Scenes 2001
is disclosed under photos.
  All writing for Behind the Scenes 2000/2001
was taken from the JDH Travel Journals.

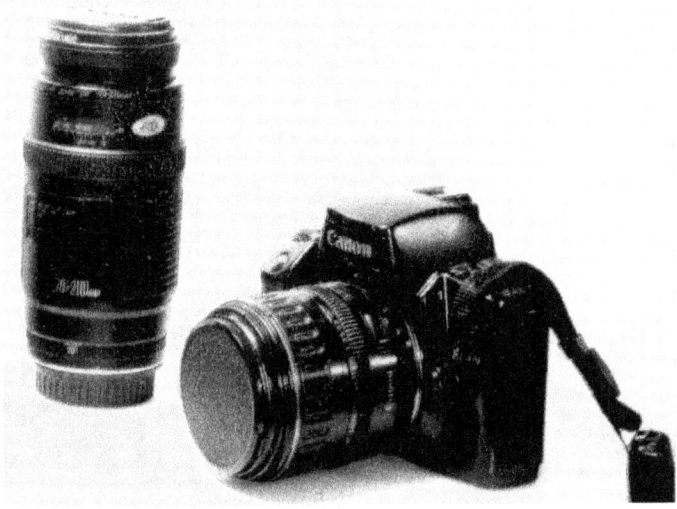

INTRODUCTION by Author

Four and a half pounds of camera equipment was packed into Interior Alaska to photograph the old mining cabin in 2000. My Cannon was a 28-80 mm with a ZOOM LENS of 70-210 mm. Everything we packed was weighed and considered for a light carry.

My experience with digital began after we had returned from our second trip to Alaska and the Northwest Territory. I actually did a comparison check on an image taken with the 28-80 Cannon camera and a "new" digital camera that I had purchased in 2002. The good old camera won hands down.

I developed an immediate interest in digital everything, however! Books were turning digital and computers made writing easy. History had its digital beginning in 1981.

To achieve a color interior with the landscape sizing the original book was limited to 212 pages. The repeat photography was best displayed by using a color "now" picture against a black and white (grayscale) "then" picture. It became pricey to purchase, thus the idea of *LAST CHANCE ALASKA 2* turning the interior into a grayscale with a more common sizing and much lower cost.

As a second publishing was considered, opportunity opened up to share several original, but edited out items and Last *CHANCE ALASKA 2* arrived with a new chapter called **DIRECTOR'S CUT.**

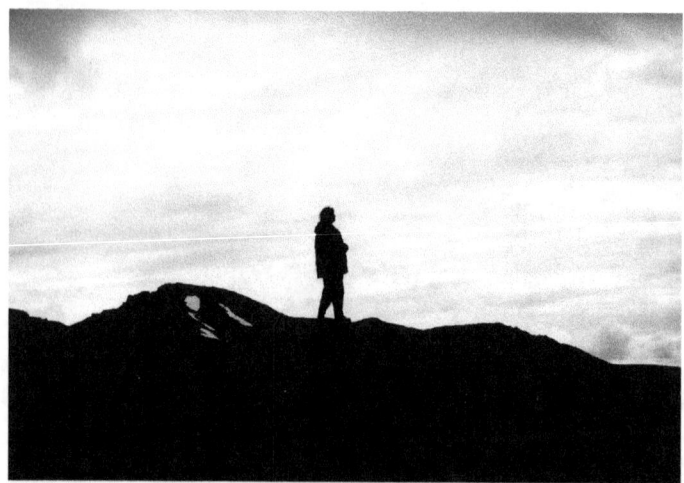

First cover: *LAST CHANCE ALASKA*

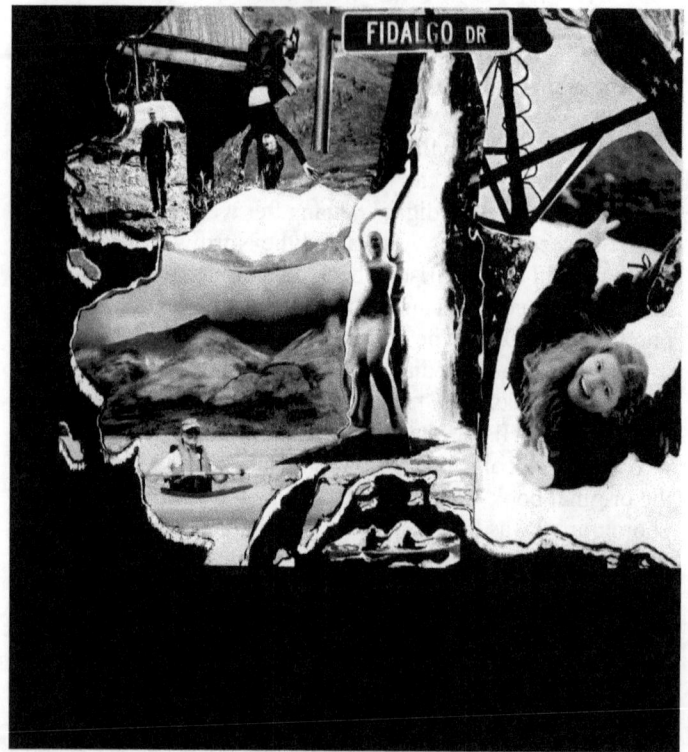

First cover: *LAST CHANCE ALASKA 2*

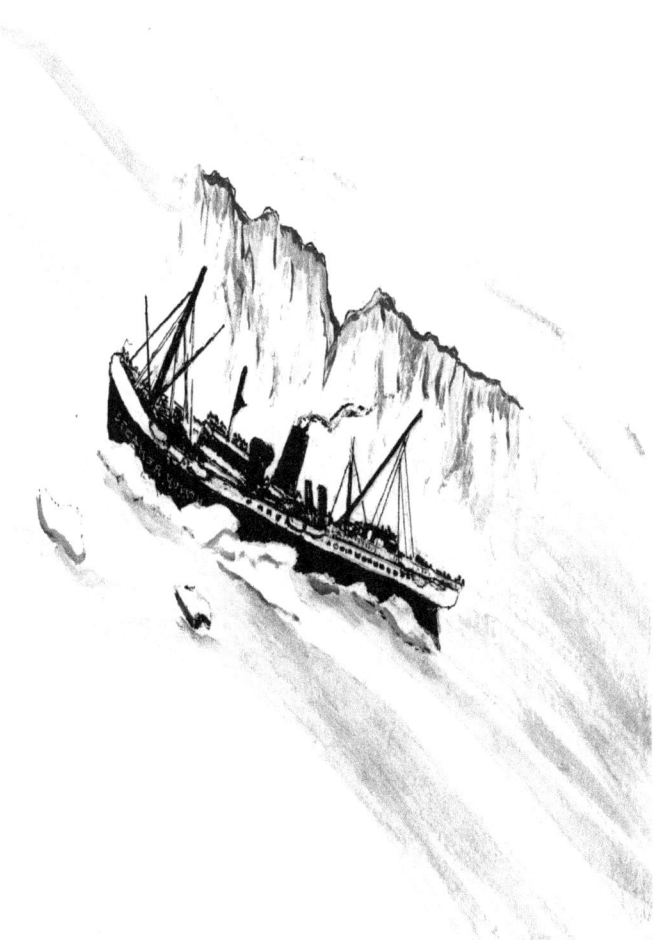

STEAM SHIP YUKON in GOLD FED WATERS

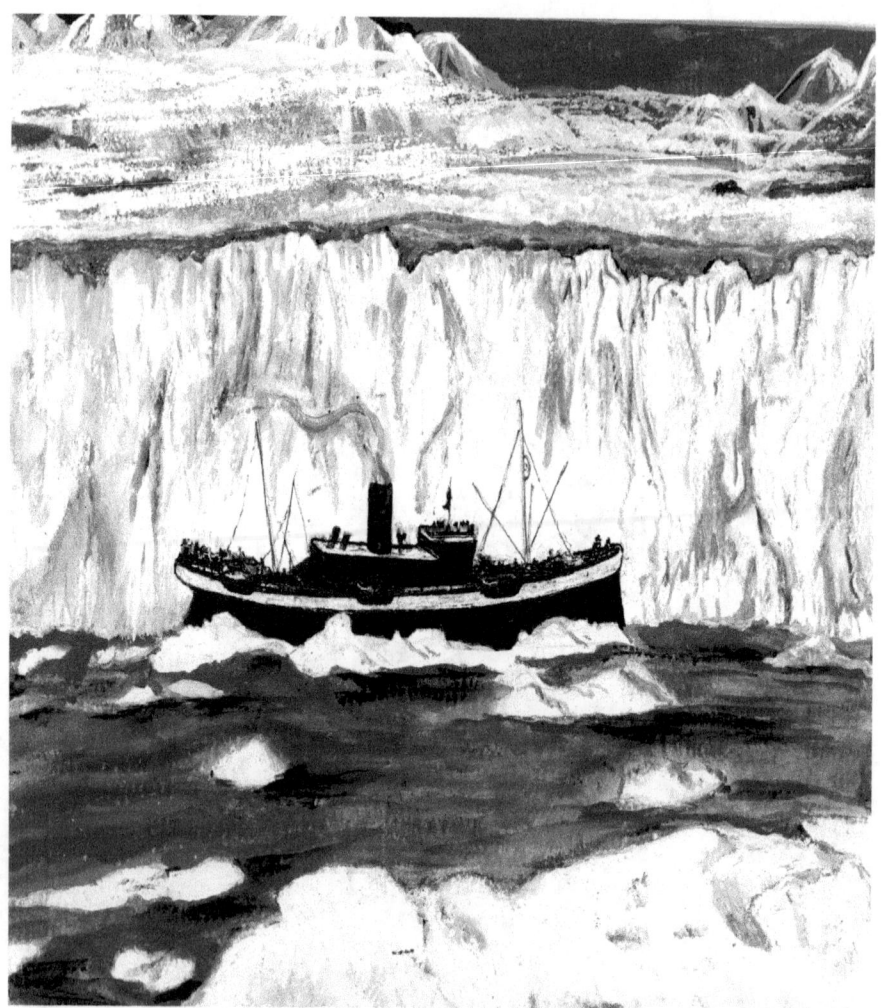

The STEAMER YUKON 1935

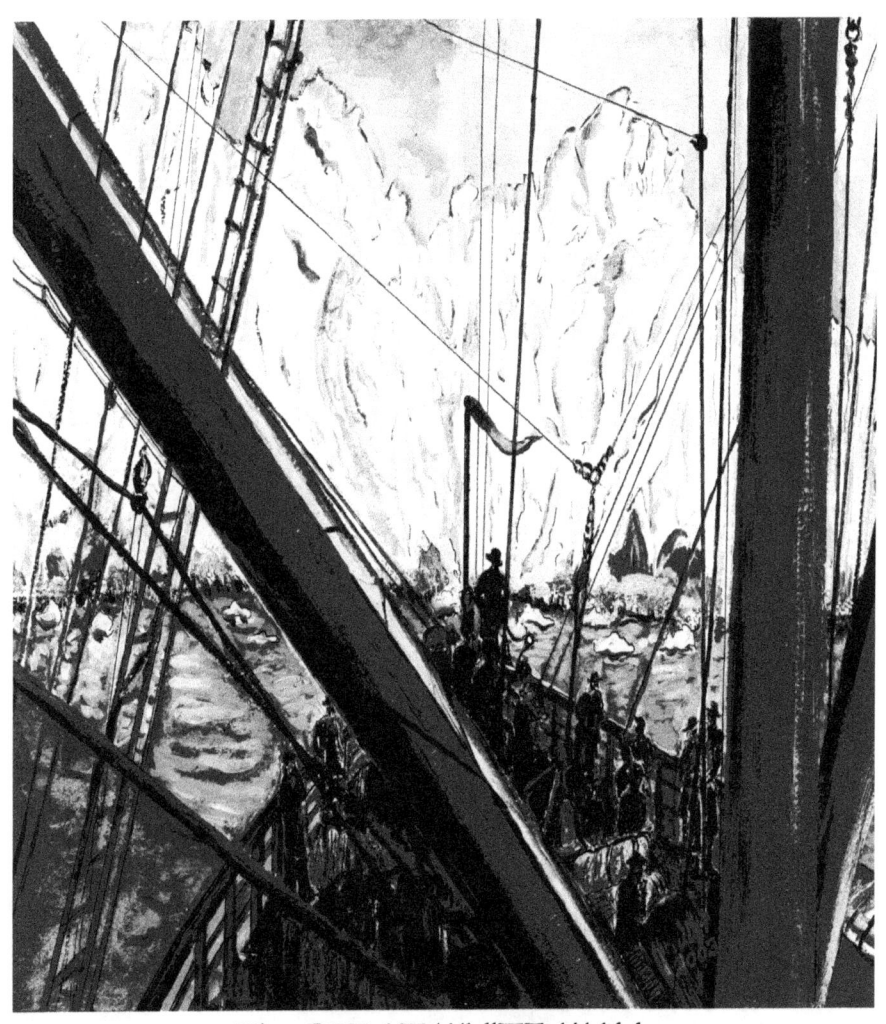

The GREAT WHITE WALL

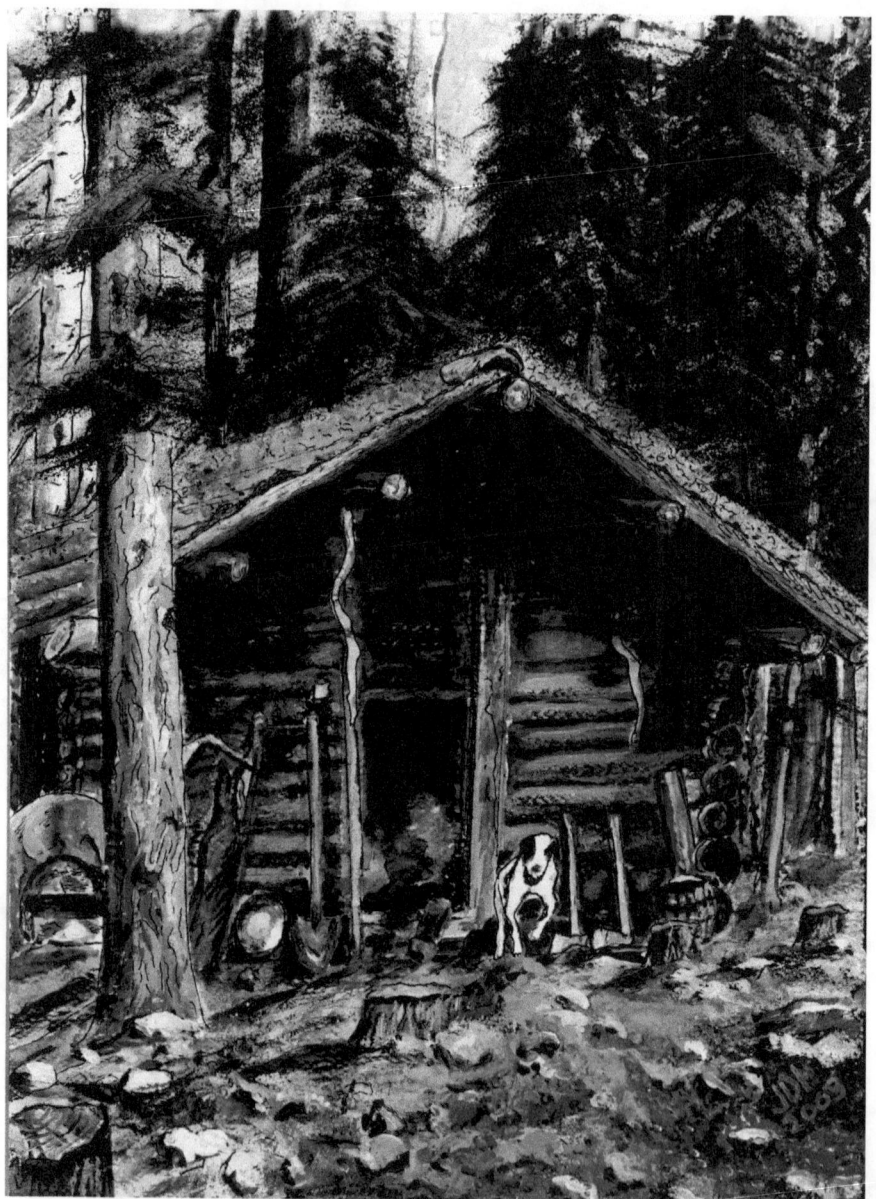

The CABIN on the CREEK 1935

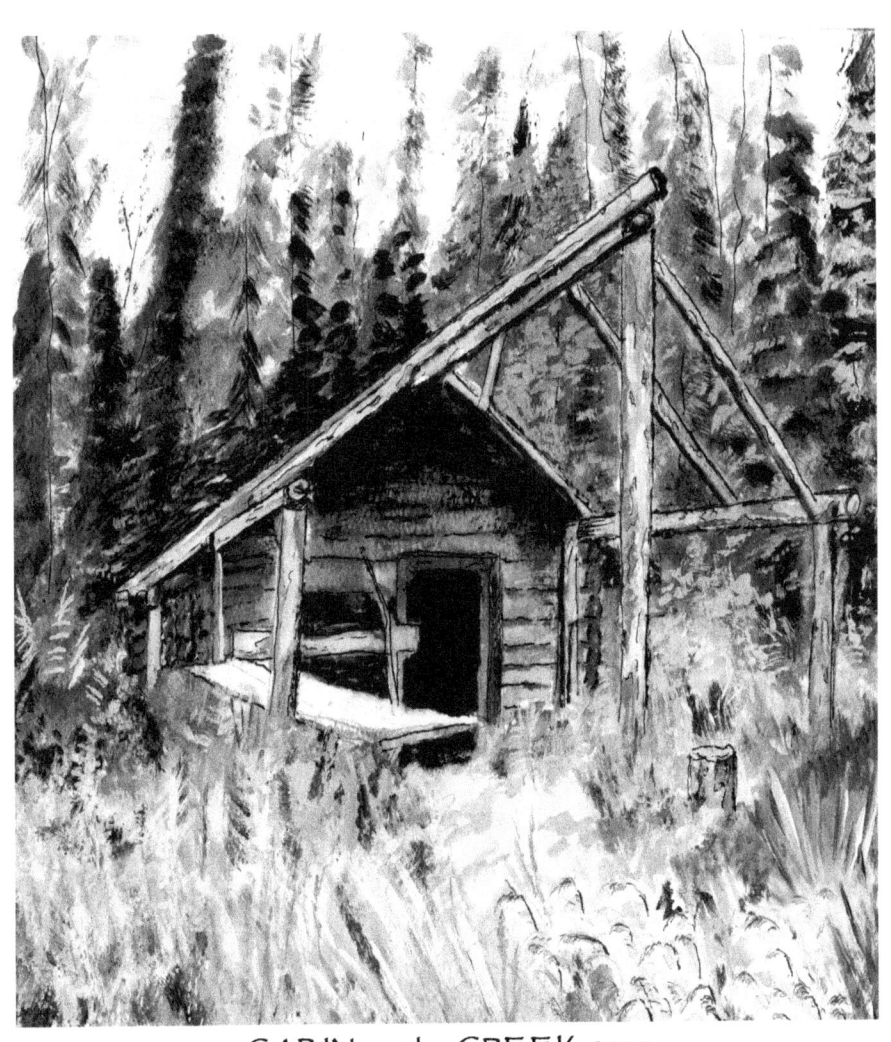

CABIN on the CREEK 2000

Matanuska Valley, Alaska
1936

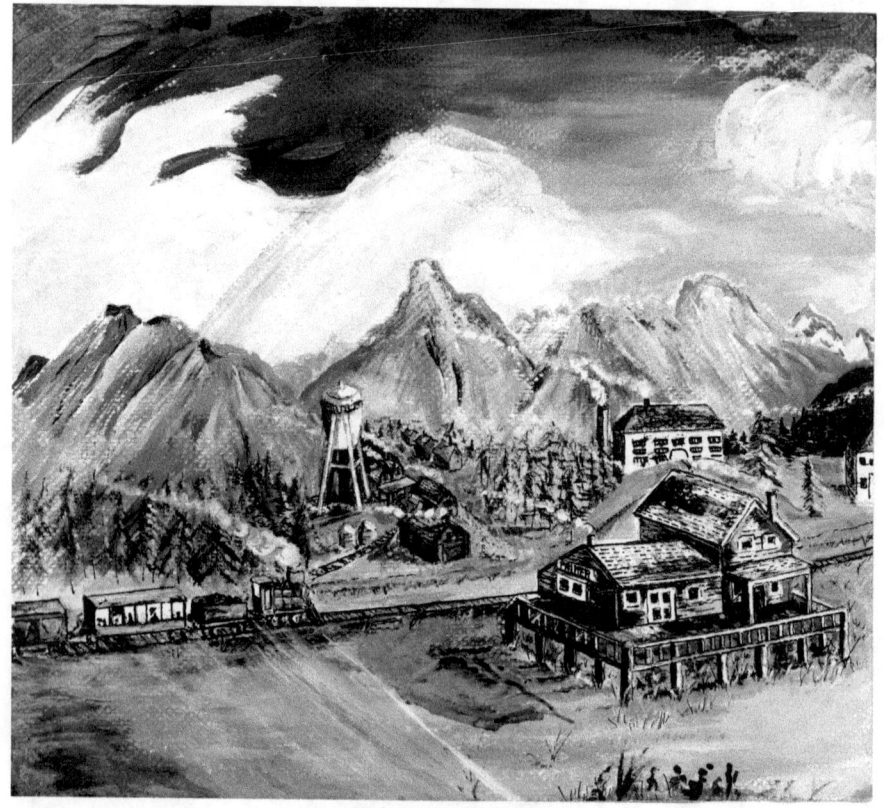

HAPPY VALLEY

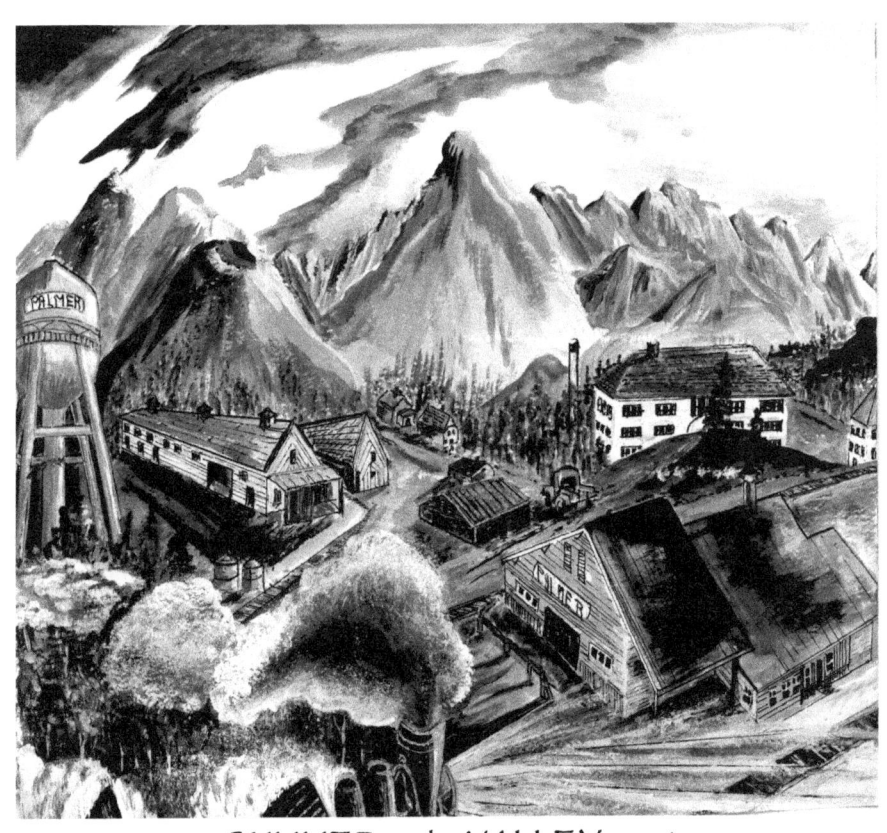

SUMMER in the VALLEY 1936

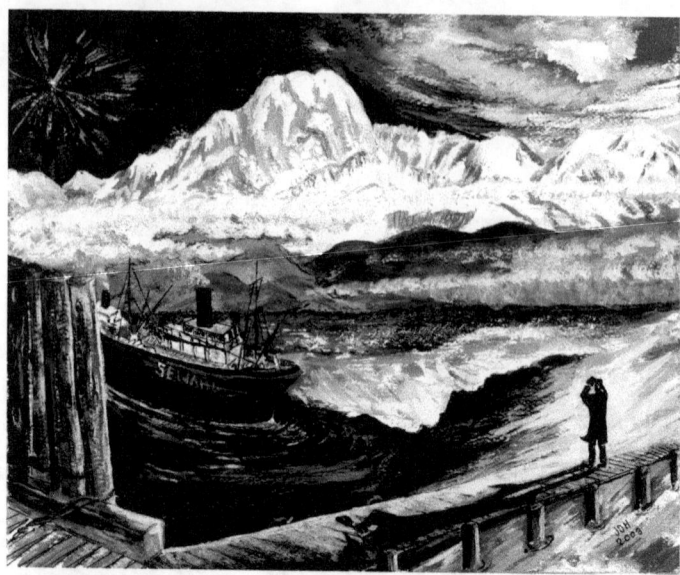

North Star

A prospector viewing the northern skies while waiting for his ship to dock. After studying it for a while, I realized the ship needed to be larger. Rather than paint another picture I digitally revised it by placing an enlarged ship into a copy of the painting (below). It worked and turned out to be one of the best illustrations in *LAST CHANCE ALASKA*.

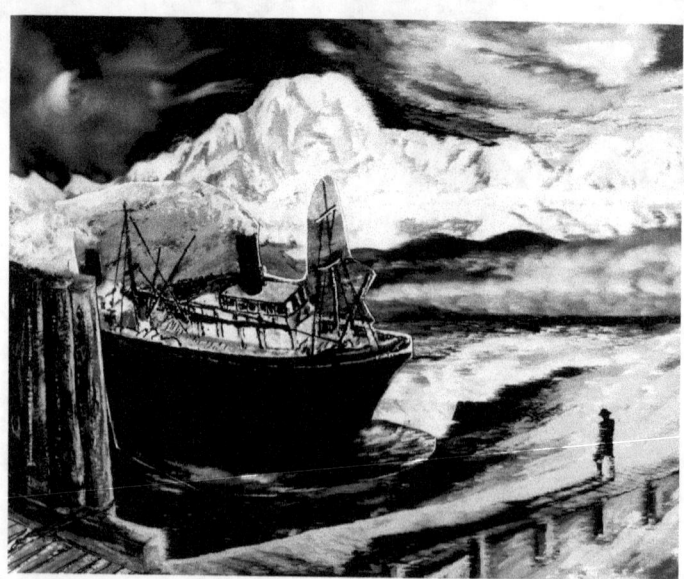

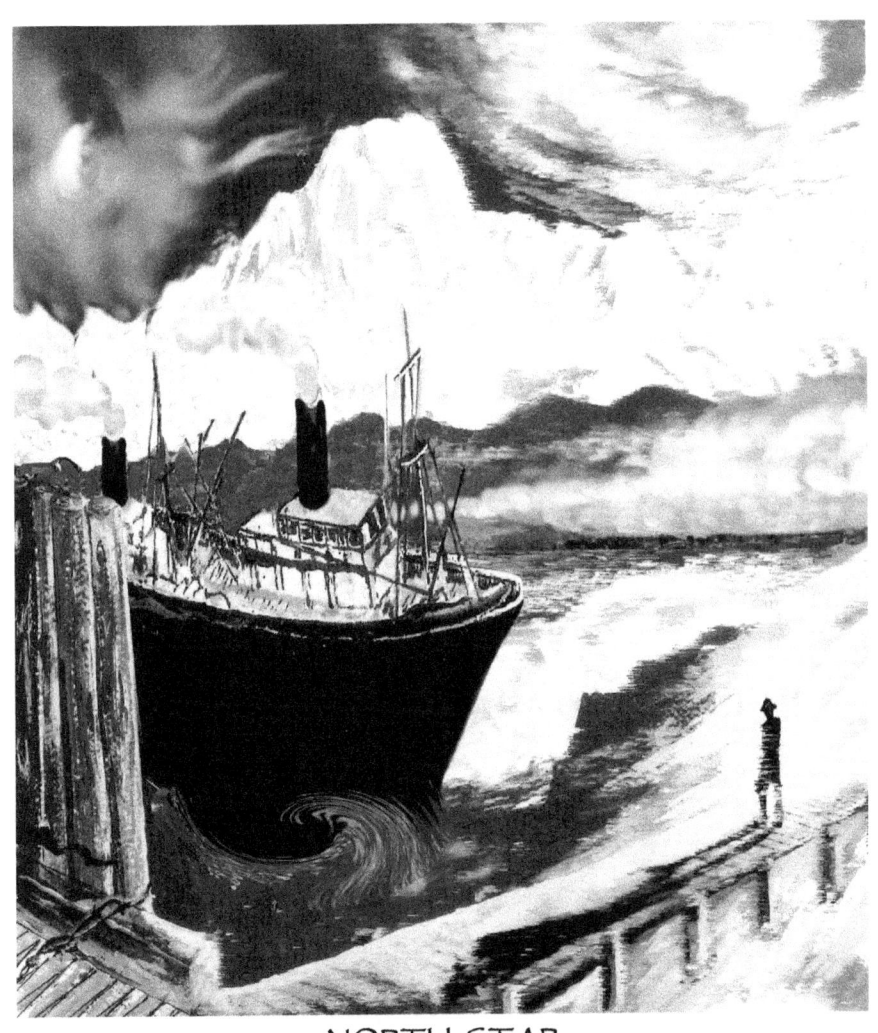

NORTH STAR

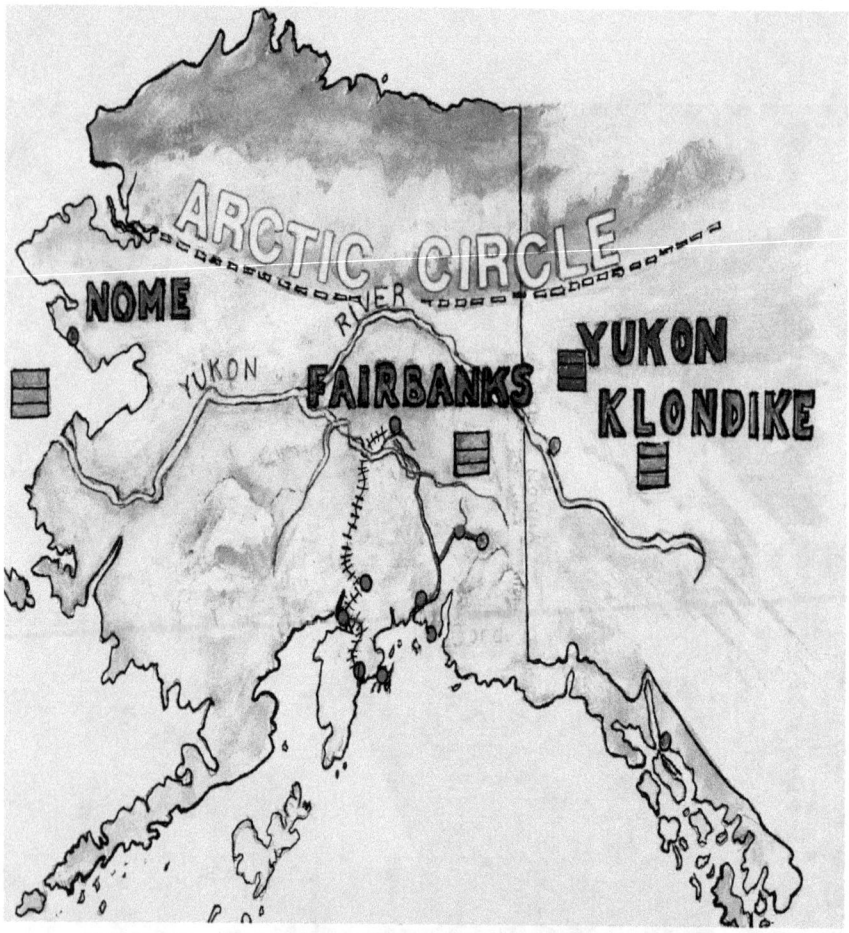

Map (not to scale): Alaska 1935-36 with Repeat Photo locations
(including GOLDBUG game mines)

This map was replaced and a more detailed map was used
to represent the 1935-36 journey of RAD.
When Douglas got back, to the lower northeast he created
a board game called Goldbug with each player running his
own gold mine. The mines were named NOME,
FAIRBANKS, YUKON and KLONDIKE.
Privately playing Goldbug in the 1950's created a lot of
excitement and fun. Regretfully, TV games have now taken
over and changed the way families entertain themselves.

194

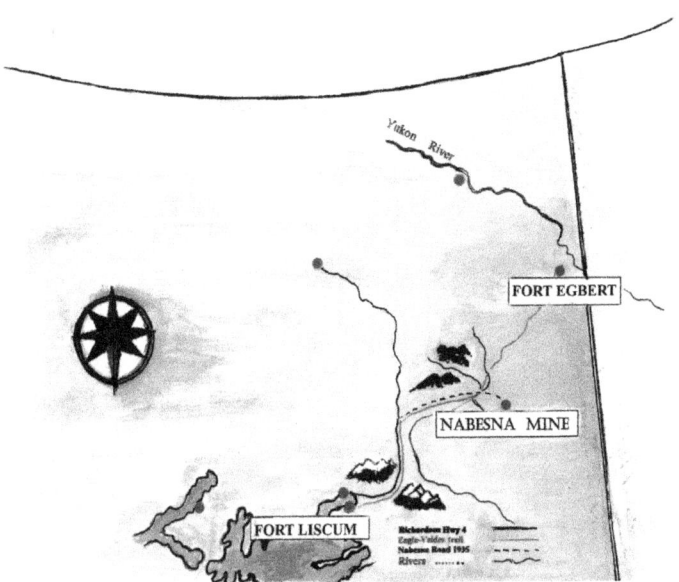

MAP 1899 (not to scale) EAGLE VALDEZ TRAIL, HIGHWAY 4, Rivers and 1935Towns.

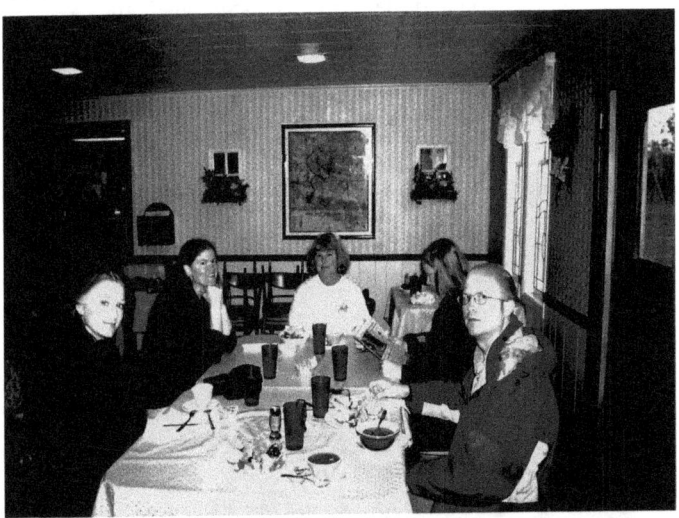

Heather, Alison, Jill, Diane and Ken at the COPPER CENTER RESTAURANT near Glennallen, Alaska. 2000   UEH

There it was on the wall behind us, the map we had been looking for. A 1934 map not depicting the Glenn Hwy. It was a map of the Copper River Region and general vicinity published by the Seattle Alaska Map Co.

195

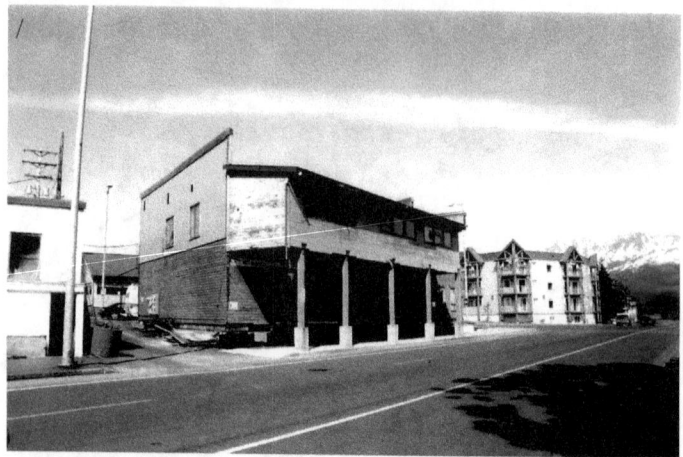

SEWARD DEPOT, Alaska 2001   Photos JDH

In 1903 the Alaska Central Railroad Co. began construction of a track system in Seward Alaska. It traveled past Alaska Nellie's Homestead — now a Roadhouse — to the upper Turnagain Arm. Goods were taken by boat at high tide and dog sled to Eklutna and the Matanuska-Susitna Valley — long before the colonists arrived.

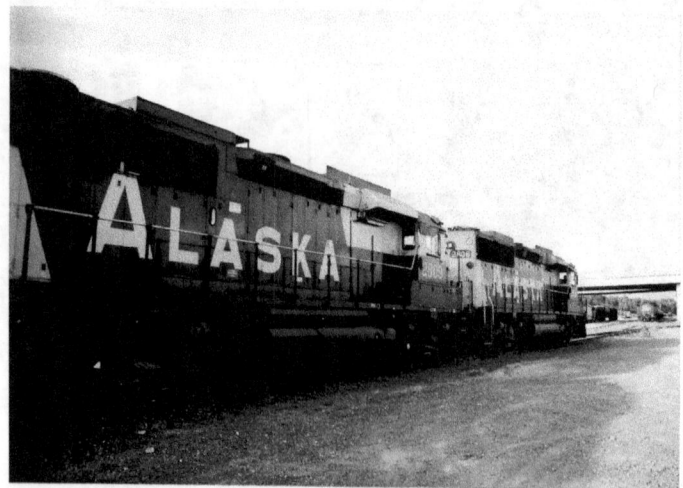

TRAIN YARD, Anchorage, Alaska 2001

In 1914, the government bought the now Northern Railroad Co. and moved its headquarters to Ship Creek — later called Anchorage. Over 470 miles of an all-weather route began.

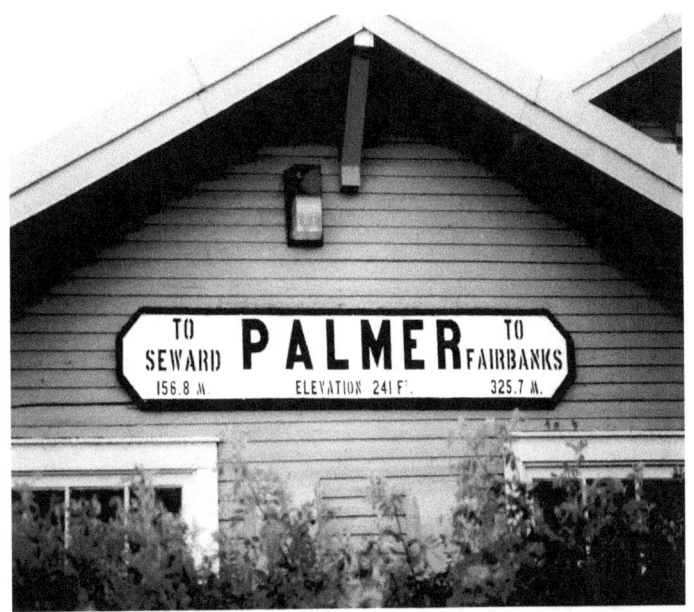

PALMER DEPOT, Alaska 2001   Photos JDH

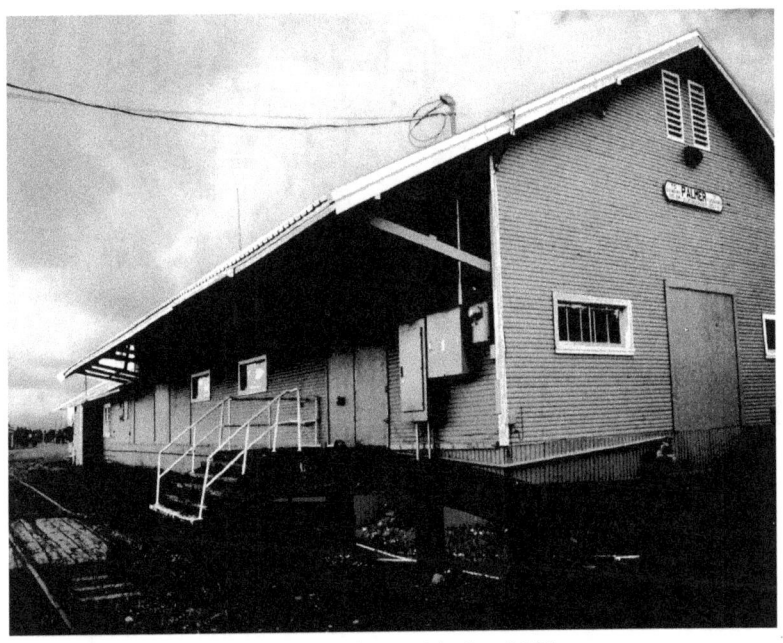

TRAIN STATION, Palmer, Alaska 2001

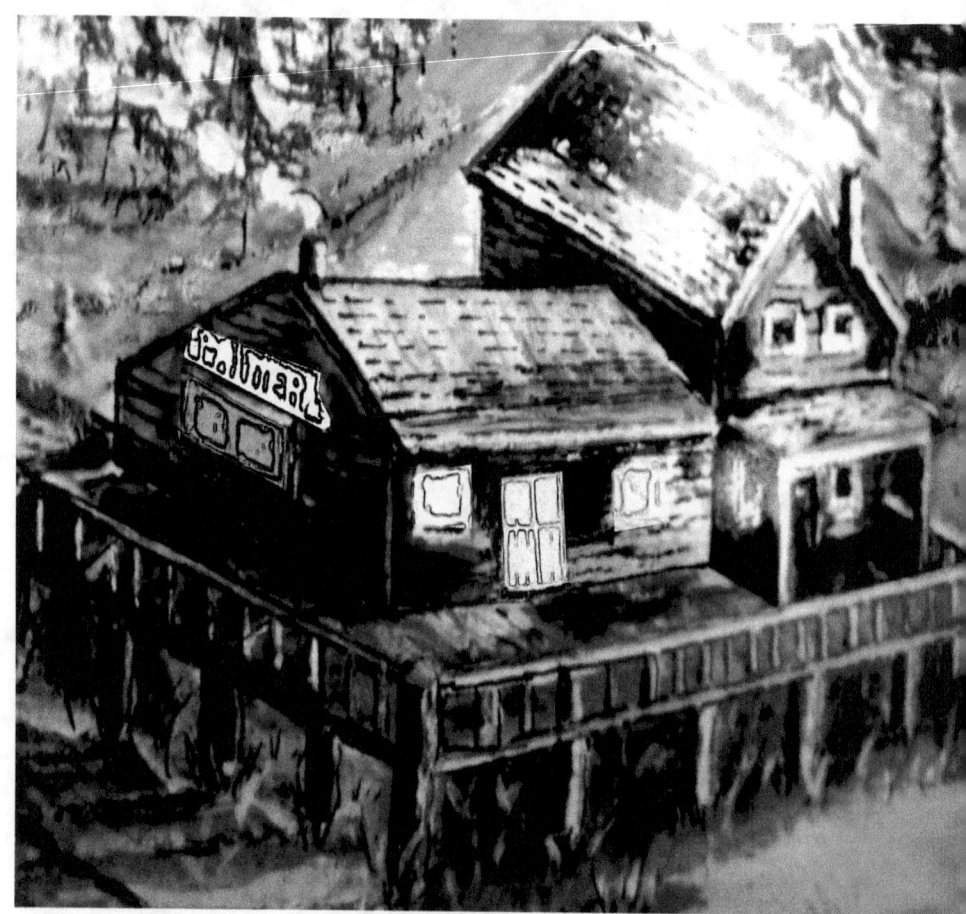

MATANUSKA VALLEY DEPOT, 1936

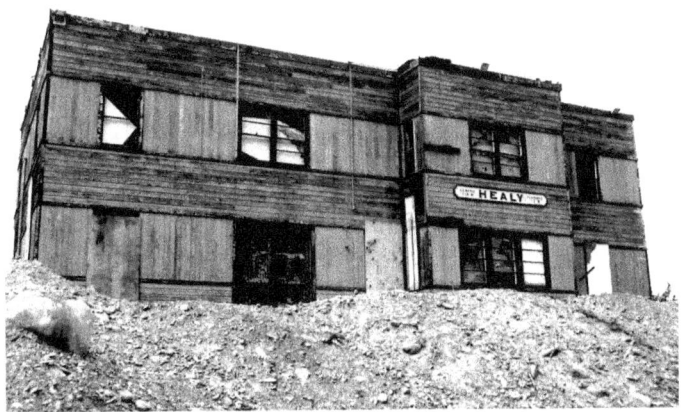

The HEALY DEPOT (relocated), Alaska. 2001   Photos JDH

The Healy depot sat stoically on top of a hill awaiting its renovation. The depot was once located close to the "old" Alaska Railroad tracks.

In 1923 the final golden spike was driven at the north end of the 700-foot-long Mears Memorial Bridge built over the Tanana River as part of the state's railroad project. This was the only link between Fairbanks and Seward until the George Parks Highway was finished in 1971.

In 1936 , a train stopped en route to the Matanuska Valley from Fairbanks and a few passengers disembarked. Was the sun shining on Mount McKinley (20,320 feet) that day, as the train continued down through the interior?

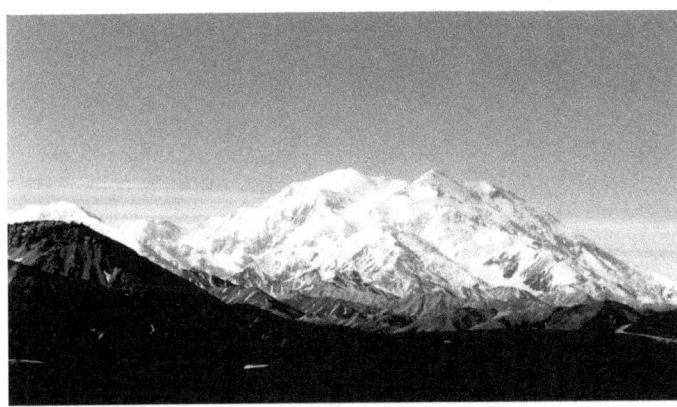

Mount McKinley, Alaska 2001

199

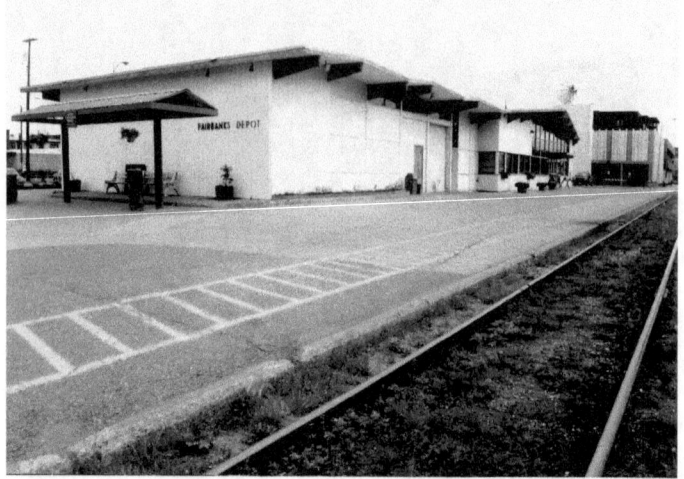

FAIRBANKS DEPOT (current), Alaska 2001   JDH

RAILROAD EXPANTION?
  A railroad line from Fairbanks to Delta Junction is under construction. It is unclear the length of time needed to complete the project.
  There are other interesting proposed connections to the nearby lower 48 states. As of now, some governments do not want to commit funds, but the Yukon government *is* interested. It was proposed to base in Carmacks, Yukon and travel from Delta Junction, Alaska to Hazelton, British Columbia. This line would make its way through Watson lake, Yukon and Dease Lake, British Columbia.
  Another scenario would route it from Delta Junction, Alaska, again using Carmacks, Yukon as the hub. This line would go through Watson Lake, Yukon and down through Fort Nelson, British Columbia. It would continue to Peace River, Alberta with a southern base at Fort McMurray. The time frame of the lower 48 proposals are still in work.

2 YEARS of INCREDIBLE ALASKA

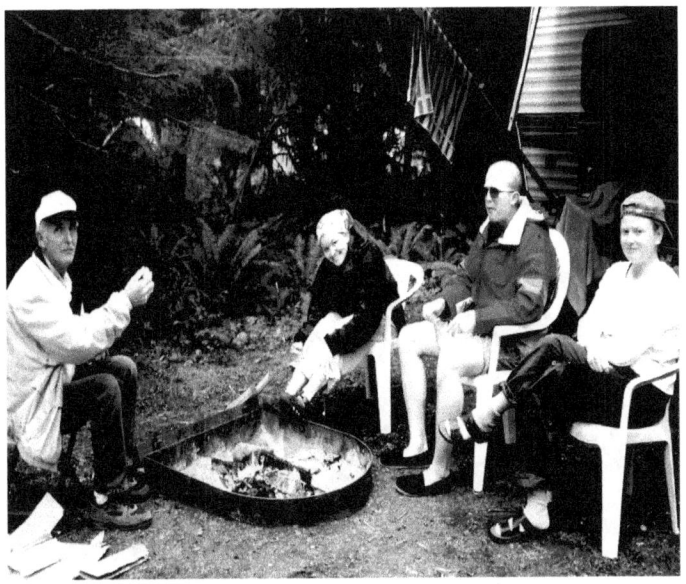

IRON CREEK STATE PARK, Washington. 2000   JDH
HIKERS: Emory, Diane, Ken and Alison

Friday-Sunday, July 21—23, 2000
Relocated to a KOA for travel preparation on Sunday.

CONTENTS
BEHIND the SCENES 2000

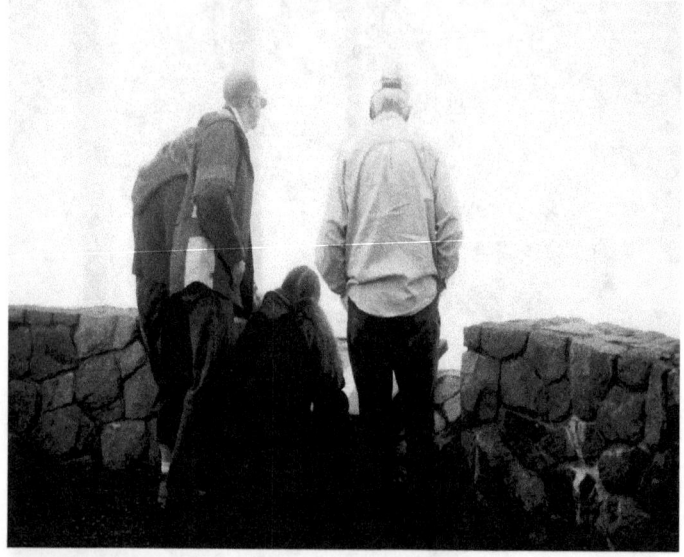

Washington State

"So, we're going to hike where?"

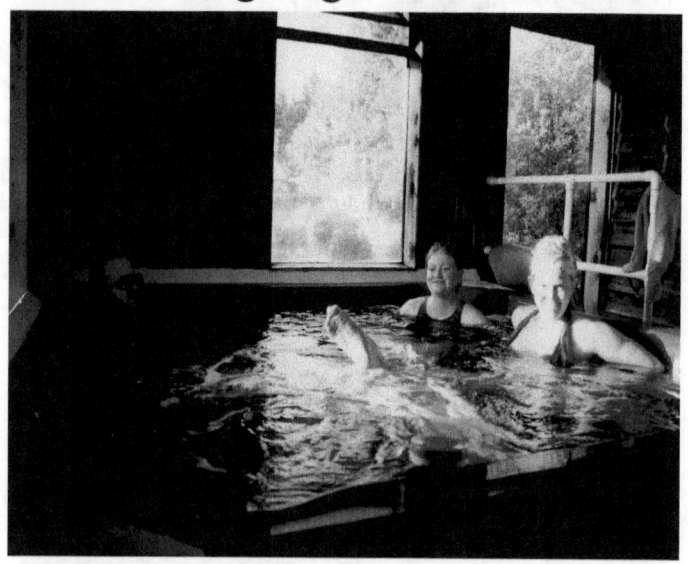

"What? No electricity?"

The next day the group was on an Alaska Airlines jet flying to Anchorage.

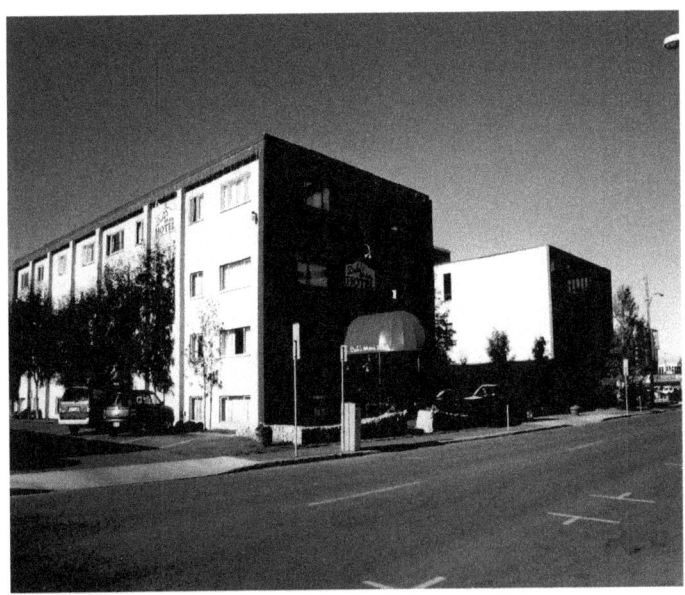

Duke's 8th Ave Hotel, Anchorage, Alaska.. July 24, 2000

July 24, 2000

A little apprehension prevailed because of a recent accident down by San Diego, CA. An Alaska Airline plane plunges into the sea. Playing it safe, we arranged two separate flights. Ken went with us.

The time of the first arrival is approximately 3:49 pm. We lost an hour. Later we all took a shuttle bus named Borealis to our 8th Ave Hotel, checked in and picked up our rental vehicle.

The little apartment that we had rented had a kitchen, so we went out to a food store and picked up groceries for 3 nights.

July 25, 2000

First thing the next morning, Emory and I headed to the visitor center to find out information on the 4th Ave. 1936 RAD photo. We were sent to the archives area of the Anchorage Museum. A man from the BLM met with us at the archives area and was extremely helpful in arranging our repeat photo of the 4th Ave. 1936 RAD photo. Also, the Government Hill 1936 RAD photo area.

The three hikers had other ideas of fun, and were busy arranging a kayaking trip on Lake Eklutna—just 40 miles north of downtown Anchorage.

July 25th continued

That afternoon we gathered together everyone and headed to Fourth Street to take the first Alaska repeat photo. They were entertained setting themselves up on the street while I snapped shots and took some video. Alone, Emory and I went to Government Hill to check out that photo potential. We found out the area we would be shooting had dropped during the 1964 earthquake.

Later, Emory and I headed to the airport to pick up the last hiker. She was coming in on Northwest from New York. Her plane ended up being about 2 hours late because of Tornados in Minneapolis. It was after 2 am before she arrived, but she was in good spirits in spite of the delay.

We all slipped in to a sleeping apartment.

July 26, 2000

Driving north forty miles was our first time out of Anchorage and all eyes were open. Eklutna Lake was a considerable distance in off the main road. A drive on a state park kind of road. It was worth it, though. The lake was a Turquoise blue, very cold at 45 degrees and had a depth of 300 feet. Eklutna Lake was 8 miles long before reaching the Eklutna Glacier.

There was a delightful lakeside trail leading to the Eklutna Glacier and beyond. Thirteen miles in, one way. Eight to the Glacier and five additional miles after that. Emory and I chose a long walk on the trail instead of kayaking.

An instructor gave the kayakers a quick crash course in safety. She mentioned that if you tip you would probably only have 15 minutes before dying, because the water was so cold. Also the Eklutna Glacier can calve causing waves that could tip you. Another issue due to it being in a valley, the winds and storms can pick up quickly without notice and can send you into the water.

The four hikers went out for four hours and we were glad to see them returning. Our walk was fun, but we didn't have any weapons and we were concerned about bears. It really was very remote.

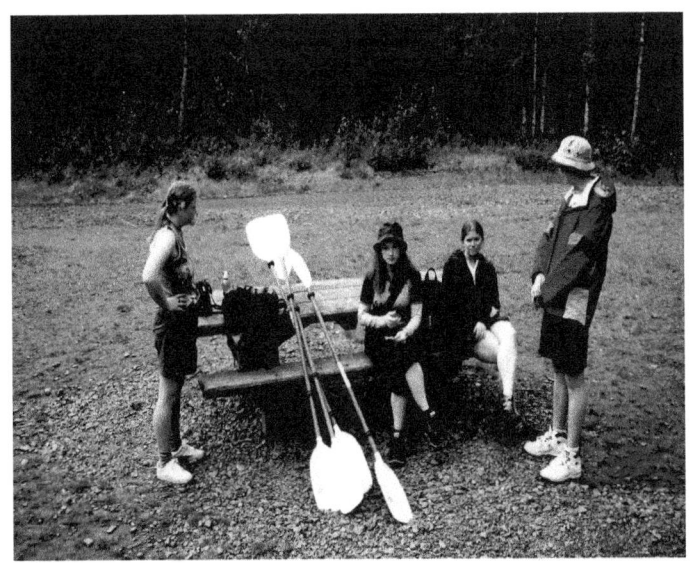

Diane, Heather, Alison and Ken, Eklutna Lake, AK. 2000   JDH
—Listening to the crash course in Kayaking safety.

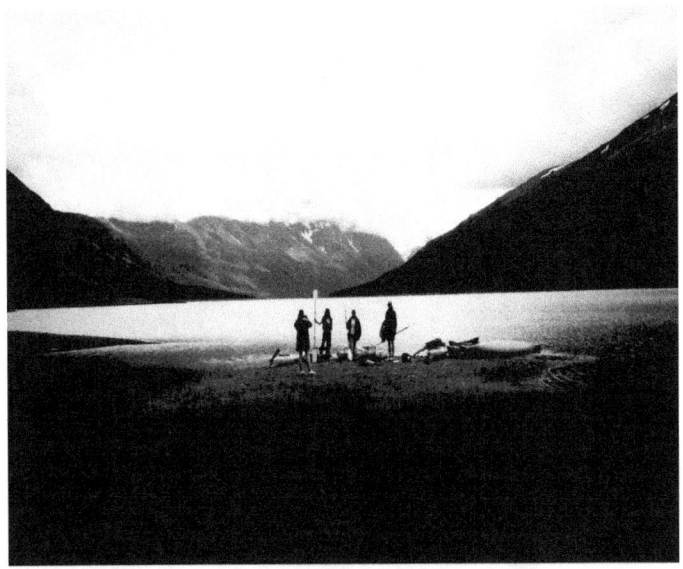

"Fifteen minutes, huhh? I'll swim to shore."

July 27, 2000

Now, the most north from Anchorage the hikers will travel in the year 2000.

For amusement during the packed "rental van" road trip up to Hatcher Pass, everyone was given a nickname—mocking out the new Survivor show on TV. Jokes were frequent. It went as follows:

> Ken was *T-Moo* (master organizer)
> Alison was *Sunny*
> Diane was *Willow*
> Heather was *Aerostar*
> Emory was *Grey Ghost*
> Jill was *Bear Food*

After a brief stop in Palmer to refresh and get directions, we began to head up. The mountains were pretty awesome! Many pictures were taken. Everyone was overwhelmed by the beauty of it all. It was like arriving at some Swiss chalets in the Alps—and the GOLD MINES!!!

It rained in the mornings and became sunny for a short time in the afternoon.

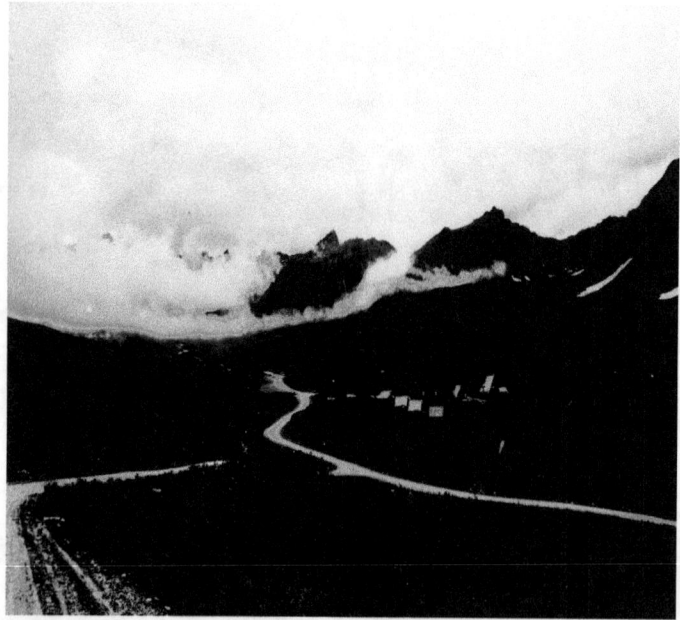

Hatcher Pass Lodge, Alaska July 27, 2000

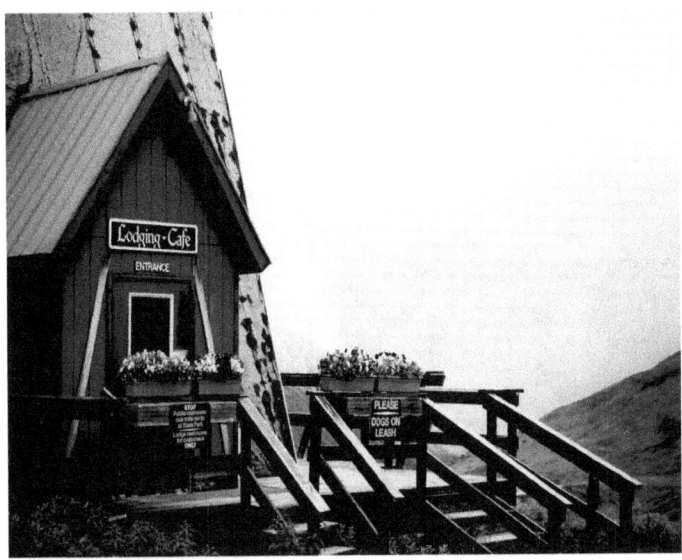

Hatcher Pass Lodge, July 27, 2000

There was an ulterior motive for choosing this lovely spot. There were some 1936 photos to duplicate. "Go where the stories live," I kept saying to myself.

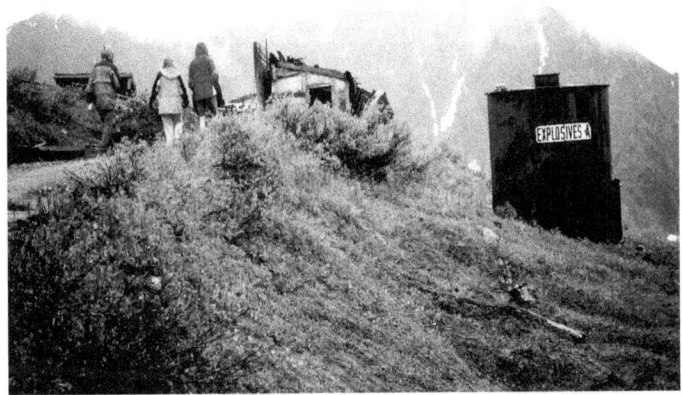

..That afternoon we hiked up to the Gold Cord Mine and made several trips to the summit to locate the rock two young Matanuska Valley teens stood on for that 1936 bathing suit picture. The clues were in the mountain tops.

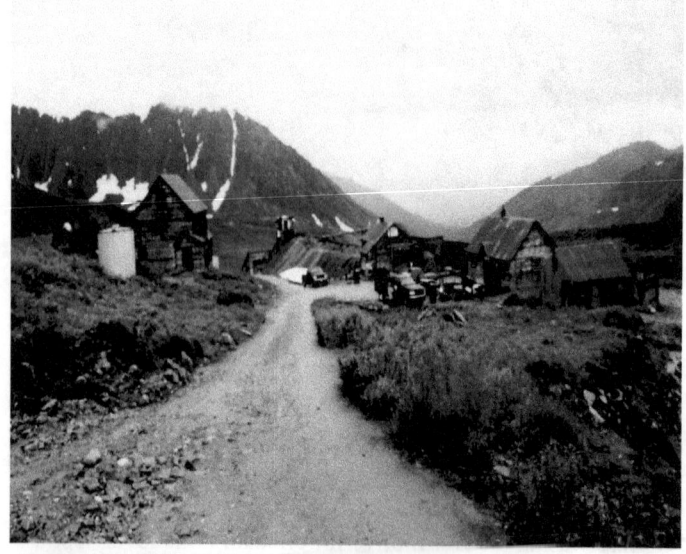

The Gold Cord Mine, Hatcher Pass, Alaska. 2000

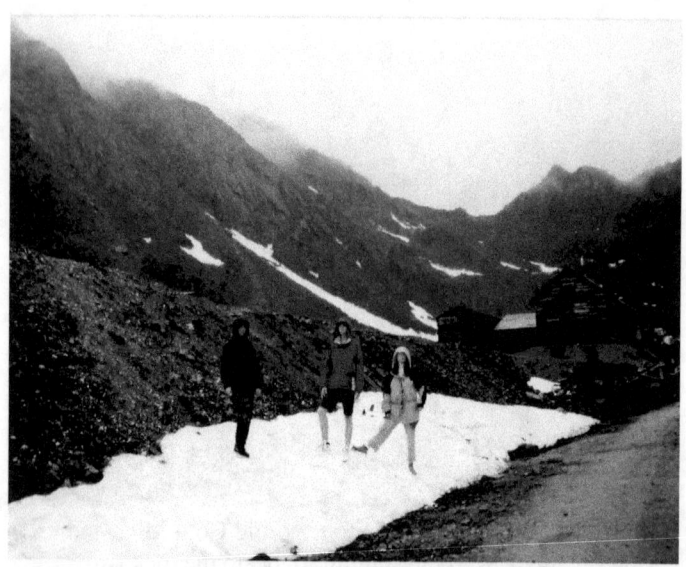

Hikers: Alison, Ken and Diane chose their own kind of amusement and hiked off by themselves.

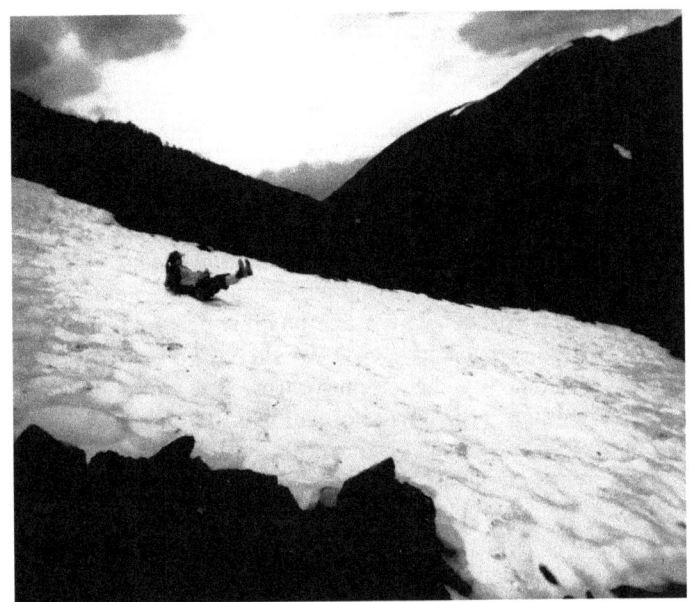

Diane sliding down Marmot Mountain, Hatcher Pass, Alaska.

Friday, July 28, 2000

"It was cold and raining."

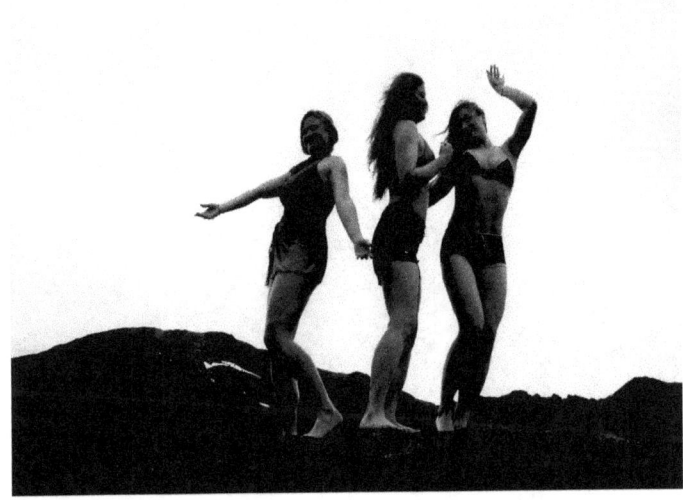

All ran to the summit rock from a warm car for an unforgettable photo shoot.

Friday, July 28, 2000 continued

It was after that rainy photo shoot that we continued on over the mountain pass to the little town of Willow. Somewhere beyond the Willow Creek Mine, we took a picture of what we thought might be the Lucky Shot Mine. The location seemed right. The road coming down was terrible. It went on forever with nothing at the bottom except a blue port-a-potty. The area one of the hikers got their nickname from. Yes, we drove away and left a hiker behind!

July 29th the prospector (RAD) would have been 99 years old and he was the reason we were here in this spot. Somehow I must relay this information into four over stimulated "brain cases" blazing with excitement in a world they were now collectively apart of.

We had dinner together that evening at the lodge and made plans for Ken's birthday breakfast on Sunday. The girls were already creating his gift.

Saturday, July 29, 2000

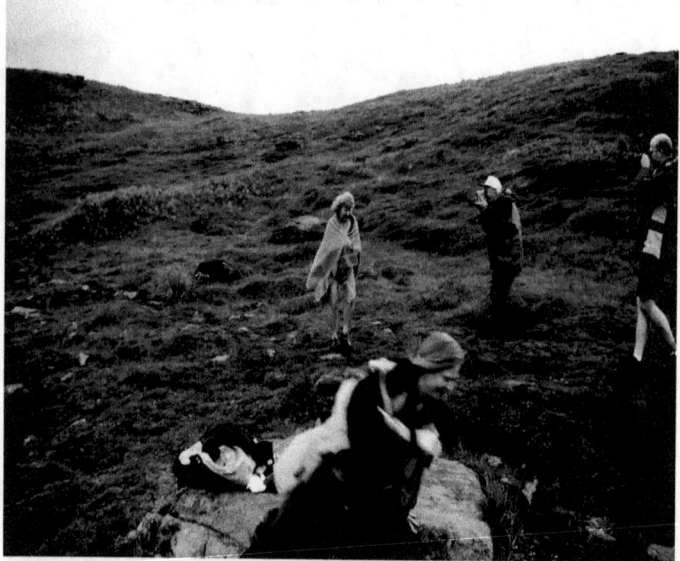

Cleary Summit Lake, Hatcher Pass, Alaska. July 29, 2000
Jill (author) becoming a member of the Polar Bear Club.

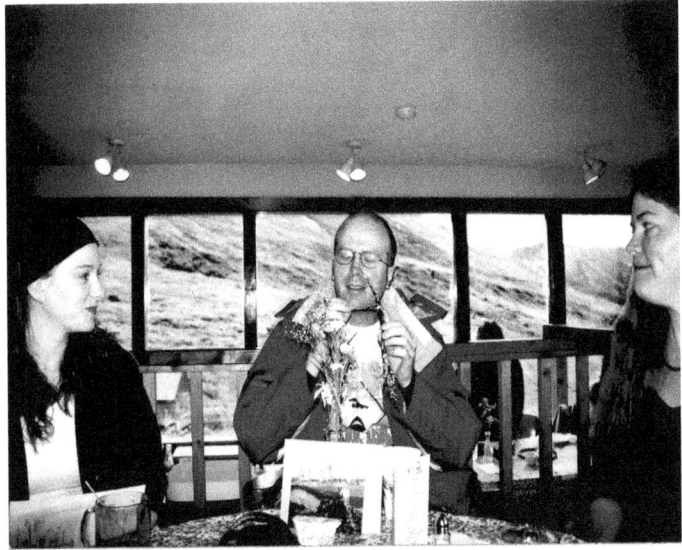

The birthday breakfast began in earnest. The gift of "Stick Boy" was a huge success. All was well at the Hatcher Pass Lodge in Alaska that morning.

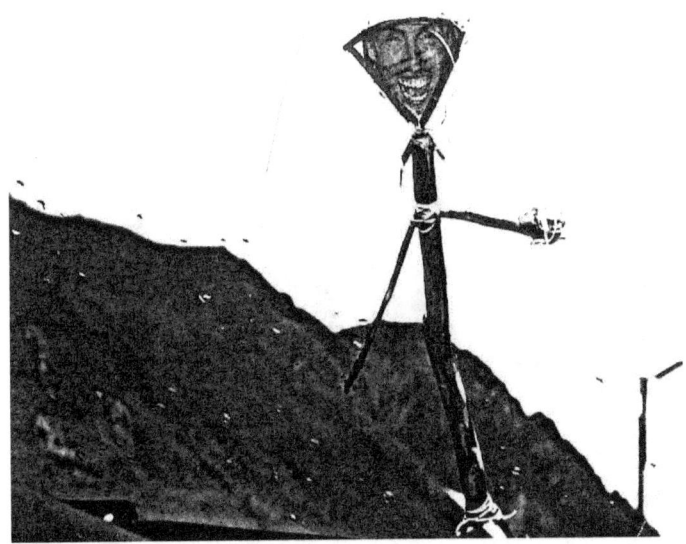

STICK BOY began a personality all his own. He even came with his own voice compliments of Heather.
"But now what we really came here for…"

211

Sunday, July 30, 2000 continued

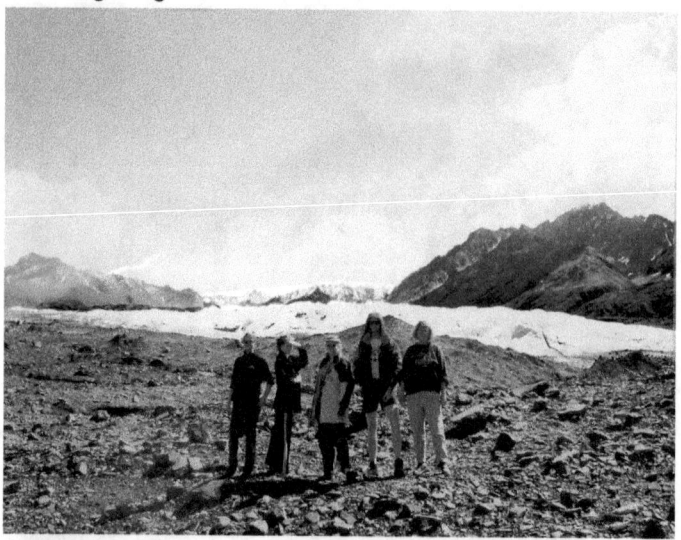

On the way over to Glennallen to pick up some directions at the BLM, we were diverted by a unanimous vote to turn right and follow the sign to walk on the Matanuska Glacier.
Above are the photographers responsible for taking the photographs for *Behind the Scenes 2000* including the photographer who took this photo. All standing on the Matanuska Glacier, Alaska.

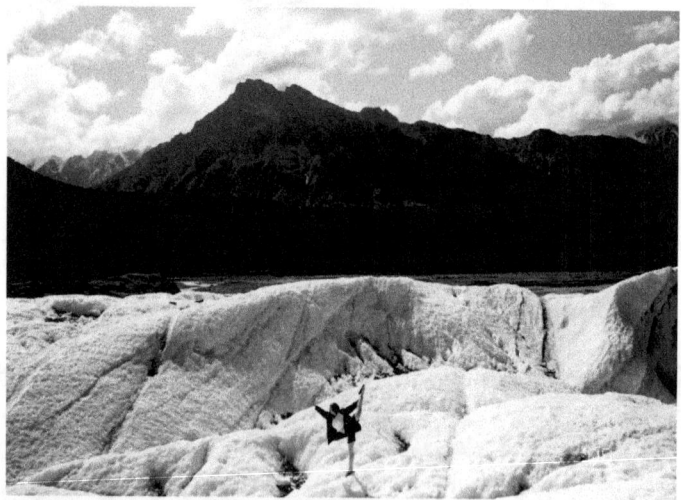

Hiker: Heather strikes a pose on the Matanuska Glacier. They allowed visitors to walk on their own, unattended.

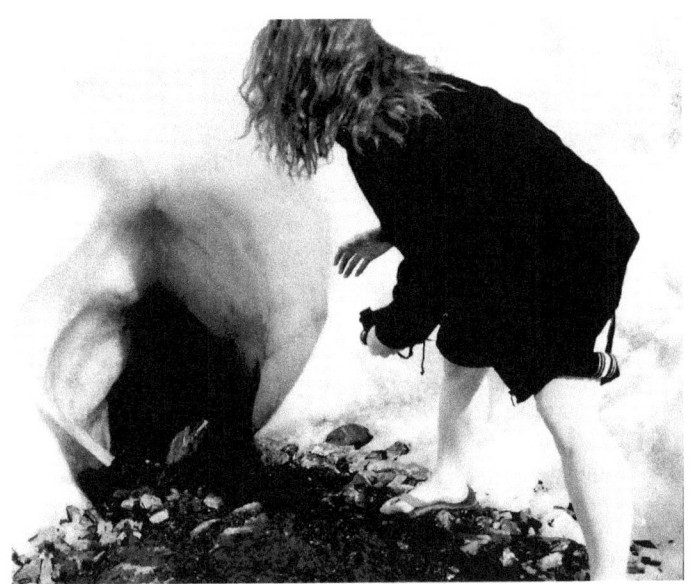

Hiker: Heather looks down a glacier tunnel leading to an underground flow of icy cold water.

Dangerous, but very exciting. Hazards were everywhere!

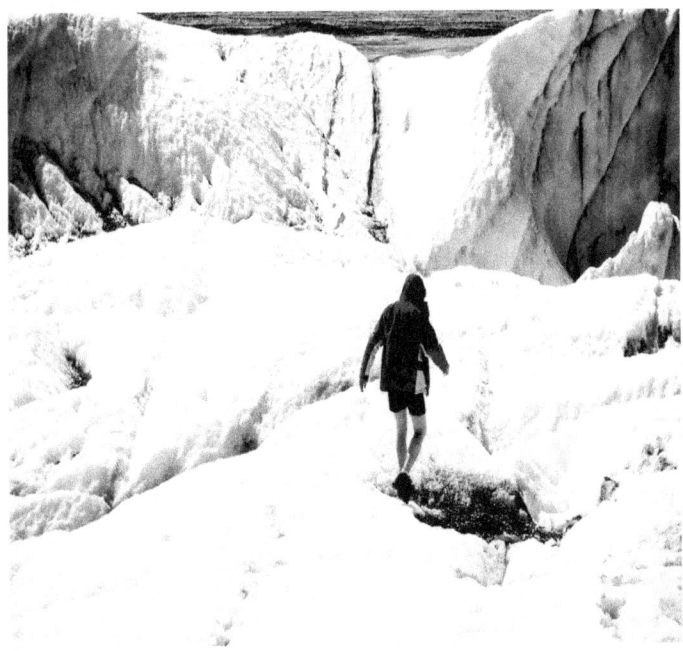

Hiker: Ken walks by an ice-break to the right and a crevasse to the left.

Sunday, July 30, 2000 continued

The Wrangell-St. Elias National Park mountain range began to come into view, as we headed east toward Glennallen. Silence took over and each had to deal with their own thoughts of what might be ahead. So this was Alaska!

As we reached the Caribou Café, had some dinner and studied the maps from the BLM that were waiting there for us on the door as per phone call. We knew we had a job to do. All were committed. No more talk of Stick Boy, T-Moo, Willow, Sunny, Aerostar, Grey Ghost and Bear Food. Bear food was now <u>all too real</u>! Continuing on, passing an incredible valley view of Mount Sanford on the right and unfamiliar trees on the left, we began looking for the trailhead. After several failed attempts at locating it, we picked up the cel and called the BLM. It was a tricky find. Now for setting up and preparing our packs.

The rooms were very spacious and very new. Strangely out of place, but we weren't complaining. Most who book here were interested in the Wrangell -St. Elias National Park.

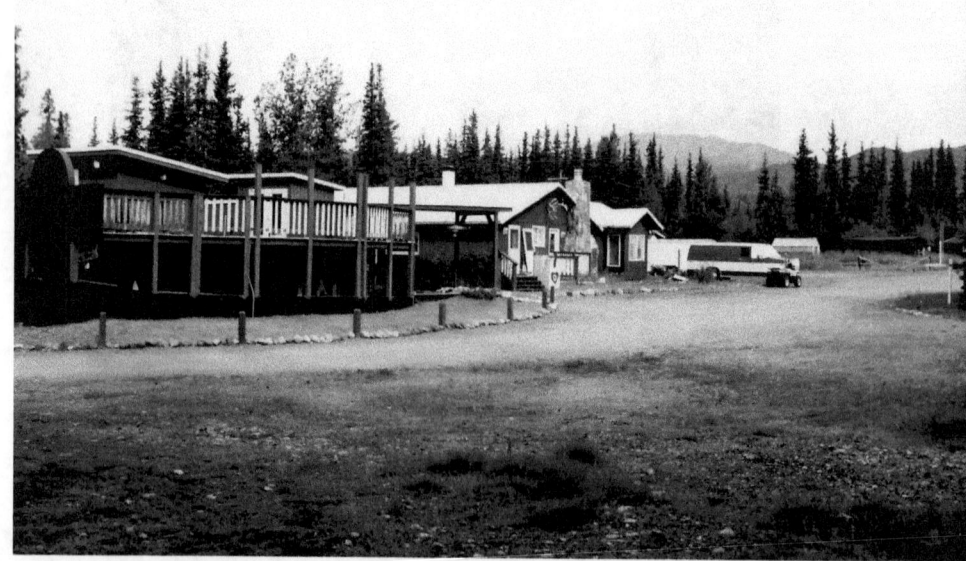

The Hart-D-Ranch, Slana, Alaska. 2000

This ranch did not exist in 1935. RAD stayed down the road at the Slana Road House on Nabesna Rd.

214

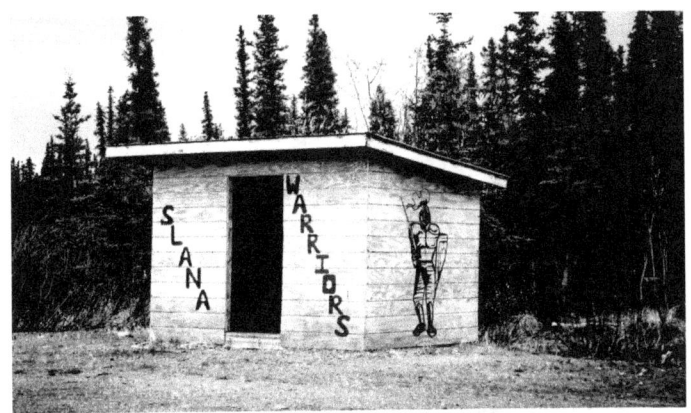

Perhaps a bus stop and shelter for the Warriors on Nabesna Rd.

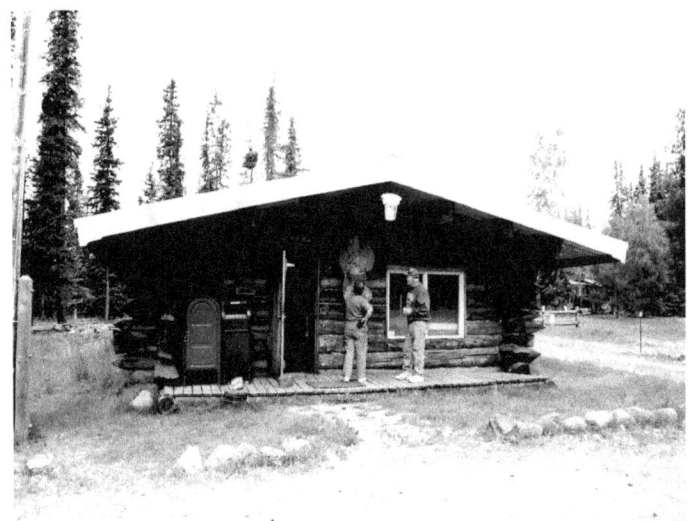

The Slana Post Office, Slana, Alaska 2000

The owner of the Hart-D-Ranch was also the post mistress for many years (above). A great place to prepare for our hike. The four young adults were pleasantly surprised to find this modern facility in the middle of no where.

The evening before the hike, there was a great energy moving about. With backpacks opened up, weapons being loaded and food supplies distributed, everyone went about somberly planning how they would survive. The cool weather and the rain were our enemies more than the grizzlies and black bear. Rain and coolness could lead to hypothermia.

215

Monday, July 31, 2000

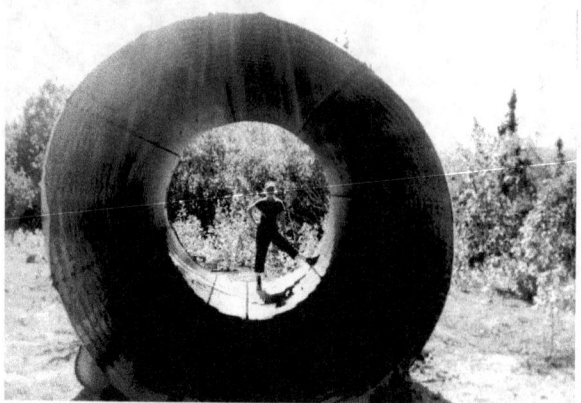

Hiker: Diane stands inside a piece of pipeline at the trailhead.

THE AHTELL CREEK TRAILHEAD

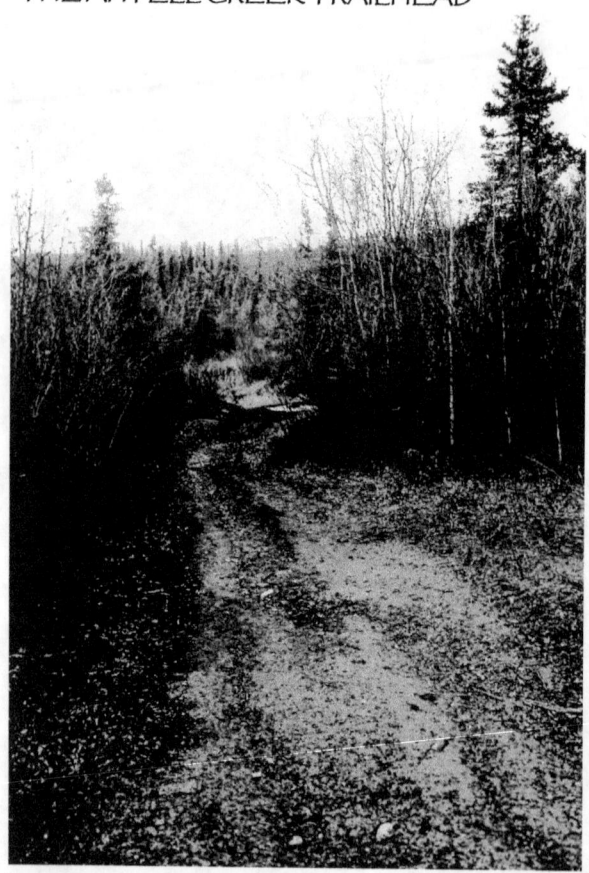

THE HIKE BEGINS

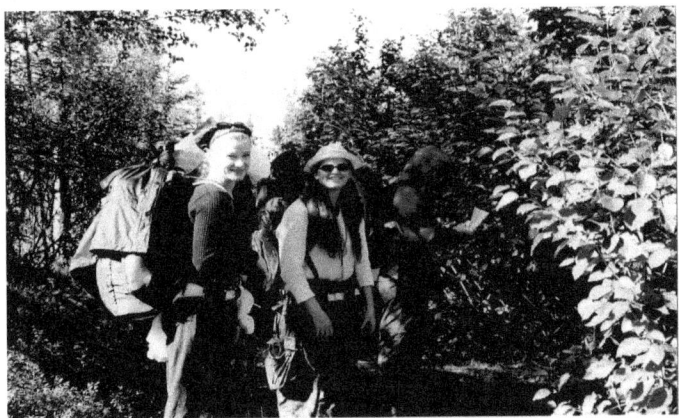

Hikers: Heather, Emory, Alison and Ken beginning the Ahtell Creek Trail in Slana, Alaska.

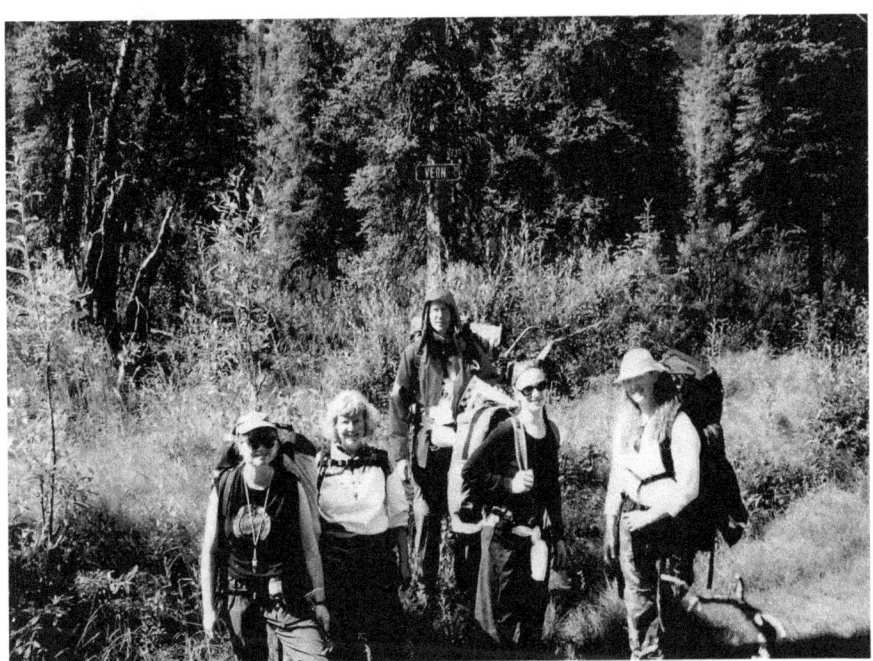

The trail seems to end. It appeared that the four-wheelers had taken a more northerly route to enter due to all the water and mud. If it weren't for the four-wheeler tracks every now and then, we might have been misled several times.

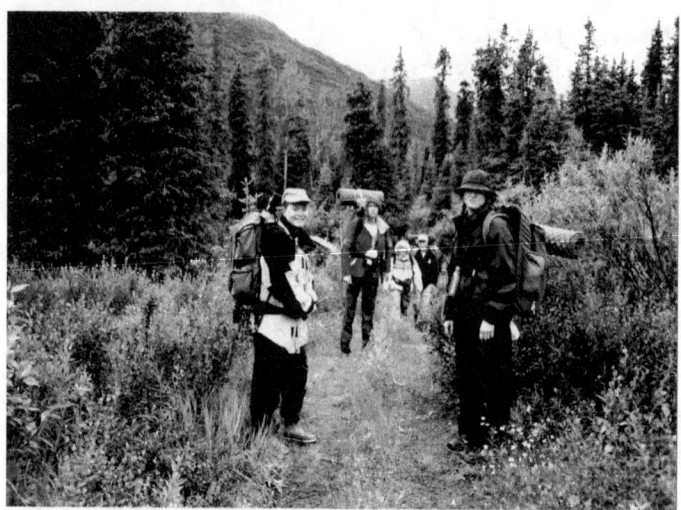

Hikers: Diane, Ken, Jill, Emory and Heather on the Ahtell Creek Trail, Alaska. 2000

The bonus pictures in the new *DIRECTOR'S CUT* chapter reflect the hike to the cabin, views from behind the gold mining cabin, the Grub Stake Creek Mining cabin, the BLM preparing to head back, setting up our campsite at the cabin, an additional "Casual Cabin Portrait" and fording the Ahtell Creek back out.

The documentation of our hike to the cabin is in Chapter III of this book. However, the following additional photos have been selected to boost the storyline of the event. Locating the old 1935 gold mining cabin was an important find.

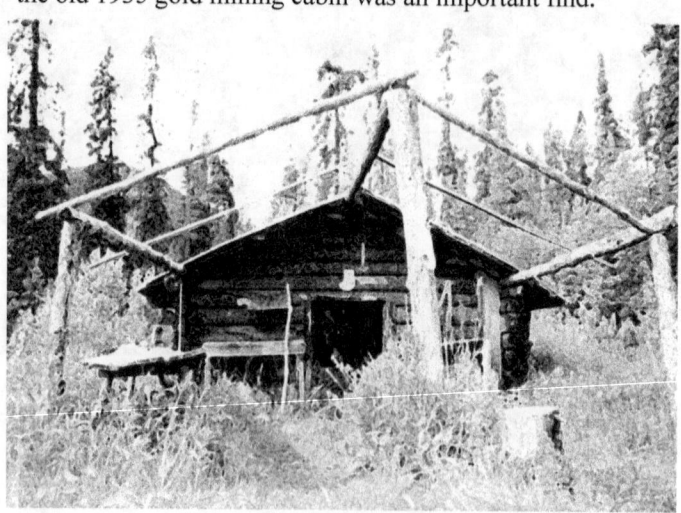

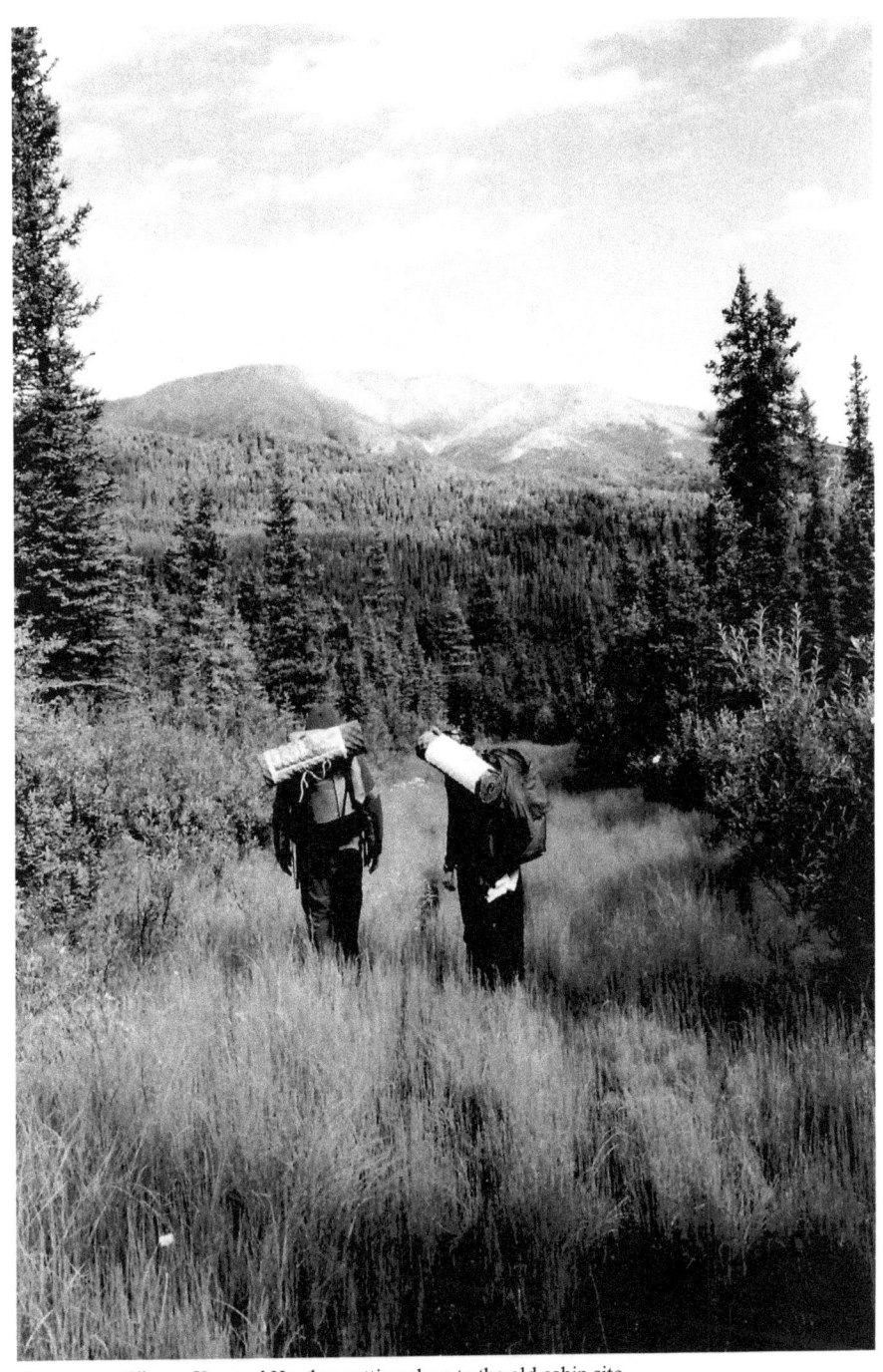

Hikers: Ken and Heather getting close to the old cabin site.

Monday, July 31, 2000 continued

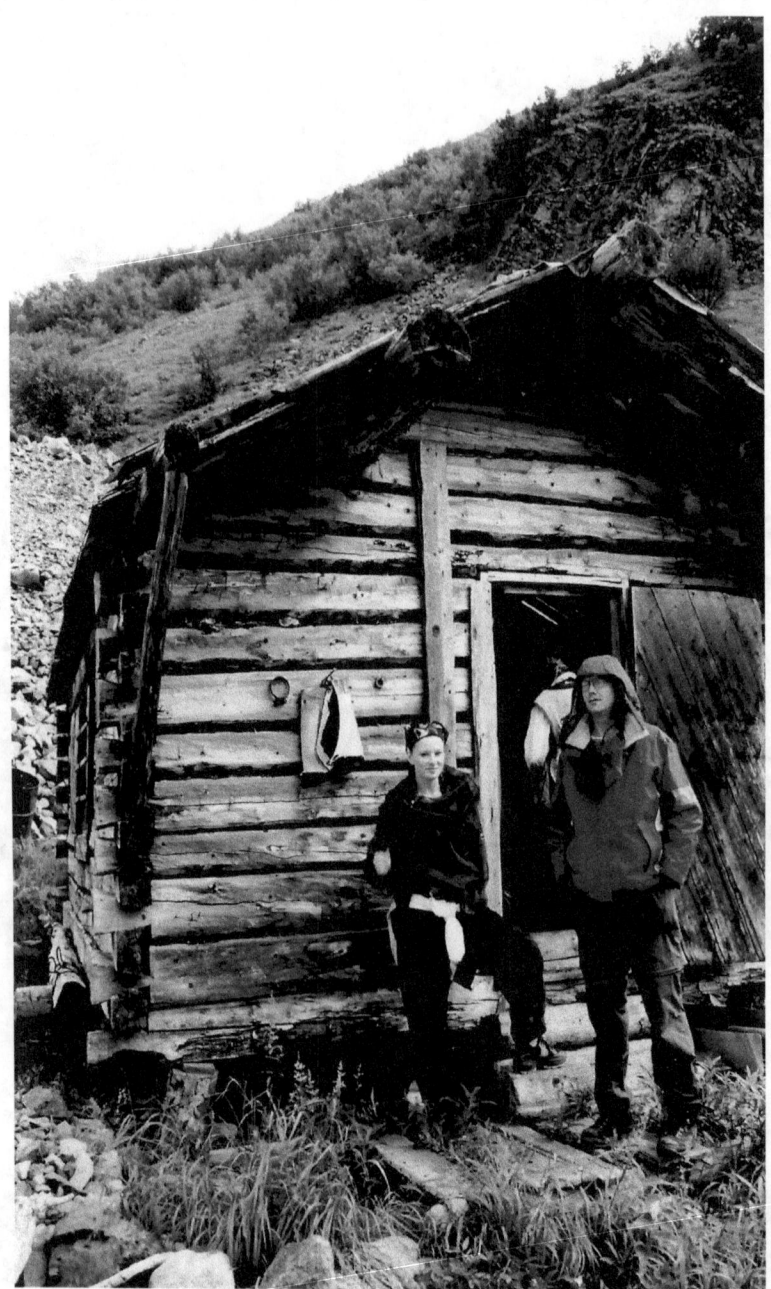

The Grub Stake Creek Gold Mining Cabin. Hikers:
Heather, Ken and BLM Specialist. 2000

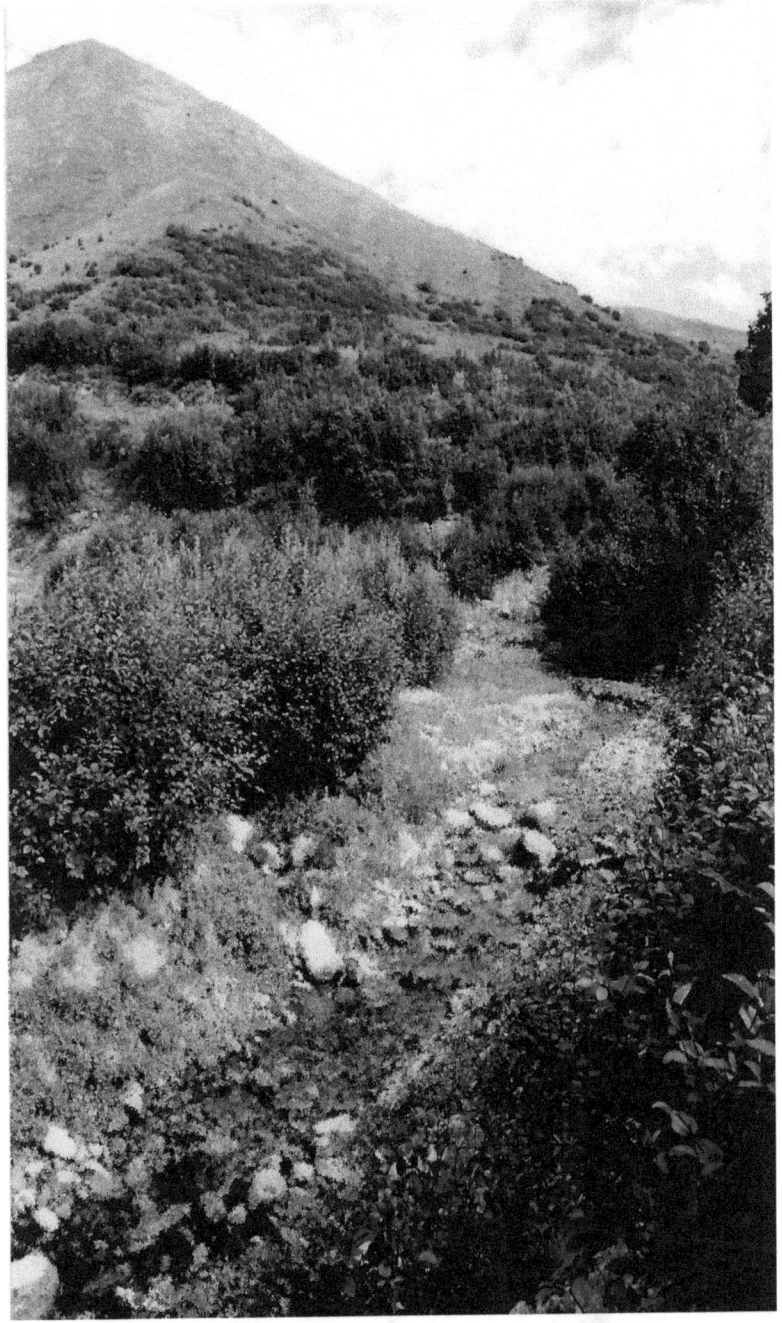

Monday, July 31, 2000 continued

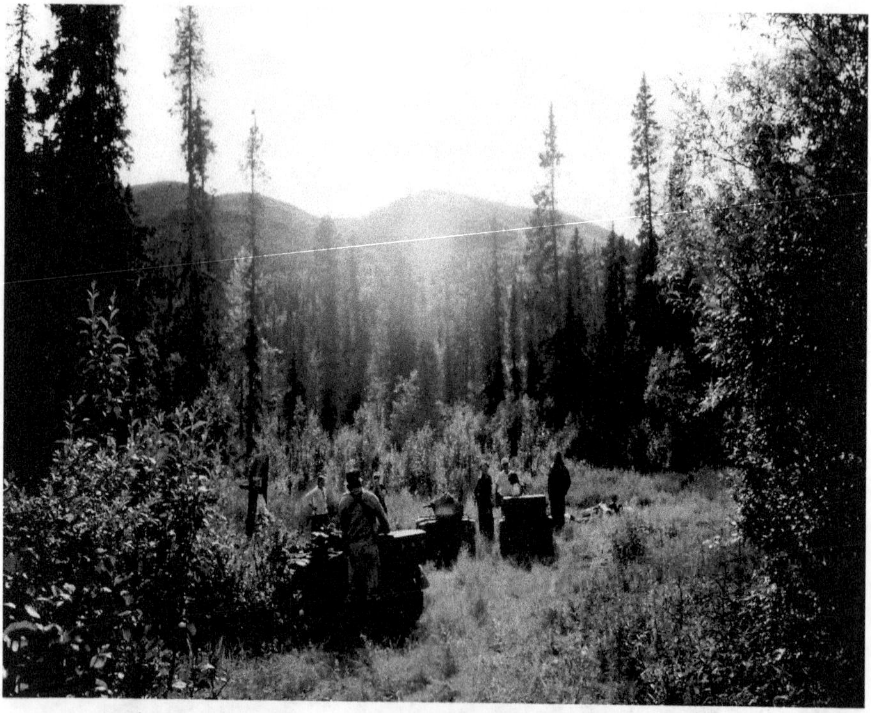

The BLM Specialists prepare to leave. The hikers are now all alone! Ahtell Creek Valley, Alaska 2000

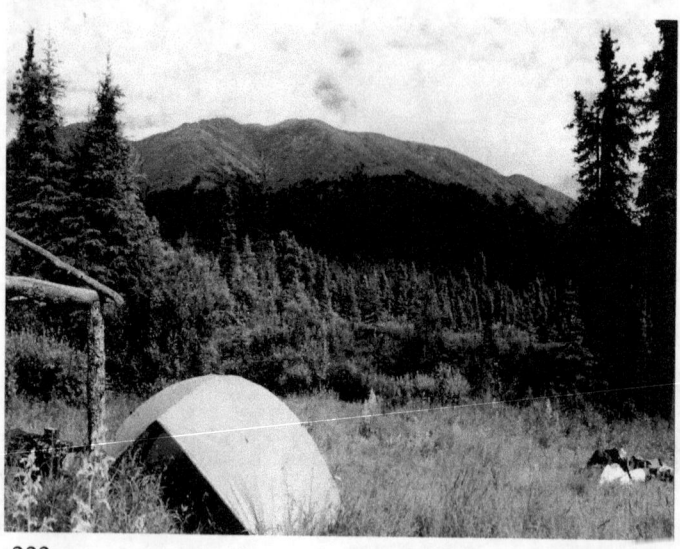

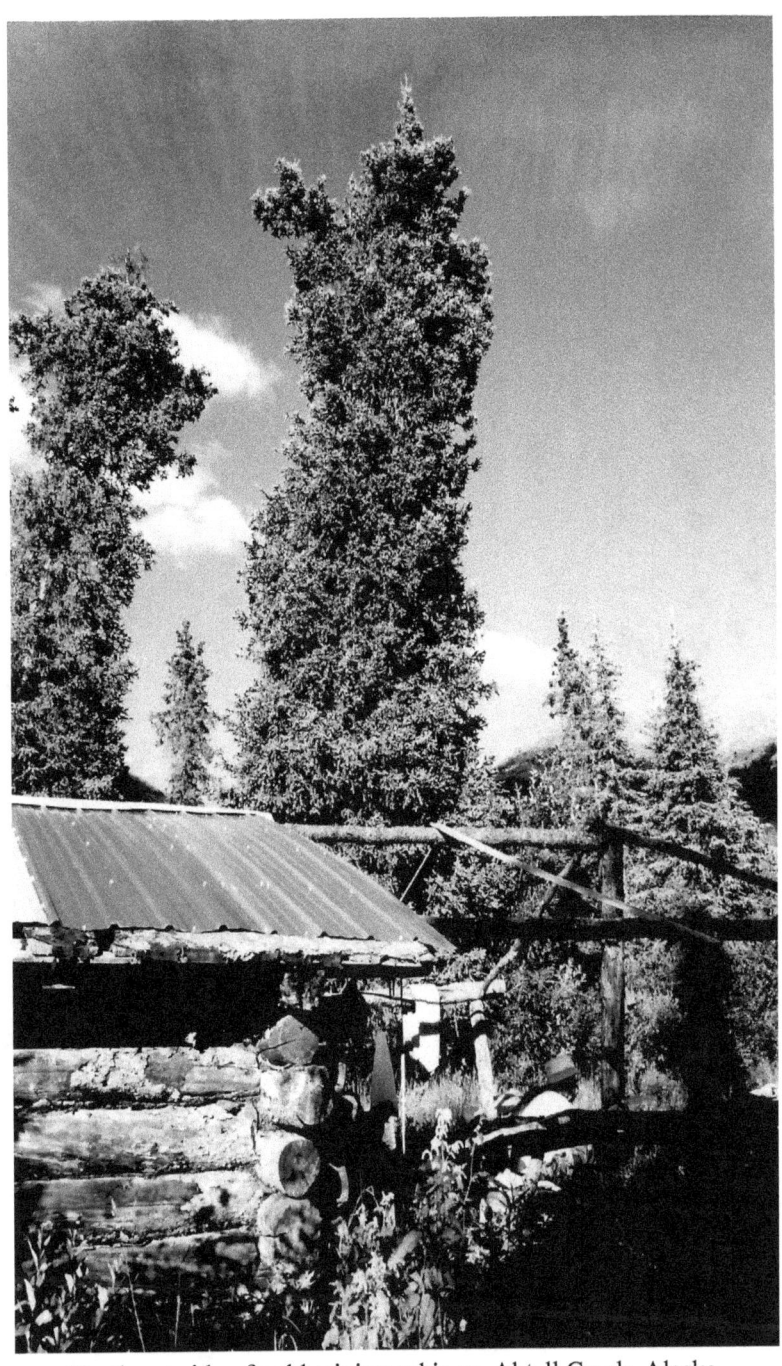

Northeast side of gold mining cabin on Ahtell Creek, Alaska.

Monday, July 31, 2000 continued

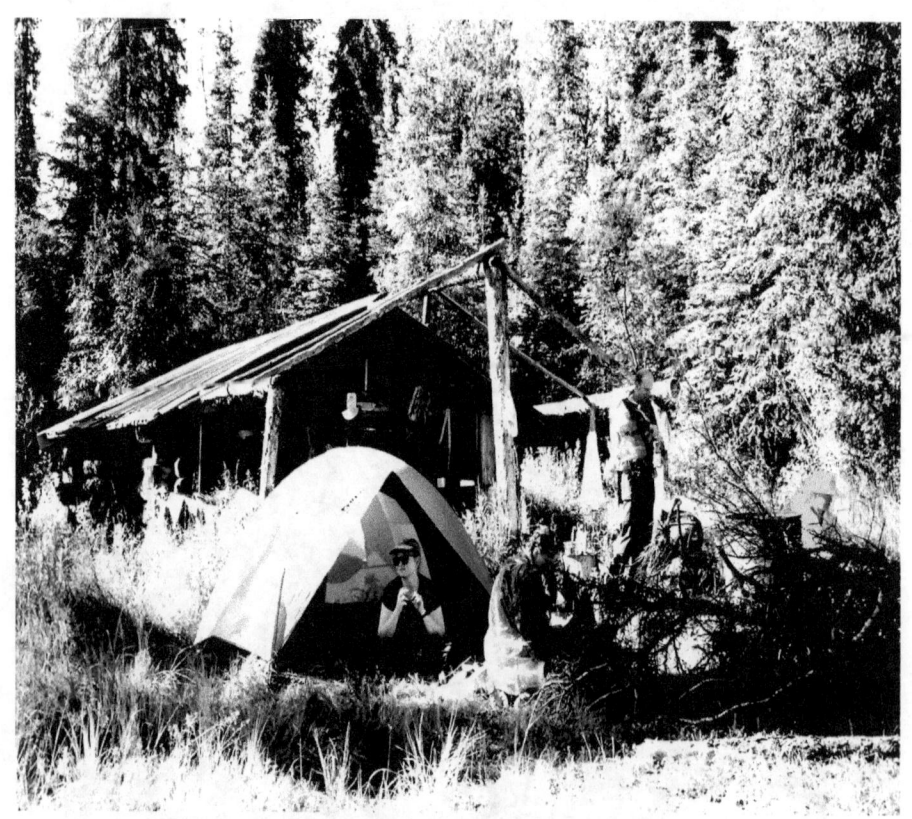

Unplanned Cabin Portrait 2000
AHTELL CREEK CABIN, Alaska

Tuesday, August 1, 2000

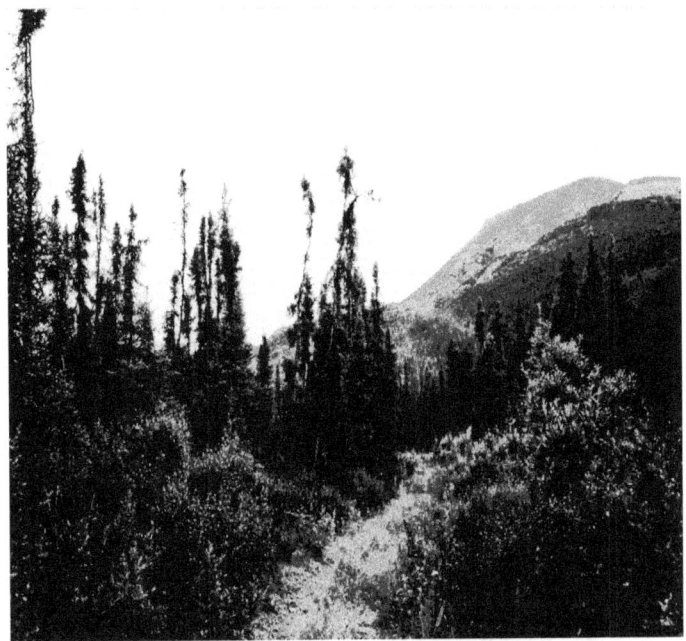

Eight mile trail back.

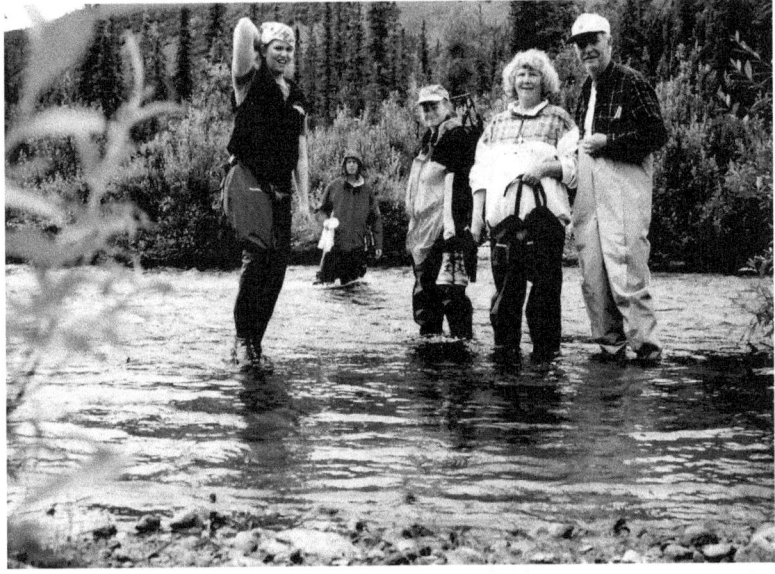

Fording the Creek out...Hikers: Alison, Ken, Diane, Jill and
Emory / Slana, Alaska

225

Tuesday, August 1, 2000 continued

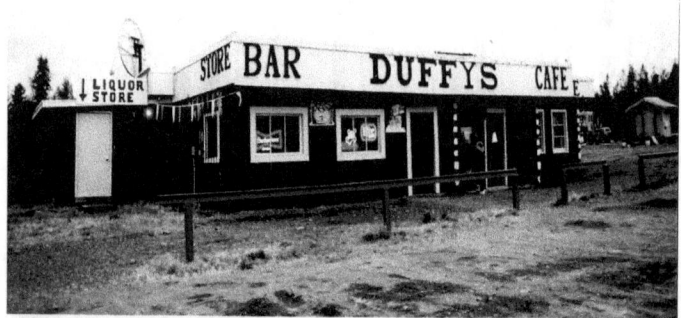

That evening we all went over to Duffy's Café to celebrate.
They ran out of hamburger meat, but the lady down the street
ran over with something else. There were cheers and a
thumbs up when she came through the door. No one
questioned what it was? (Below) hiker Ken enjoys his food.

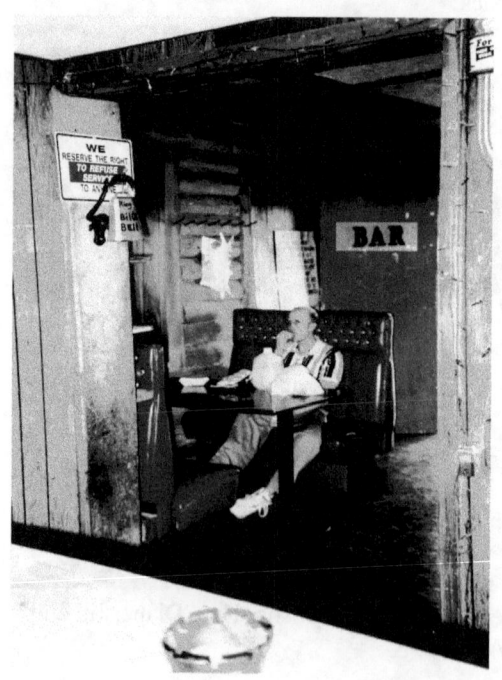

Wednesday, August 2, 2000

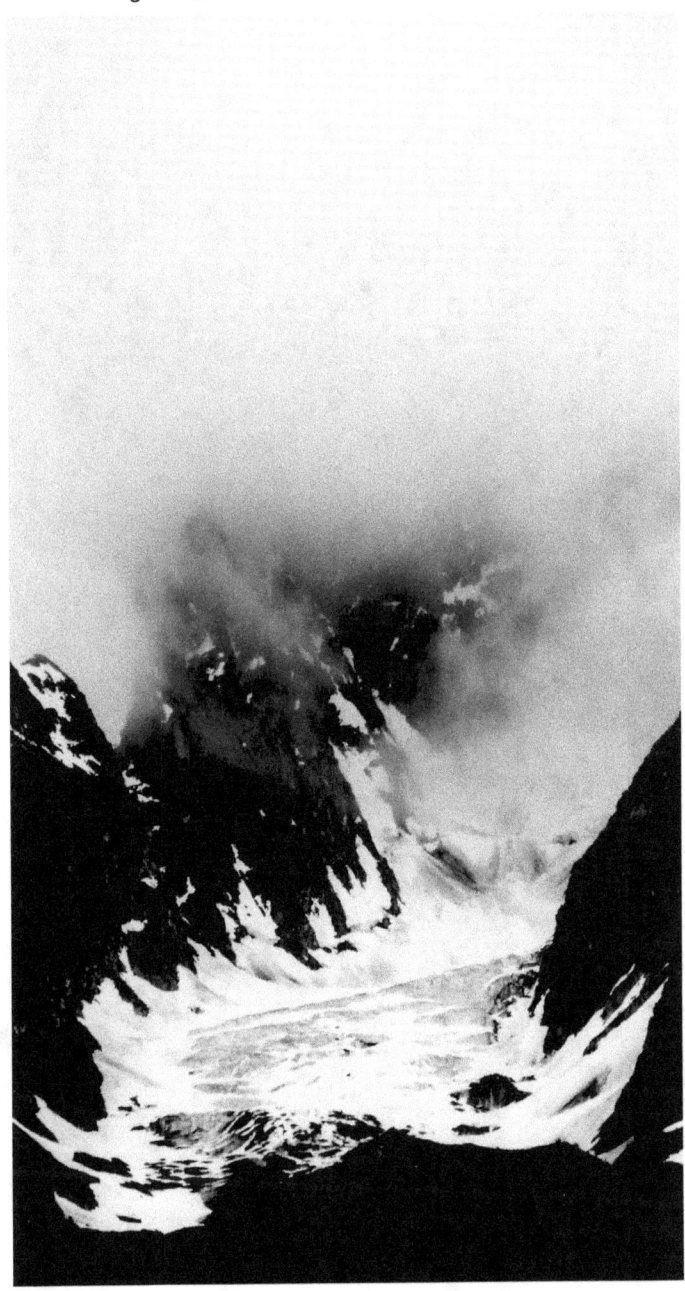

Heading to Valdez on the Richardson Highway.

Wednesday, August 2, 2000 continued

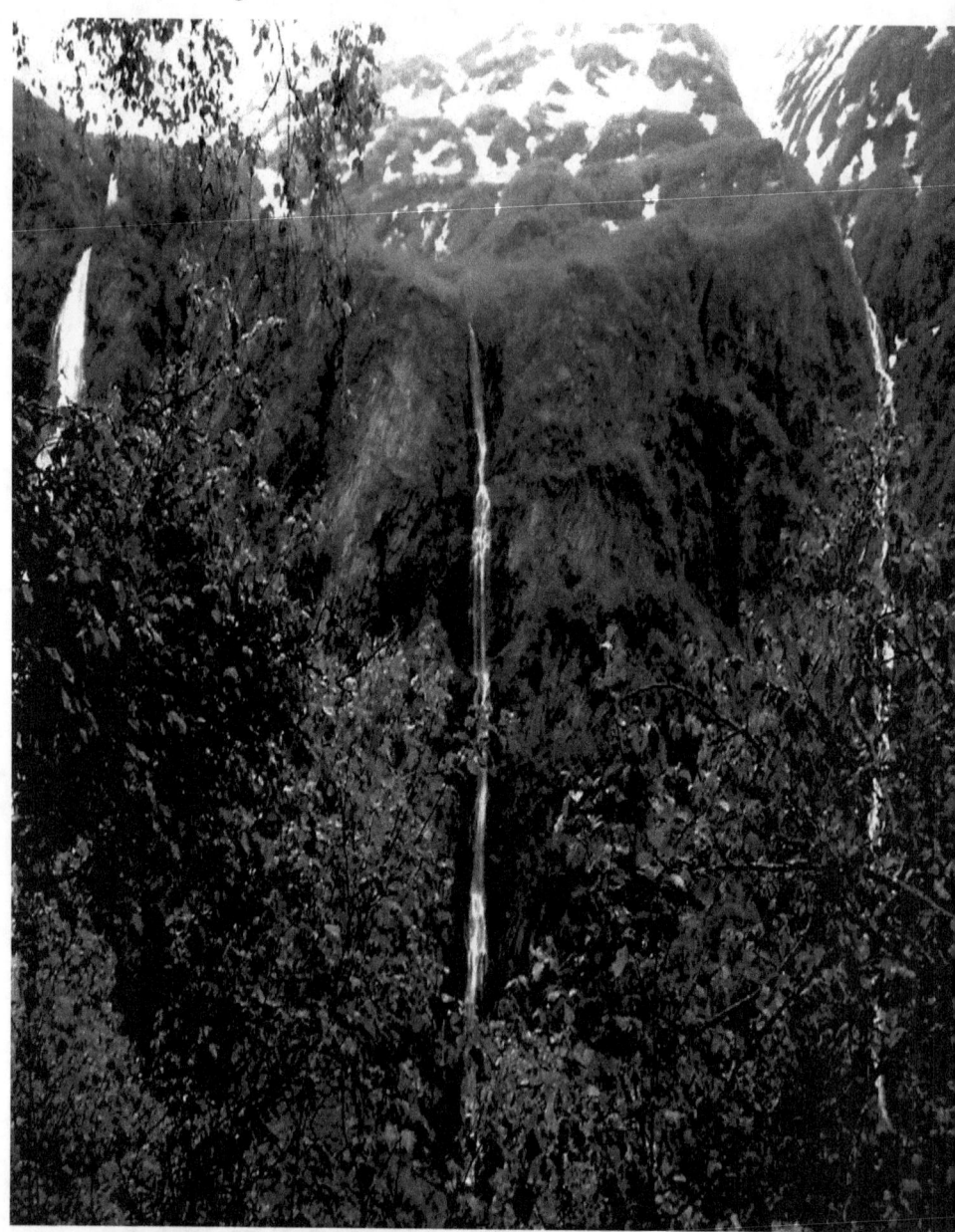

Thompson Pass, Alaska. 2000

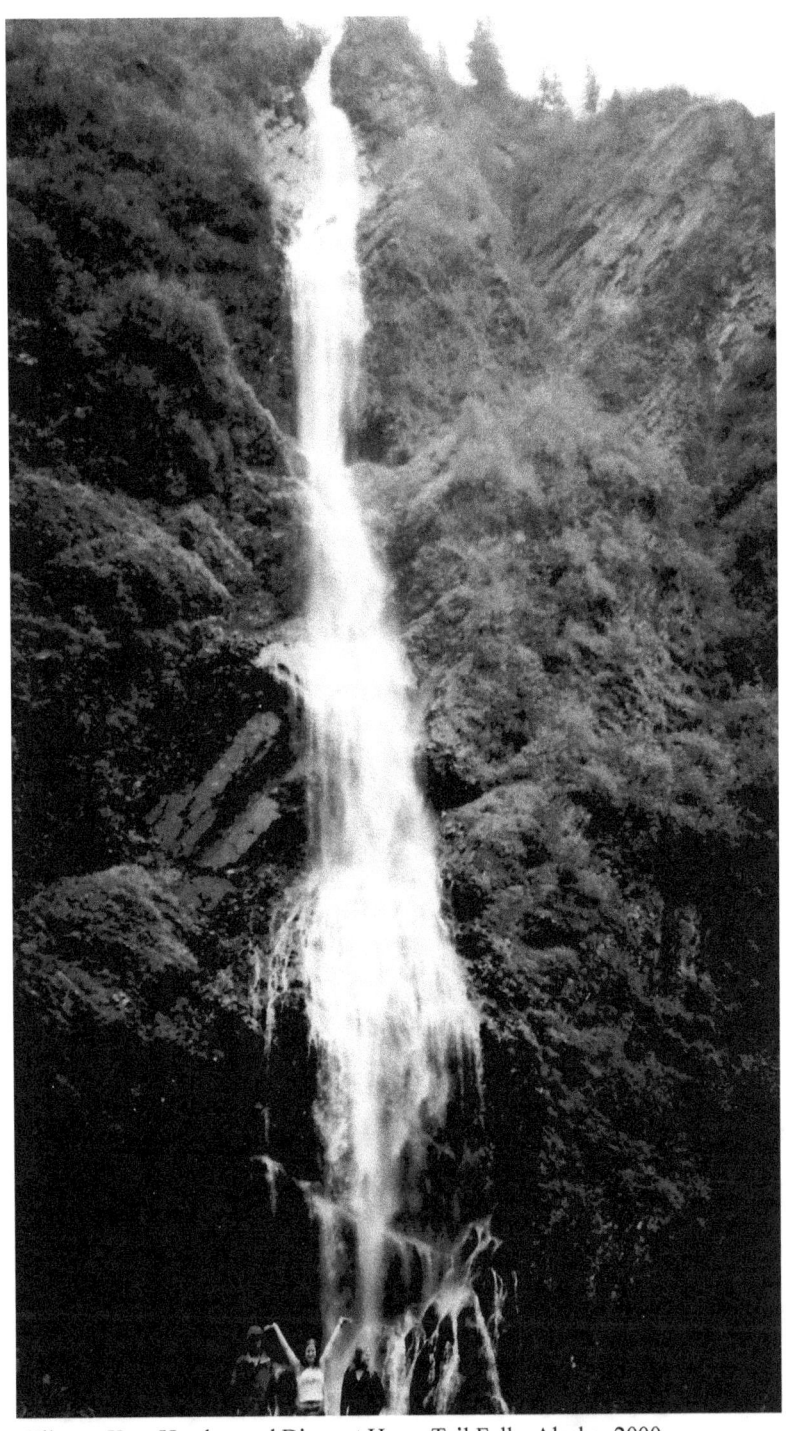

Hikers: Ken, Heather and Diane at Horse Tail Falls, Alaska 2000

2050?

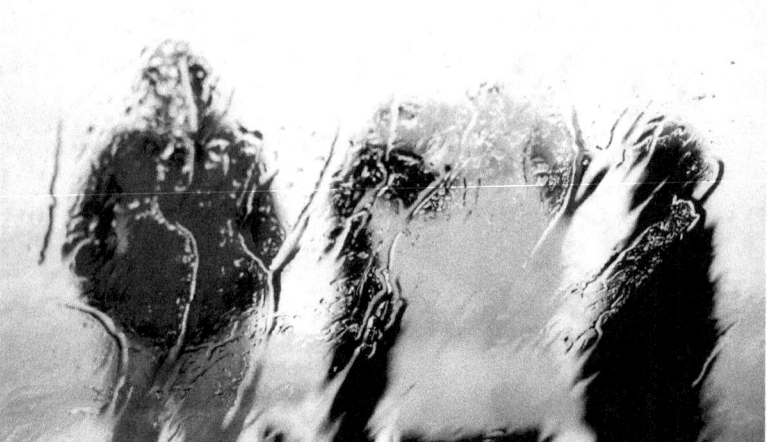

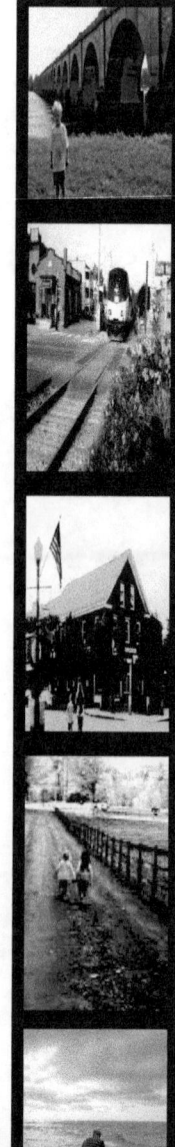

Thursday, August 3, 2000

We all headed for the nine hour Columbia Glacier Cruise with a stop at Growler Island for lunch. The Columbia Glacier was very far back and had poor visibility, but we did get an extremely good view of the Meares Glacier.

Friday, August 4, 2000

Early Friday morning we drove Heather to the local airport, as she had a scheduled flight to New York from Anchorage.

Saturday, August, 5, 2000

Three hikers ferry over to Whittier. Time to fly back.

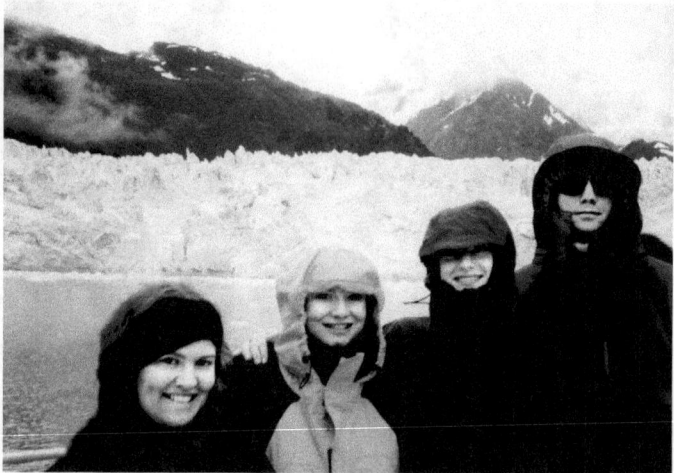

Hikers: Alison, Diane, Heather and Ken in front of the Meares Glacier.

Wyatt
Erin & Grace

230

12 MORE DAYS 2000

- ANCHORAGE *August 5*
We rented a black truck-camper.
- PALMER *August 6,7*
Stayed at the Mountain View RV / hiked up Lazy Mountain
- DENALI NAT'L PARK *August 9, 10*
- FAIRBANKS *August 11, 12, 13*

"Like going back in time"—the slow arrival of the Parks
Highway in 1971 held the area in a *sort of* time warp. Once
in the town of Fairbanks we began to notice things were not
as we had expected. Our small campground was all dirt and
very muddy. The attendants all looked like prospectors from
the gold rush days—long beards, long hair, old dirty clothes
and a certain swagger in their walk. Wow, I guess we are
now gold rushers. The first thing we did was attempt to
locate the illusive News Boy Mine. After reaching the
Cushman Bridge and heading to the Steese Highway, *I* began
to feel claustrophobic—like reaching the North Pole (the end
of the Earth) with no other place to go—beginning to feel
closed in like, "take me to another planet."

It was apparent that we would be returning next summer,
The truck-camper turned south and headed thru the Delta.

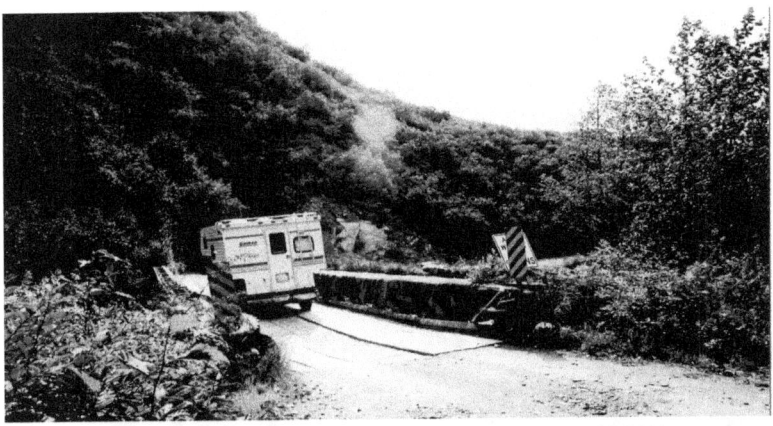

Beginning of MINERAL CREEK, Valdez, AK. August 15, 2000   JDH

- VALDEZ *August 14,15,16*

Some fantastic pictures of the Smith Stamp Mill were taken
in Mineral Creek on the 15th. We also hiked out to the
Valdez Glacier area, but failed to come close to the face.
- ANCHORAGE *August 17*

Fly back to Seattle, WA.

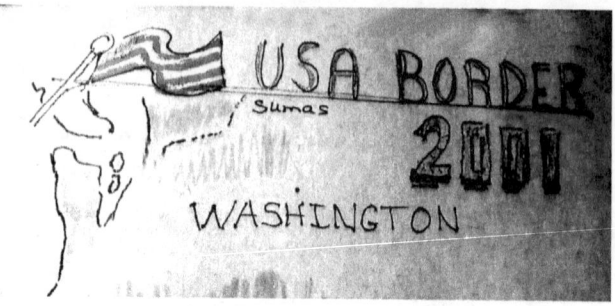

OUR RETURN TRIP
- Tuesday, May 15, 2001

ODOMETER 23,955 / 37.01 full tank / 155.9 per gal Diesel
We entered Canada from Sumas, Washington and camped at
or near the following towns:

CONTENTS: CANADA

- Boston Bar, BC May 15
- Lac La Hache, BC May 16,
- Prince George, BC May 17, 18
- Chetwynd, BC May 19
- Fort Nelson, BC May 20
- Liard Hot Springs Provincial Park, BC May 21
- Watson Lake, Yukon May 22
- White Horse, Yukon May 23, 24
- Carmacks, Yukon (stop only)
- Pelly's Crossing, Yukon (stop only)
- Dawson City, Yukon May 25, 26, 27 & 28

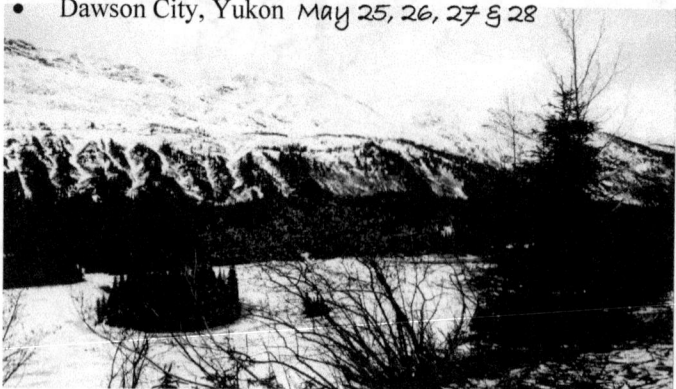

PINE PASS, N of Prince George / S of Chetwynd, BC. 2001   JDH

BOSTON BAR, BC

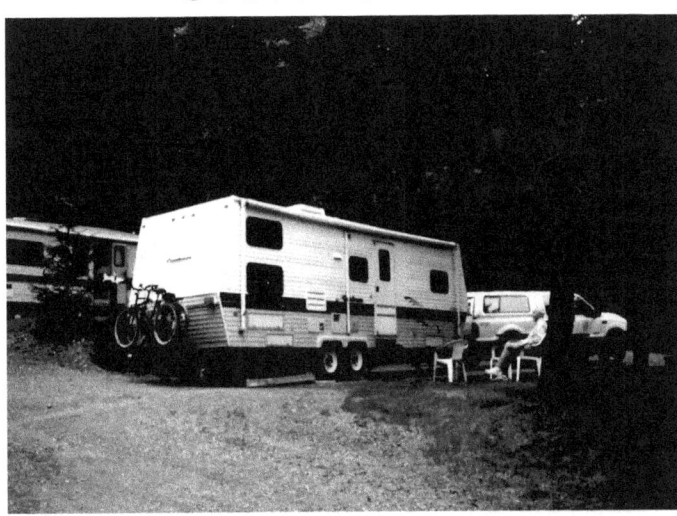

Tuesday, May 15, 2001   Photos JDH

Shortly after crossing the border, we stopped in Chillwack, BC and bought a bike rack. We also went to a bank to exchange our American dollars to Canadian money. Then off to Swallows for some coffee and a coke.

We drove through the Fraser Canyon where there were snow capped mountains everywhere, reminding us of Valdez, Alaska.

south of LAKE LA HACHE, BC

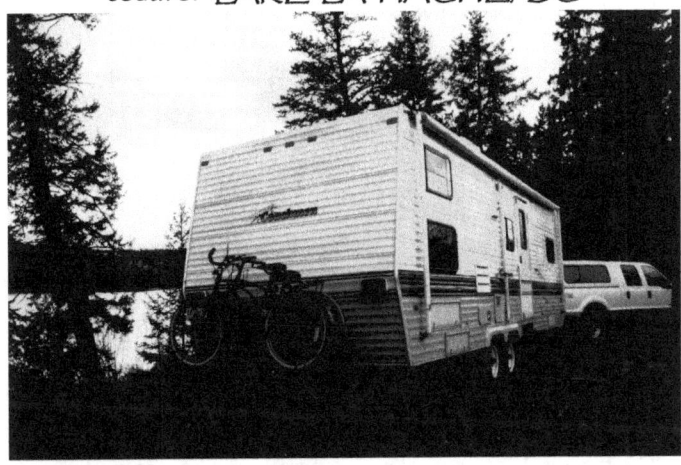

Wednesday, may 16, 2001

Trains everywhere! Rocky Mt. / Pacific Railroad / Canadian Northern Pacific. Fraser River below in canyon.

233

south of PRINCE GEORGE, BC

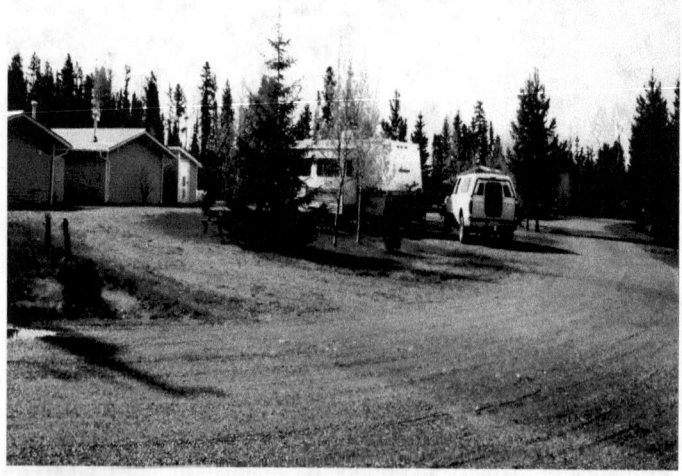

PRINCE GEORGE, BC campground. 2001   JDH

Thursday & Friday, May 17, 18, 2001

Heading to Prince George on 97 and still following the
Fraser River up. It is 45 degrees and hailing outside. It sort
of reminds us of Fairbanks, Alaska.

We bought some honey and some real maple syrup. Later
we visited the Fraser-Fort George Regional Museum.
Interesting.

It is at this campsite near Prince George that we dreamed up
driving to Inuvik, NWT. Inuvik is just south of the Beaufort
Sea. We will work out the particulars up in Dawson City,
Yukon

Saturday, May 19, 2001

It snowed last night. The gas ran out in the camper. It went
down to 45 degrees inside. Outside it was 34 degrees.

We are driving up to PINE PASS followed by Chetwynd,
BC. ...just saw a black bear nibbling at the side of the road.

The time is 12:35 pm. The temperature is beginning to
drop...as we made calls to home, voices on the phone were
getting more and more distant.

CHETWYND, BC

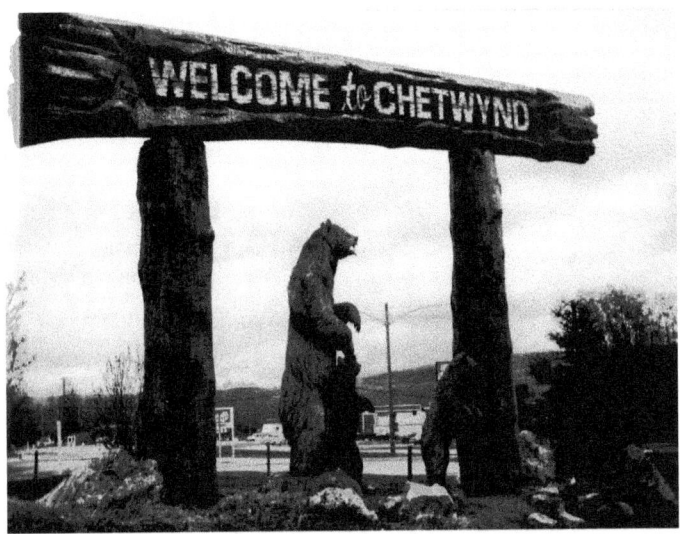

Late that afternoon after driving the pass, we arrive in Chetwynd to resupply.

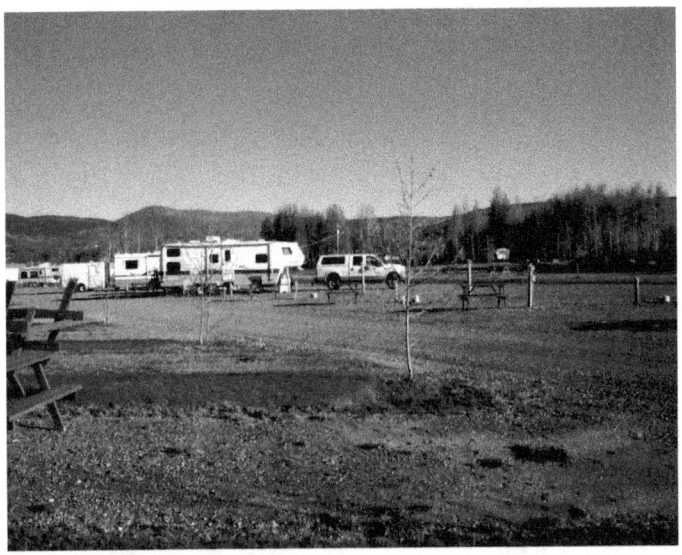

CHETWYND campground, BC 2001   Photos JDH

Sunday May 20, 2001

This morning heading out of town past the lumber yard on 29, we saw a wolf limping along in the woods.

PEACE RIVER, BC

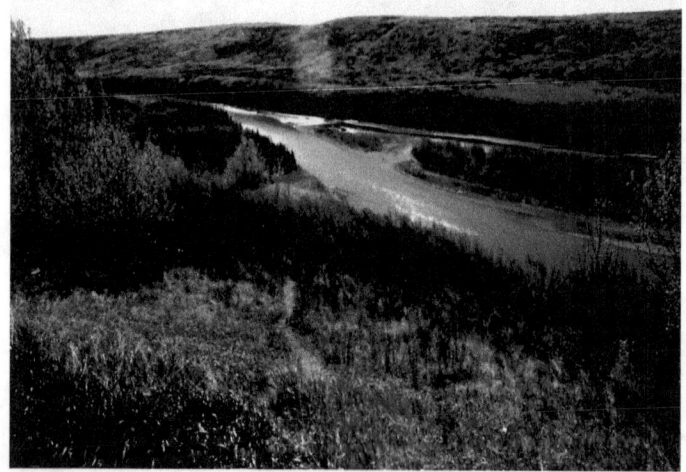

PEACE RIVER, BC north of Chetwynd and Hudson's Hope   Photos JDH

Sunday, May 20, 2001

Traveling NE along 29, we came to the Peace River overlook. There was a lovely campground on the R with a view of the Peace River. But, we were very determined to get to Fort Nelson, so kept on going to our next wet and muddy campsite without water and sewer.

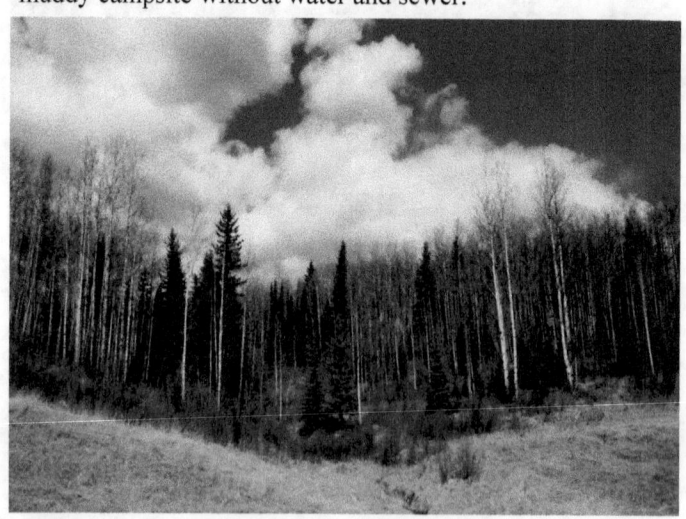

236

FORT NELSON, BC

Monday, May 21, 2001

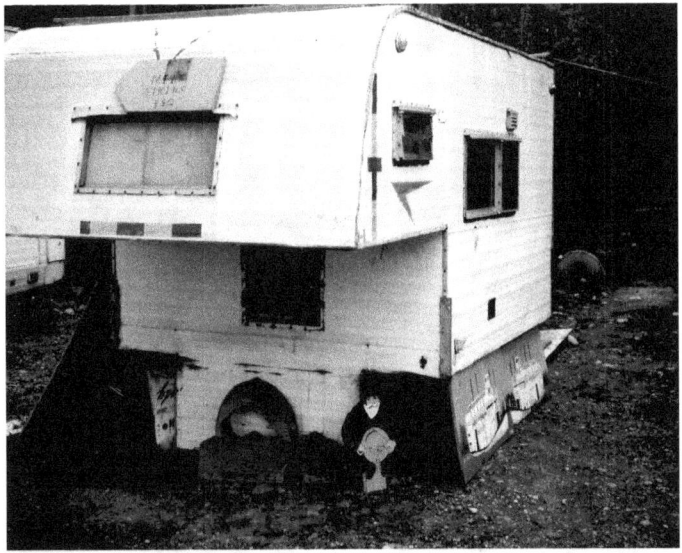

FORT NELSON BC campground 2001   Photos JDH

By now our camper needed a good washing, so we took a picture of our neighbor's truck-camper instead.

The site *did* have electric and cable, which came in handy on our way back...September 10th, 2001.

SUMMIT LAKE, BC

Tuesday, May 22, 2001

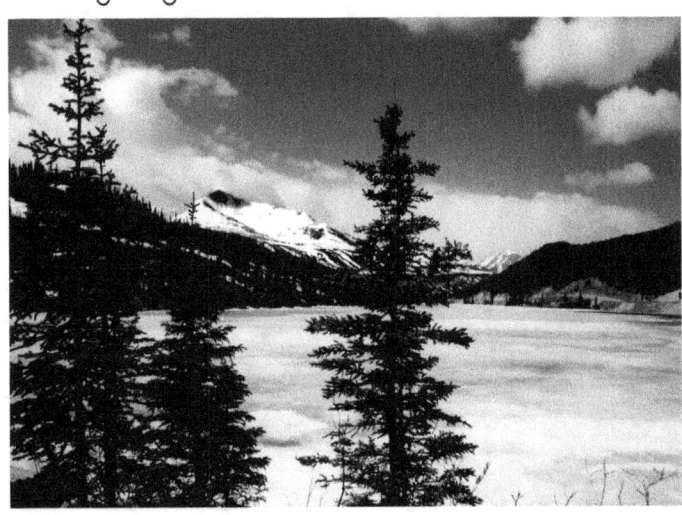

MUNCHO LAKE, BC

Monday, May 21, 2001

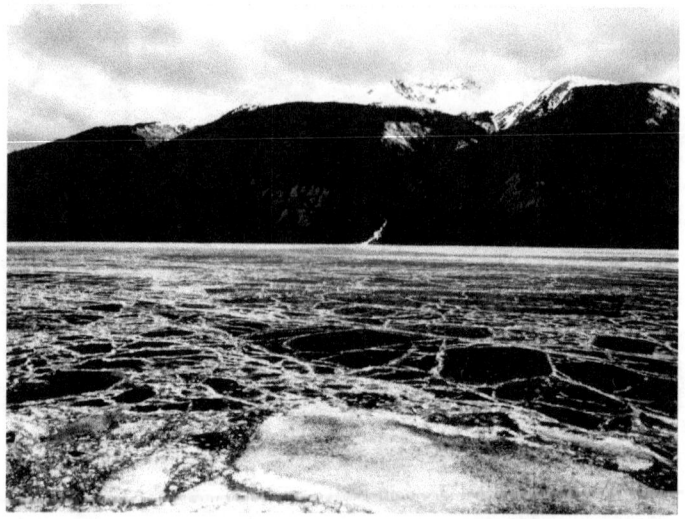

Photos JDH

Driving by Summit Lake on our way to Liard Hot Springs, we saw two moose up on a hill, two beaver dams, an elk and several big horns. There were snow covered craters everywhere. The temperature was 43 degrees at 12 noon. Many fine-looking birch trees. It was a good day. Today is Queen's Day.

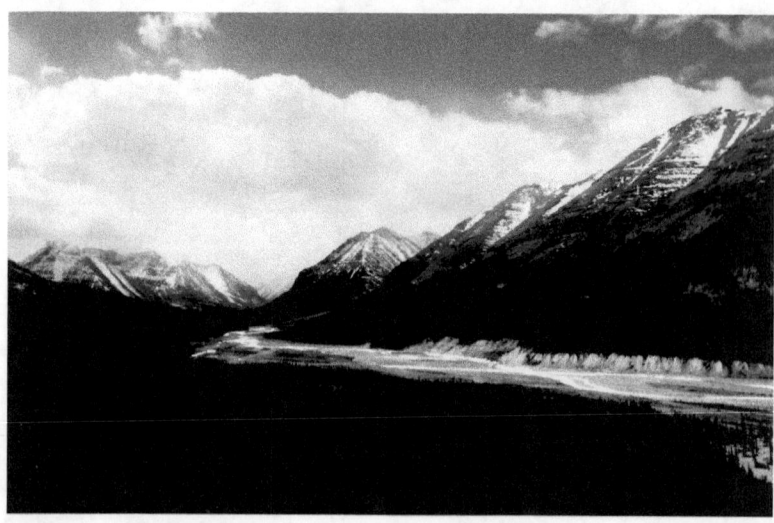

LIARD RIVER HOT SPRINGS, BC

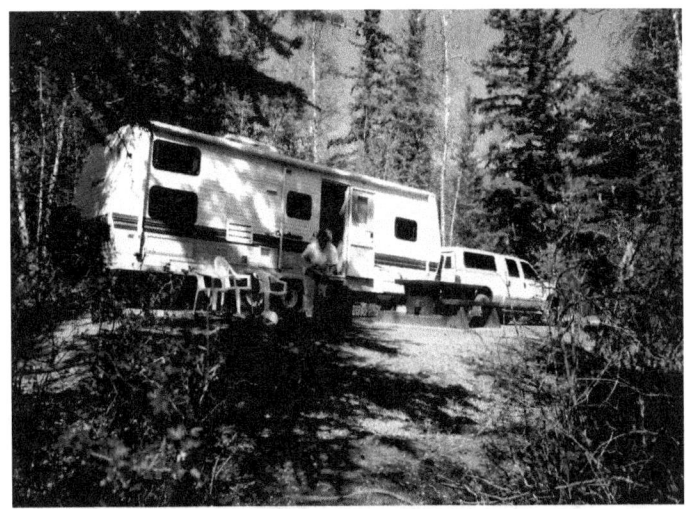

LIARD RIVER HOT SPRINGS PROVINCIAL PARK   Photos UEH

We took the boardwalk to the Hot Springs and saw a moose along the way. Our campsite was private and up on a hill. The fire was going when we pulled in, so we just kept it going. There was plenty of firewood. We roasted veggie dogs later in the evening. Bear watch signs were everywhere. On the way out we saw a buffalo grazing.

This is where Chris Mc Candless stayed on his way to Alaska. Subject of book and movie, *"INTO THE WILD."*

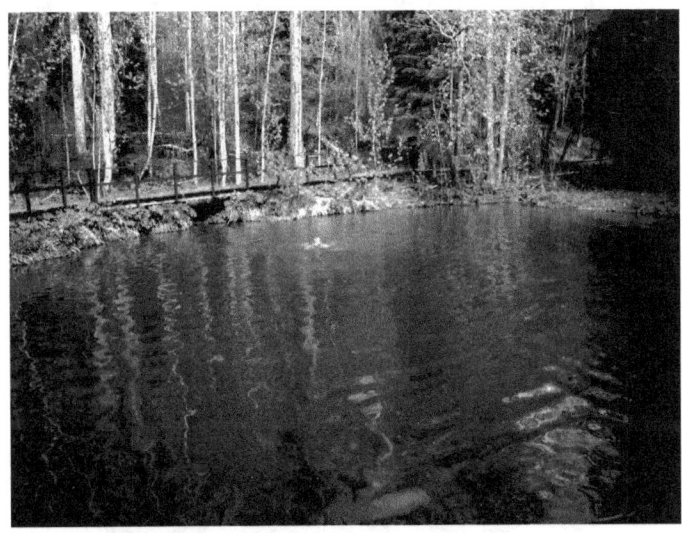

LIARD HOT SPRINGS, BC. Monday, May 21, 2001

WATSON LAKE, Yukon

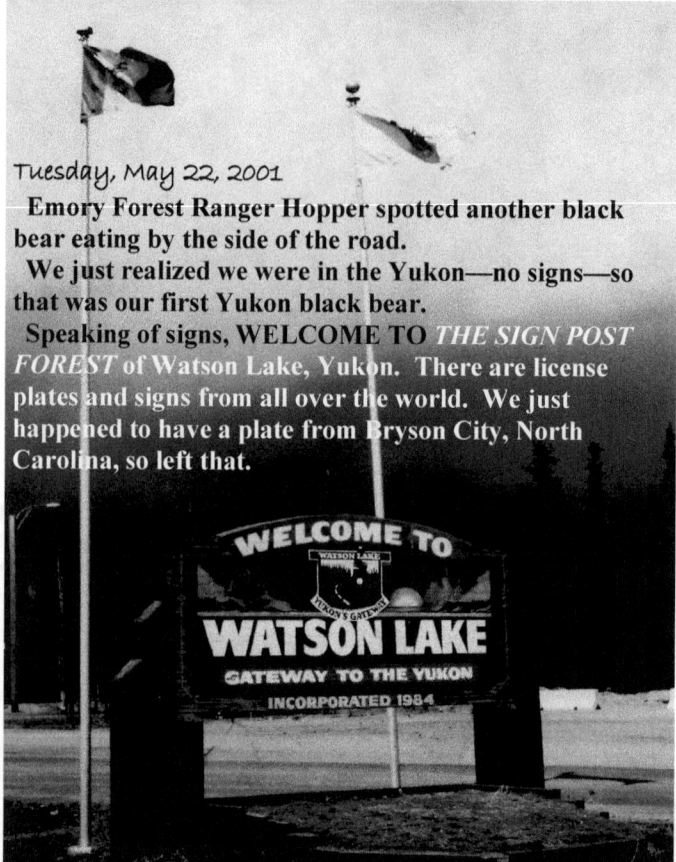

Tuesday, May 22, 2001

Emory Forest Ranger Hopper spotted another black bear eating by the side of the road.

We just realized we were in the Yukon—no signs—so that was our first Yukon black bear.

Speaking of signs, WELCOME TO *THE SIGN POST FOREST* of Watson Lake, Yukon. There are license plates and signs from all over the world. We just happened to have a plate from Bryson City, North Carolina, so left that.

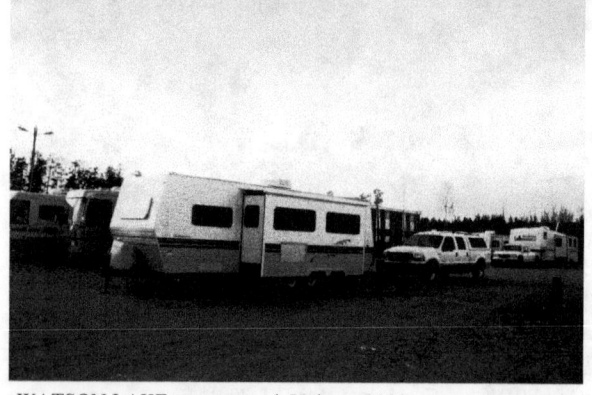

WATSON LAKE campground, Yukon. 2001   Photos JDH

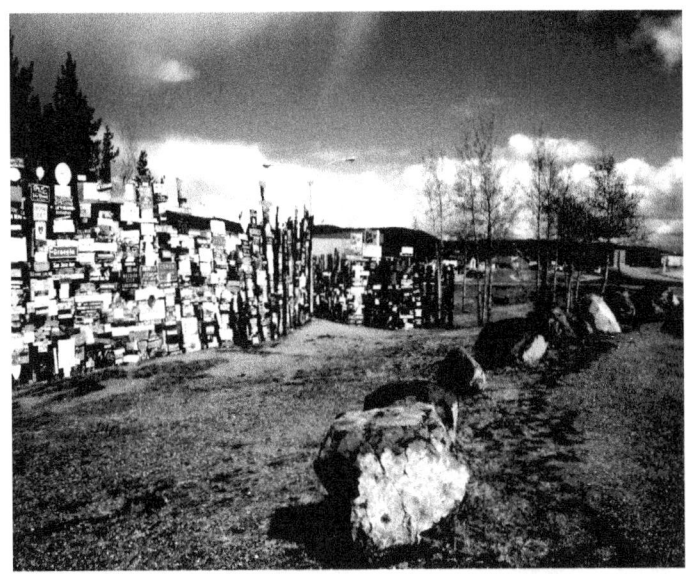

The Sign Post Forest, Watson Lake, Yukon. 2001   JDH

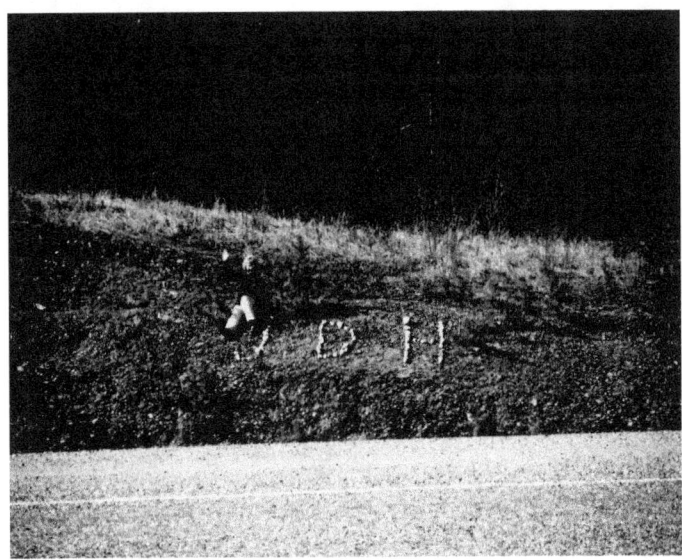

Author waving after leaving her mark. 2001   UEH

Wednesday, May 23, 2001

On the way out, we noticed people were writing their initials in stones. Everyone was leaving their mark, one way or another. Finally arriving into the Yukon created an excitement in the air like no other.

Wednesday, May 23, 2001 continued

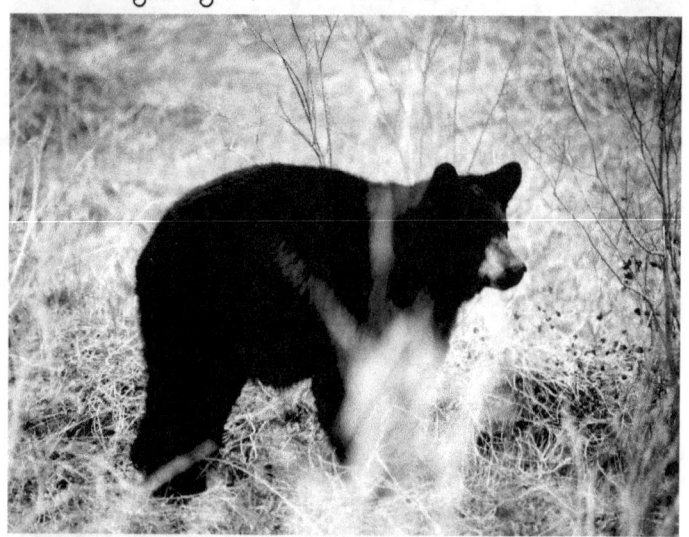

Another YUKON BLACK BEAR, Alaska Highway   Photos JDH

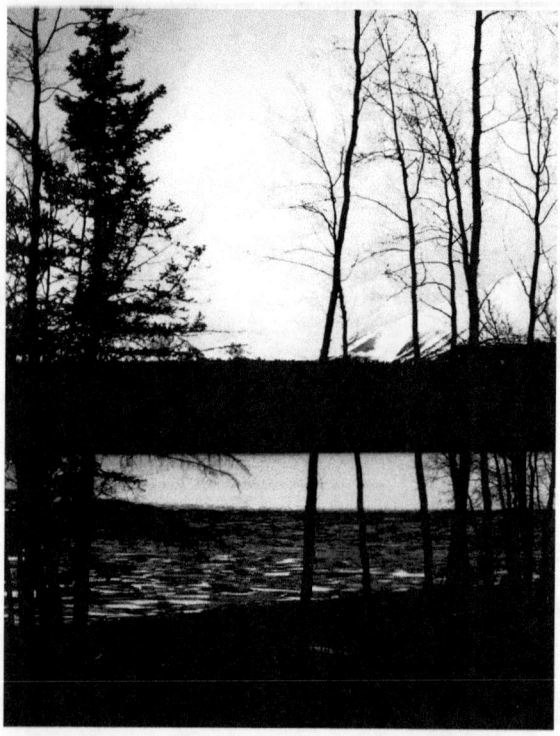

The ALASKA HIGHWAY—Watson Lake to Whitehorse

WHITEHORSE, Yukon

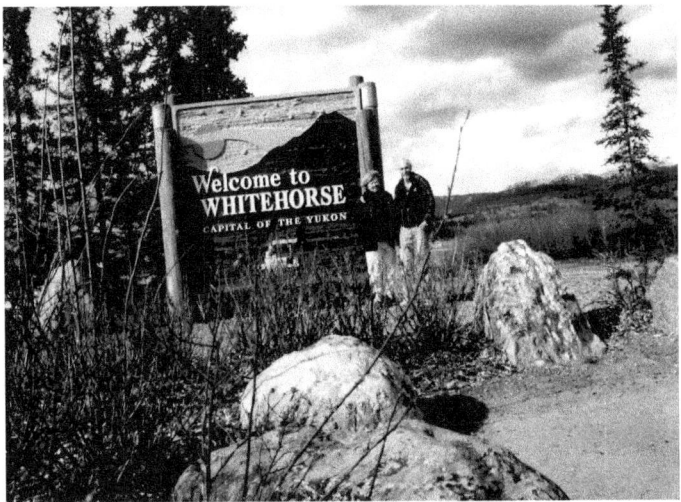

Adventurers Jill and Emory   Timer

We passed signs for the Continental Divide heading to Whitehorse, Yukon (on the Alaska Highway). The temperature was 36 degrees, the time was 11:54 pm. If conditions were like this for the prospectors in 1898, they were noticeably horrible (for them and their horses). It was very windy just after Teslin. Electric shocks seem to be common place. Everything you touched gave you a shock.

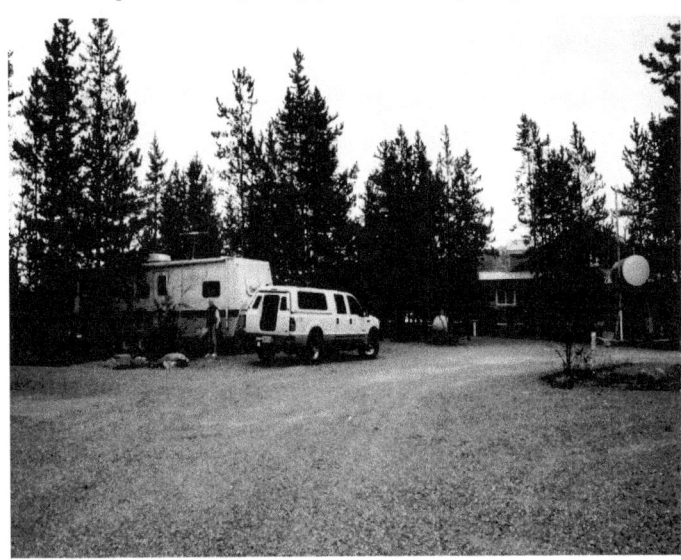

WHITEHORSE, YUKON campsite. 2001   JDH

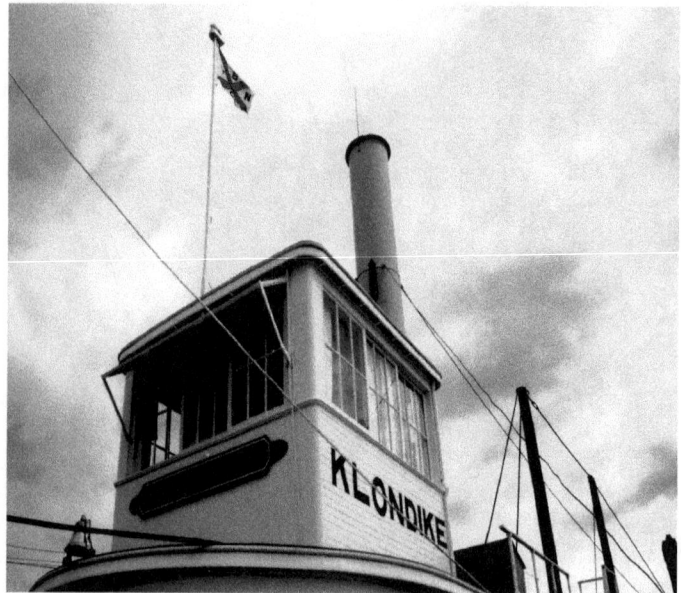

KLONDIKE PADDLEWHEEL II, Whitehorse, Yukon. JDH

Thursday, May 24, 2001

We took the Klondike Paddle wheel II tour on Thursday. The original boat began in 1927 until it crashed on a sand bar circa 1936. The Klondike II was built from the hull of the first boat and in six months it was back in service. We also visited the Klondike Riverboat exhibit and later in the day, visited the Beringia Interpretive Center. Both extremely informative of a time gone by. One period of time circa 100 years ago and the other of a time dealing with the Land Bridge Theory of 20,000 years ago.

Time: 12:37 Snow flakes falling through the air. The ice brakes on the Yukon River at Whitehorse in late May. I guess we won't be boating up to Dawson City.

CHOICES

Which way to go from Whitehorse, west 277miles to Beaver Creek (and the Alaska border) or north on the Klondike Highway to Dawson City? In 1979 the entire Klondike Highway was gravel. In 1982 pavement was laid down up to Carmacks. We kept with the plan and turned north.

244

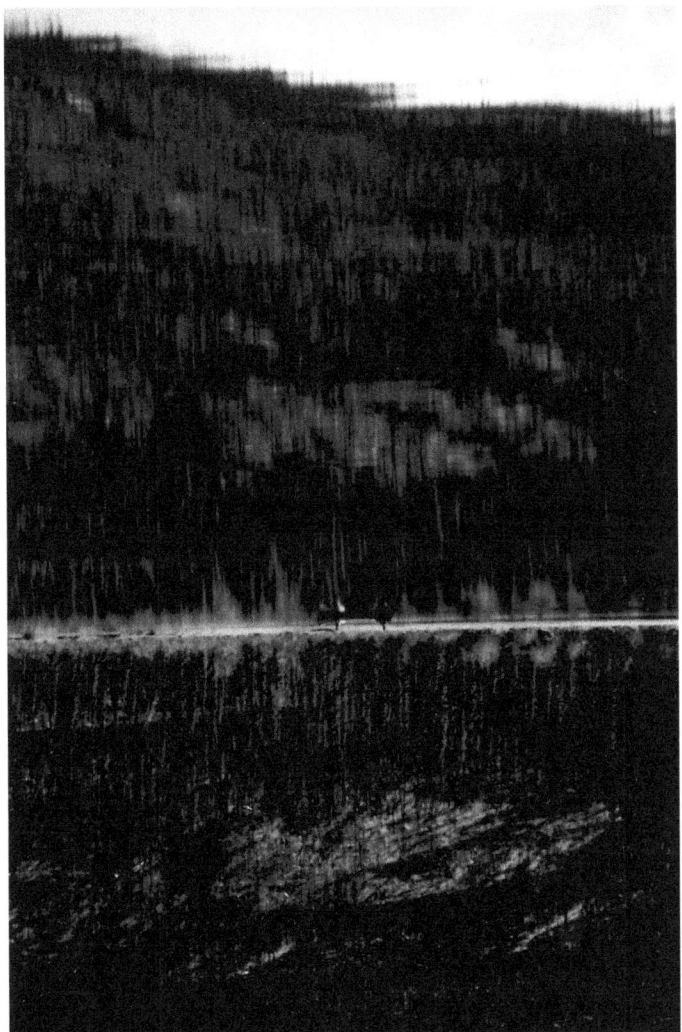

LAKE LABERGE, YUKON, a lone canoeist and his son fishing.

Friday, May 25, 2001

Heading north on the Klondike Highway to Dawson City, we did not expect it to be soooo desolate. Where have all the campers gone? Nothing like the road from Watson Lake to Whitehorse. There were many periodic stopping off places for gas and food.

Lake Laberge is a widening of the Yukon River north of Whitehorse. A river made famous by Robert Service and his poem, *"THE CREMATION OF SAM MCGEE."*

245

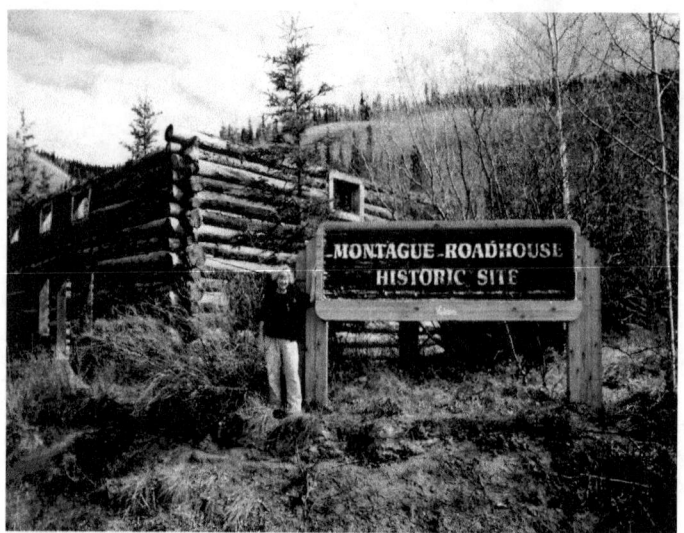

Author (south of CARMACKS), by the HISTORIC MONTAGUE
ROADHOUSE, Klondike Highway, Yukon.   UEH

Friday, May 25, 2001 continued

According to a local Carmacks resident, George Carmack
was the main man in the Klondike gold discovery. If it
weren't for the discovery of Gold in 1897, we wouldn't be
here driving this desolate road to Dawson City. The
prospector, Randolph Angus Douglas, would not have made
his journey to Alaska in 1935—entering from Valdez—and
there wouldn't be any pictures or reason to publish a book.

Inside this Montague Roadhouse was some scribbling on
the wall of a fellow traveler saying, **"I'M A LONG
WAY FROM HOME."**

FOOTNOTE:

Interestingly, Carmacks was considered in the Alaska-
Canada Rail link Project—WPYR from the University of
Alaska, Fairbanks. It would connect Whitehorse to
Carmacks from either Haines or Skagway. A project
undertaken by two graduate students. A very well laid out
plan—Carmacks being just one of the legs being mentioned.

Impressive, and a good read. Permafrost and seasonal deep
freeze were studied. Costs were also estimated.

The confluence of the Yukon and Nordenskiold Rivers
is where N Tutchone traded and fished in mid-late 1800's.

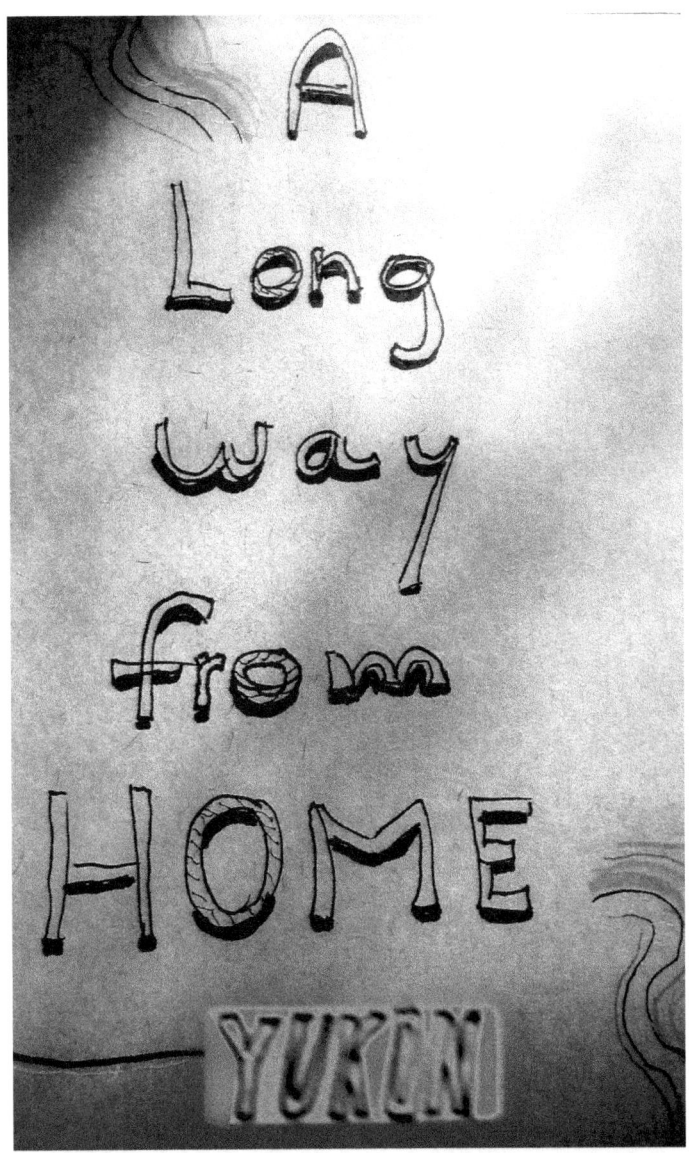

North of Carmacks, the road becomes a two-lane narrow "old stagecoach route."

There had been a very bad forest fire. Signs were asking travelers to report fire. Maybe it is the burnt trees, but it is beginning to look a lot like tundra with no hills or mountains. A land void of animals. They were probably driven out or killed by the fires.

PELLY'S CROSSING, Yukon

Friday, May 25, 2001 continued

Pelly's Crossing and a little piece of "unreal". The warmth of the sun, the picnic tables, the snow white birch trees, the crow warbling like a mockingbird, the old long-haired white and black dog sleeping in a spot of sun from that big orange ball in the sky and the voice of *JEWEL* asking Adrian to come out and play—" *I'm sensitive and I'd like to keep it that way.* " That was PENNY"S PLACE deep in the heart of the Yukon. Our veggie burgers never tasted better.

The Pelly River is a tributary of the Yukon River and considered part of the northern valley of the Great Tantina Trench.

Locals believe that the ravens are spirits of the dead. Two ravens can be seen of top on the Pelly's Crossing sign.

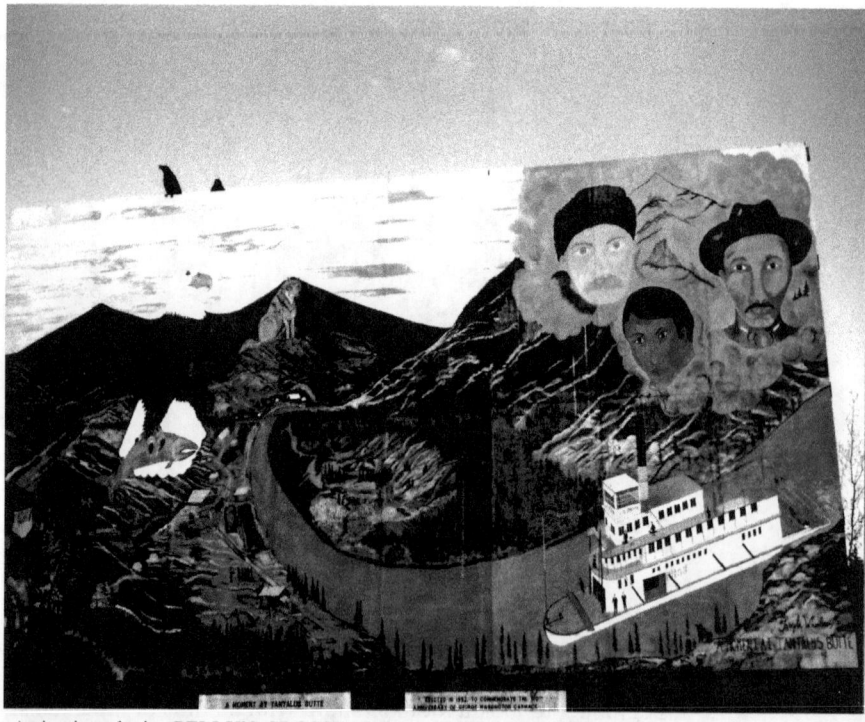

A sign introducing PELLY'S CROSSING along the Klondike Highway, Yukon. 2001   JDH

TANTINA TRENCH, Yukon

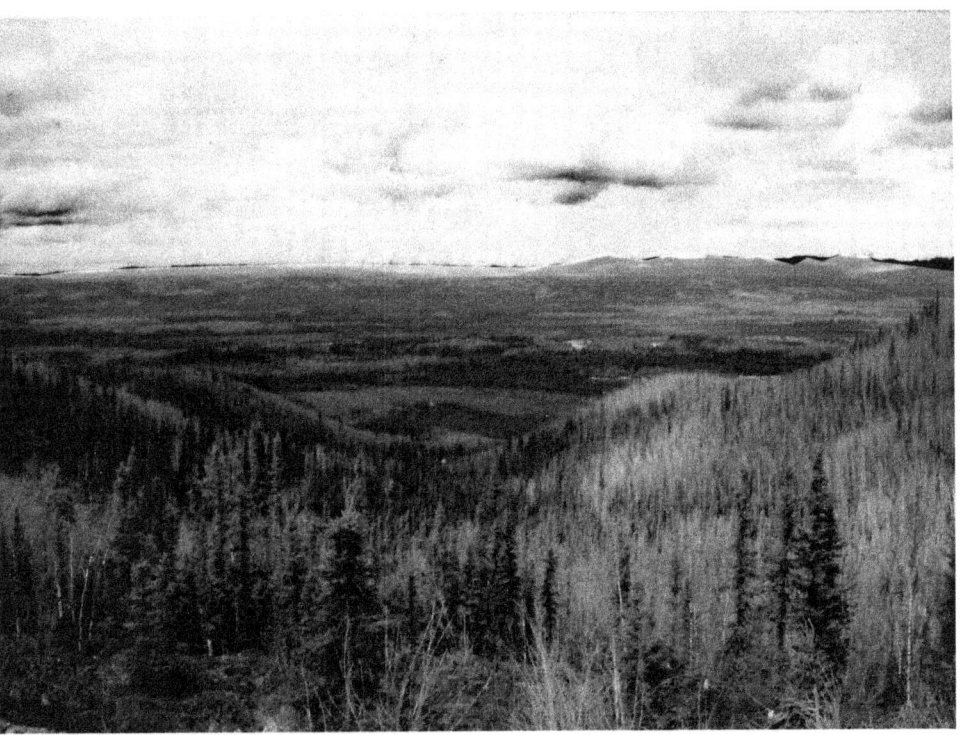

TANTINA TRENCH, Yukon. 2001   JDH

NEW MEANING for THE WORD VAST!

The southern valley of the Tantina Trench drains into
the Liard River—going south-eastward, then eastward,
merging with the Mackenzie River at Fort Simpson, NWT,
eventually heading back north for the long journey to the
Arctic Ocean.

The trench is actually a great fault in Western North
America. It extends 600 miles from south-eastern Yukon to
the Yukon Flats in Alaska.

Besides its awesome view, it provides a natural wildlife
corridor for animals hunting and looking for water.

Besides the natural wildlife corridor the "trench" is known
as the Klondike "gold fields," and to prospectors everywhere
with time and desire it is the ultimate place to strike it rich.

Besides the Klondike "gold fields", it is a geologist's
DREAM COME TRUE — so many years to study.

249

THE DEMPSTER HIGHWAY, Yukon

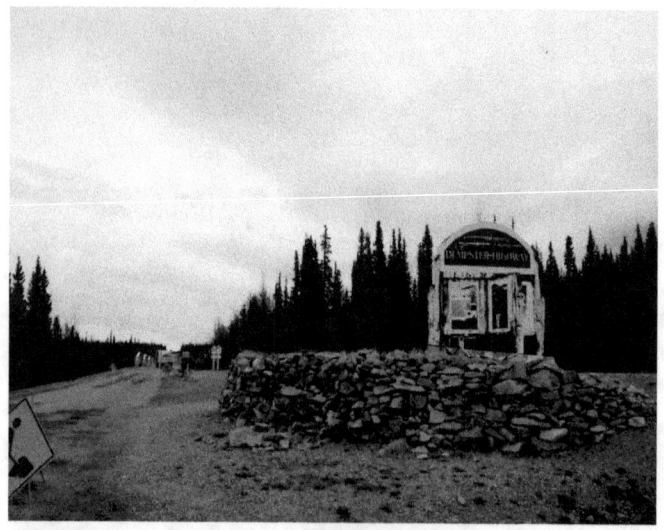

DEMPSTER HIGHWAY, Yukon. 2001   JDH

Friday, May 25, 2001 continued

All of a sudden, there it was—the Dempster Highway heading all the way to Inuvik, NWT.

The signs made it abundantly clear—**"FERRIES CLOSED DUE to ICE"** and we would have to wait until our return trip to drive to Inuvik and fly to Tuktoyaktuk in the NWT—ultimately, reaching the Beaufort Sea and the Arctic Ocean.

DAWSON CITY, Yukon

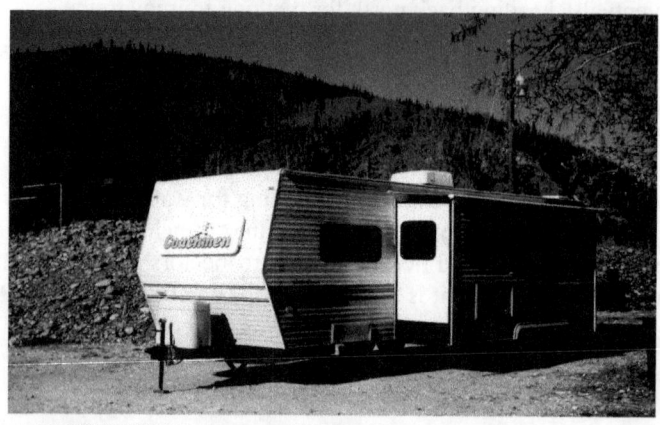

A DAWSON CITY campground, Yukon.   JDH

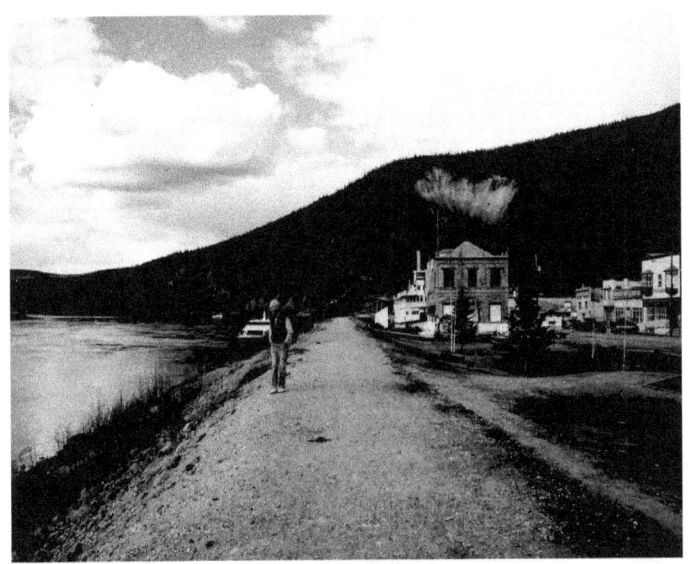

YUKON RIVER (L), DAWSON CITY (R), Yukon. 2001 JDH
Emory, walking where prospectors arrived to look for gold
over one hundred years ago.

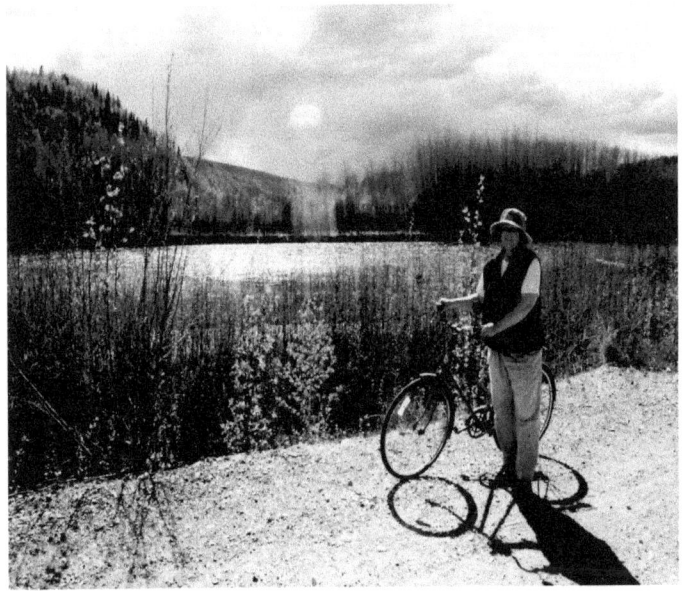

A Yukon River bikeway. 2001 UEH
Jill making the bike-rack pay off. This bike has not seen its
last days yet.

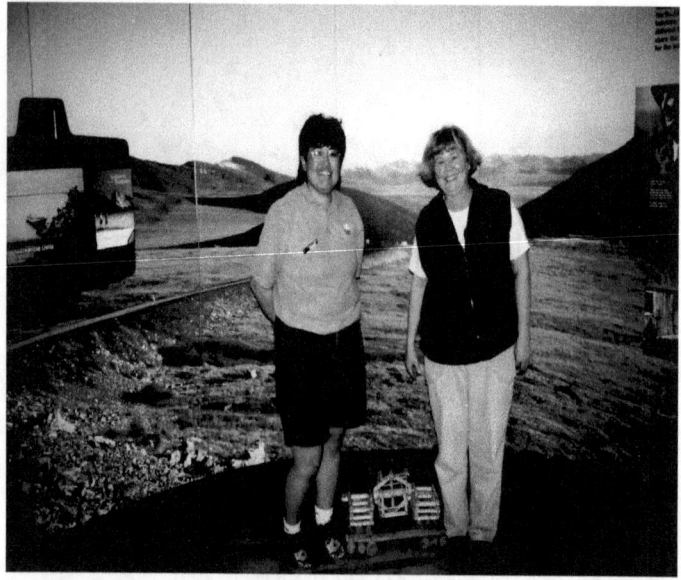

Dawn and Jill, DAWSON CITY, Yukon. 2001   UEH

Saturday, May 26, 2001

My friend, Dawn from the Tourist Building for Northern Tours. Meeting my first Inuvik resident, asking many Questions and sealing our fate for the end of our trip.

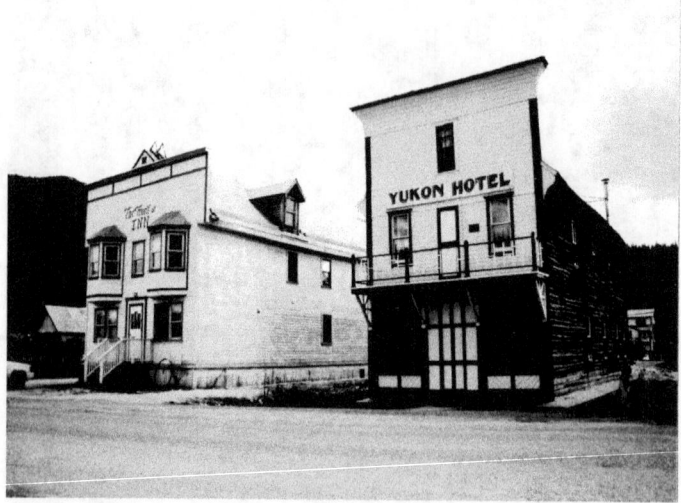

Permafrost is hard on the old buildings in Dawson City.   JDH

FATE of the PRINCESS SOPHIA

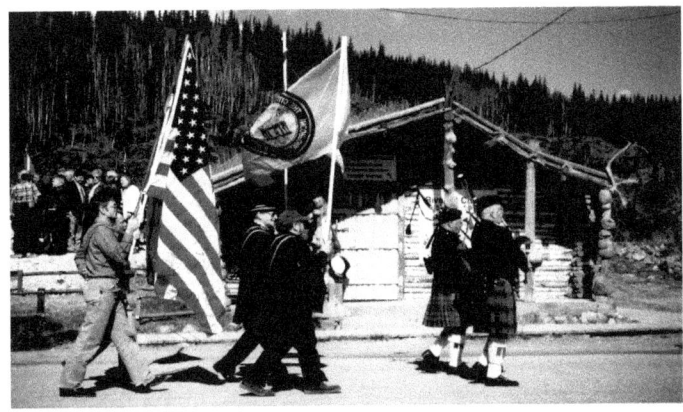

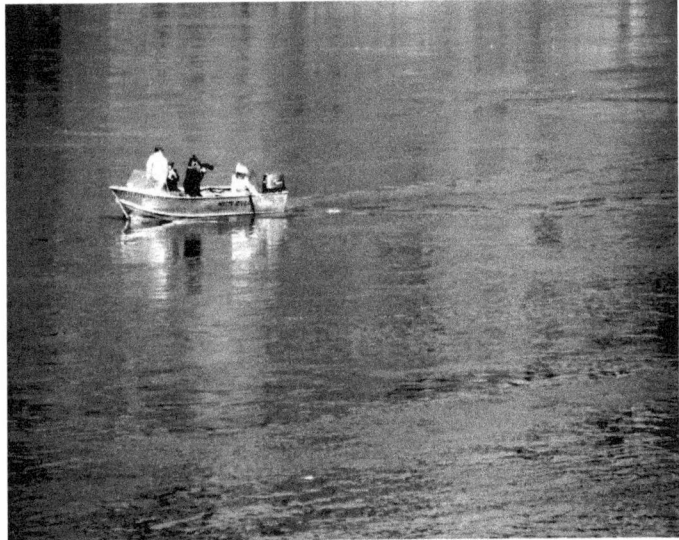

A wreath was laid into the YUKON RIVER.   Photos JDH

We were fortunate enough to arrive in town the day before a plaque was dedicated to the Princess Sophia and the 343 passengers who lost their lives near Juneau, AK. in 1918. A lone dog swam to a nearby island. The only survivor.

FOOTNOTE:

Dawson City was incorporated on January 9, 1902. A Trans Continental Trail was established in 1992. Over 14,000 miles of trail winding around the Dempster Highway and on up to Tuktoyaktuk. It can be hiked in St. John's, New Foundland, Labrador, Victoria and British Columbia. It was 80 percent complete as of 2001.

MIDNIGHT DOME, Yukon

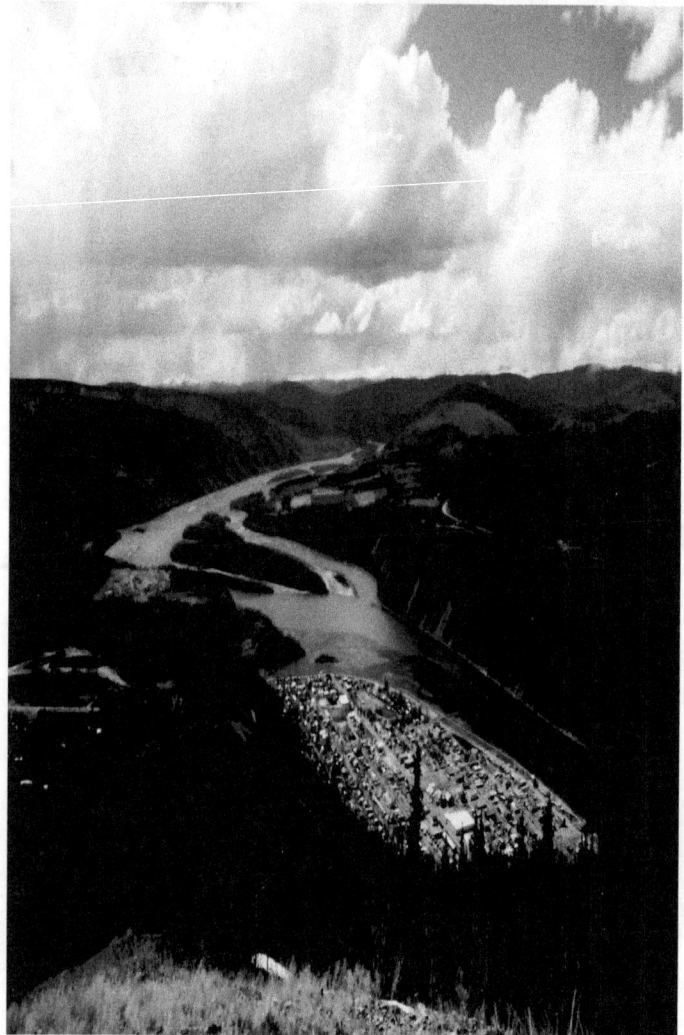

MIDNIGHT DOME, Dawson City & Yukon River looking SE. 2001   JDH

Saturday, May 26, 2001 continued

This afternoon we drove to the Midnight Dome above the city of Dawson and took some pictures. We also visited the forestry station.

Two books were purchased. One by Jack London and one of the Princess Sophia disaster. Today we plan to visit Jack London's cabin—can't wait!

JACK LONDON CABIN, Yukon

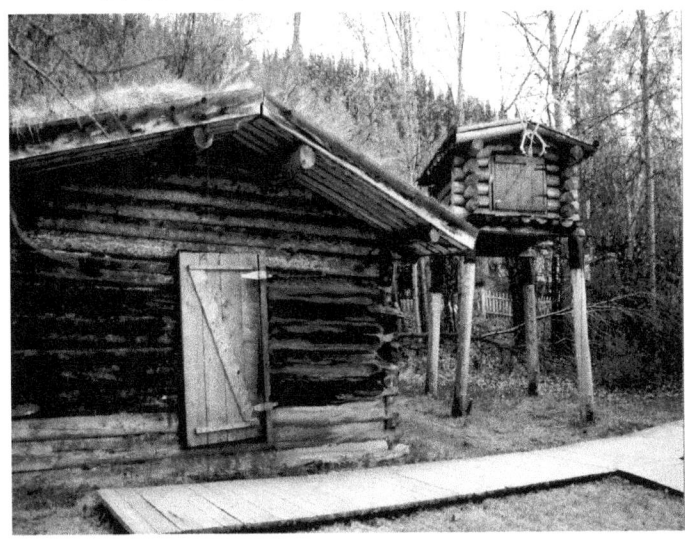

JACK LONDON'S CABIN, Dawson City, Yukon. 2001   JDH

Jack London's Klondike cabin was located on Henderson Creek in the Yukon. It was relocated in 1969. It was decided to use half of the original logs, building two identical cabins. One built and relocated to Dawson City, Yukon and one built down in Oakland, CA. in Jack London Square. Jack London was an animal activist. In 1885, (age 9), he had a portrait taken with his dog, Rollo.

On July 12, 1897 (age 21) he sailed to join the Klondike Gold Rush. It was here he wrote *Call of the Wild, White fang, To build a fire & Love of Life*

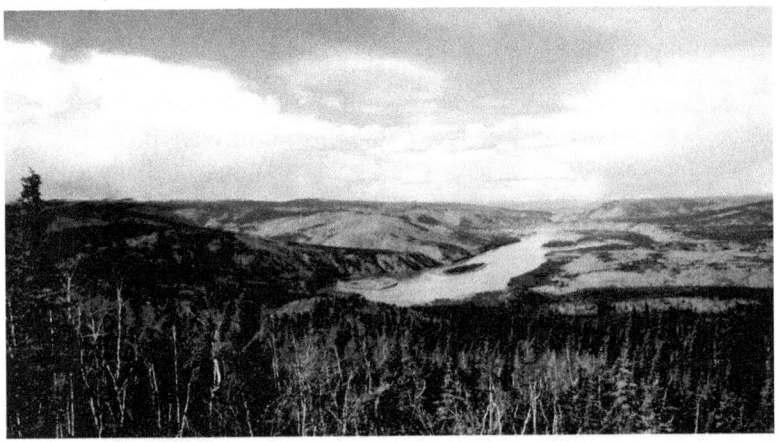

DOG ISLAND (where they keep the huskies during summer months), Midnight Dome, Yukon—looking NW. 2001   JDH

255

ROBERT SERVICE CABIN, Yukon

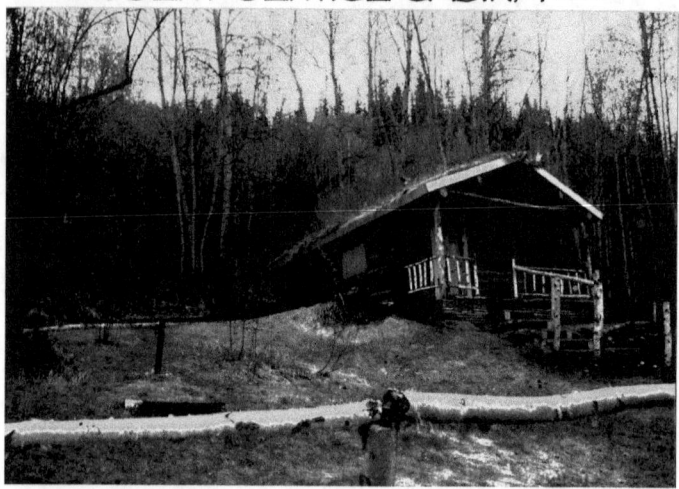

ROBERT SERVICE CABIN, Dawson City, Yukon. 2001   JDH

Saturday, May 26, 2001 continued

Service did not locate into Dawson City until 1908, ten years after the Gold rush had begun. He entered by way of White Pass (Skagway) and the Yukon Route in 1900, residing in the early frontier town of Whitehorse listening to the tales of the prospectors.

Other prospectors made entries from Nome, AK, the all-Canadian Route (Pelly River) and the all-American Route (Valdez Glacier). In 2001 we made our way up via the highways of BC and the Klondike Highway—mining for photos.

BONANZA CREEK, Yukon

The Bonanza Creek was originally called "Rabbit Creek." A creek that was a tiny tributary of the Klondike River. In August of 1896 the cry went out that gold was discovered on this tiny tributary and boom towns sprang up *overnight!!!*

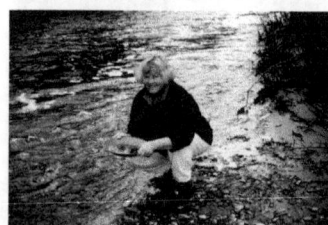 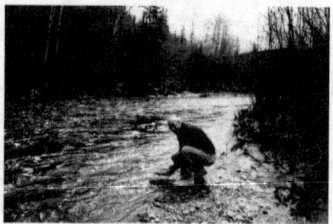

Jill and Emory panning for colors on Bonanza Creek. Note : Emory has his glasses on. 2001   UEH & JDH

TRIBUTE to the MINER, Yukon

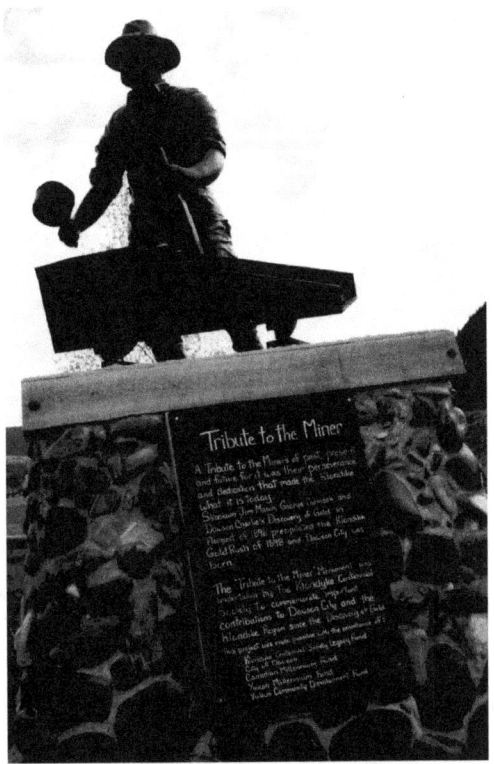

A wonderful tribute, Dawson City, Yukon.   .JDH

A native American named Shookum Jim Mason, made the discovery but it was decided to let an American named George Carmack take credit for it as the authorities might be reluctant to recognize a claim by a native American. The tribute plaque lists Mason first, however. Page 246 has been left in, favoring Carmack. Dawson Charlie was Carmack's bother-in-law, and also was there.

THE KLONDIKE RIVER, near Dawson City, Yukon. 2001   JDH

257

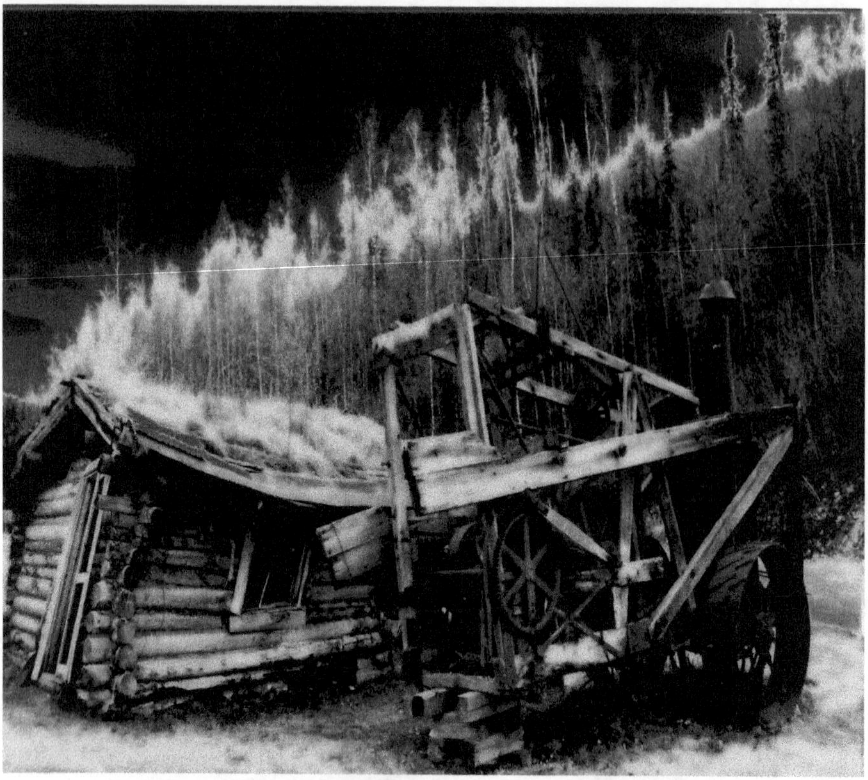

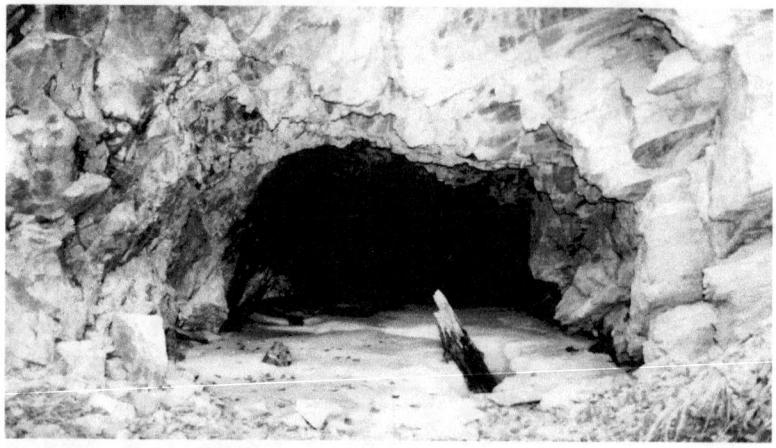

Sunday-Monday, May 27, 28, 2001
BOOM TOWNS with no more reason to be. In 1898. the
area population was approximately 40,000. In 2011 the area
population was 1,319.

Bonanza Creek area, near Dawson City, Yukon. 2001   Photos JDH

DREDGE 4, Yukon

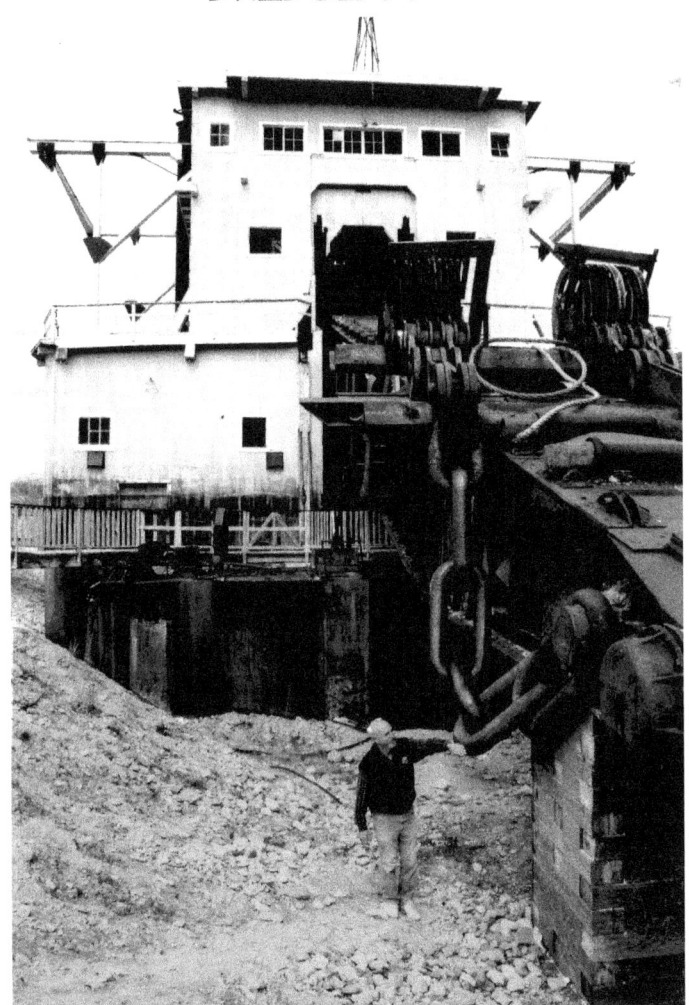

STATISTICS
Length   Width   Height
140 ft.   65 ft.   76 ft.
Displacement-3000 tons
Digging Depth
-57 ft. below water level
-14 ft. above water level

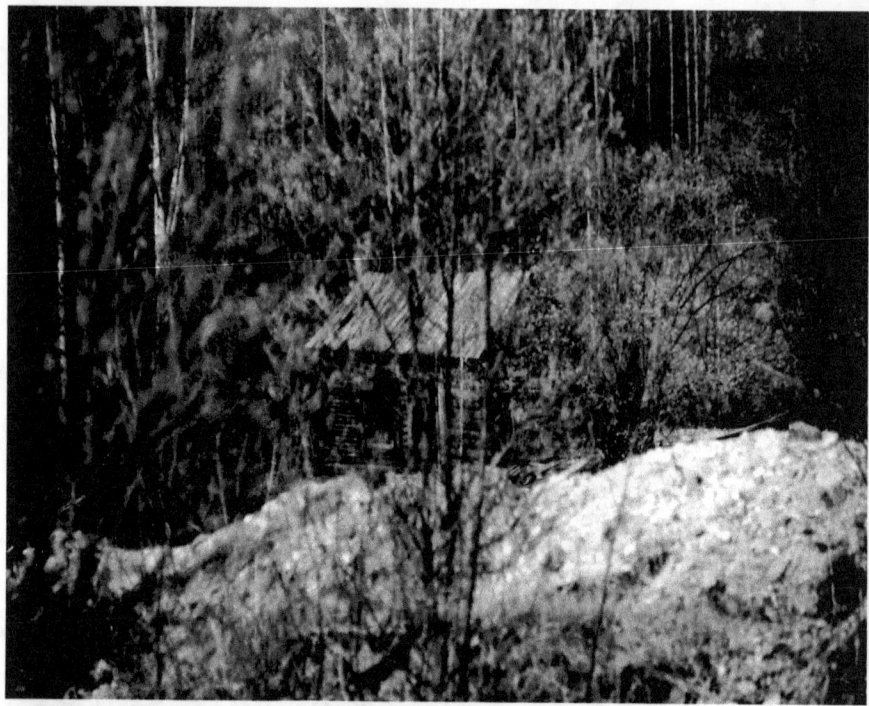

Sunday-Monday, May 27, 28, 2001 continued
   Just a matter of time—now a cabin sits as a shadow in the woods and an old bridge crossing the Bonanza Creek is barely reflecting in an area once bustling with placer miners.

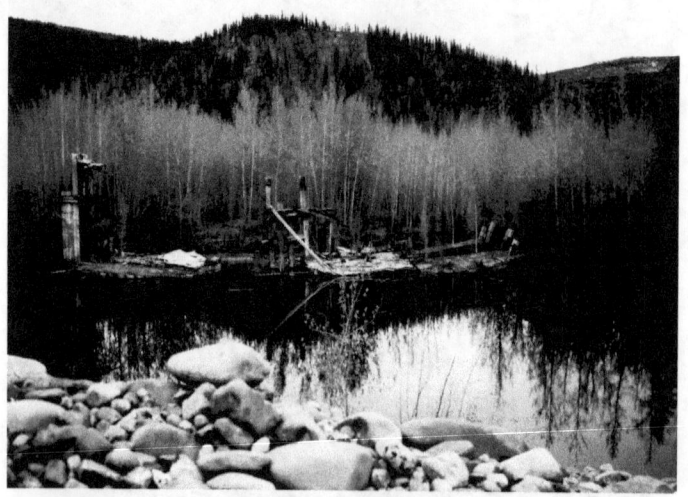

The BONANZA CREEK area, Yukon. 2001   Photos JDH

GOLDFIELDS of the YUKON

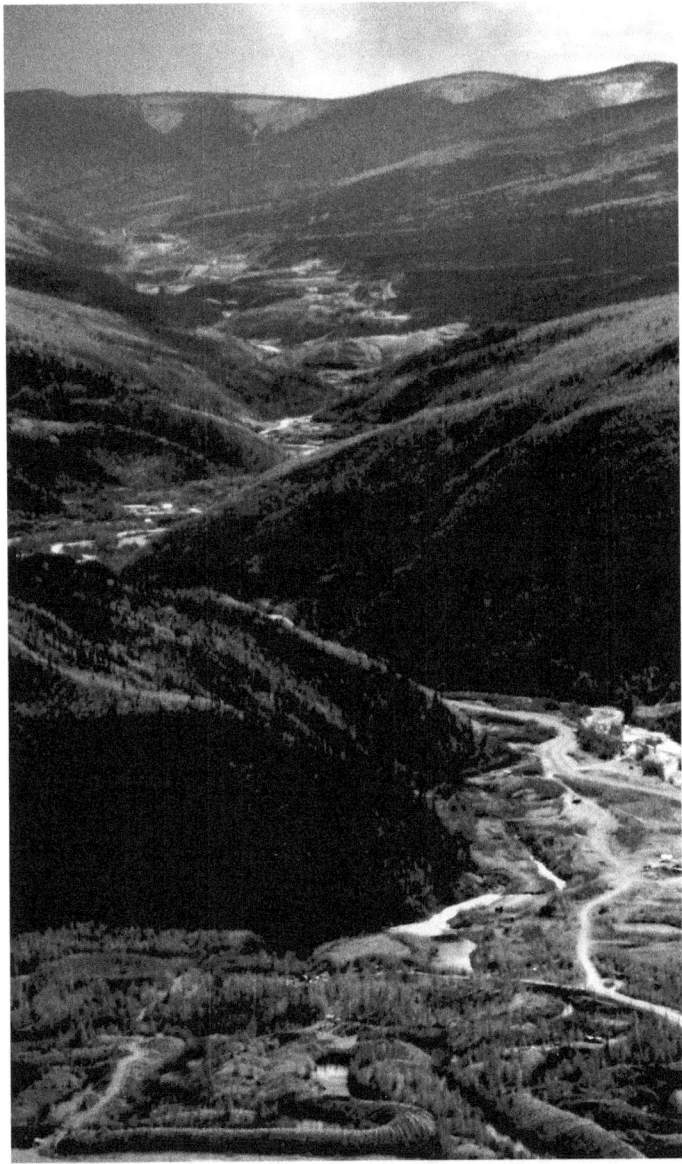

A MIDNIGHT DOME PHOTOGRAPH of Bonanza Creek.   JDH
(Gold dredge tailings can be seen in the forefront)

Monday, May 28, 2001
We took a ferry to West Dawson and drove up the hill to take photographs from the other side. Tomorrow we head to the Alaska border by way of TOP of the WORLD HWY.

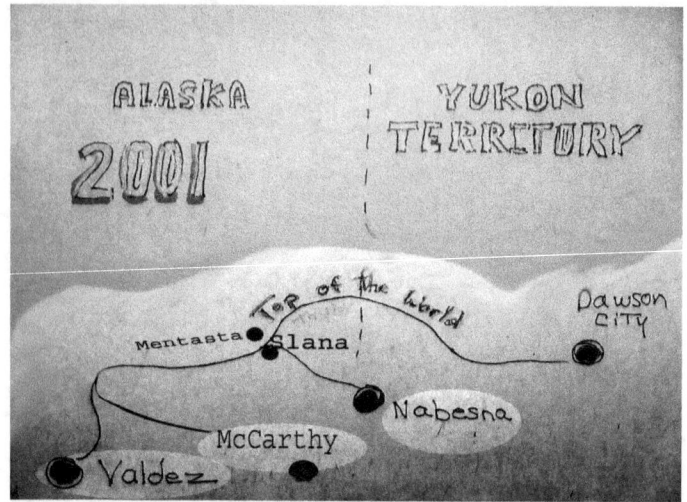

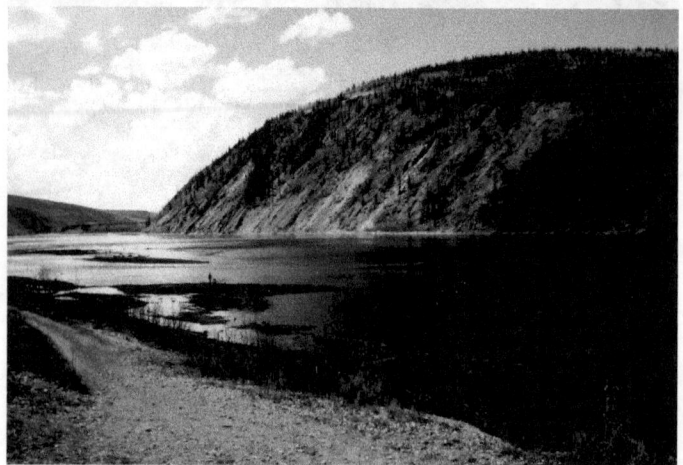

YUKON RIVER, eastside, Dawson City, Yukon. 2001   JDH

Tuesday, may 29, 2001

In the distance, up on the hill is the road to the USA border and the TOP of the WORLD HIGHWAY. It was a very cold start. What a drive! We had to detour because of an avalanche. There were two other spots where the snow was about 12 feet deep and ready to slide—no guard rails and a drop off. This put us behind schedule on very small roads in the middle of nowhere, pulling a 30 foot travel trailer with a 19 foot truck. "GO at YOUR OWN RISK" the sign read.

We stopped at Chicken and had some chili, saw our first porcupine and camped at Tok for the night.

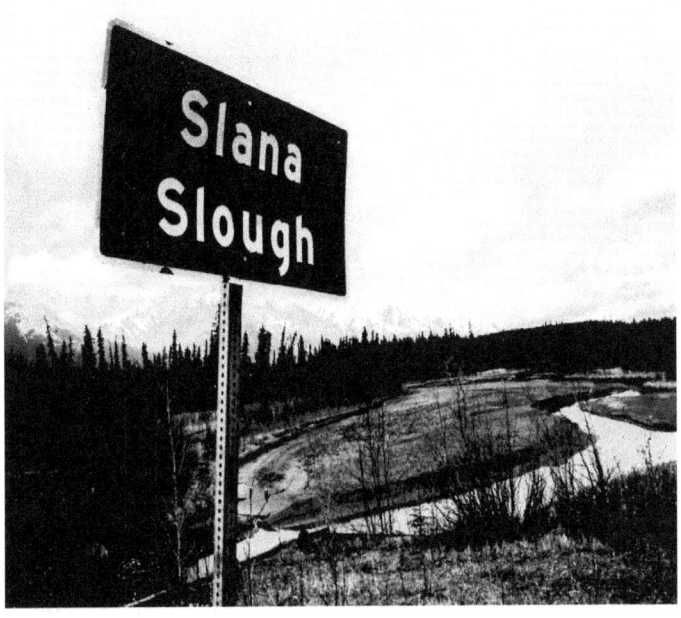

CONTENTS: SLANA SLOUGH, Alaska

GOOD to be HOME

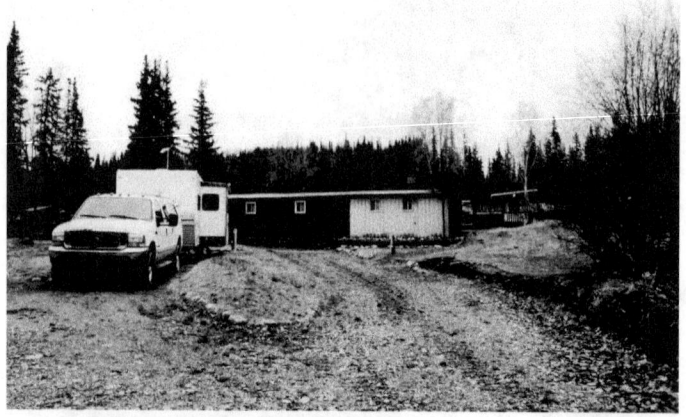

Hart-D-Ranch, Slana, Alaska. 2001   JDH

Wednesday, May 30, 2001

Arrived at the Hart-D-Ranch, this time to camp instead of booking one of those remarkable rooms. Mary was busy as usual—painting, plastering and tiling her rooms. She also carves statues and creates artwork which she sells. I might ad, very exquisite artwork. Much of her clientele are from Europe.

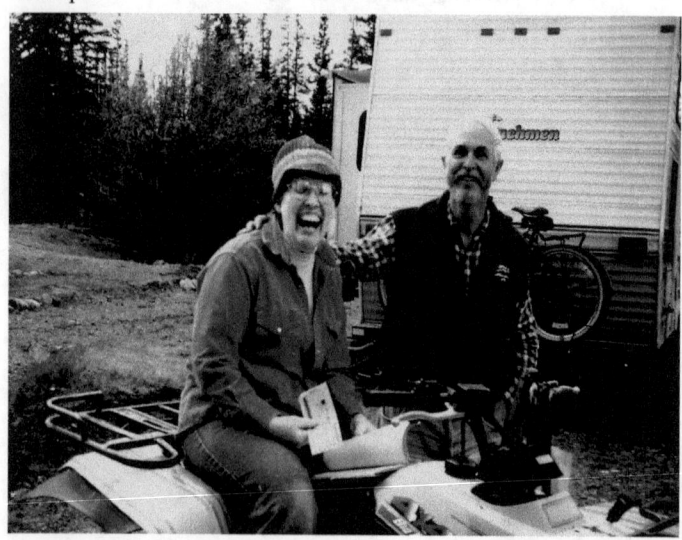

Mary D-Hart and Emory at campsite, Slana, Alaska. 2001   JDH

THE OLD ROADHOUSE

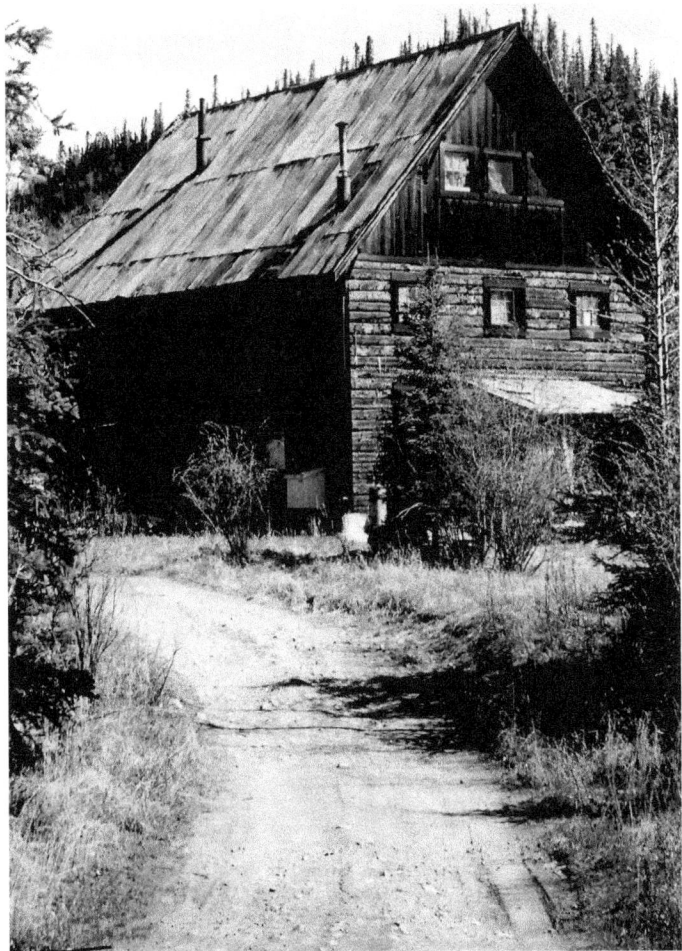

ROADHOUSE, Nabesna Rd., Slana, Alaska. 2001   JDH

We went over to visit Angus DeWitt this afternoon. He was so pleased to meet us. He introduced us to his two dogs Smokey and Goober. We got an invite to meet him behind his house tomorrow to watch his fish wheel being placed into the Copper River, where it converges with the Slana River.

Later, we rode our bikes down Nabesna Rd. a ways—noticed how awesome the sun was shining on Mt. Sanford and biked back for the camera...Also drove back to the Ahtell Creek trail head for a peek and slipped in the mud. The time was 7:00 pm with a temp of 50 degrees—it began hailing as we left.

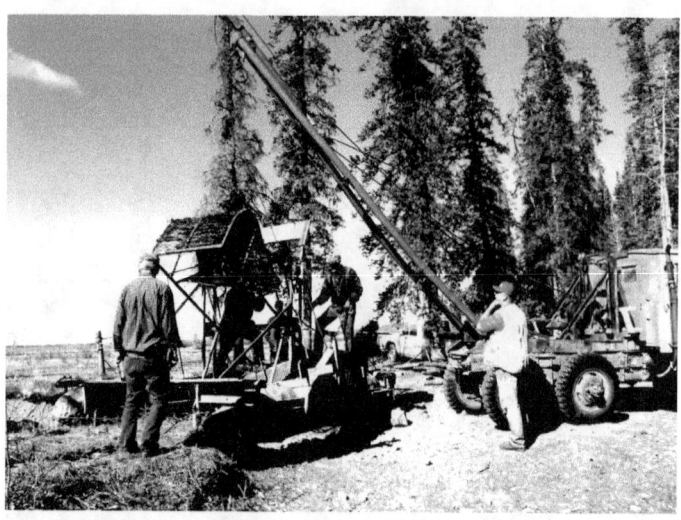

Thursday, May 31, 2001

We met Angus down by his fish wheel in the morning..
Eight or nine other men (1 teen) were there to help. They
were using an old World War II truck without brakes to
lower the wheel into the water. Angus's wheel was lowered
second.

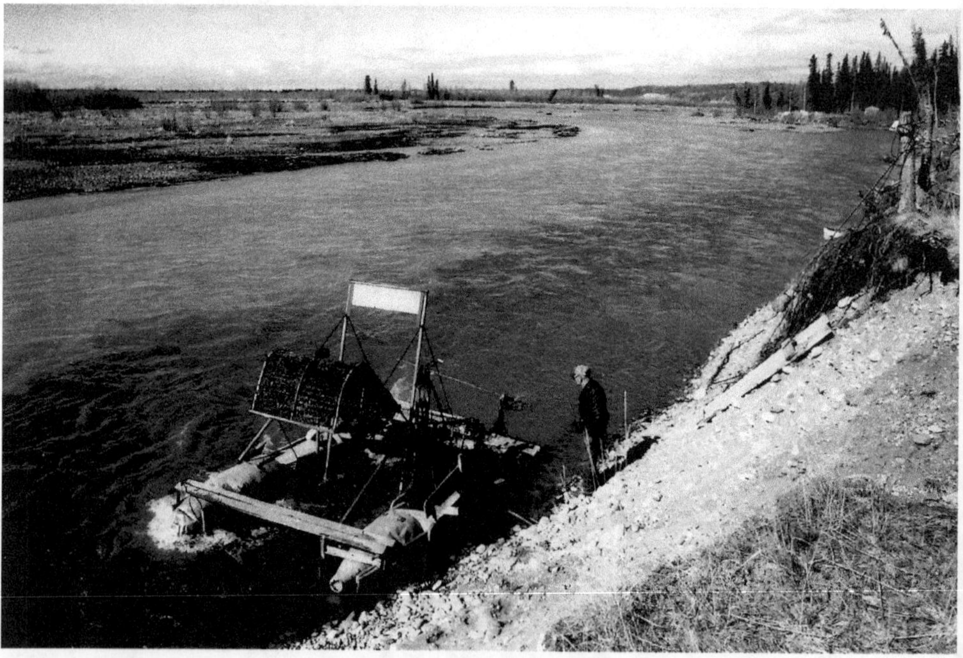

Angus by his fish wheel, Copper River, Slana, Alaska. 2001   Photos JDH

CHATINA

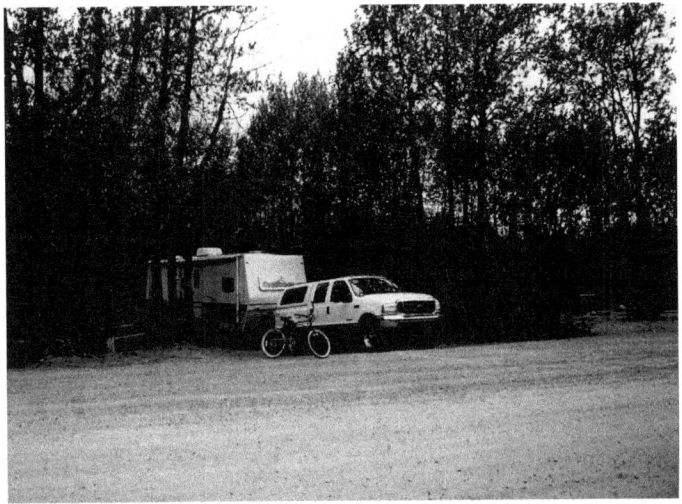

CHATINA campsite, Wrangell-St-Elias Nat'l Park, Alaska 2001   JDH

Thursday-Friday, May 31, June 1, 2001

After driving Route 10 (Edgerton Hwy) to Chatina, we booked two nights (dry) at a local campground, before taking the challenge of McCarthy Road. A challenge car rental places do not allow.

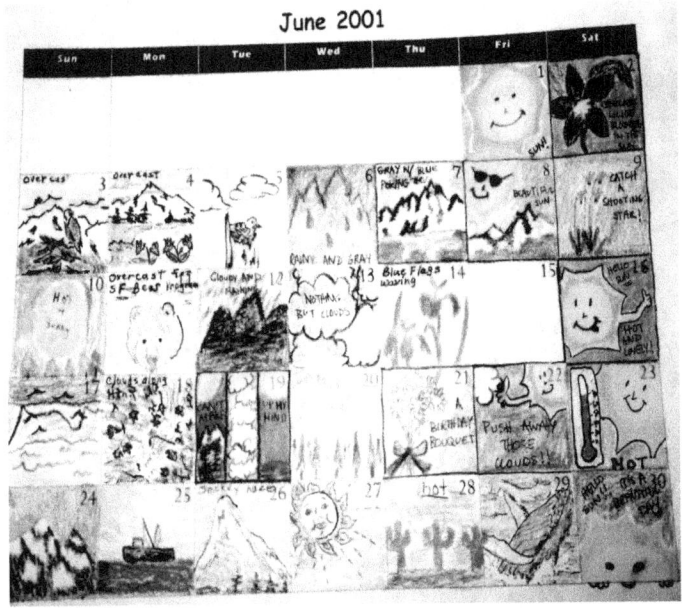

Courtesy of the Forest Service BLM office, Valdez, Alaska 2001   JDH

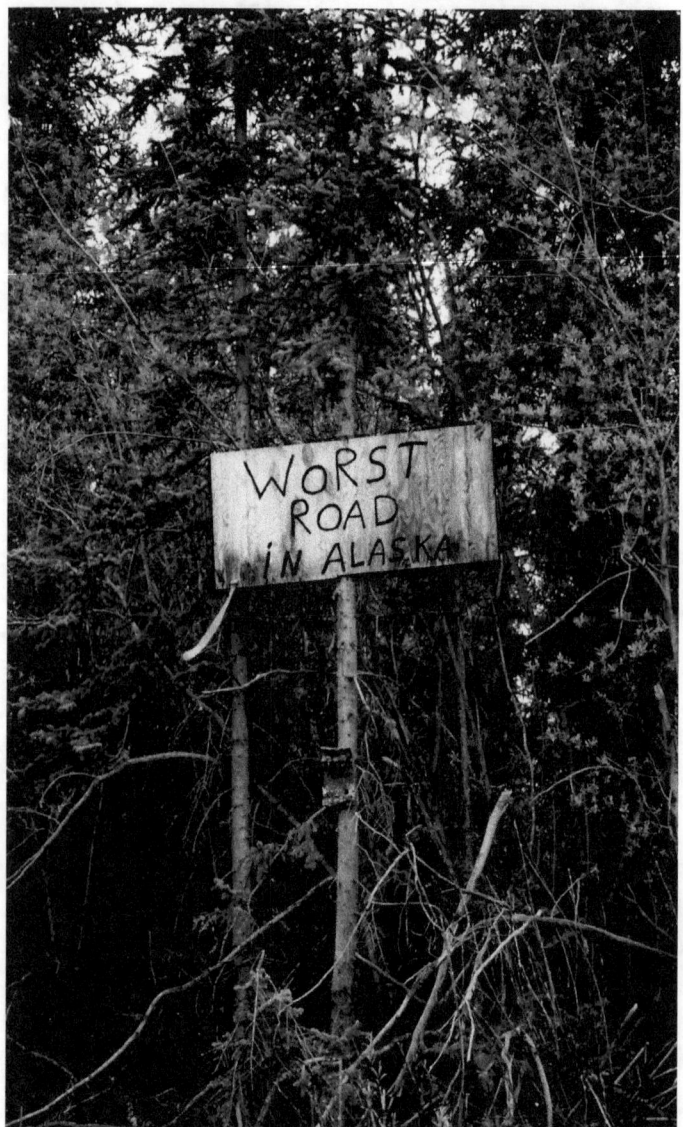

Friday, June 1, 2001

All sixty miles of the McCarthy Road were incredibly bumpy. A terrible ride! We rode on the north side of the Chatina River all the way to McCarthy.

The old Kuskulana railroad trestle was very interesting. It was a tall structure made of wood with an inscription by an unknown visitor...the ties, the ties, the ties, the ties, the lies, lies, lies, lies...

268

McCarthy Road, Alaska

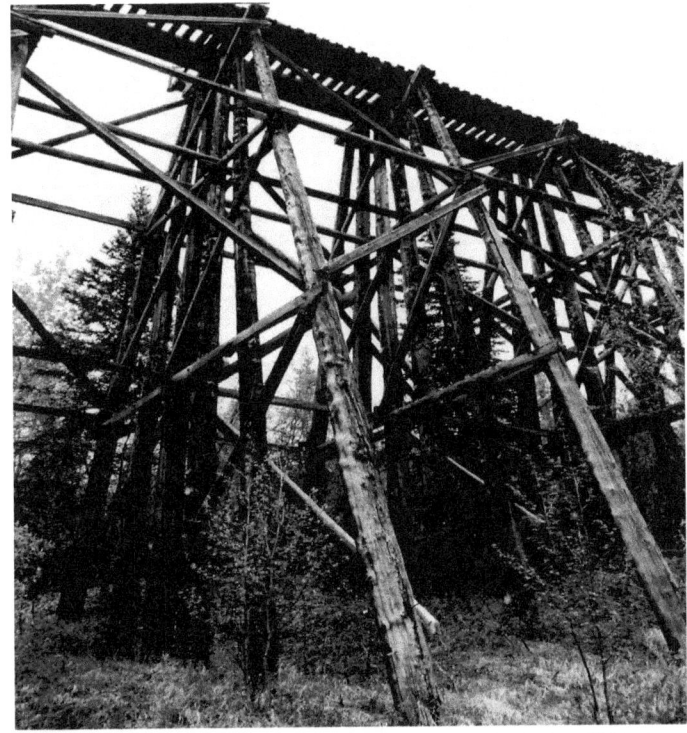

KUSKULANA RAILROAD TRESTLE, McCarthy Rd., Alaska. 2001

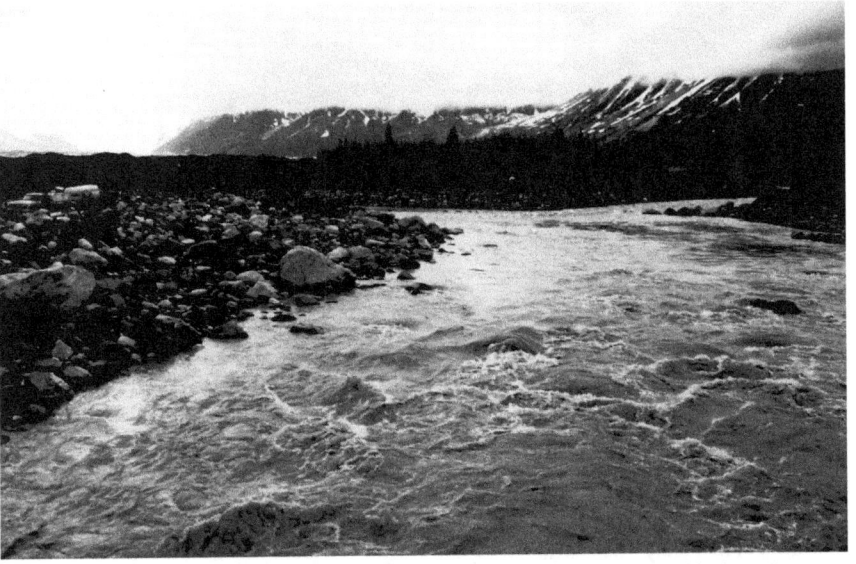

End McCarthy Road—looking N on Chatina River. Root Glacier to L, McCarthy and Kennecott mine area to R. 2001   Photos JDH

269

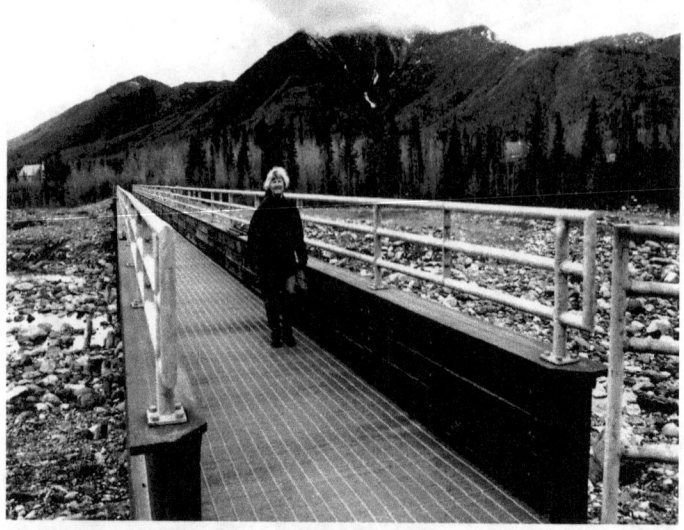

Author (Jill) walking over the Chatina River. 2001 UEH

Friday, June 1, 2001 continued
This is not the BRIDGE TO NOWHERE, but it is the footbridge to the old town of McCarthy and the deserted Kennecott Copper Mine area.

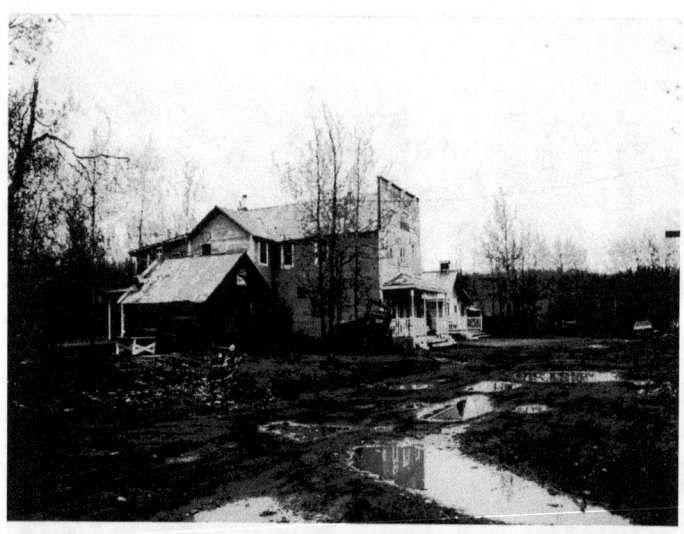

Old town of McCarthy, Alaska. 2001 JDH
A shuttle van drove us the 4.5 miles over to the mine.

270

KENNECOTT COPPER MINE, Alaska

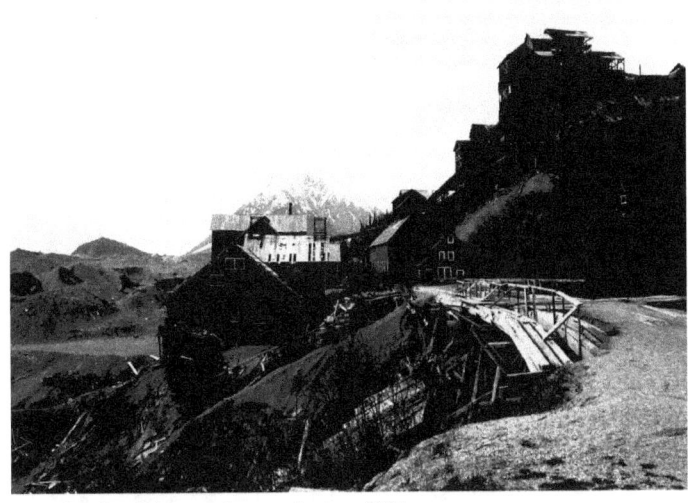

Another foot bridge to the actual mine. 2001   Photos JDH

The buildings at Kennecott were deserted and very red.
You might say it was a privilege to be able to walk around
and photograph them. The red barn color made for excellent
Photography—not achievable in this grayscale edition. The
misspelling covered in detail page 16.

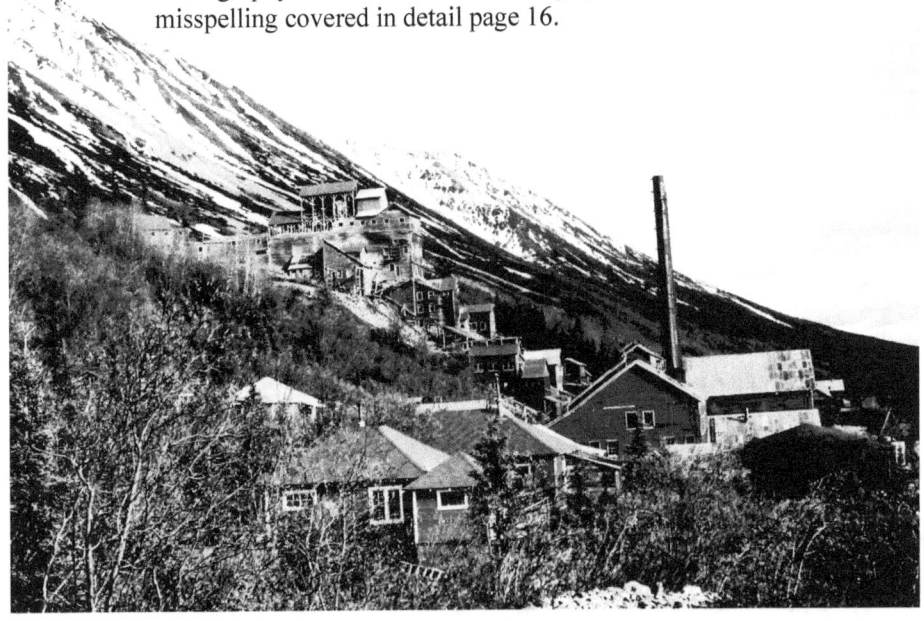

The MINE

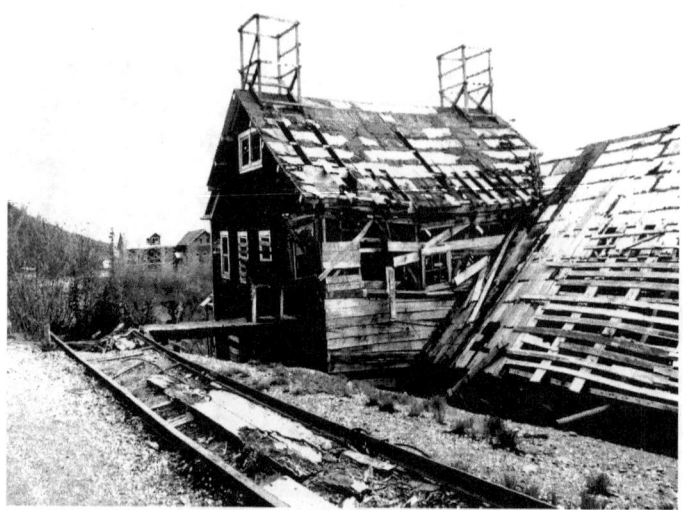

Friday, June 1, 2001 continued
In 1911 the first shipment of ore by train began. In 1938 the last train left Kennecott, as ore was largely exhausted and the area became a ghost town.

A hundred and ninety-six miles of rail remained on the north and west sides of the Chatina and Copper Rivers, ending in the coastal town of Cordova, Alaska.

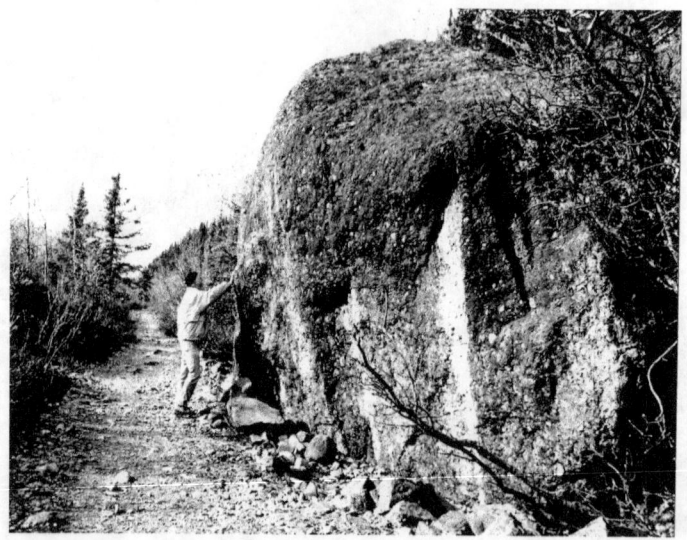

Ulys E. examines a large rock from the glacier gravel fan. 2001   Photos JDH

GRAVEL FAN

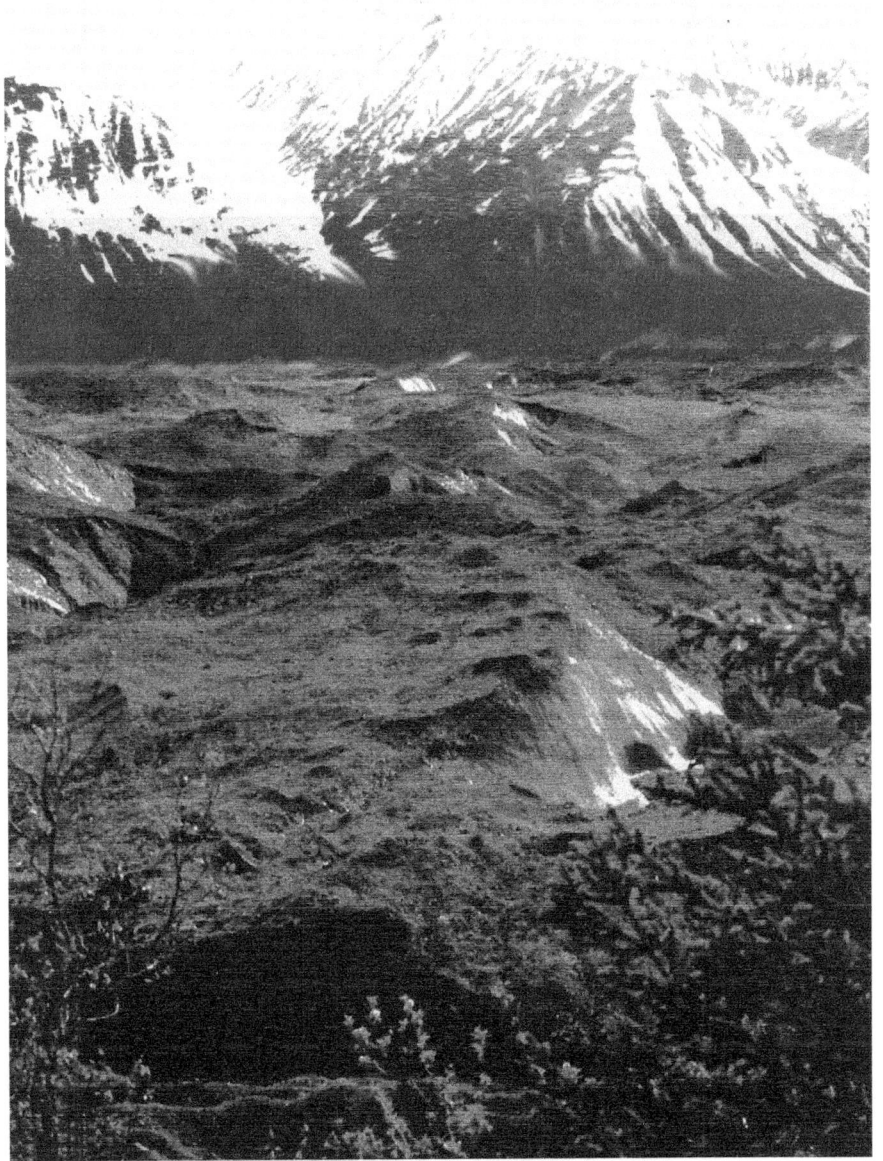

WHEN GLACIERS COLLIDE

Gravel fan from Root and Kennicott Glaciers, Alaska.
photo taken from a trail at the Kennecott Mine area.
June 1, 2001   JDH

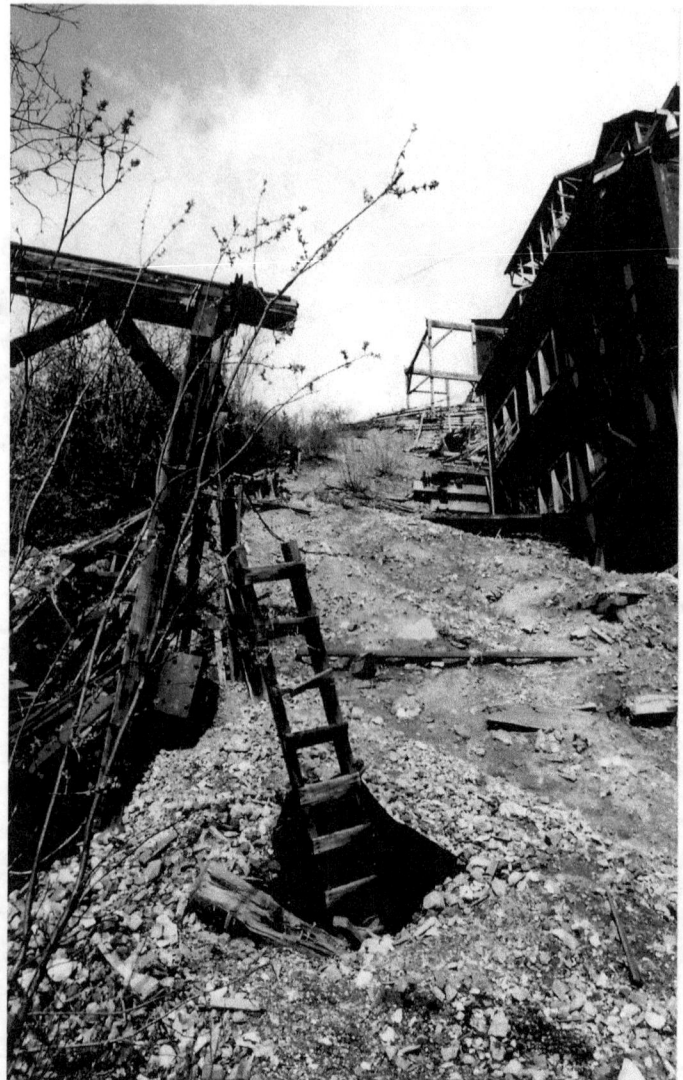

KENNECOTT COPPER MINE, Alaska. 2001   JDH

A GHOST TOWN?

Friday, June 1, 2001 continued

From 1932-1952 a family of three stayed on as watchmen to the Kennecott Mine facility. After a brief restart and the earthquake of 1964, the mine became a National Historic Landmark. In 1986 it became official. Truly a treasure!

KUSKULANA GEORGE, Alaska

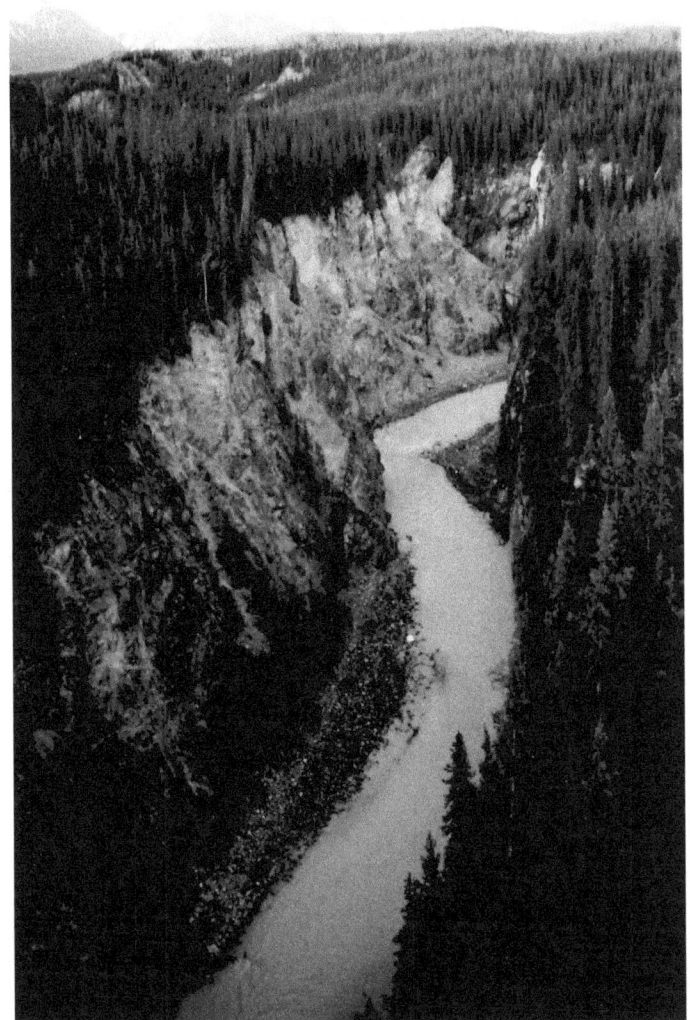

The KUSKULANA RIVER, Mc Carthy Rd., Alaska. 2001 JDH
A decade ago this gorge was a popular bungee jumping spot.

Friday, June 1, 2001 continued

It was getting late and we needed to get back to our second night of camping at Chatina—nestled in the confluence of the Copper and Chatina Rivers.

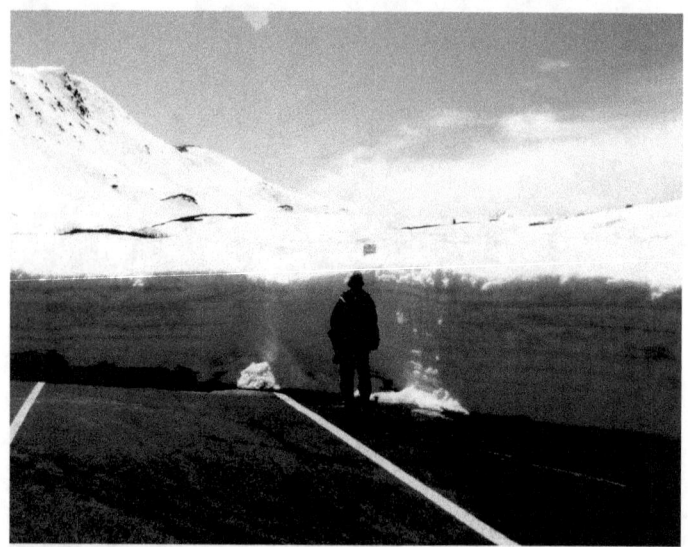

Author (Jill) in front of Worthington Glacier, Alaska. 2001   UEH

Saturday, June 2, 2001

The pass was beautiful and breathtaking as always. Maybe this would be a good place to take the summer solstice photograph.

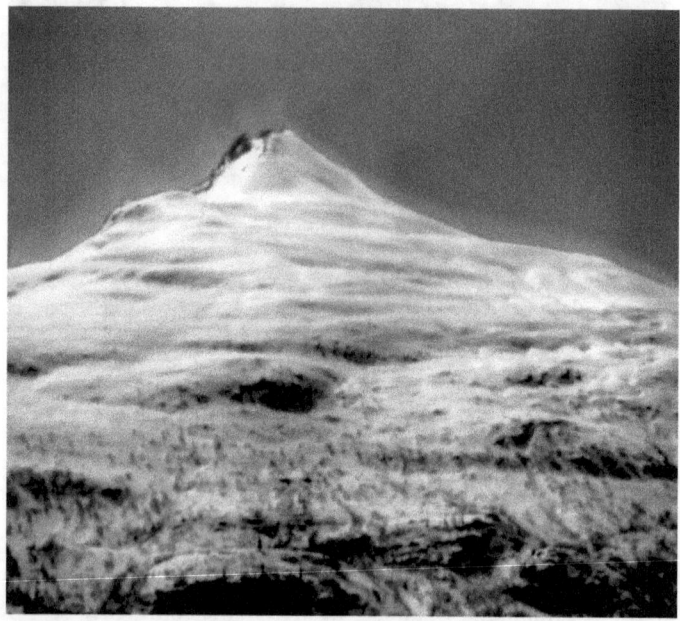

Thompson Pass area, heading to Valdez, Alaska. 2001   JDH

VALDEZ, Aerial View

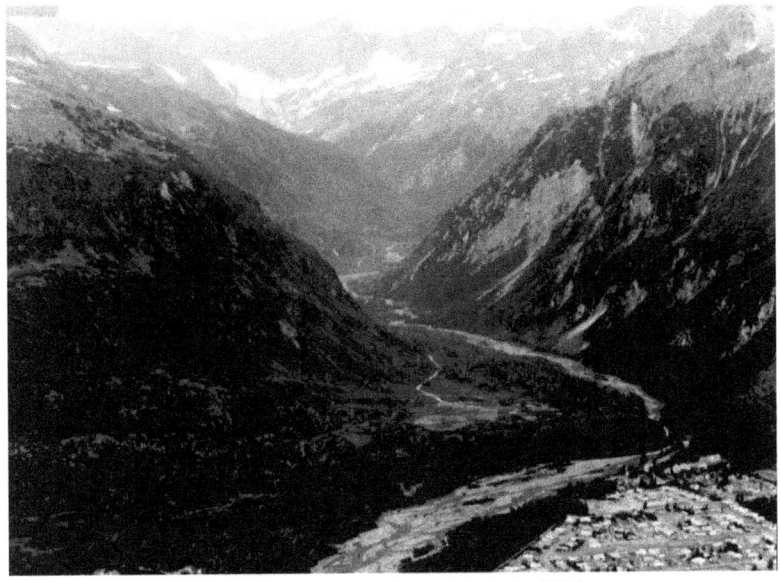

VALDEZ, Alaska (Alpine Aviation aerial view). 2001   JDH

CONTENTS: VALDEZ DAYS
Order of activities—some without photographs

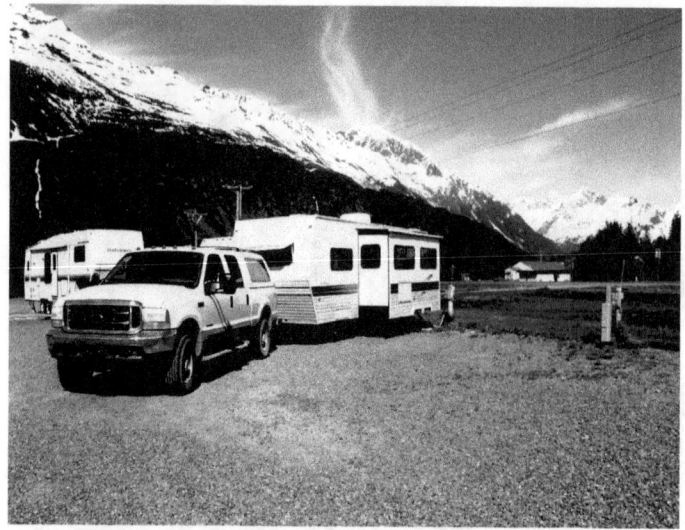

EAGLE'S REST, Valdez, Alaska. 2001   Photos JDH

ANIMAL SHELTER in DISTANCE

Saturday-Sunday June 2 and 3, 2001

This weekend was spent cleaning up the camper and the truck and recouping. Monday I will visit the Animal Shelter and walk some dogs.

DOCKSIDE

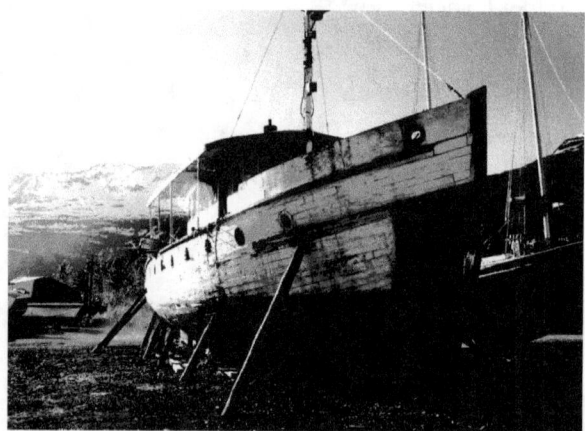

An intriguing old "dockside" boat which has been since demolished. We also hiked the 1.7 mile Dock Point Loop Trail to photograph the *TREE FAMILY*.

278

The VALDEZ ANIMAL SHELTER, Alaska

Monday, June 4, 2001

At the Animal Shelter, we met Flash for the first time along with three Rot-Lab pups. We walked all of them. They were so glad to see us. That evening a new camper arrived behind us — a pipeline worker, using his dog to guard his camper. The cry went out and the cry was heard. Animal control handled it brilliantly. The dog ended up with a dog house and a run for the entire summer along side of the camper. He also was witnessed walking his dog by a neighbor—"ONE FOR SPOT!"

The moral of this story is if you travel long and far enough, eventually you will see something you do not want to see.

MILE HIGH and the VALDEZ GLACIER

Wednesday, June 6, 2001

Determined to locate the Valdez Glacier, we passed the mountain known as "Mile High" and passed the field of yellow dandelions—so that is where R. A. Douglas became interested in dandelion greens. Growing up, he boiled them like spinach and insisted we clean our plates.

Further back we were able to get closer to the first body of water without the blasting signs stopping us. We walked completely around it. No trail, just steep banks.

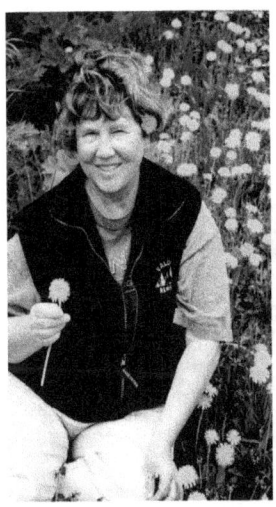 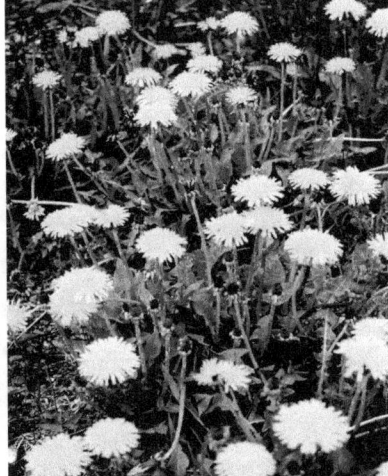

Author, Jill in field of dandelions   Photo UEH

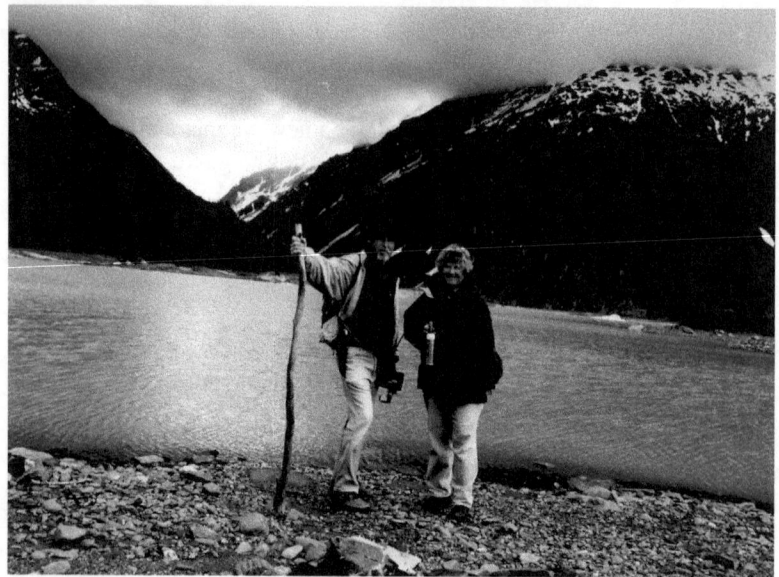

WHERE'S the GLACIER? Emory and Jill (Author) 2001

Thursday, June 7, 2001

We had just arrived in town and this was another attempt at locating the Valdez Glacier.

It was not until August 22, 2001 that we finally located the terminal moraine of the Valdez Glacier. It was not easy. Two moraine photos can be seen on pages 76 & 77.

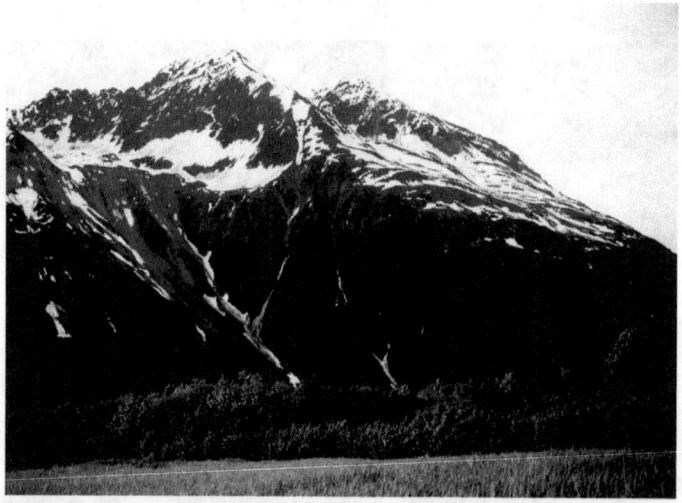

The CHUGACH MOUNTAIN RANGE and a Valdez mountain nicknamed "Mile High." Local airstrip in forefront. 2001 JDH

TOWN MOUNTAIN HIKE

Friday, June 8, 2001

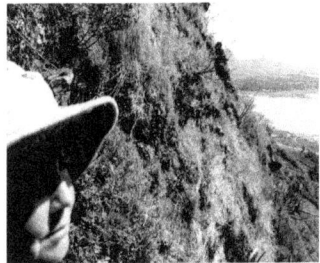
Jill and Emory

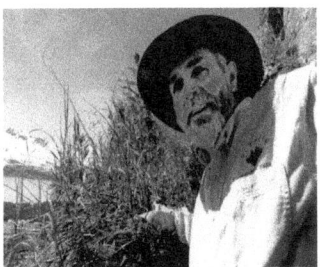
and decision to abort. 2001

It was said that if another tsunami came the high school students were to climb the town mountain all the way to the top. They practiced. The rope at the top looked old and weathered like the clothesline in my childhood backyard. Knots were tied every 2 feet.

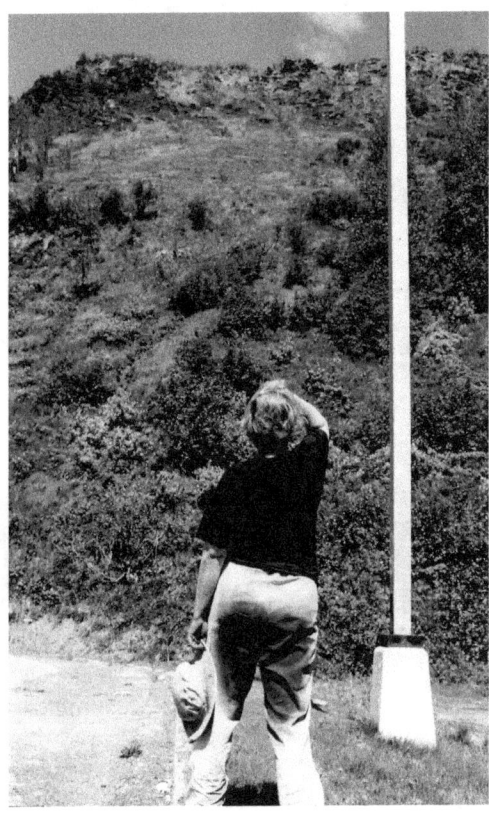
Author (Jill) looking at the Town Mountain.   UEH

Water Tower Trail

Saturday-Sunday, June 9—10, 2001

Took a brake on Saturday, after locating the 1935 Sugar Loaf Mountain Shot. Sunday, bathed 3 pups at the shelter and walked dogs.

Later, we decided to hike up Trail 2 of the Town Mountain behind the Mineral Creek water tower This was the back trail and supposed to be easier. It wasn't. The trouble with this trail was that it kept going out onto curvy, straight down cliffs. There were also two rope areas going up steep sections. We conquered the first one and half way up the second, Emory said, "I didn't leave anything up there." I said, "I hear you" and we headed down alive and well to hike another day.

Monday, June 11, 2001

Celebrated our anniversary by taking the Alyeska Pipeline Tour on the other side of Valdez Bay and had dinner at the Pipeline Club. Fresh salmon, yum!

SOLOMON GULCH TRAIL

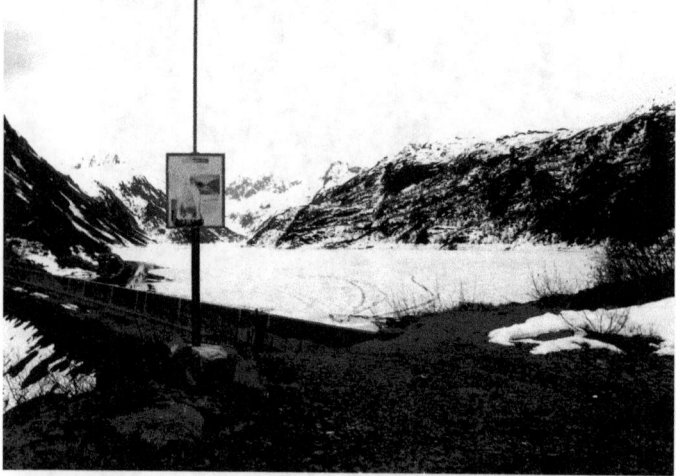

Wednesday, June 13, 2001

Hiked the 1.7 mile trail, a mile past the fish hatchery. It was a steep uphill hike. No bears. Two government employee trucks passed, checking on the dam.

This area was the site of Fort Liscum in 1899 during the gold rush and before Alaska was a state. The Valdez-Eagle Trail head began here—heading to Fort Egbert near Eagle.

OLD MILITARY TRAIL

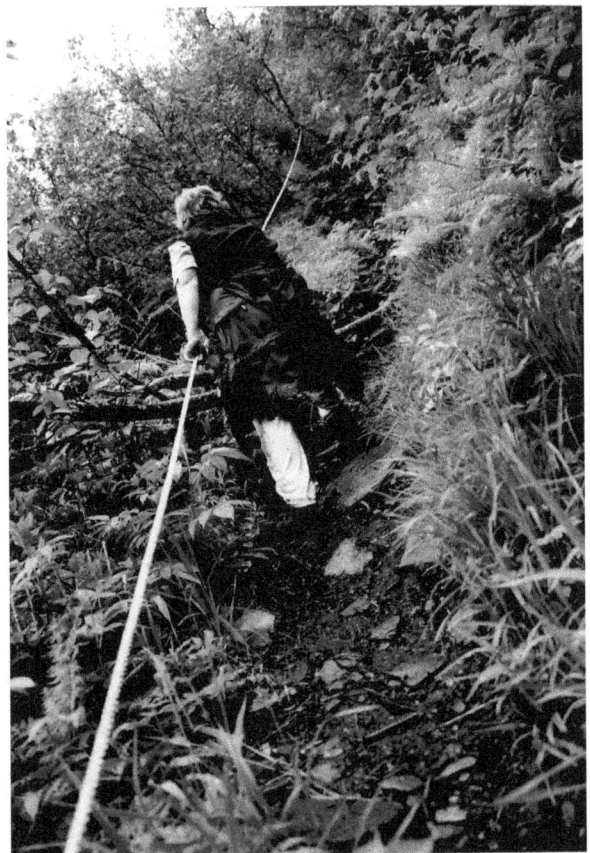

Author hiking Military Trail, Keystone Canyon, AK. UEH

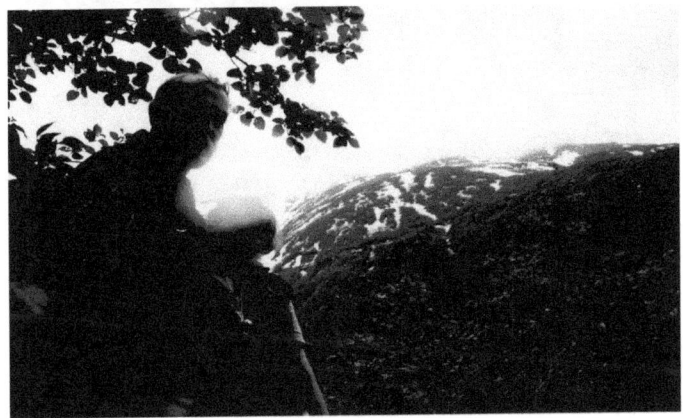

Emory and Jill across from "Three-Falls." west side.   Timer

Thursday, June 14, 2001

SHOUP BAY TRAIL, Alaska

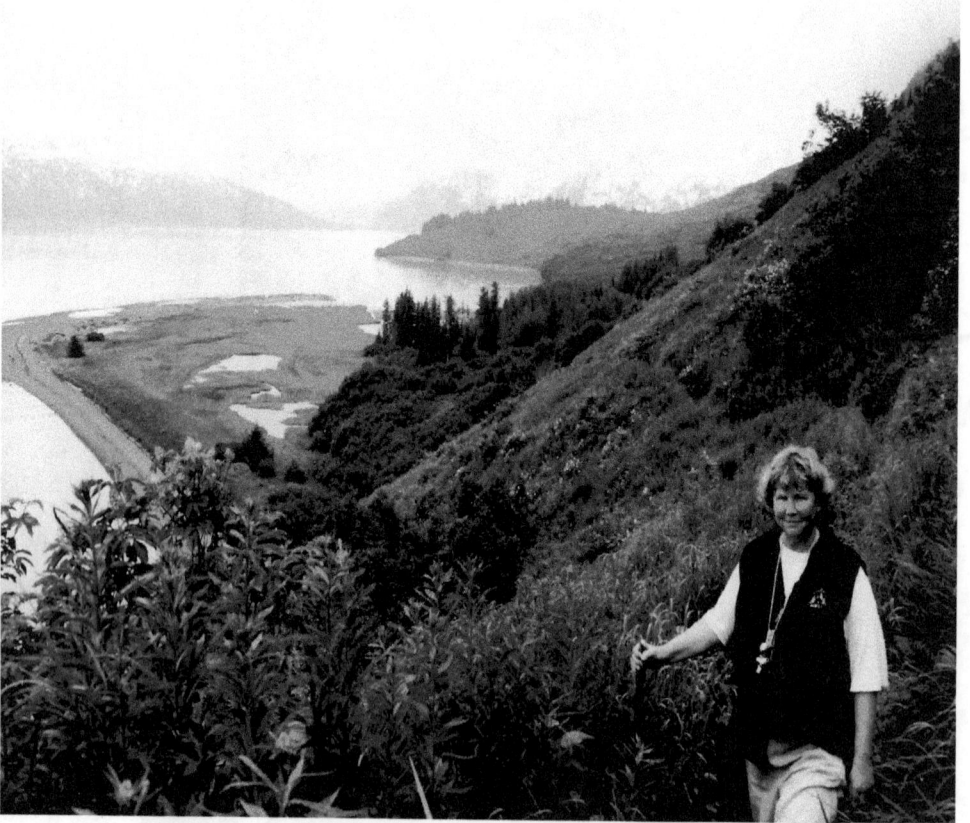

Author, GOLD CREEK L on SHOUP BAY TRAIL, Valdez, AK. 2001 UEH

Sunday, June 17

An old Scottish saying from a noble clan—
"be prepared." The Author is wearing bear bells, a whistle and carrying a big stick.

GOLD CREEK, Alaska

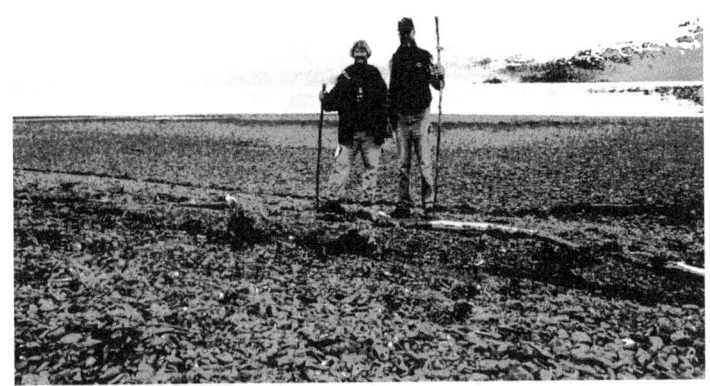

GOLD CREEK, Alaska — Author (Jill) and Emory. 2001   Timer

An aerial photograph, a photo from the Shoup Bay Trail, a photo on the ground at Gold Creek and in an egg reflect what life is like from different vantage points.

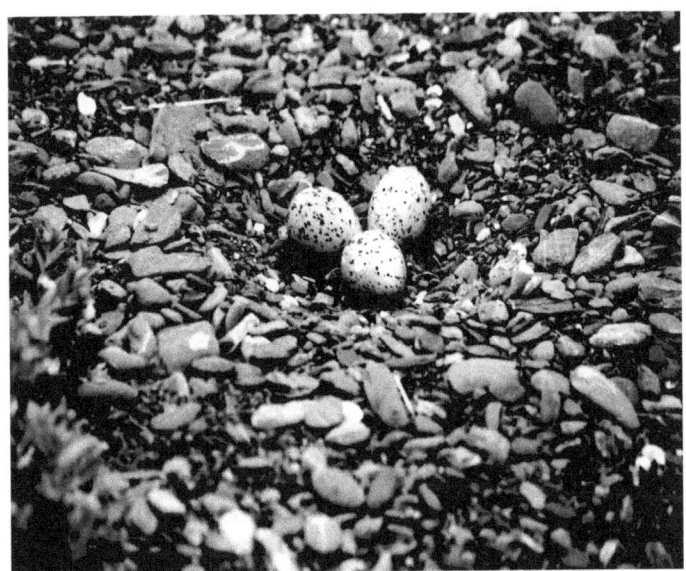

GOLD CREEK, Alaska. 2001   JDH

SUMMER SOLSTICE 2001

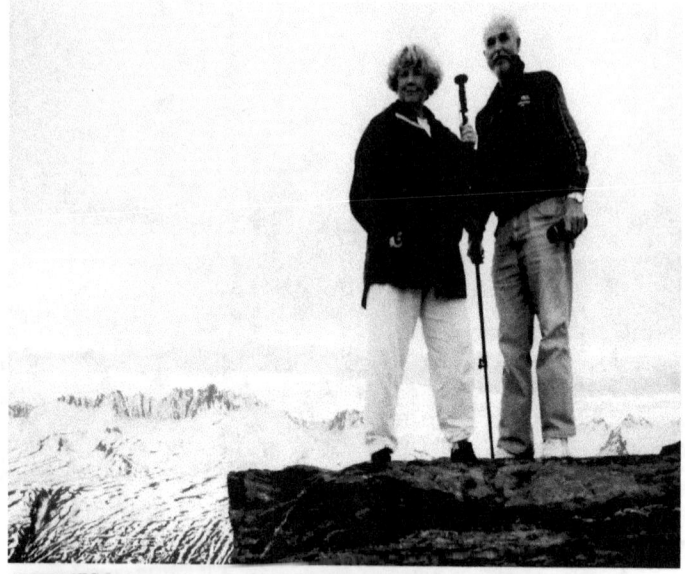

THOMPSON PASS, Alaska. Author (Jill) and Emory. 2001   Timer

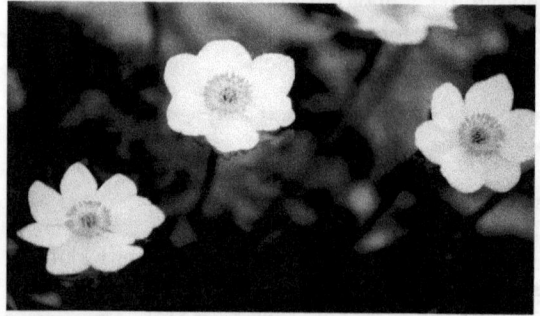

Wildflowers on the pass, summer solstice. 2001 JDH

Wednesday-Thursday, June 20, 21, 2001

It was very cold, quiet and snowy up there. We were surprised that the sun set very close to where it rose. 3:00 am

Friday-Thursday, June 22—28, 2001

Jill attended the last frontier playwrights workshop at the college. We both helped paint the Animal Shelter a happy dandelion yellow and visited the original old grave yard.

Now preparing for the loop trip, we relocated the camper to a dry area in the back and delivered Spot's (dog) picture to the Valdez Animal Shelter. Spot ran the streets of Old Valdez for several years before yielding to an unknown end.

286

LOOP TRIP, Alaska

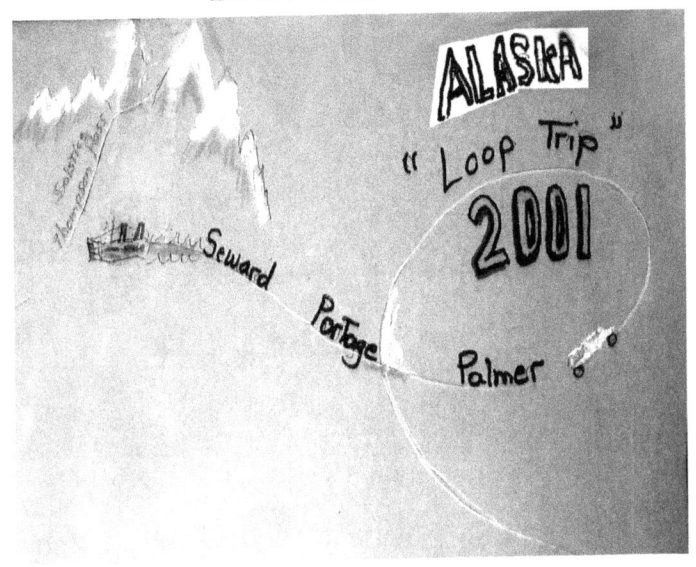

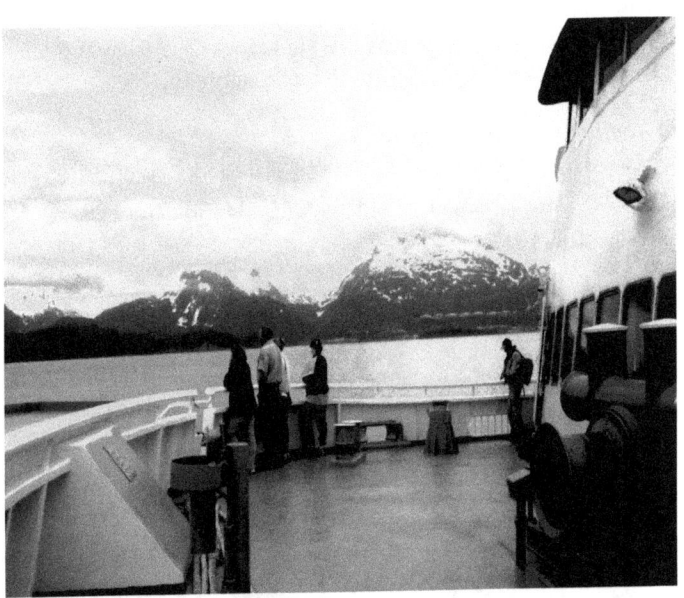

The TUSTUMENA FERRY, Valdez, Alaska. UEH to right. 2001   JDH

FRIDAY, June 29, 2001

At 5:30 am, we locked up the camper at Eagle's Rest and headed for the Ferry Terminal. It was a 12 hour trip over to Seward.

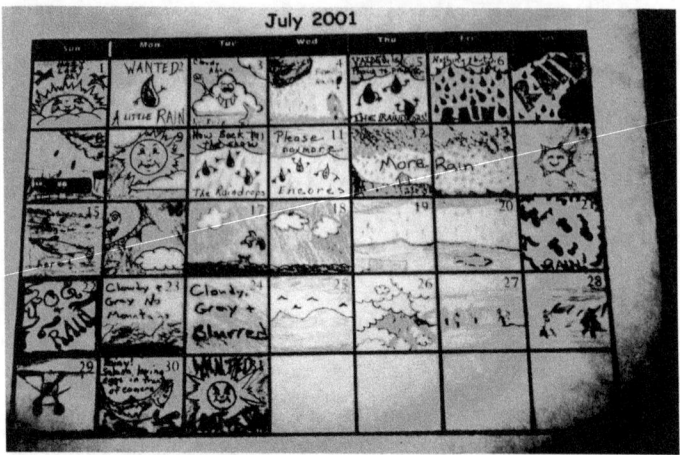

Courtesy of the Forest Service BLM office, Valdez Alaska. 2001   JDH

CONTENTS: LOOP TRIP (ODOMETER 29,574)

Friday, June 29– Wednesday, July 25, 2001

Our Alaska Loop Trip was traveled clockwise from Valdez, using our truck for transportation and camping.

The following areas are highlighted:
Seward, Portage Glacier, Whittier, Girdwood, Palmer, Wasilla, Denali, Nenana, Fairbanks, Circle Hot Springs, Circle & the Delta.

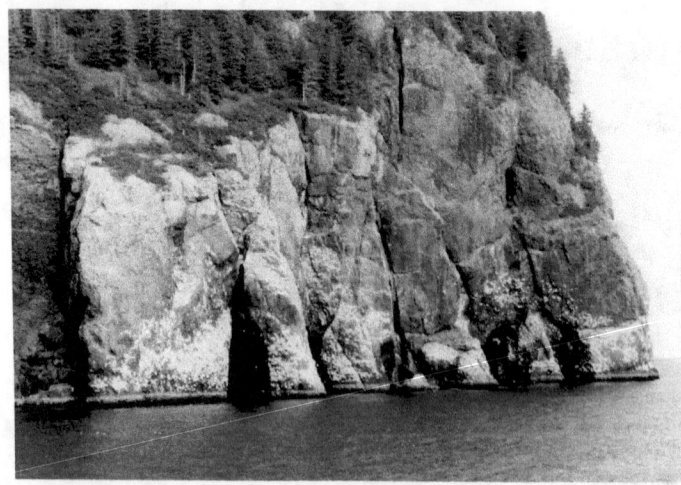

RESURRECTION BAY, from ferry. 2001   JDH

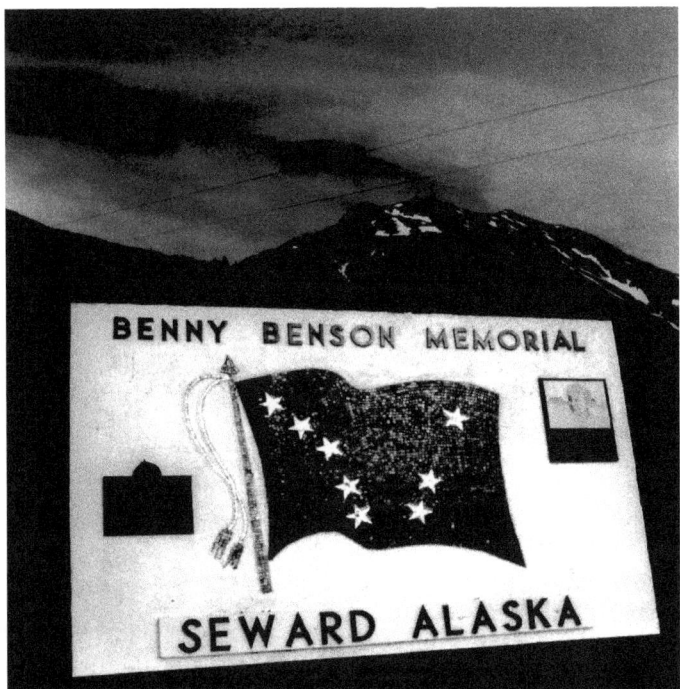

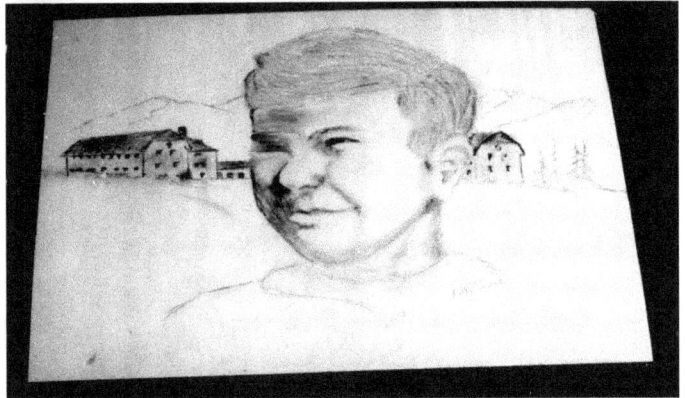

At four years of age, Benny lost his mother and was soon placed into the Methodist Jesse Lee Home on the Aleutian Islands. In the seventh grade he designed this flag. He submitted the flag with the following writing:

"The blue field is for the Alaska sky and the forget-me-not is the Alaska flower. The North Star is for the future state of Alaska (the most northerly in the union). The big dipper is for the Great Bear, symbolizing strength."

LOWELL CREEK FALLS, Seward

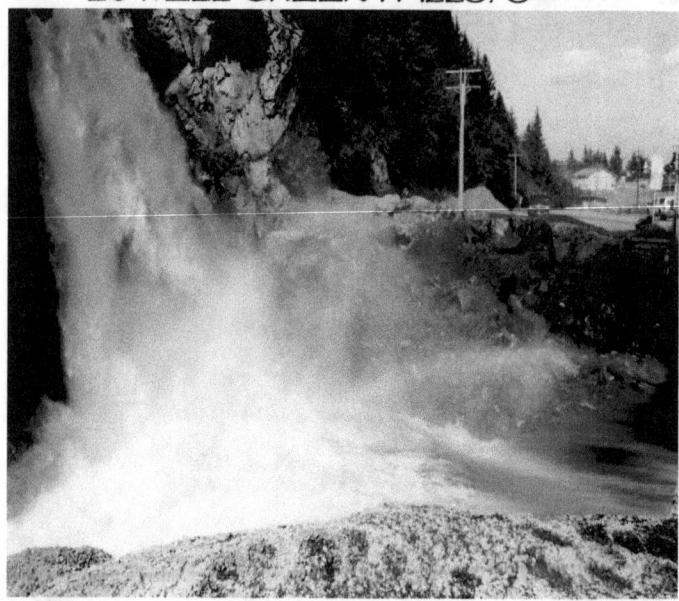

LOWELL CREEK FALLS on Bear MT., Seward, Alaska. 2001   JDH

Out at Lowell Point there is a rainbow to the R. of the falls.

Saturday, June 30, 2001

We arrived the night before at 6:30 pm It was our first night sleeping in the truck. Seward is the home of Marathon Mt. There is a race up the 3,020 ft Mt. every July 4th.

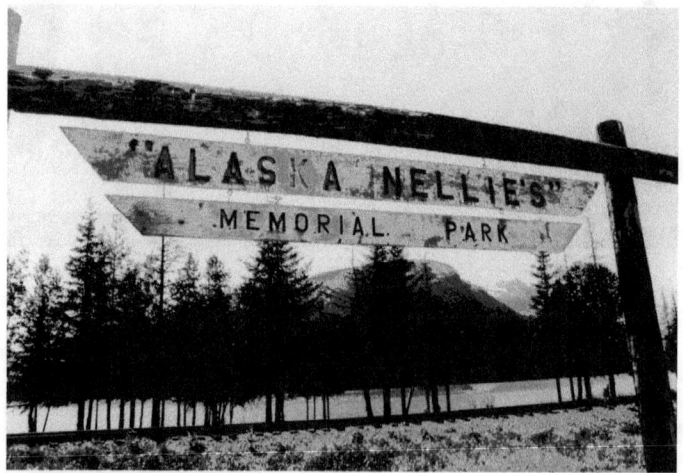

ALASKA NELLIE'S B&B, Rt 9 to Portage Glacier, Alaska. 2001   JDH

Sunday, July 1, 2001

290

PORTAGE GLACIER, Alaska

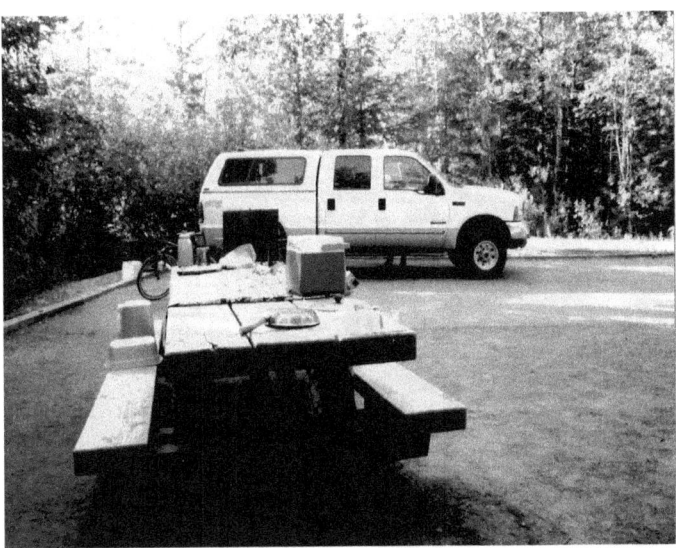

WILIWAW CAMPGROUND, Portage, Alaska. 2001   JDH

This was one of our favorite "Truck" campgrounds. Some of LCA 's best writing was inspired here. The trees by our campsite were Black Spruce and Cottonwood. Alder was the brush of the trails. /

Monday, July 2, 2001

Visited the Portage Lake Recreation Center and booked a Portage Glacier Tour. Saw the Portage Pass where people used to cross in the earlier days from Whittier.

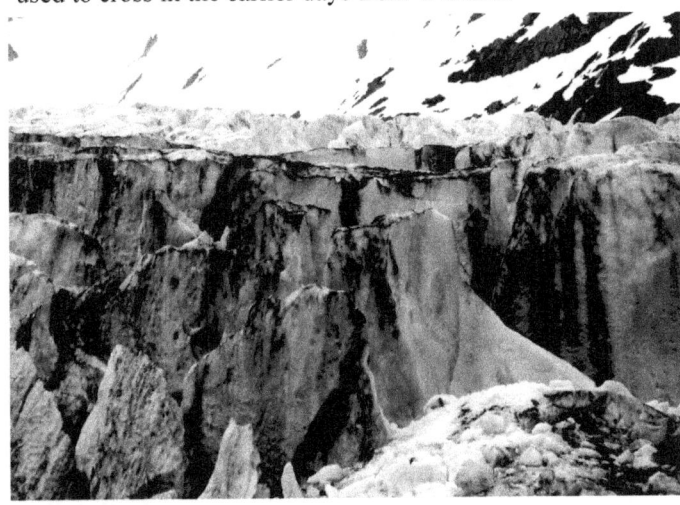

PORTAGE GLACIER TOUR, Portage, Alaska. 2001   JDH

WHITTIER, Alaska

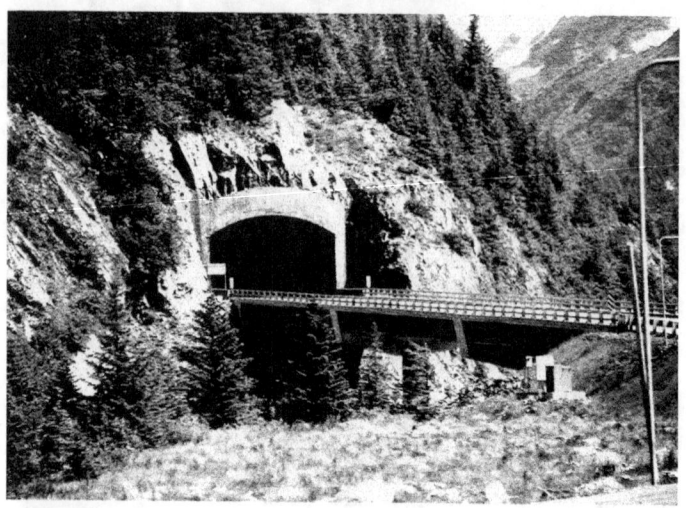

WHITTIER-PORTAGE TUNNEL, Alaska. 2001   JDH

In 1943, the ANTON ANDERSON MEMORIAL TUNNEL was completed. Seward and Anchorage were no longer the only railroad ports. In the year 2000, cars went thru the tunnel for the first time. We are fortunate to have some "2000" footage traveling through it with our rental van.

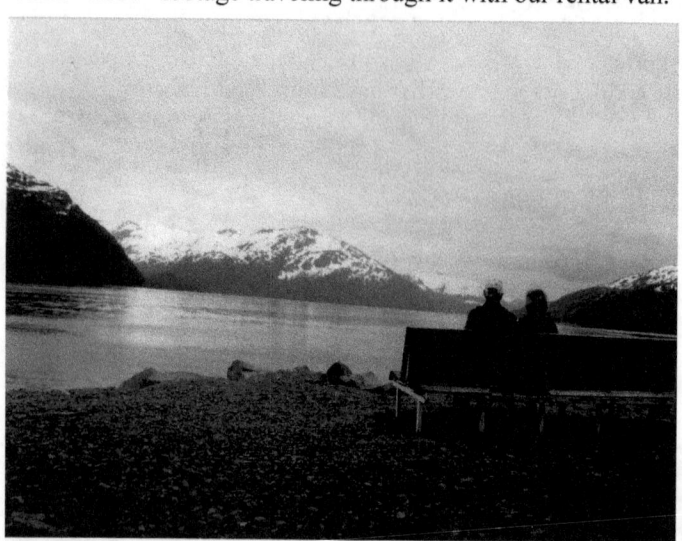

Emory and Jill, Whittier dock area, Alaska. 2001   Timer

July 2, 2001.

First days of our Alaska LOOP TRIP.

PORTAGE PASS TRAIL, Whittier

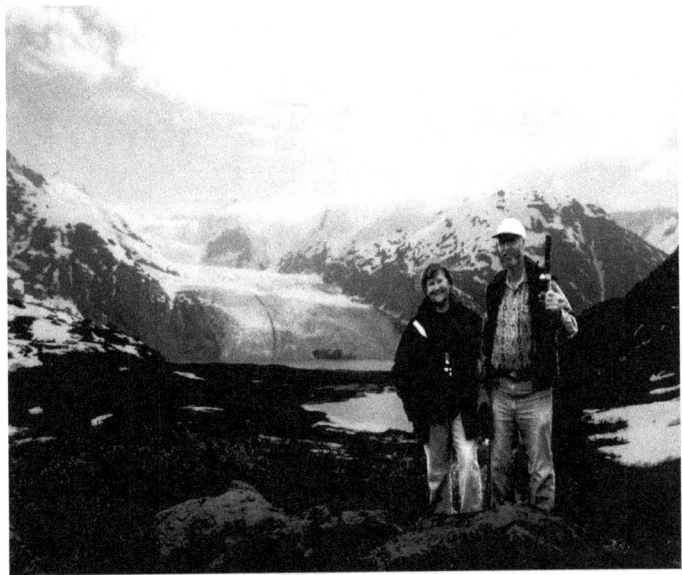

Author (Jill) and Emory on Portage Pass Trail, Whittier, Alaska. Timer
Standing above the Portage Glacier—all the while keeping an eye on a nearby black bear.

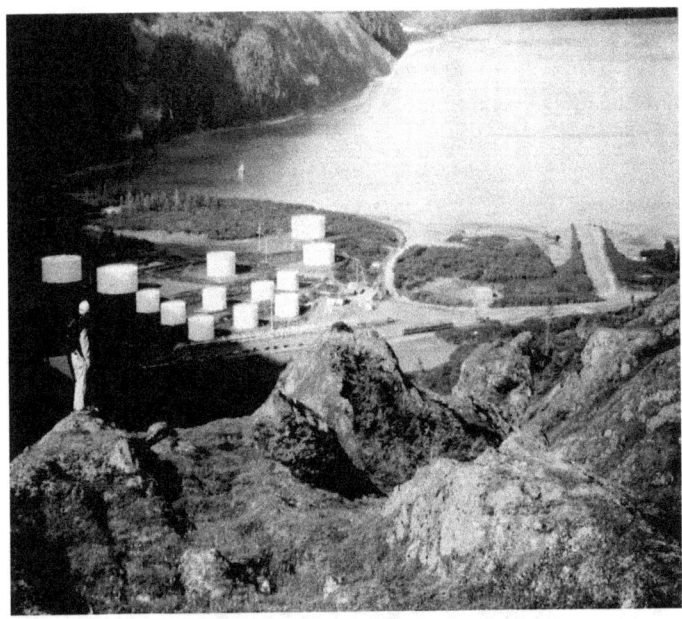

UEH on PORTAGE PASS TRAIL, Whittier, Alaska. 2001 JDH
Both enjoying a spectacular view of Whittier, Alaska.

293

GIRDWOOD, Alaska

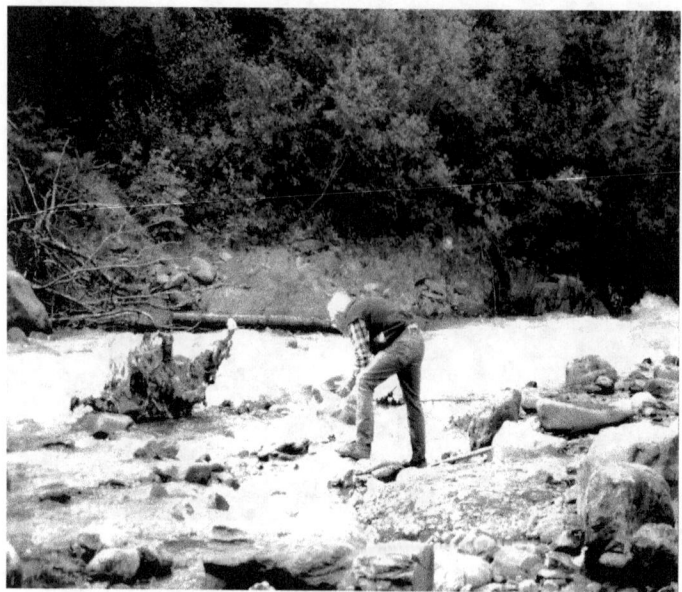

UEH seriously panning Crow Creek for gold, Girdwood, Alaska. 2001

Monday-Tuesday, July 2—3, 2001
We toured the mining site and walked to both #1 And #2 panning sites where Emory really got into it!!!

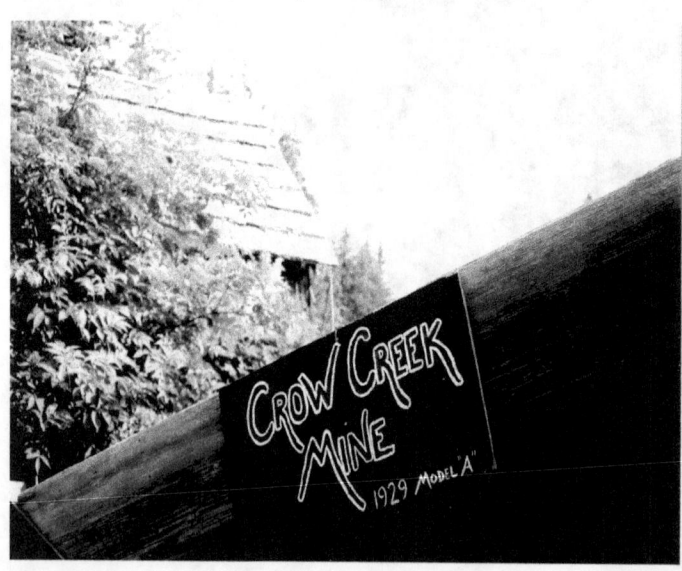

Photos JDH

CROW CREEK CAMPSITE, Girdwood

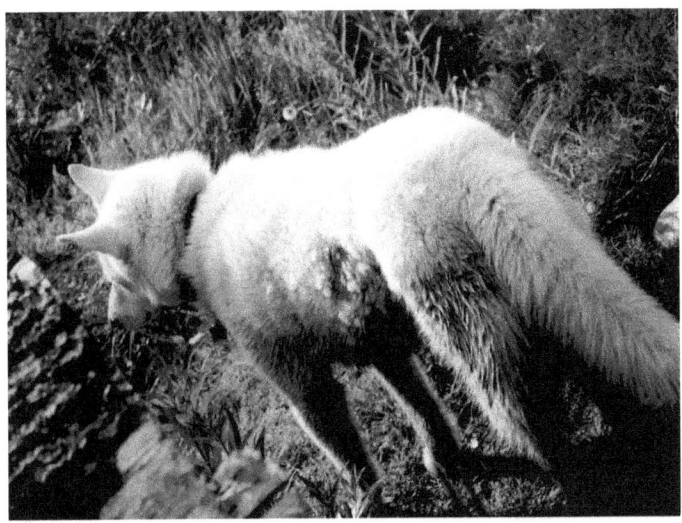

A friendly white shepherd hosted the campground., Girdwood, Alaska. 2001

Yes, he got a snack!

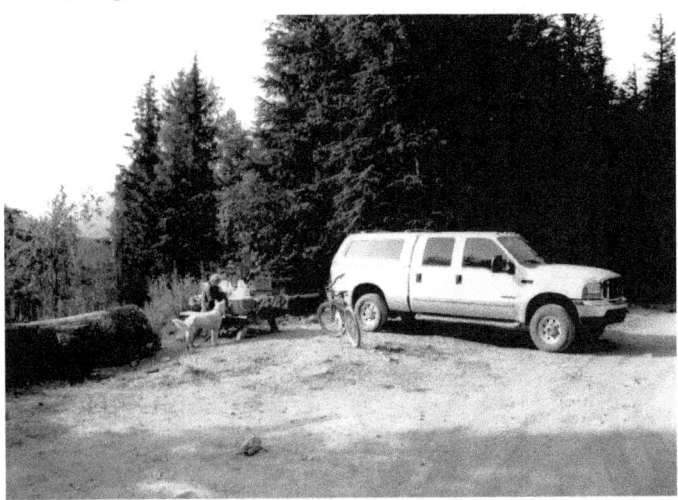

Our CROW CREEK CAMPSITE, Girdwood, Alaska. 2001   Photos UEH

On the drive west up Turn Again Arm we came upon a tidal
bore. It was a large wave of about 6 feet coming across the
water toward Portage. It was 4 out of 5 stars. Impressive.

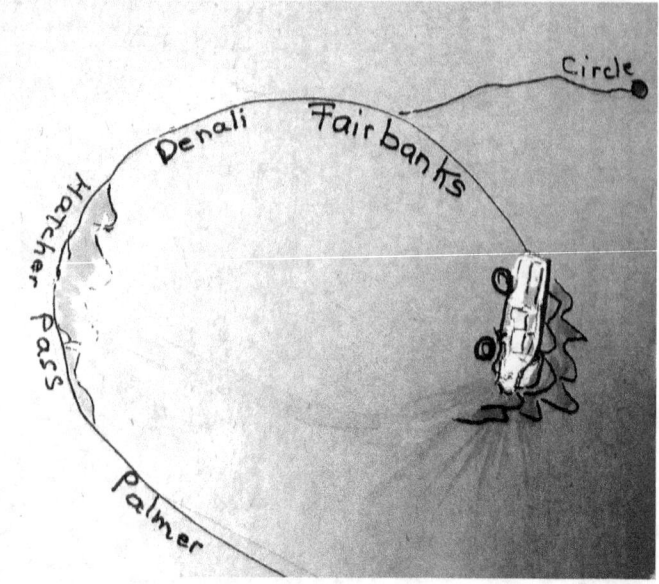

PALMER, Alaska

Wednesday-Thursday, July 4—12, 2001

We stayed at three different campsite locations in Palmer.

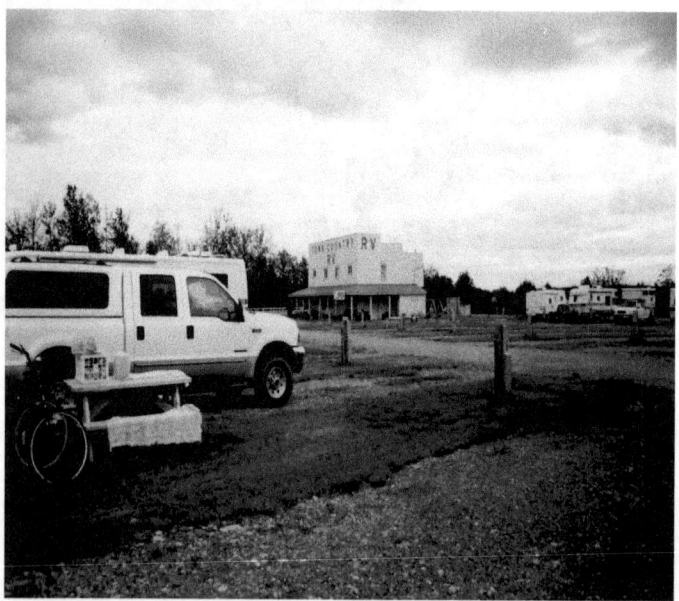

Town and Country RV, Palmer, Alaska. 2001   JDH

A CALL to the COLONISTS

Wednesday, July 4, 2001

We hiked the Butte. The Knik Glacier, the Knik River-Arm and the Matanuska River seen from the top (pgs 158, 159)

Thursday, July 5, 2001

Saw a movie in Wasilla.

Friday, July 6, 2001

Walked the old bridge by Pioneer Mountain in the rain.

Saturday, July 7, 2001

Talked with the "Colony Kids" that were available. Patty Wiesenberger was in the hospital. She autographed a book I had purchased, *"WE SHALL BE REMEMBERED."* She said her father told her to "Jump off the train and you will be the first colonist to arrive in the Matanuska Valley." This story is in the book. Patty identified Ina Belle in the Summit Rock photograph on Hatcher Pass and let us know that Stella, her (older) sister was living in Wasilla.

Tiny and Gerry (also in *"WE SHALL BE REMEMBERED"*) were of great assistance at the COLONY HOUSE as was Patty in making contact with Ina Belle's older sister, Estella.

Sunday, July 8, 2001

Drove to Hatcher Pass to revisit the Gold Cord Mine and the Hatcher Pass Lodge. Parked and hiked up a ridge trail above Summit Lake all the way to the snow line on a high peak. A lot of summit lakes up here!

Monday, July 9, 2001

Contact was made. Ina Belle was visiting. Tues. at 1:00.

Tuesday, July 10, 2001

What a day this was! A prominent family, indeed. Got to see the Alaska flag given to them by Benny Benson.

TIME RUNNING OUT

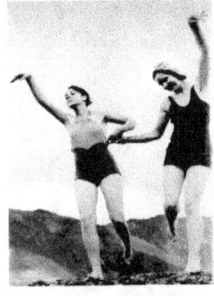

Virginia & Ina Belle
Hatcher Pass, Alaska
1936   Photo by RAD

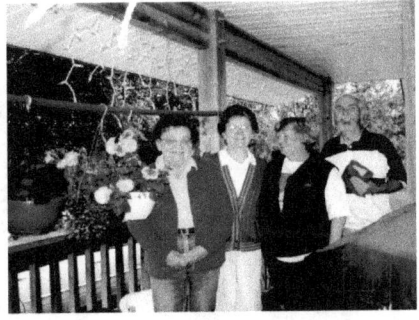

Estella, Ina Belle, Jill and Emory
Wasilla, Alaska 2001   Photo by Kathy of CA.

297

DENALI NATIONAL PARK, Alaska

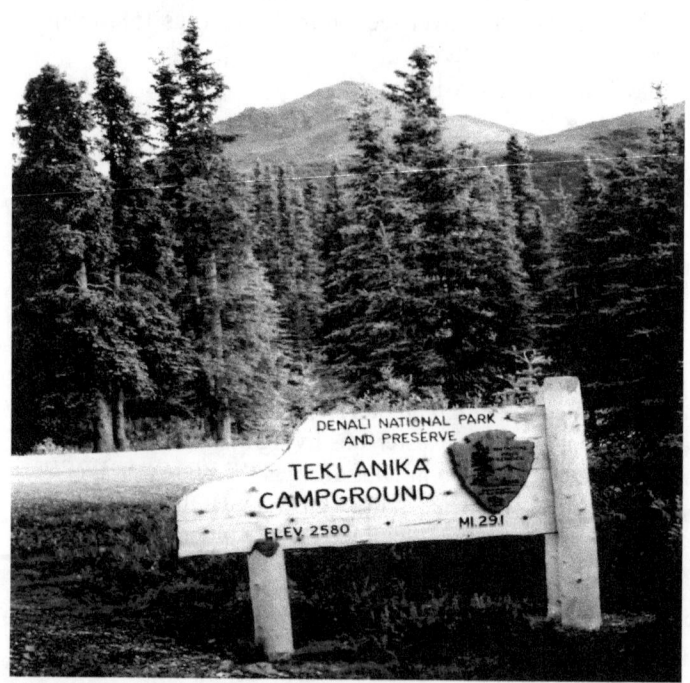

Thursday-Sunday, July 12—15, 2001

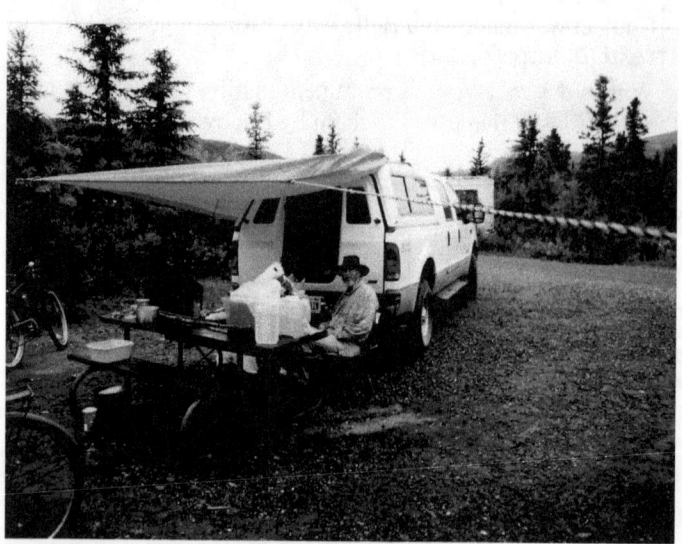

Emory enjoying our campsite, Denali N. P., Alaska. 2001   Photos JDH

THE MOOSE TALE

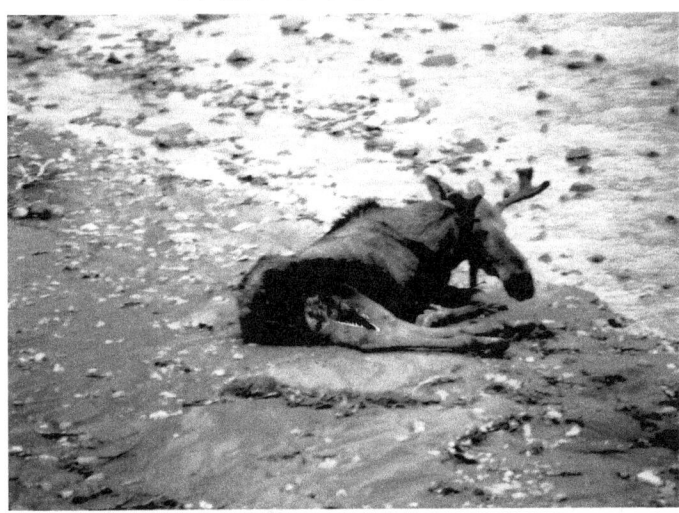

The MOOSE still alive by Teklanika Bridge, Denali Nat'l PK. 2000....JDH

A year ago we had visited the park and stayed at Savage River Campground. This is where we witnessed for several days the slow take down of a moose by some wolves. If the tourists and their buses hadn't kept the wolves away, they would have taken him down much quicker. Nothing natural about that!!!

In 2001 we came back.

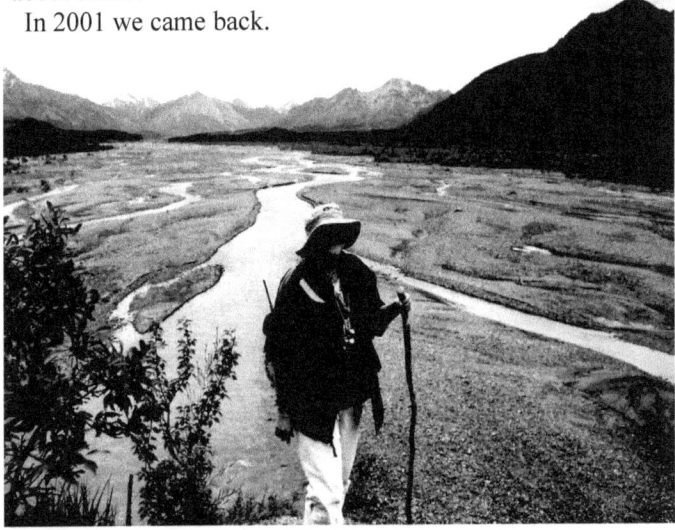

Author looking for the moose remains, Tek Delta. Denali. 2001   UEH

Friday, July 13, 2001

No bridge. We had walked 6 miles in the wrong direction.

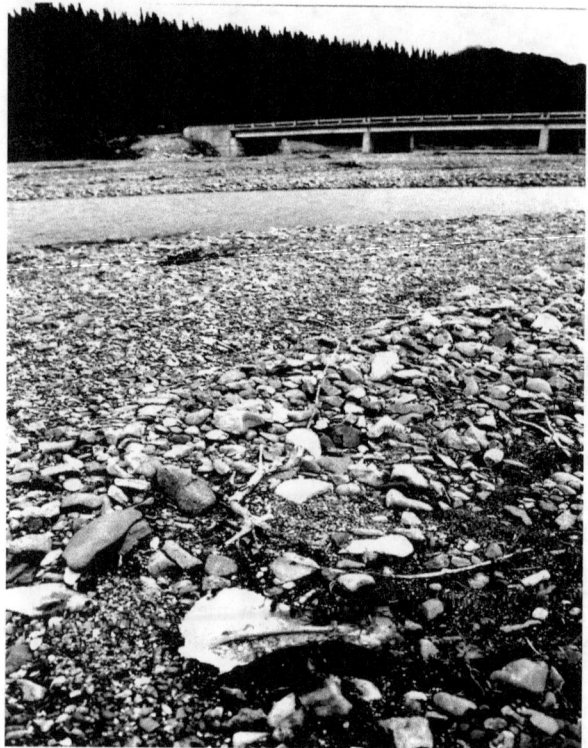

MOOSE remains located at Tek Bridge. 2001   JDH

Saturday, July 14, 2001

After our Friday walk, we took our bikes a long ways trying to locate the bridge. Someone finally knew where it was and directed us in the right direction. That evening Emory climbed the bluffs behind our campground to try and see Mount McKinley. He couldn't.

Saturday it was raining in the morning. We had to muster up enough nerve to get out in the rain and put up the tarp before breakfast. Done.

After riding our bikes 2 miles to the bridge, we got our backpacks on and walked the right way this time to the Tek Bridge. We looked for any sign of remains and finally found part of a hip bone. We photographed it and decided that tomorrow we may pack it up to the top of the bluffs for a proper burial.

Sunday, July 15, 2001

Our bus trip to Wonder Lake began at 8:30 am. The weather was beautiful.

MOUNT McKINLEY

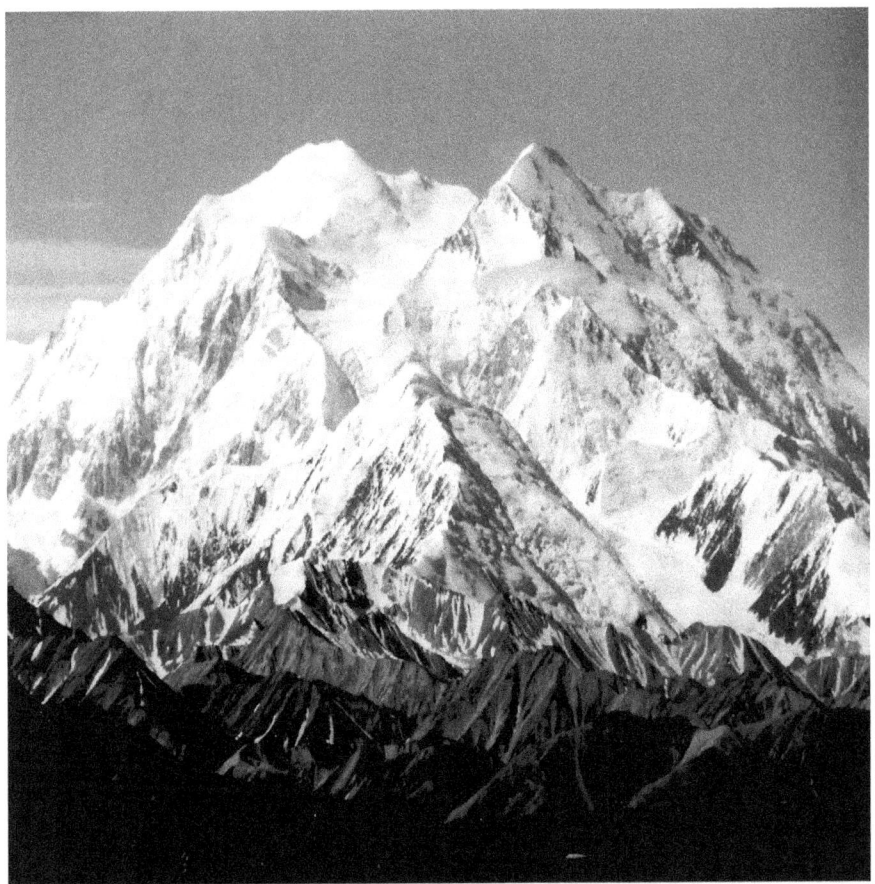

MOUNT McKINLEY Elevation 20,310 ft. Denali N P.   July 15, 2001   JDH

Our guide said that it had been four years since Mount
McKinley was visible all day long. July was known for two
days during the month that the mountain was partly visible.

A PLAN at POLYCHROME

The Wonder Lake bus let us off at the Polychrome look-off
where Emory packed one mile down to the Tek Bridge to
pick up the Moose remains. He met me back at Polychrome
and we walked to the trailhead of the bluffs overlooking our
campsite at Teklanika Campground.

We were tired, but trekked up the mountain gladly to take
the "Tek Moose" home.

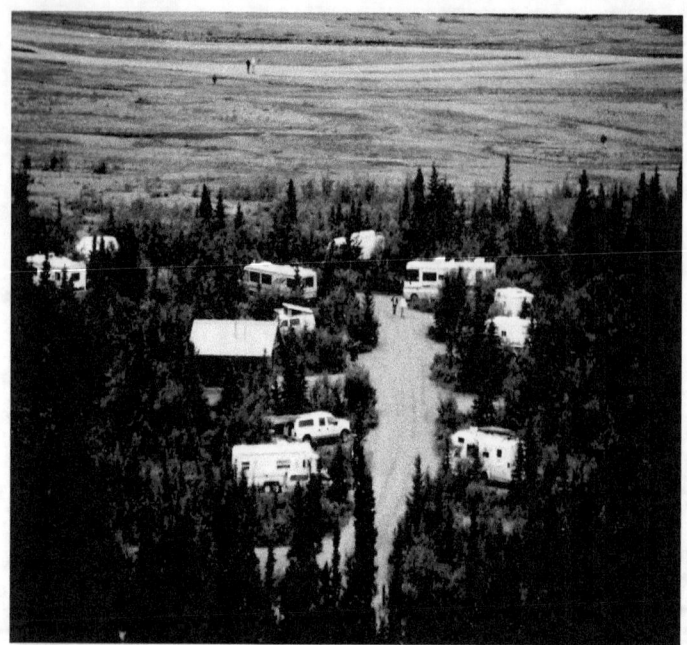

TEK CAMPGROUND, Tek Delta, Denali, AK 2001
Our campsite is second up on the left.   Photos JDH

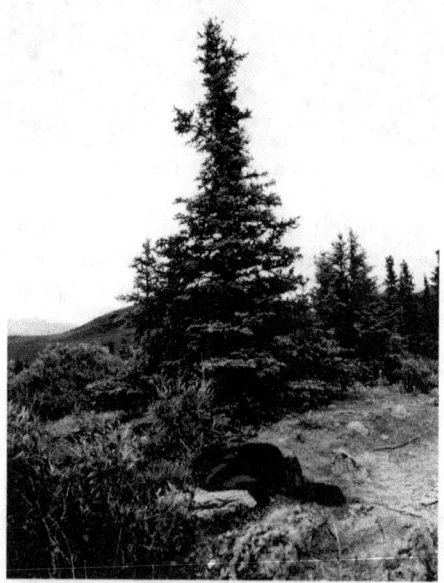

The site has been selected high on the
bluffs of the Tek Campground.

GUARDIAN of the TEK DELTA

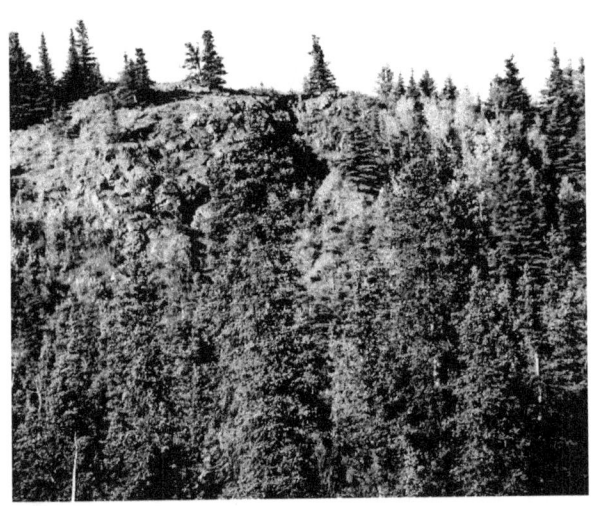

TEK MOOSE TREE, R of crack. 2001   Photos JDH

Sunday, July 15, 2001
DENALI NATIONAL PARK

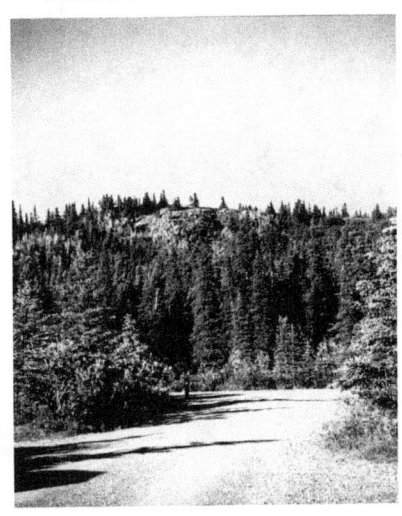

To STAMPEDE TRAIL Healy, Alaska

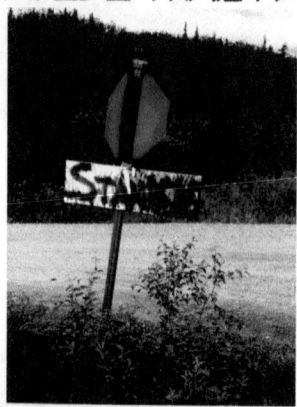

STAMPEDE ROAD   Photos JDH

Monday, July 16, 2001

A hand written sign saying "HAPPY BIRTHDAY" with today's date on it was at the beginning of Stampede Road. This was a road of no return for Chris McCandless who has a book written about his experience — *"INTO THE WILD."* The Teklanika River was flooded. A river he could not cross to get himself out.

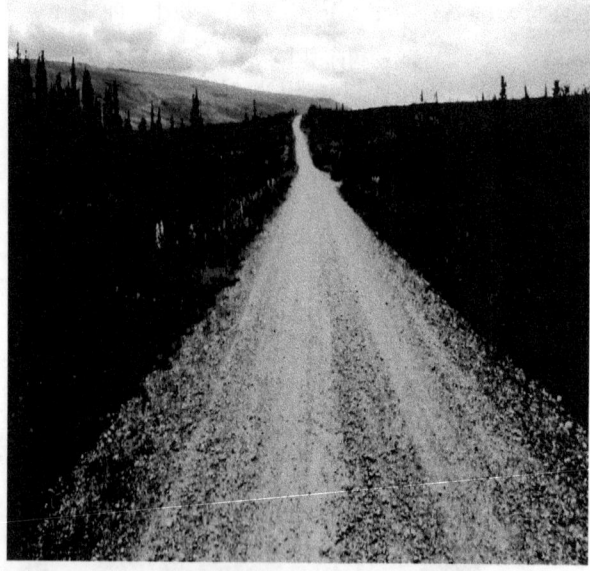

Stampede Road, Healy, Alaska.

NENANA, Alaska

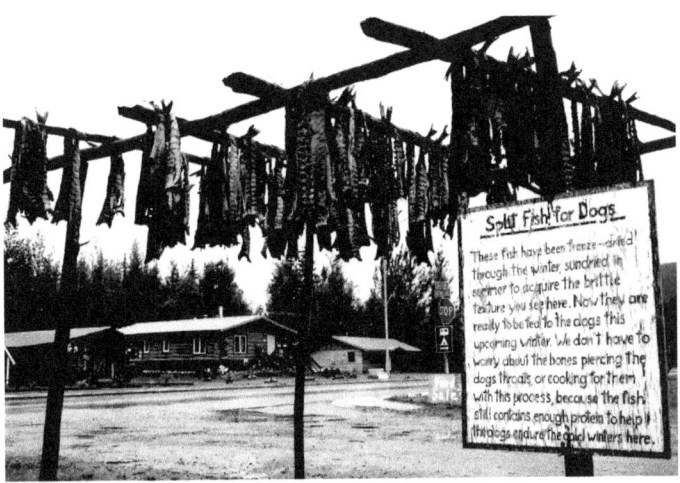

"Fish" for dog food, Nenana, AK. 2001   Photos JDH

Tuesday, July 17, 2001

Our first *real* shower since the Denali experience at the Nenana Valley RV Park. A miniature cashe, snow boots for Emory and a print of Mt. McKinley were purchased at a yard sale across the street from the campground.

At the visitor center we bought one ticket to the ice classic—May 1, 2002 12:59 pm. Didn't win. However, on July 15, 2001 we *did* win and the magnificent Mount McKinley was photographed presenting a timely tribute to The Moose Tale.

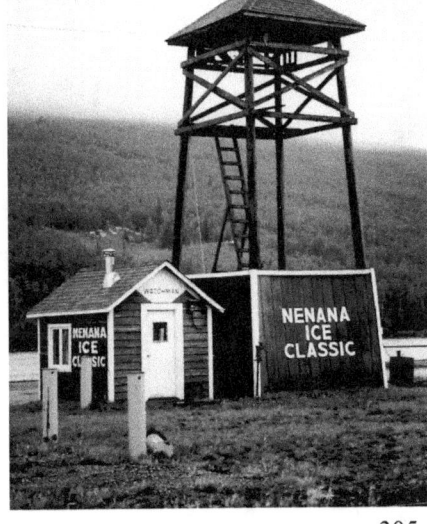

FAIRBANKS, Alaska

Wednesday, July 18, 2001

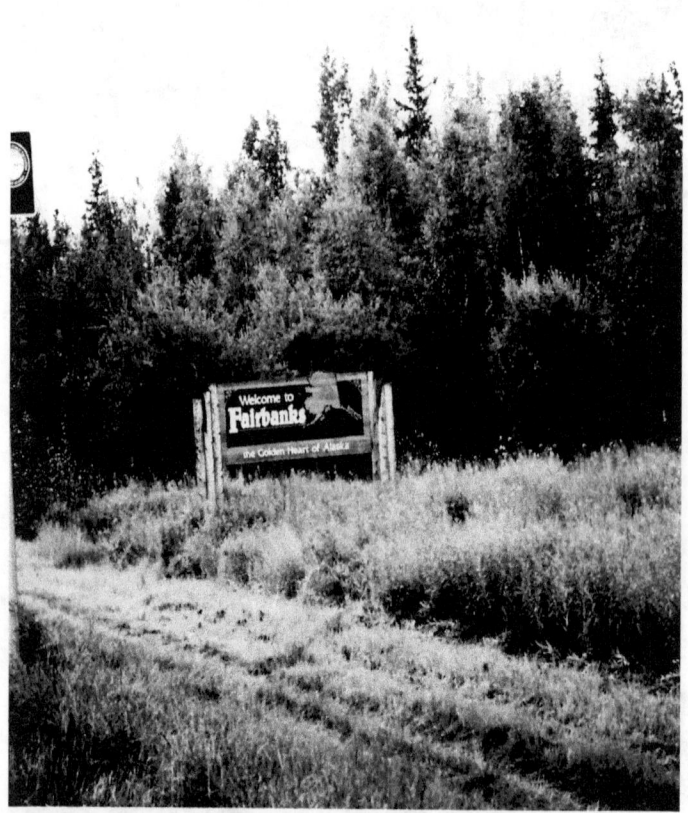

Traveling N, George Parks Hwy, Fairbanks, Alaska. 2001   JDH

This is the only photo taken from our traveling truck. We are now 362 miles from Anchorage (ODOMETER 28,697). Memories of feelings from the previous year came rushing back. Not for claustrophobics.

River's Edge RV Park, Fairbanks, Alaska

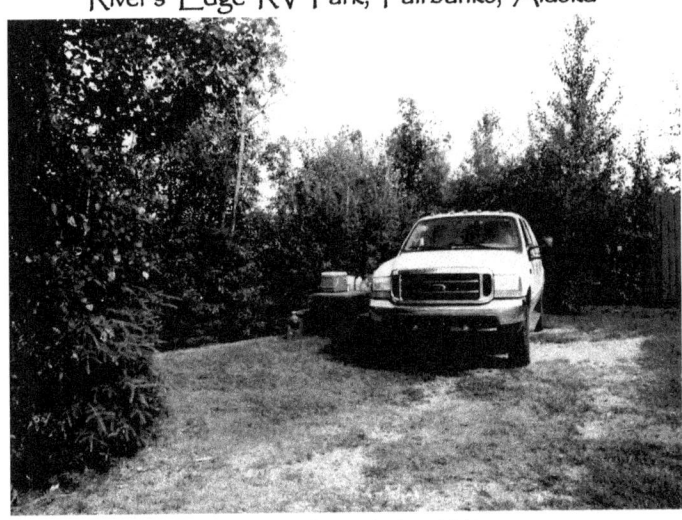

River's Edge RV Park, Fairbanks, Alaska. 2001   JDH

Wednesday-Sunday, July 18—22, 2001

Five days of activities ensued — covered in previous chapters. We worked on locating gold mines and capturing repeat photography before driving out to the circle area for two days.

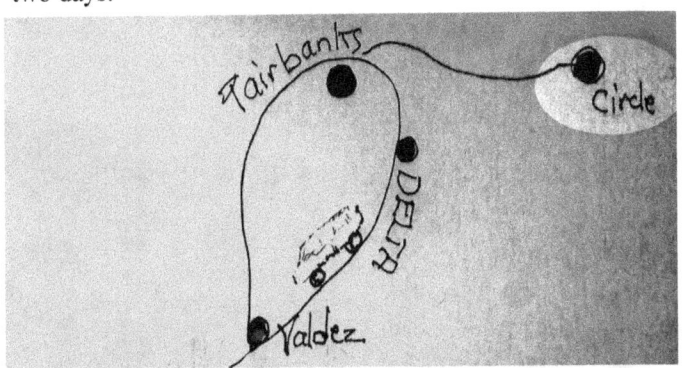

EAGLE SUMMIT, Steese Highway

57 degrees, mile 107.1, Elev. 3, 685 feet, time 5:13 pm.
— one word, "GRANDEUR." We climbed up on a ridge to the left of the view and, yes, "The grandeur of it all." A wonderful location for a summer solstice visit.

We traveled on and stayed two nights at the Arctic Circle Hot Springs Gold Camp.

Sunday, July 22, 2001

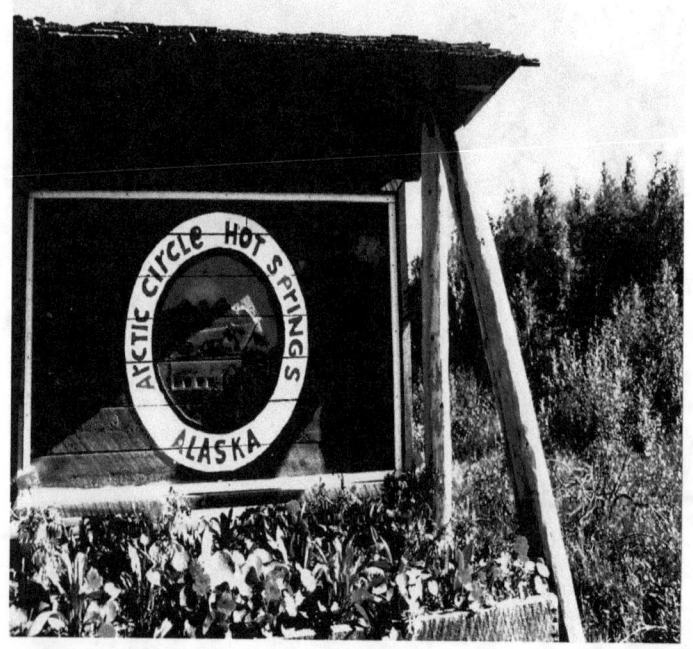

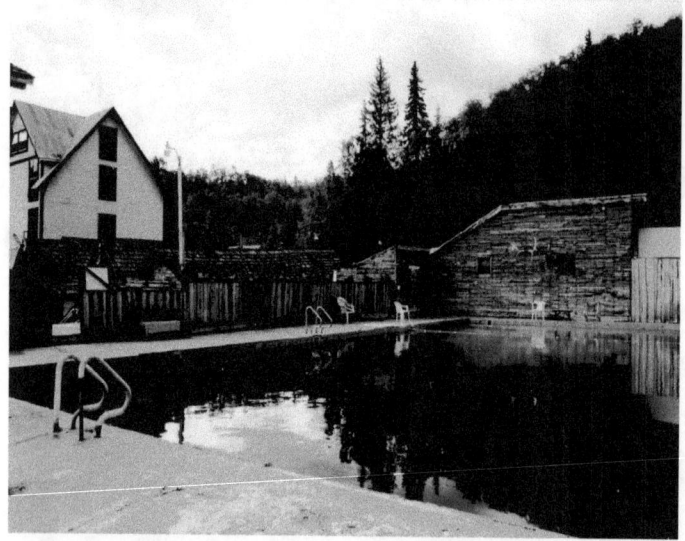

Arctic Circle Hot Springs, Alaska. July 22, 2001....Photos JDH

ARCTIC CIRCLE HOT SPRINGS, Alaska

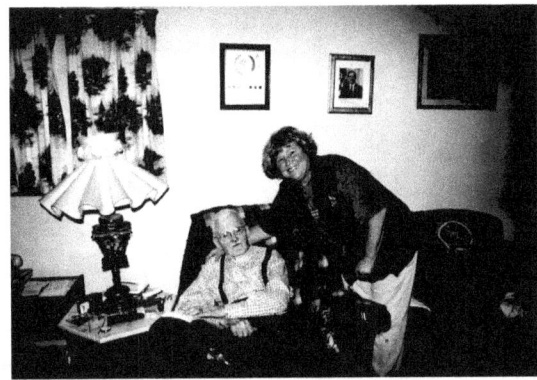

Harrie Hughes w. Author (refer page 119)....UEH

Monday, July 23, 2001

Harrie Hughes was a resident here. He was 102 years old. He talked to us about the Gold Rush days and World War II years in Alaska.

In the lobby of the main lodge there was a very long rectangular green war dept. map of the Steese Hwy. from 1927. It accessed Fairbanks to the Yukon River—162 miles.

YUKON RIVER, Alaska

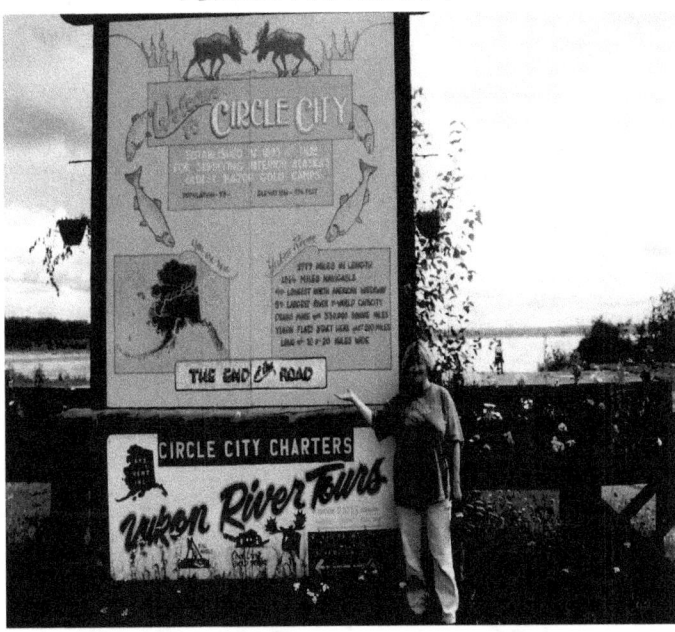

Author and the YUKON RIVER, Circle, Alaska. 2001   UEH

DOWN the DELTA, Alaska

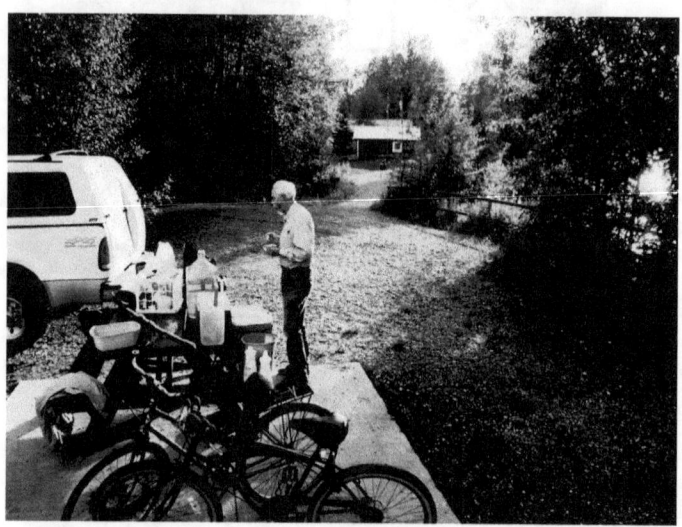

UEH at RIKA'S ROADHOUSE campground. 2001 JDH

Tuesday, July 24, 2001

There is fireweed everywhere along the Delta River. It signifies the end of summer for locals when the red flowers reach the top. The Tanana Ferry traveled to Fairbanks along the Tanana River circa early 1900's.

Route 8 goes from Paxson to Cantwell (164 mi. to Denali).

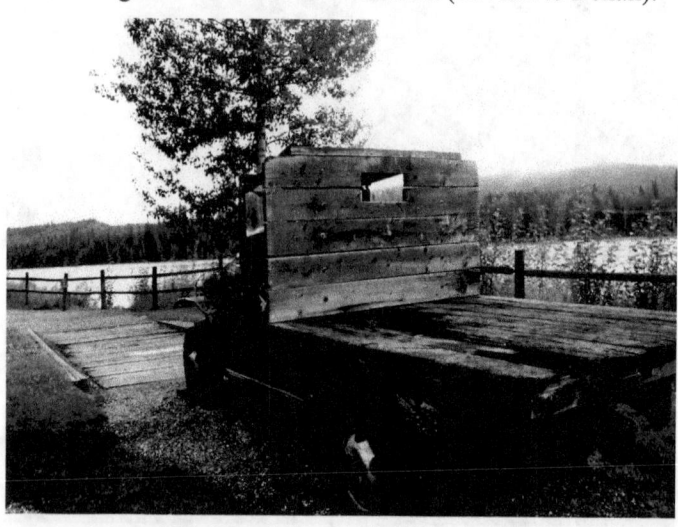

END of the LOOP TRIP

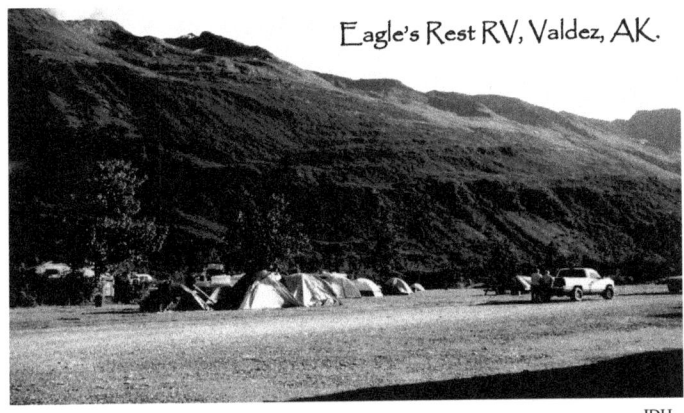

Eagle's Rest RV, Valdez, AK.

JDH

CONTENTS

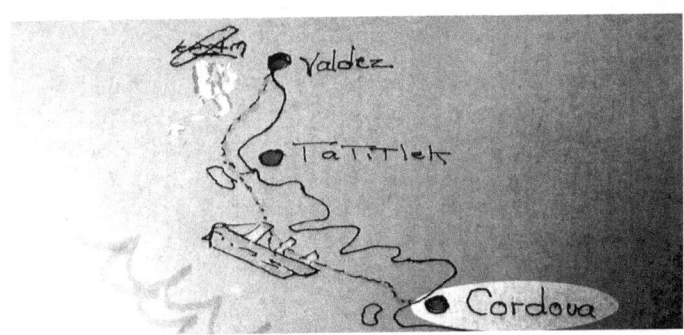

311

JEFF'S FISHING TRIP INVITE, Valdez

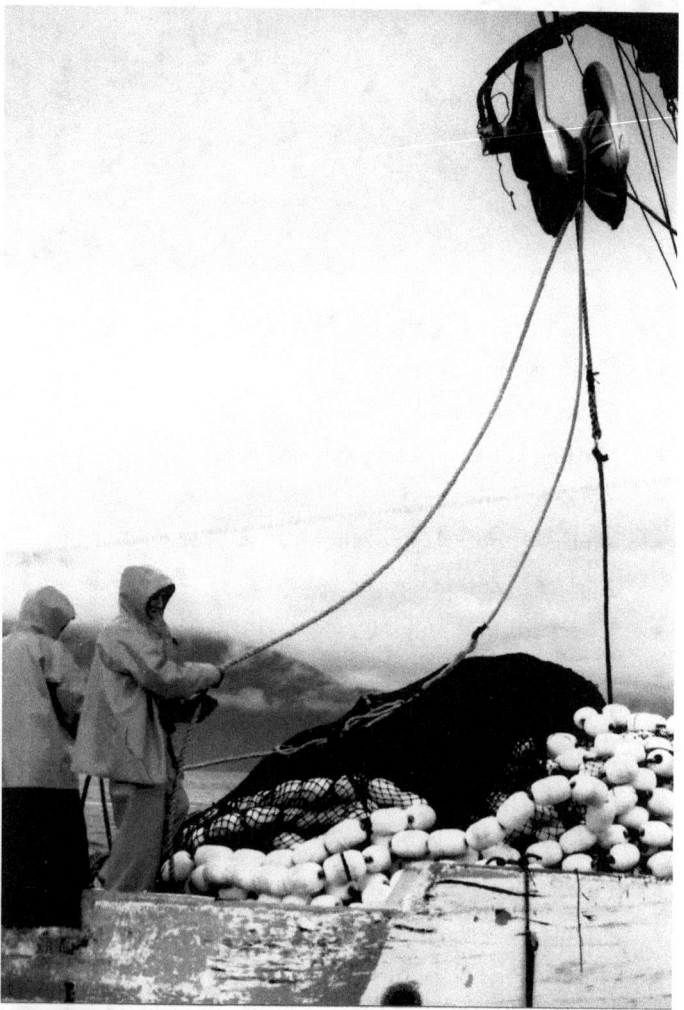

Thursday, July 26, 2001

After unloading everything from the truck to the camper, we headed off up the Bay with Jeff and a friend and a case of Miller. The Miller was the bait, but I didn't understand at the time. We found out that Jeff was the owner of Eagle's Rest RV and someone owed him a favor. He headed to a commercial fishing rig to collect and he did just that. We saw about 10 whales and some sea otters by the time we reached Prince William Sound.

A CAMPGROUND FISH FRY, Valdez

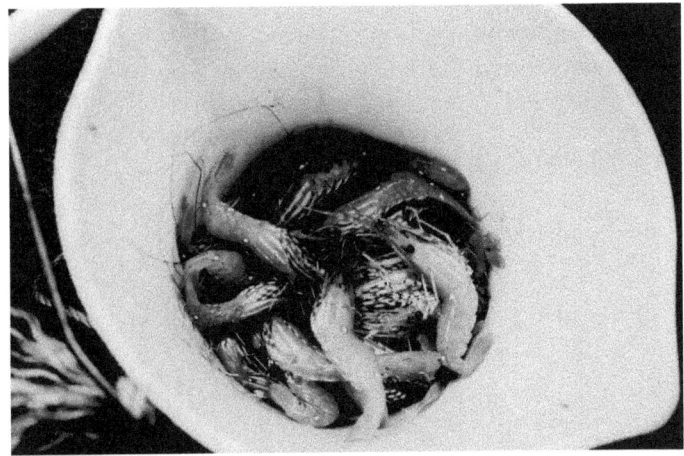

Jeff invited the entire campground to a fish fry — yes!!! That weekend we returned to the shelter and spent some time walking Dublin. Later we cleaned up the camper. What a mess!

There was a meeting at the shelter about the Gold Rush Parade. Found out that I was in charge—oh well.

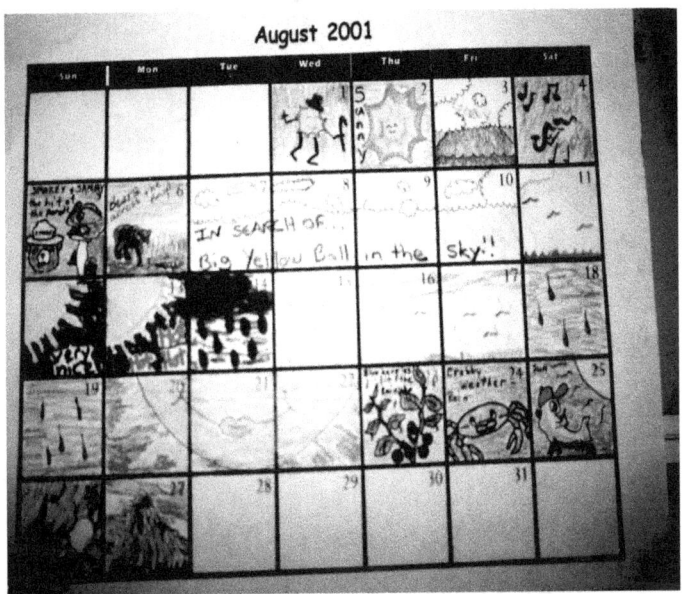

Courtesy of the Forest Service BLM, Valdez, AK 2001   JDH

Wednesday, August 1, 2001
Dublin looses—I went swimming.

DIRECTOR'S CUT Behind the Scenes 2001

Thursday-Saturday, August 2—4, 2001

Drove to Mineral Creek to picture chase. Emory got the truck lubed and Saturday we drove to Thompson Pass for a black and white photo shoot for the book. Emory fishes at Worthington Lake, Jill writes.

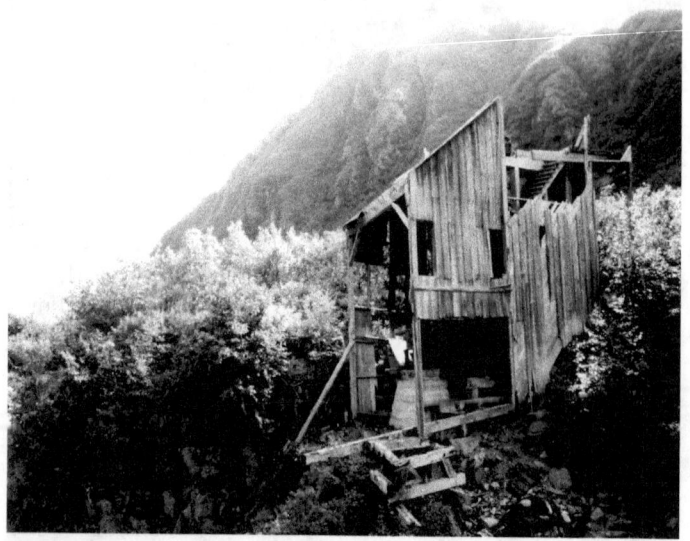

The SMITH STAMP MILL, Mineral Creek, Valdez, AK. 2001   JDH

Thursday

We began hiking further back and noticed that some prospectors had set up camp there. It appeared that they were using the old wood from the Stamp Mill to keep a fire. It really angered Emory that they were so uncaring about the old mill. Let's say a strong wind came up suddenly and blew things around a bit. We reported what they were doing to the authorities in town when we got back.

We continued on trying to cross the water to the mountain range on the other side of the creek to the left. In the early 1900's there used to be a small bridge. After getting a little wet, we were able to venture up the mountain to the left a ways looking for some kind of path. None.

There were suppose to be many black bears in this area, so one last quick photograph (on R) was taken of the area leading up to several gold mines—3,000 foot level and we hiked back out—keeping in mind we did have to pass by that Stamp Mill again.

FAR up MINERAL CREEK, Valdez

FINAL PHOTO

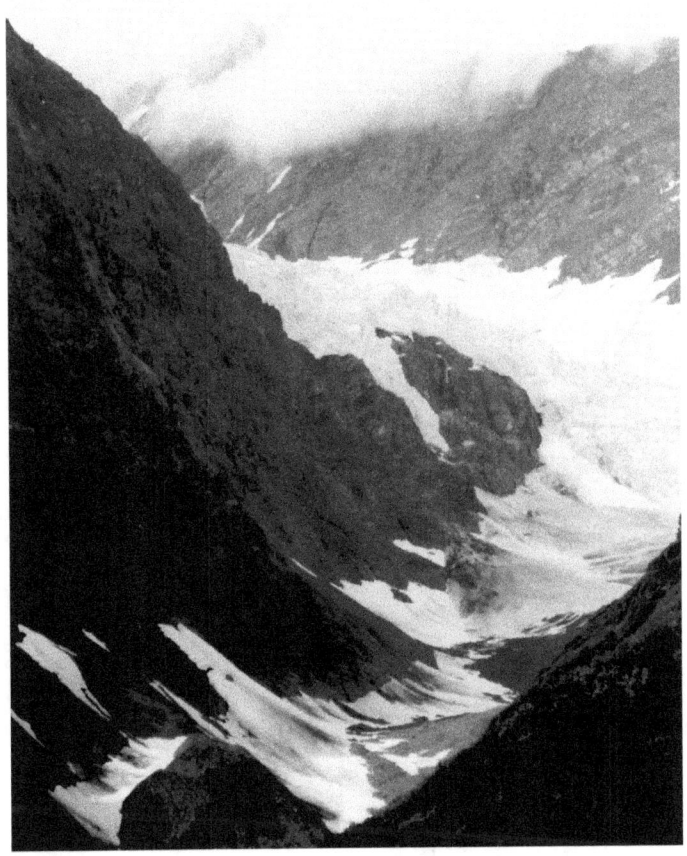

LAST PHOTO TAKEN past Stamp Mill, Valdez, AK. 2001   JDH

GOLD RUSH PARADE, Valdez

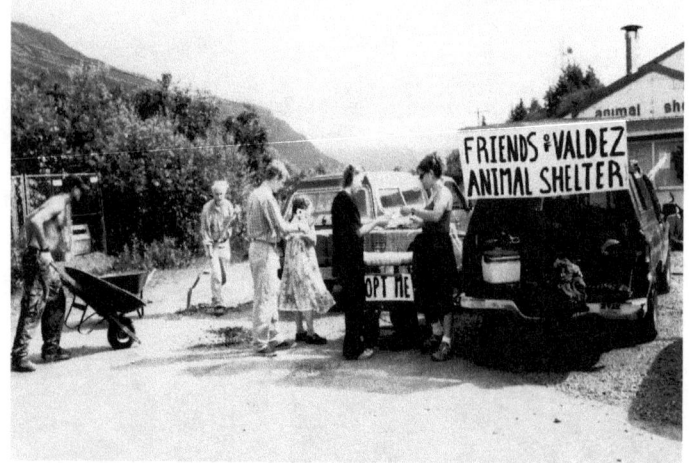

FVAS prepares for the parade. UH with shovel, 2001   JDII

Sunday, August 5, 2001

Denali, the dog, Pulled his owner Shanna on her skate board. It was an interesting spectacle. The white shepherd was also involved.

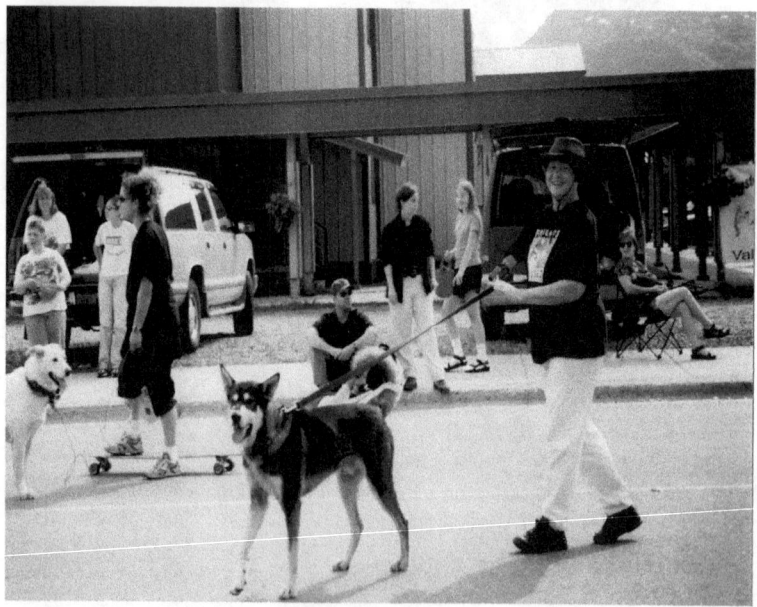

Author walking Shanna's dog, Denali. Shanna on skateboard. 2001   UEH

316

A SECOND PLACE WIN

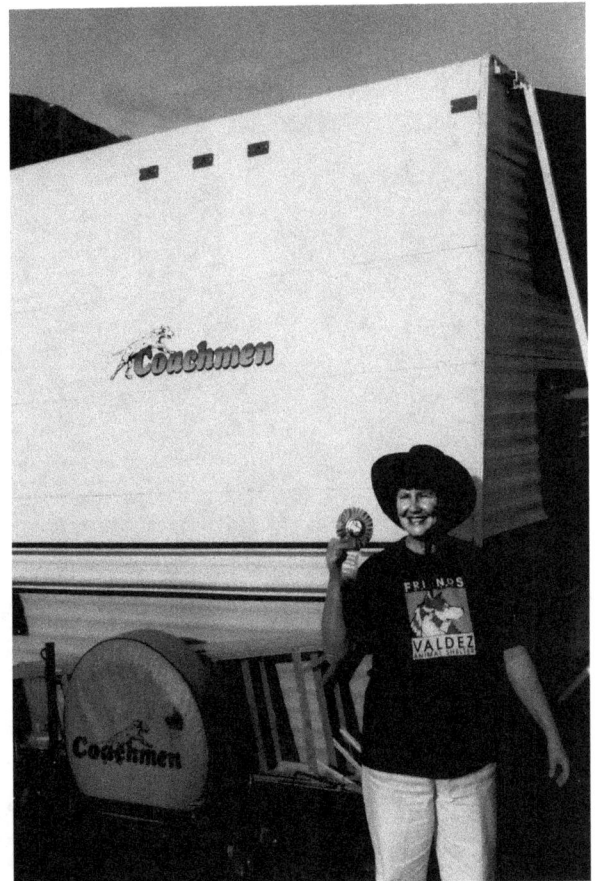

Author—very proud of our second place win! 2001   UEH

There was an air force band playing at the town picnic and the food was great. We sat with our friends from FVAS.

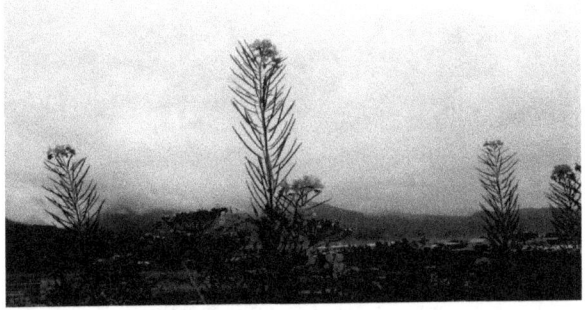

Reminders everywhere that time was running out...

Monday, Aug 6, 2001

RAFTING KEYSTONE CANYON, Alaska

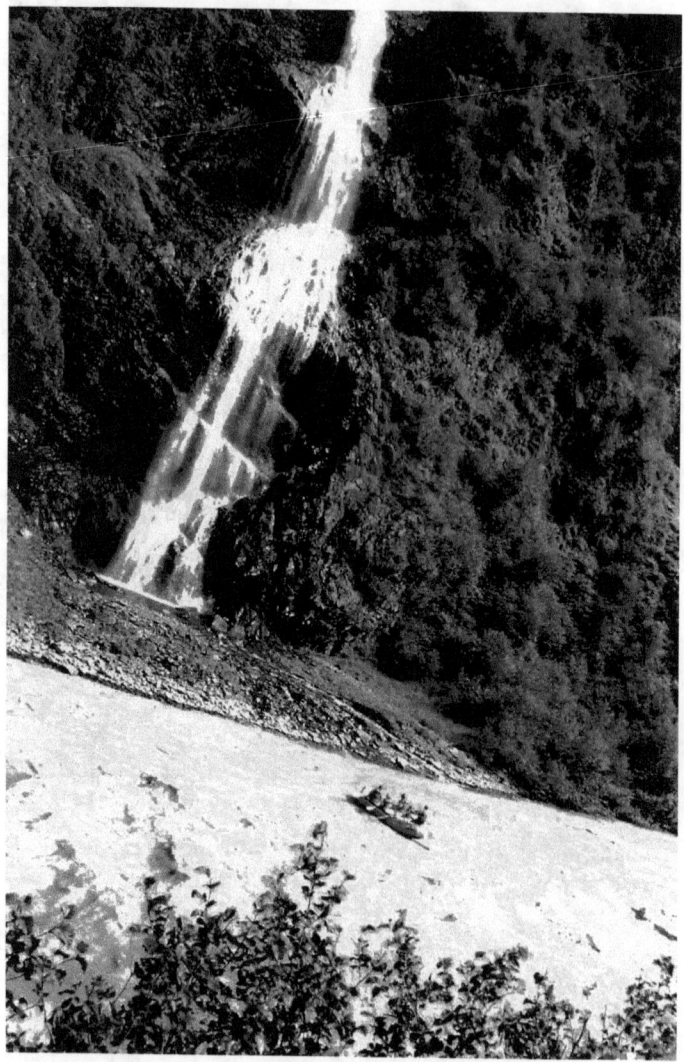

Jill in raft, KEYSTONE CANYON, ALASKA. 2001   UEH

Tuesday, August 7, 2001

We both went to the shelter. I walked the Husky named Fidalgo. Later we visited the Salmon Hatchery on the other side of the Bay. Emory went fishing at Allison Point.

BEAR CREEK BRIDGE, Alaska

Flooding destroyed the bridge in 1925. A new bridge was built in 1943. An extension of the old Military trail we did not hike.

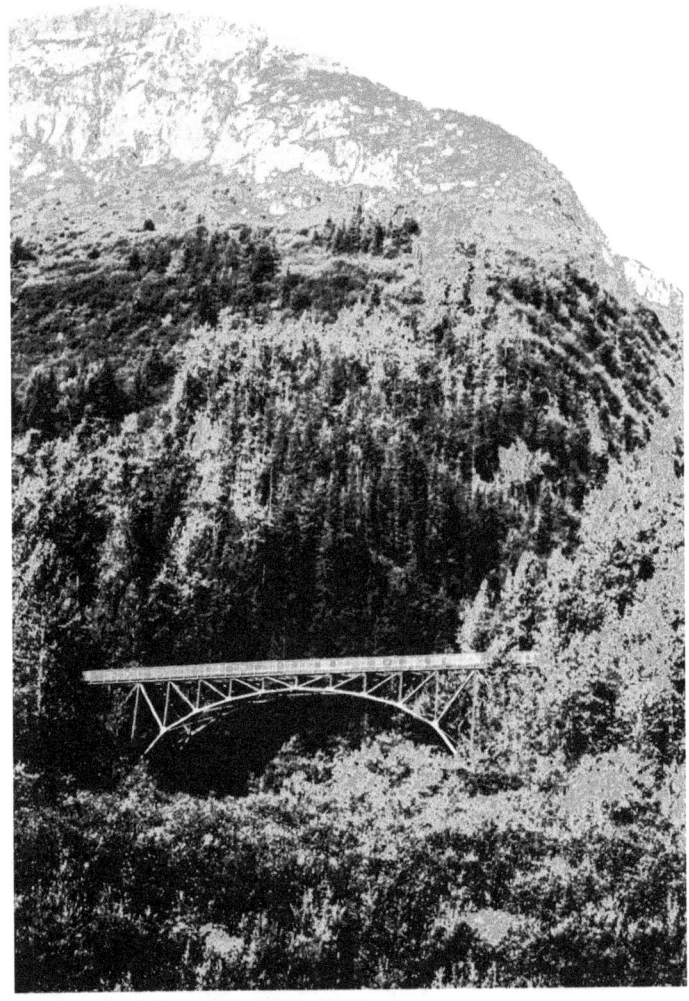

BEAR CREEK BRIDGE, Alaska. 2001   JDH

Wednesday-Friday, August 8—10, 2001

I attended the Animal Control Convention and am now a member of the Alaska Animal Control Officer Association.

Saturday, August 11, 2001

Fishing at Worthington Lake, visited Bear Creek Bridge (above) and Jill swam at Valdez High .

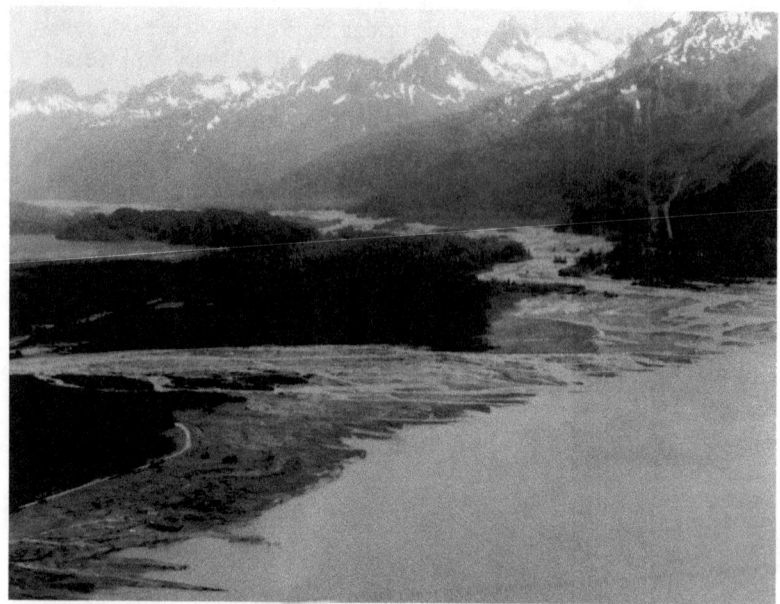

Aerial photo of OLD VALDEZ, Alpine Aviation, 2001.   JDH

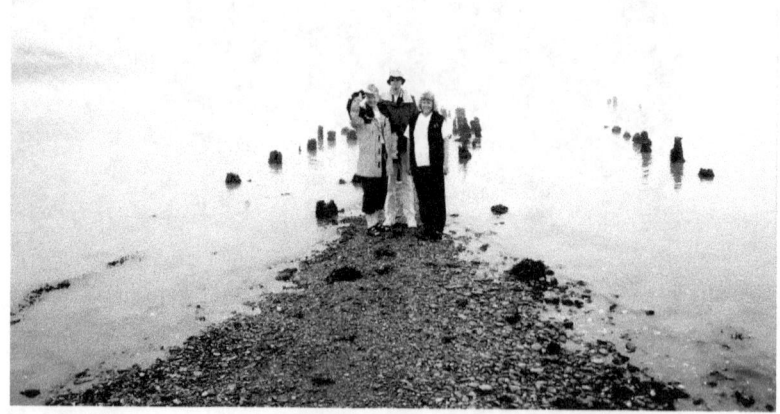

Photo by UEH

A year ago in 2000 Diane, Ken and Jill (Author), stand at the site of the original dock area of OLD VALDEZ. In 1964 the land sunk and changed the dock area forever due to an extremely high tsunami from a 9.2 earthquake.

320

TOWN RELOCATED AFTER the QUAKE

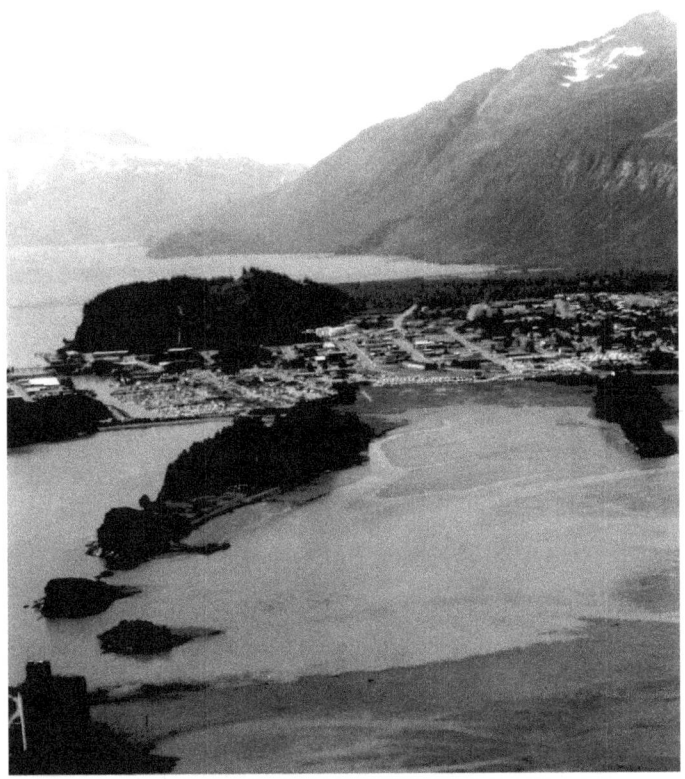

ALPINE flyover w Chuck LaPage, Valdez, AK. Aug. 13, 2001   JDH

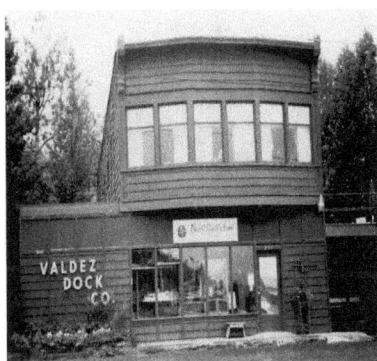

Bob's dad owned the DOCK BUILDING
which has since been relocated.   JDH

August, 16, 2001
  We have lunch with
Bob Kelsey at the Sr.
Center in Valdez.

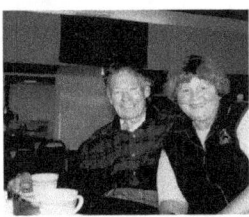

Bob Kelsey w Author UEH

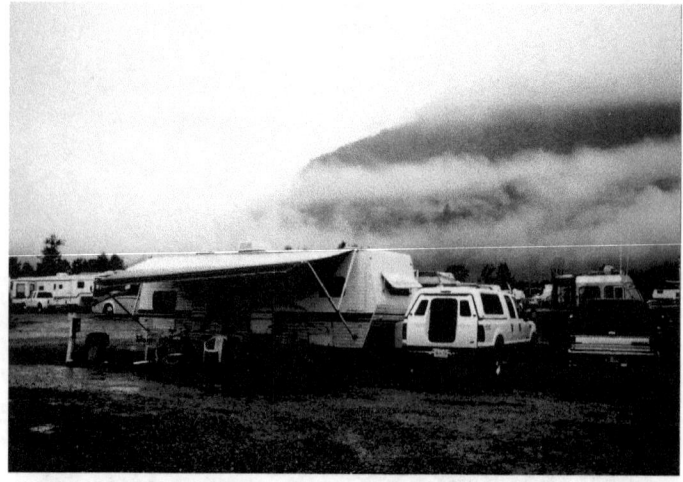

EAGLE'S REST, Valdez, AK. 2001   Photos JDH

CORDOVA DAY TRIP

Friday, August 17, 2001

We took our bikes down on the Bartlett Ferry. $9.00 one way for each bike. The trip took about 6 and a half hours because we made a stop at a village called Tatitlek. A village with a population of 200. A couple of dogs came running down to meet the ferry. They fed them sausage from the kitchen. The passengers watched from the upper deck. A small, foggy interesting place.

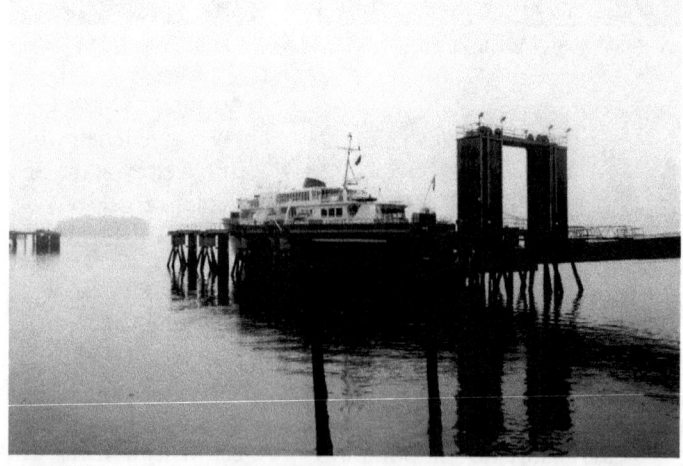

CORDOVA DOCK, Alaska. 2001

CORDOVA, Alaska

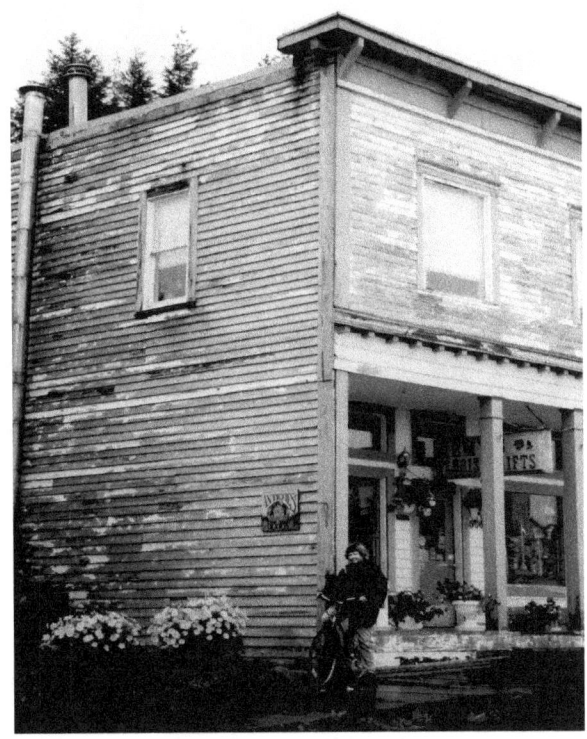

Author in front of local Cordova flower shop. 2001   UEH

Friday, August 17, 2001 continued
"Cordova was hilly and had a lot of canneries," said Jill.
We got to see a video of the town history at the museum and
wished we would have had enough time to go to the Child's
Glacier about 48 miles outside of town.

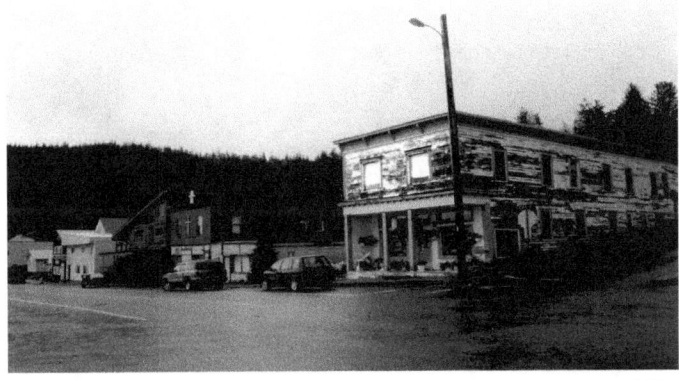

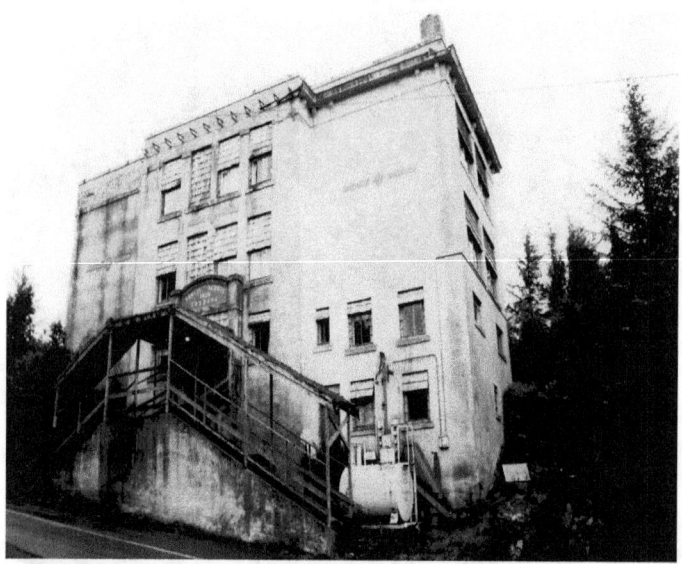

Old Cordova Public School 1925, Cordova, AK. 2001   Photos JDH

Friday, August 17, 2001 continued

The "Million Dollar Bridge" was a long taxi ride or car rental ride away, as was the Childs Glacier. The intent of this bridge was to run a highway from the bridge up the west side of the Copper River to the Copper mines—NEVER HAPPENED!

It was raining so we did not venture that far. We *did* get to eat at the Light House Inn and bike around the "dock area" for pictures before using up our five hour port time.

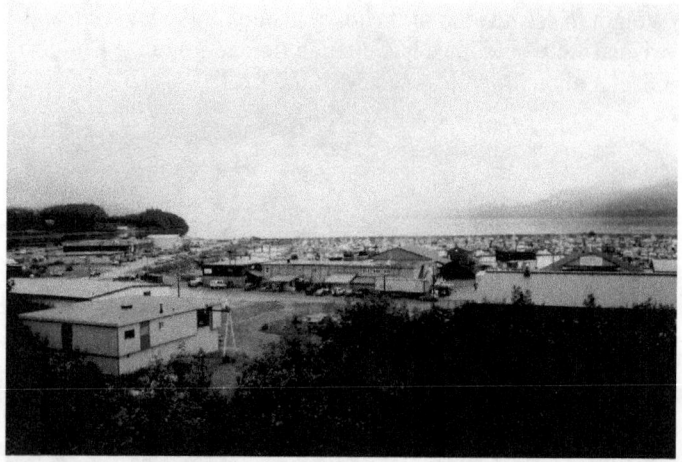

CORDOVA PANORAMA, Alaska. 2001

324

CORDOVA continued

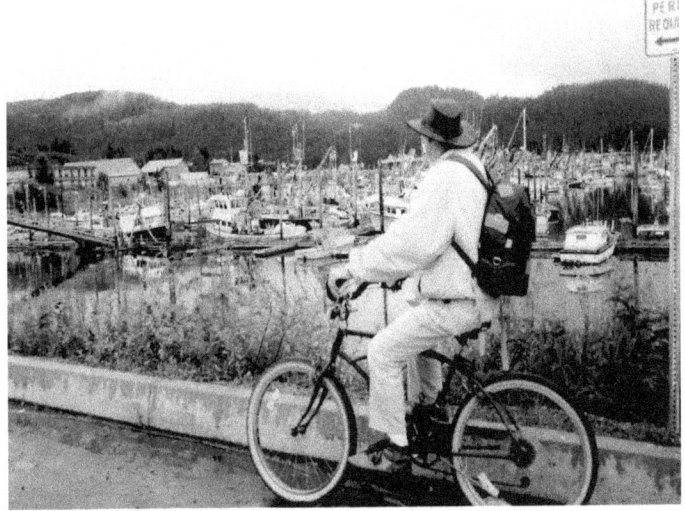

UEH riding the Cordova dock area. 2001   Photos JDH

It took five hours for the trip back to Valdez, but we didn't have to stop at Tatitlek this time. All and all it was a very long day of about 20 hours.

"Wait a minute, is that fire weed I see below?" Yes, fire weed was also visiting Cordova. I think it is trying to tell us something.

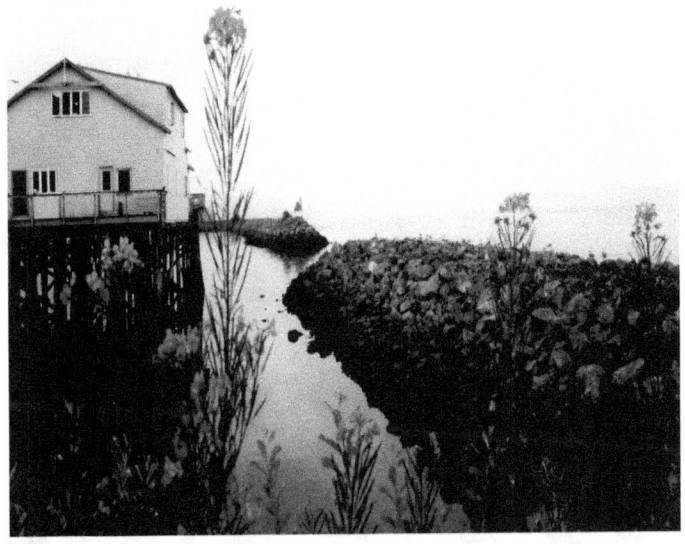

Fire weed at the Cordova dock area. 2001

THE FACE of the VALDEZ GLACIER

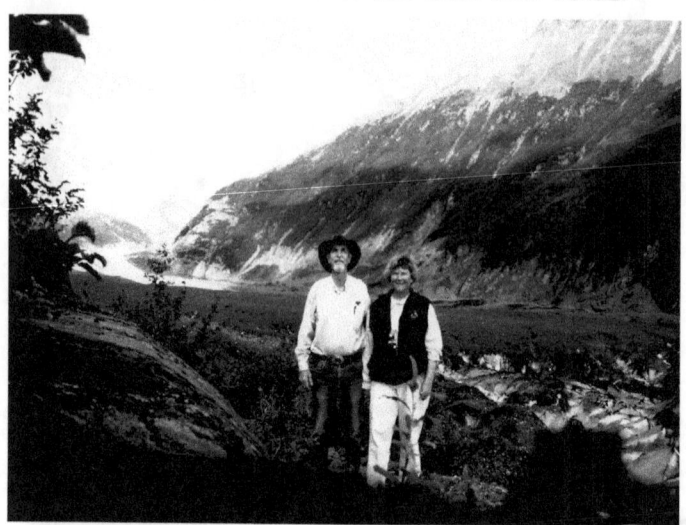

UEH & JDH, TERMANAL MORAINE of the Valdez Glacier. Aug, 2001

Saturday-Saturday, August 18—25, 2001
   Two trips to the glacier were made, FVAS had its garage sale behind the Police Station (split 50/50 domestic violence/ animal shelter), it rained (Jill swam), Emory went fishing at Worthington Lake and Allison Point, Jill labeled pictures, and Emory hiked on the Shoup Trail without bear spray!

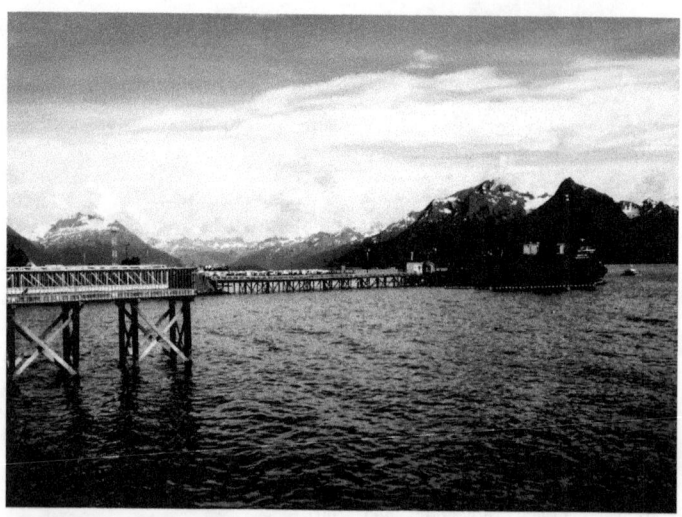

Emory fishes at VALDEZ DOCK area. 2001....JDH

EXPANDING HORIZONS

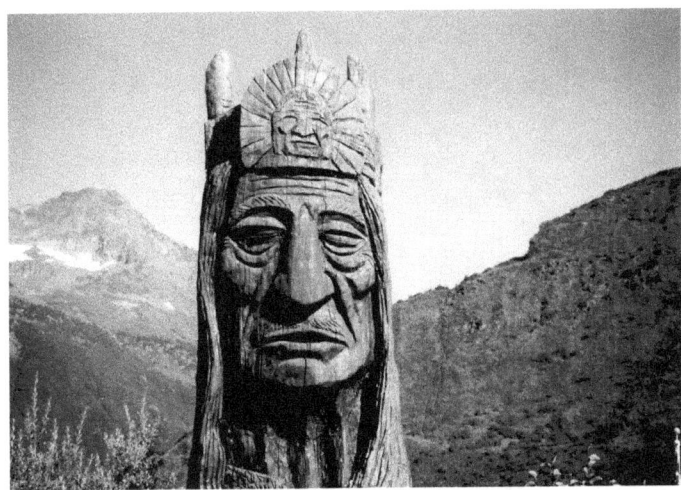

PROTECTING PRINCE WILLIAM COLLEGE, Valdez, AK. 2001

This remarkable carving looks out onto Prince William Sound and the waters leading to it. Behind the carving is the Town Mountain Trail.

We can not stop expanding our horizons. It seems to be unstoppable. Up in the air, out into the sound, ferrying to Whittier, Seward and Cordova, the loop, the beginning of the Valdez Glacier, Thompson Pass, the Shoup and Gulch trails—some reaches going far back in time. Worthy of note, a pattern is setting in—a very strong human instinct has taken over—like a switch has been turned on. Fascinating.

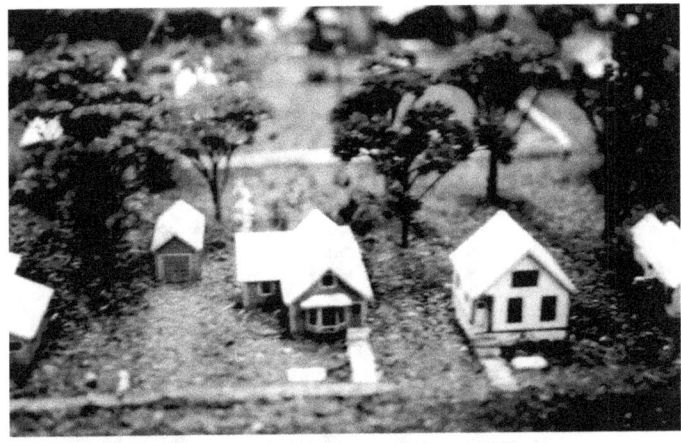

ANNEX MUSEUM, miniature "old" town display. 2001   Photos JDH

The house on the left is where RAD left his dog, Spot. This was Lee Albin's house.

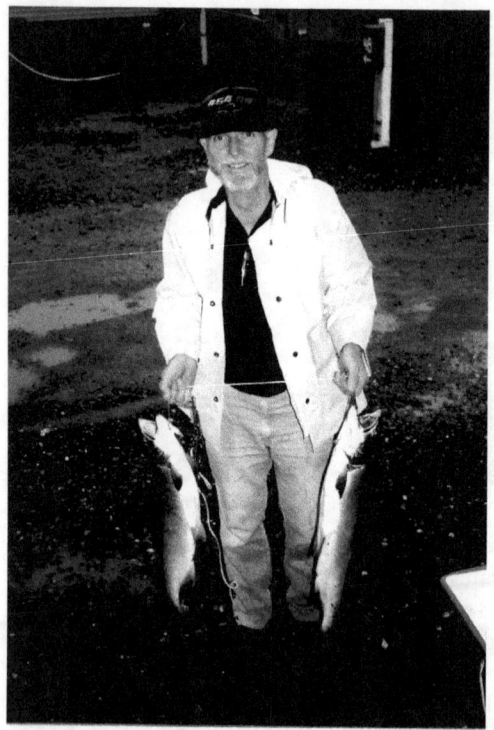

UH fishing at Allison Point. 2001   Photos JDH

Sunday, August 26, 2001

FVAS PICNIC

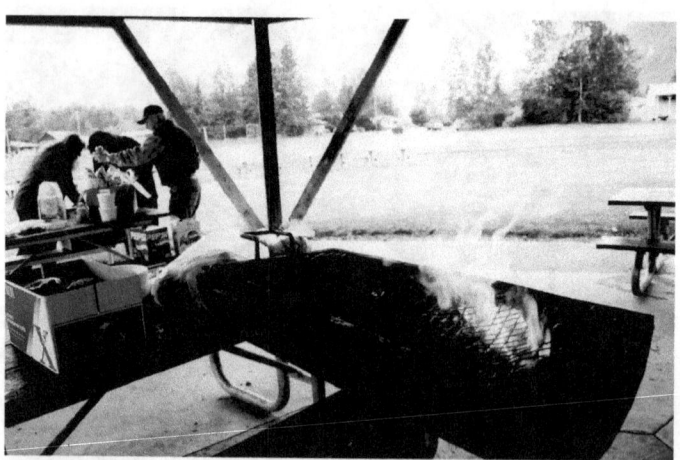

It was cloudy, but didn't rain. It was quite cool. You could tell winter was coming. The picnic was well attended.

SAYING GOOD BYE

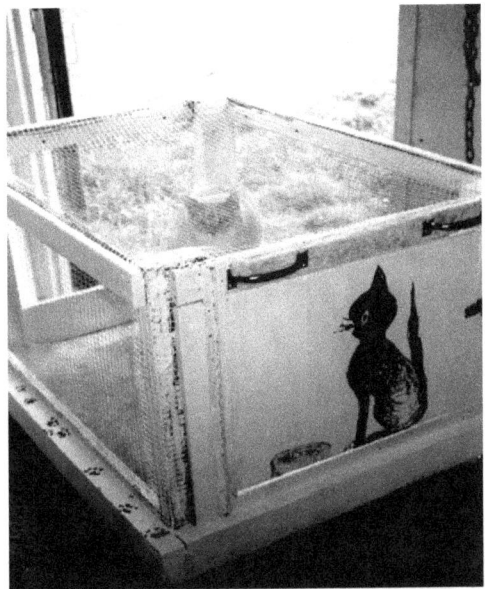

Emory gave the cats at THE VALDEZ SHELTER a gift. A rolling screened in porch for them to get some fresh air. Everyone liked it, especially the cats.

Monday, August 27, 2001

When the snow first falls on Sugar Loaf, there will be about 6 more weeks before winter—42 more days before snow touches the ground of Valdez.

ODOMETOR 30,631

We head to the pass for the last time.

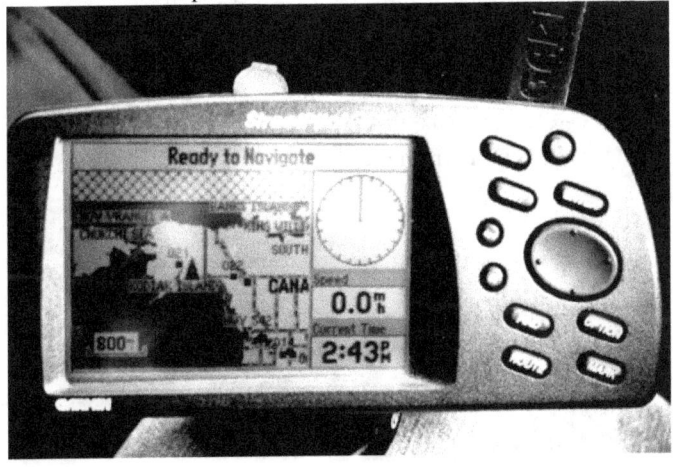

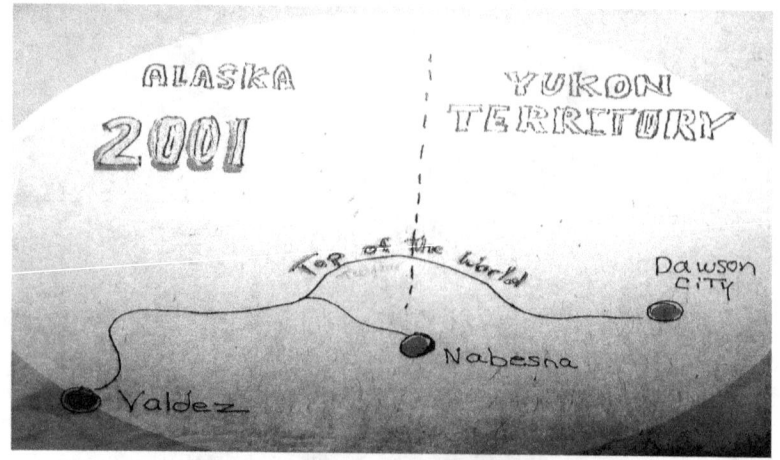

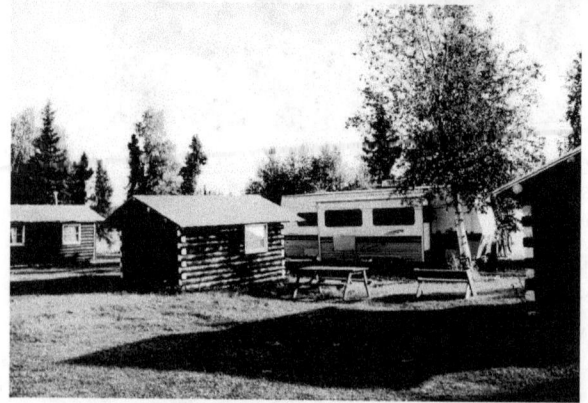

GRIZZLY LAKE RANCH, Tok Cutoff, AK. 2001   Photos JDH

Monday-Wednesday, August 27, 28 & 29, 2001
   Listened to tapes of Harry Heinz and how he made it up
to Slana the same summer that RAD did. His uncle was
Laugh'in Ole (in RAD Diary). This was a good insight to the
way it was back in 1935. We were also fortunate to witness
the large gold scale from the Nabesna Mine (below).

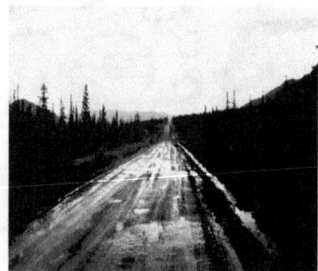

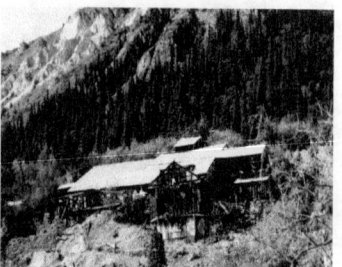

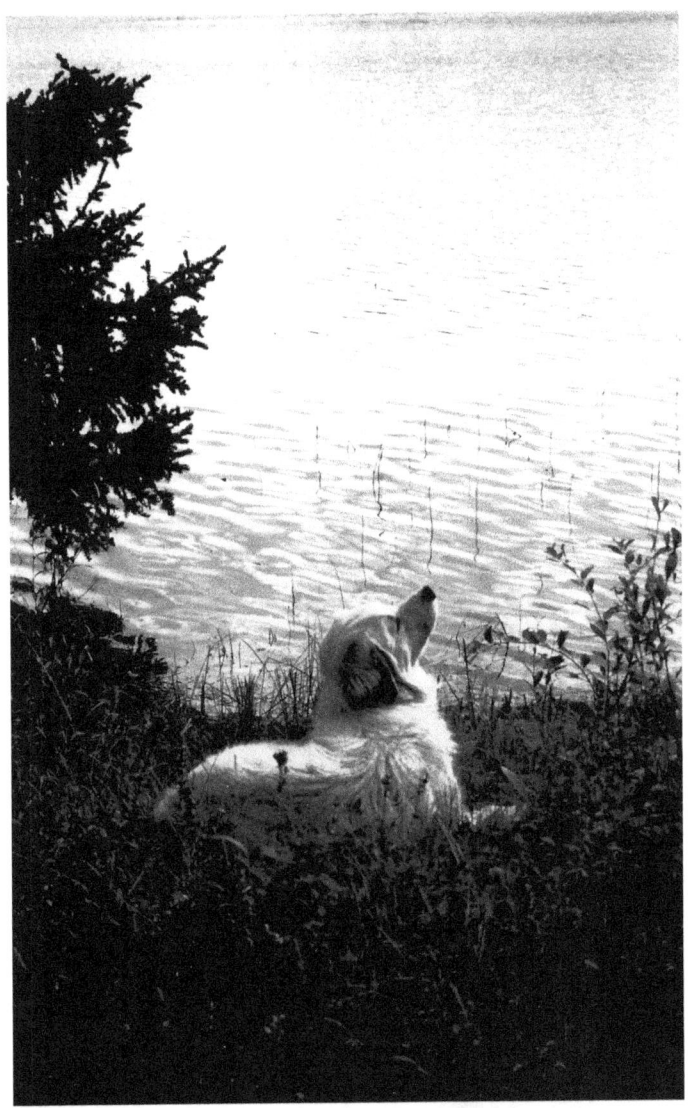

Lambie, Great Pyrenees mascot at Grizzly Lake Ranch, AK. 2001   JDH

Thursday, August 30, 2001
  On the way out, we stopped at Mentasta (mile 82) at the
Athabaskan Native American Village to meet with Katie
John. She was an elderly Athabaskan who was related
to Guy John in RAD's diary. Katie helped author
THE HEADWATER PEOPLE.
—then on to the Tok Village RV for our last Alaska night.

331

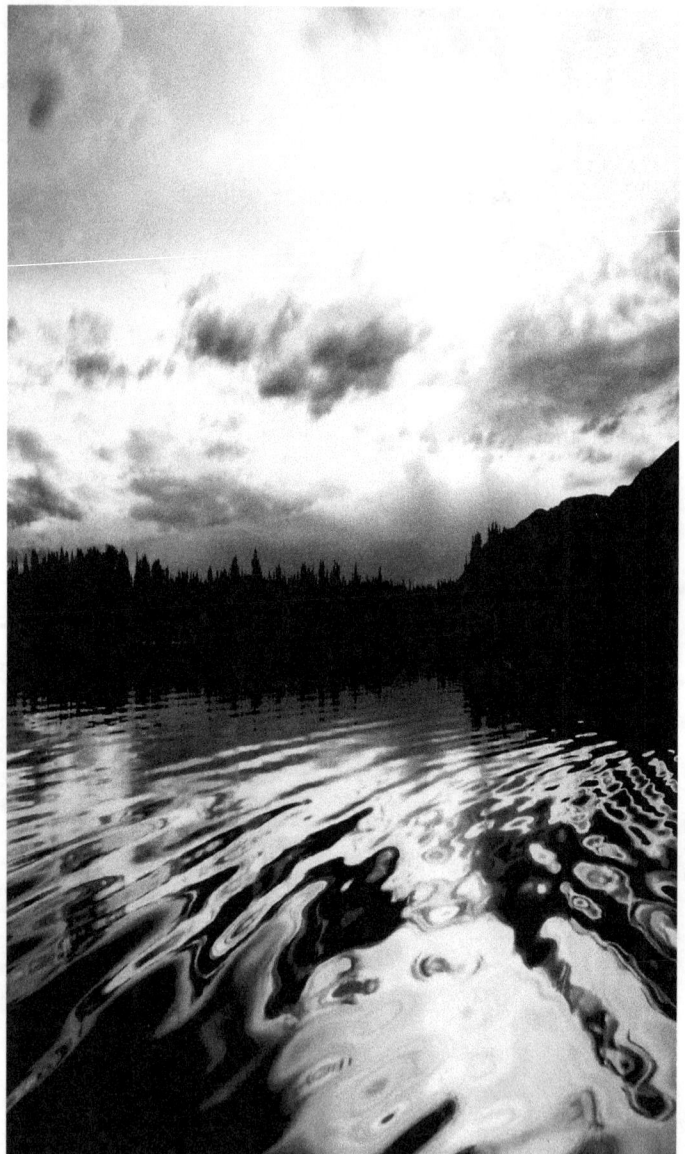

Grizzly Lake on Tok Cutoff, Alaska. 2001   JDH

Friday, August 31, 2001

With the sound of loons still ringing in our ears, we drove east toward the Canadian border.

ODOMETER 31,116

THE TREE FAMILY

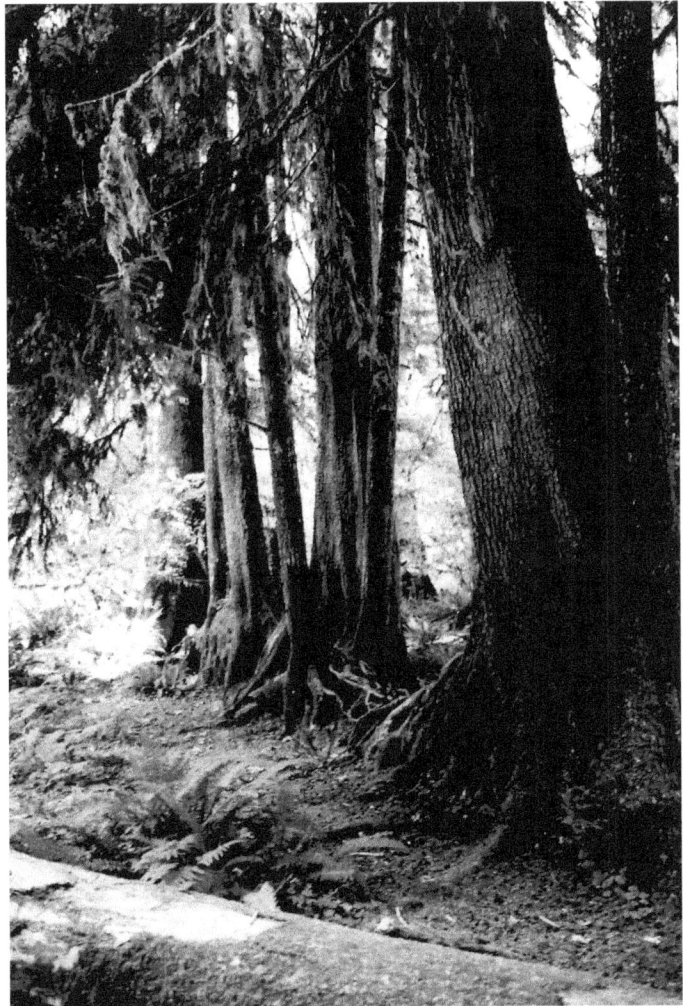

HOH RAIN FOREST, Olympic National Park, WA. September, 2000 JDH

When a tree falls in the forest, the owl sees it, the deer hears it and the bear smells it...

The prospector's only son Daniel passed away on December 24, 2016. I would like to dedicate this page to him. Daniel was my only brother and a big fan of *LAST CHANCE ALASKA*. He always created the appropriate cairns on the trails of life for his family to follow.

—— Daniel Randolph Douglas ——

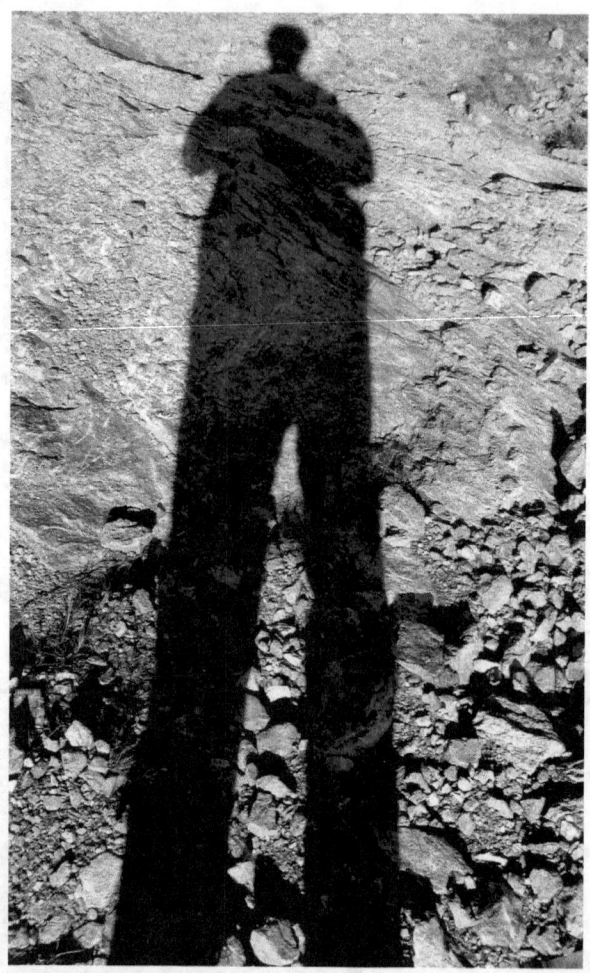

September, 2016   Photo by Author

Top of MOUNT MANSFIELD, Vermont

Fifteen years later, I am standing on top of Mount Mansfield looking out over a land soon to be covered in white. The distance becoming ever greater from that hike in the Alaska Interior to locate a little cabin in the woods lived in by Randolph Angus Douglas in 1935.

Only one final book project to complete. A book to be titled, *DRIVING THE DEMPSTER—as* white becomes green and green becomes white.

Record what you see — record what you hear.
film, write, draw, paint—capture and cry out.

334

www.ingramcontent.com/pod-product-compliance
Lightning Source LLC
Chambersburg PA
CBHW051440170526

45166CB00001B/53